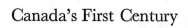

Canada's First Century

BOOKS BY DONALD CREIGHTON

The Empire of the St. Lawrence
British North America at Confederation
Dominion of the North
John A. Macdonald
Volume I   The Young Politician
Volume II   The Old Chieftain
Harold Adams Innis: Portrait of a Scholar
The Story of Canada
The Road to Confederation
Canada's First Century

Canada's
First
Century

1867-1967

Donald Creighton

MACMILLAN OF CANADA

TORONTO

Printed in Canada by the T. H. Best Printing Company Limited
for The Macmillan Company of Canada Limited
70 Bond Street, Toronto

Acknowledgements

I should like particularly to acknowledge the help I have received from two persons in the writing of this book. My son, Philip W. B. Creighton, has kindly assisted me in the collection and checking of the statistical material. My old friend, Dr. Eugene A. Forsey, has given me the full benefit of his critical genius and his vast knowledge of Canadian history. He has read my manuscript with scrupulous care, detected a number of errors and imperfections, and made many valuable suggestions for improvement. I am greatly indebted to him for his generous help: it is one more of the many gifts of a long and valued friendship.

Donald Creighton

Contents

Illustrations

Except where otherwise noted the illustrations have been provided by the Public Archives of Canada.

Between pages 68 and 69

'Child Canada Takes Her First Steps'
Sir Alexander Mackenzie
Sir John A. Macdonald by J. W. Bengough
Riel addressing the jury
'Let the Big Chief Beware'
   (by permission of Rapid Grip and Batten Ltd.)
D'Alton McCarthy
Honoré Mercier
'Dignified Attitude of the Liberals': 1891 election
'Quebec Gets a Show': 1895
Farewell to the Manitoba Transvaal Contingent, 1899
Emigrants leaving for Western Canada, 1902
Wheat in Saskatchewan
Sir Wilfrid Laurier by Henri Julien
   (The National Gallery of Canada, Ottawa)

Between pages 164 and 165

'The Real Emergency'
Henri Bourassa by J. H. Lemay
'Looking Our Way': 1911
'Don't Be Scared': 1914
'How Laurier Leads Quebec': 1917 election
   (by permission of the Winnipeg Free Press)

Canada's First Century

CHAPTER ONE

Confederation and Expansion

THE TOWN had not been built to be a capital. It had been made a capital after a stiff competition with other, more favoured rivals. But for the new nation that had just come into being it was a not inappropriate choice. A small, northern frontier town, set at the edge of a vast expanse of territory that still awaited occupation and development, it was in many respects a miniature of the new nation as a whole. The great pine forests which had first brought the timber merchants up the river sixty years before still loomed over the settlement that had been built to exploit them. To the north, across the deep valley of the Ottawa and beyond the low-lying meadows on the other side, the Laurentian hills rose slowly, deliberately, in ridge after darkening ridge of pine trees. The forest had created Ottawa. It had brought profits and jobs to the timber barons, the sawmill owners, the lumberjacks and raftsmen, as well as to the forwarders and merchants who supplied and served them. The forest had brought the town into being; but the town was slowly and relentlessly devouring the forest, and the signs of that ceaseless and savage assault upon the pine woods were everywhere about the settlement. The wide river was crowded with great rafts of logs. The banks were littered with stacks of boards and piles of dirty sawdust.

South of the Ottawa was the new capital. It lay spread out in a rectangular pattern of drab streets, lined with simple, unpretentious shops and houses, often semi-detached or strung together in terraces, and usually built of wood. Against the dark, majestic background of woods and highlands to the north,

this little centre of urban domesticity and commerce seemed
startlingly incongruous. In their own humble way, the plain
houses of the lumbermen had issued the first defiance to the
forest. But it was the grant of capital status and the construction of the Parliament Buildings that gave a new dramatic
emphasis to this prime contradiction of man and nature. On
the edge of Parliament Hill, overlooking the wide, deep valley
of the Ottawa, the three great stone structures that were to
house the government of Canada had been erected. The view
from the windows from the north front of the central block
across the river to the dark, remote line of the distant Laurentian highlands was completely unobstructed. Politics and geography faced each other in an immediate and implacable confrontation. To the north and west lay the enormous expanse
of rock and water, forest and plain, which made up the half-
continent that the new Dominion of Canada had inherited
and hoped to occupy as its own. To the south stood the Parliament that must try to bring this new nation into effective
being.

⇢≫ II ≪⇠

THE PARLIAMENT, established by the British North America Act of 1867 as the central institution of the new federation, the Dominion of Canada, was the greatest, most ambitious political creation that British America had yet achieved.
It represented the people of four provinces, Ontario and Quebec – the successors of the two divisions of the former Province
of Canada – and the two Maritime provinces of Nova Scotia
and New Brunswick. These first 'Canadians' in the new sense –
citizens no longer of a mere province, but of a potential nation
– were a very small community, measured at least by the im-
mensity of the task that confronted them. The population of
the original Dominion, counted four years after the union, in
the census of 1871, was 3,485,761. The two central provinces,
Ontario with 1,620,851 inhabitants and Quebec with 1,191,516,
made up the great majority of this not very impressive total.

The 387,800 Nova Scotians and the 285,594 New Brunswickers together numbered less than a fifth of the whole.

These were, of course, not all the human resources upon which the new Canada believed it might count in the future. A vast part of British America still lay outside the Dominion. In the east were the two island colonies of Newfoundland and Prince Edward Island, which had so far declined to enter Confederation; and in the west lay Rupert's Land, the North-West Territories, and the Pacific province of British Columbia, all of which, in the circumstances of 1867, could not be brought into the union. Yet these territories, despite their enormous extent, would not likely bring any great increase to Canada's population. Newfoundland, where persistent efforts had been made to limit the number of inhabitants in the interest of the visiting fishermen, had fewer than 150,000 settlers; and Prince Edward Island, with a population of 94,021, was smaller than Montreal, Canada's largest town. The far-western community of whites and half-breeds at the junction of the Red and Assiniboine rivers numbered 12,228; and British Columbia, the most sparsely populated of all the provinces, had a non-Indian population of only 10,586.

The two founding peoples of British America were the French, who had established themselves on the St. Lawrence before the Conquest, and the English-speaking North Americans, the United Empire Loyalists, who had come up from the Thirteen Colonies and the United States during and after the American Revolution. These first inhabitants had been outnumbered, though not submerged, by the huge, successive waves of immigrants from the British Isles which had kept flooding in ever since the conclusion of the War of 1812. English and Scots had come in large and not unequal numbers; but the massive 'famine' migrations of the 1840s had left the Irish the largest of the three British groups. There was a considerable minority of Germans, settled in the Maritime provinces and Ontario, some Dutch, and a small sprinkling of Scandinavians; but the new Canada was, on the whole, a community of two languages, French and English, rather than a babel of many tongues. In 1871, the 1,082,940 Canadians of

French descent, settled mainly in Quebec and New Brunswick, accounted for 31.06 per cent of the Canadian population. The Canadians of British origin, 2,110,502 in number and thus nearly twice as numerous as the French, formed 60.5 per cent of the whole. The remainder – native Indians and Eskimo, other immigrant Europeans, Asians, and Africans, most of whom became English-speaking – totalled less than 10 per cent.

The juxtaposition of French and English had been a dominant solid fact of British America; it was to remain the prime antithesis of the new Canada. A considerable minority of French origin confronted a British majority about twice its size. The contrast between two historic national traditions and two mature philosophies of life was of crucial importance for the future; but it was far from being the only significant cultural difference that divided British American society and helped to prolong its contradictions and disunity. British America, in fact, though largely bilingual, was not bicultural; it was not a cultural duality but a cultural mosaic. The French Canadians and Acadians, established in northern North America for generations, had become a remarkably homogeneous and thoroughly Canadianized people; but the much newer English-speaking communities were complicated social mixtures which still betrayed the rich diversity of their origins. Highland and Lowland Scots, Ulstermen and southern Irish, Britishers fresh from the Motherland, and English-speaking North Americans long resident in the Thirteen Colonies had had to learn to live together through the prolonged turmoil of the settlement process. Though they had slowly become British Americans in interest and sentiment, their older national loyalties and traditions still survived; and these were often intensified and exacerbated by the sectarian religious differences which had proved such a potent divisive force in the middle decades of the nineteenth century.

Among British North Americans, sectarian religion drew even sharper lines of disagreement than race. Highland Scots and southern Irish had combined with French Canadians and Acadians to make the Roman Catholic Church the largest single communion in the new Dominion. Roman Catholics numbered over 40 per cent of the Canadian population; and this massive preponderance had both frightened and angered the various Protestant denominations. They tried, not too successfully, to unite in resistance against the claims and pretensions of Roman Catholicism; but for other purposes they remained for a long time separated in their original small fragments. Like the other immigrants, the clergy of the various Protestant communions had come to British America from both Great Britain and the United States. They had begun their work in the different colonies at different times and in varying fashions; and they were so closely identified with their mother churches that they often took part in the religious quarrels of the homeland even when, as in the case of the disruption of the Church of Scotland in 1843, the original cause of the dispute had no relevance to British America. For many years, the religious divisions of colonialism delayed the growth of united British American churches. In 1867, the Methodists, despite some earlier unions, were still divided into five separate bodies, and the Presbyterians into four.

Sectarian religion deeply affected every aspect of British American life: its influence on the development of education was profound and permanent. From the beginning education had been one of the most important collective enterprises of the pioneer community; and in all the provinces it quickly became the subject of acrimonious controversy. Those British Americans who believed that education was inseparably associated with faith and morals, and that the church ought to control instruction in all three, found themselves engaged in an unending conflict with those other Canadians who urged the separation of church and state and the establishment of national, non-sectarian schools. In Quebec, where Roman Catholic philosophy was securely dominant, the control of education was entrusted to bodies organized on religious lines, Catholic and Protestant, with the state simply providing financial assistance. In Ontario and the Maritime provinces, the younger Protestant denominations, Baptist, Methodist, and Free Church Presbyterian, exerted a determined pressure in support of secular state schools. Egerton Ryerson, the first superintendent of education in Canada West, created a public school system which was to make Ontario the educational model for most of the other provinces. But Ryerson's success, impressive though it was, was not unqualified: Irish and French-Canadian influence was pertinaciously organized in the provincial legislature to compel the public acceptance of Roman Catholic schools as a separate division of the provincial system. And in both Canada and Nova Scotia efforts to establish a secular university were resisted and in part frustrated by sectarian bodies determined to organize higher education along denominational lines.

Throughout British North America the population was predominantly rural: fewer than a quarter of the inhabitants lived in incorporated towns or villages. Montreal was a city of 107,225 people, Toronto about half that size; and the Maritime towns, including the provincial capitals, were smaller still. Most British Americans lived in the open countryside or in small villages; and the family farm became at once the main unit of economic activity and the principal agency of social security and welfare. The provinces concentrated on the production of a few staples, wheat and flour, fish, timber, and lumber; and a large part of the provincial income was derived from the export of these natural products to more mature industrial nations such as Great Britain and the United States. Wood, wind, and water had governed the economic life of colonial British America; but in the last two decades before Confederation steam had been rapidly overtaking water power as a source of energy; steamships were displacing sailing vessels on ocean and lake, and railways were competing with canals and waterways as main avenues of inland transport.

At first, the new industrial methods were used chiefly to increase production in flour mills and sawmills, industries which were closely associated with the traditional staple trades; but soon British Americans began to exploit other native raw materials in an increasingly varied list of manufactures. In 1870, only 181,679 Canadians were employed in manufacturing; and the 38,898 establishments in which they worked probably included every village blacksmith and harness maker. In the main, industry was still small and decentralized; but improved trans-

port had already brought a measure of concentration; and in
Montreal, Toronto, Saint John, and some smaller places fairly
substantial factories were producing woollen textiles, boots and
shoes, furniture, agricultural implements, and beer and spirits.
In the autumn of 1873, when the Canadian Labor Union, the
first central Canadian labour organization, held its first convention, manufacturing was represented by fifty-nine branches of
six international unions, as well as by approximately twenty
local unions. The high cost of the transport of consumers'
goods from abroad gave these new industries some natural protection; and the decline of exports from the United States during and after the American Civil War went far to ensure that
the British American manufacturers would enjoy a virtual monopoly of their home market during a vital phase in the development of provincial industry.

The British American economy was breaking through the
narrow limits of colonialism; British American society was
emerging from the disturbances and antagonisms of the frontier. The middle decades of the nineteenth century had been a
period of compromises and reconciliations: the major controversies over the relation of church and state, religion and education, had been settled. The jangling Protestant sects and the
quarrelsome British nationalities had learned to get along with
each other; and French and English had discovered that, if they
ought not to live too closely together, they equally could not
exist completely apart. The loyalties of the Old World were
yielding to the vigorous interests of the New; the immigrants
of the past were becoming the British American citizens of the
present; and the provincials of the various colonies had begun
to look beyond the boundaries of their respective provinces towards a united British America. In the past, they had always
been inclined to assume that membership in the British Empire was, in itself, a completely satisfying bond of union; but
in the last two decades they had come to realize that there were
important and exclusive interests which they shared as British
Americans and that there were great enterprises which they
ought to undertake together for the benefit of British America
as a whole. They had become conscious as never before of the

potential importance of their enormous territorial inheritance in North America. More than half the continent was theirs of which to make a nation; more than a third lay empty and waiting for occupation in the north-west. And, best of all, the railway and the other techniques of modern industrialism had made development possible on a continental scale.

It was this combination of forces that gave the movement for federation its strength and its final success.

→≫ III ≪←

THE BRITISH NORTH AMERICA ACT of 1867, the act which laid the constitutional framework for the federal union of four British American provinces, Ontario, Quebec, New Brunswick, and Nova Scotia, was a characteristic expression of their collective political experience. Its authors were the thirty-six delegates, known subsequently as the Fathers of Confederation – though some of them did not deserve the title and would, in fact, have indignantly repudiated it – who had met in conference at Charlottetown, Quebec, and London and framed the bases of the union. They were typical mid-Victorian colonial politicians who were intellectually as remote from the eighteenth-century preoccupation with first political principles as they were from the twentieth-century obsession with ethnic and cultural values. They thought of themselves as British subjects, and assumed that they were legitimate heirs of the British constitutional heritage and full participants in the British political experience. Alone among all the colonies that European nations had founded in the New World, the British American provinces had never sought to separate themselves from the Motherland. They had not followed the path through revolution to republicanism which had been first blazed by the United States and worn smooth and commonplace by a long string of slatternly South and Central American republics.

Constitutional monarchy, parliamentary institutions, and responsible government made up a political tradition which was not only British but also British American. The Fathers of Confederation assumed, without question, that this political tradition must be continued unimpaired in the nation they were creating. The calamities that had overtaken republicanism in the past twenty-five years had simply confirmed and strengthened their belief in the wisdom and efficacy of parliamentary institutions on the British model. In western Europe, the republican and liberal governments which had been born of the revolutions of 1848 had weakened and yielded to much more authoritarian and arbitrary régimes; and, in the United States, a terrible civil war had seemed to cast discredit, not only on American federalism, but also on American democracy. In sharp contrast with this tragic republican record of defeat and dishonour, the British constitution, which Walter Bagehot had just celebrated in a new book, had apparently adapted itself to new, more democratic circumstances, without ever sacrificing the continuity of its development. The Fathers of Confederation had good reason for believing that constitutional monarchy on the British model was the best government for free men that had yet been devised. They regarded the British Empire as the greatest association of free states that had ever existed.

There remained, however, the business of adapting British institutions to a union of British provinces – a union which, it was firmly intended, would ultimately extend from ocean to ocean and over a half of the North American continent. Constitutional monarchy on the British model meant parliamentary sovereignty – the concentration of political power in a single, sovereign legislature; and, if a great many British Americans, including certainly such prominent political leaders as John A. Macdonald and Charles Tupper, could have had their way, they would have preferred to see the whole of British America united in a single Parliament and government. But legislative union, however politically desirable, was not thought to be politically possible. The Fathers of Confederation believed that one legislature would be incapable of coping with the diverse needs of a number of varied and widely separated communities. The French-speaking majority of one of those regions, the future province of Quebec, wished to protect its distinctive culture with a measure of local autonomy; and the provinces of the

Atlantic region, which had not developed any system of municipal institutions, would have been left without any local government at all, if their provincial legislatures had been taken away.

No, the union could not be legislative. It would have to be federal. But, though the Fathers of Confederation recognized the inevitability of federalism, they could not help regarding it as a suspect and sinister form of government. There had never yet been a federal union in the British Empire; the United States of America was the only federal union in the English-speaking world; and in 1864-7, when the Fathers of Confederation were planning to unite British America, the United States could scarcely be considered a convincing advertisement for federalism. The republic was, in fact, convulsed by a fearful civil war, a war which seemed to prove that a federal union was a divisive form of government which might very readily break up as a result of its own centrifugal pressures. The 'federal principle', as British Americans called it then, was usually regarded as a highly potent political drug, which might prove efficacious in the cure of certain constitutions, but which must be administered in small doses, with great precautions, and never without a readily available antidote. The obvious corrective to the disruptive forces of 'states rights' was a strong central government; and this the Fathers of Confederation were determined to create. British American union, they admitted, would have to be federal in character; but at the same time it must also be the most strongly centralized union that was possible under federal forms.

This basic principle guided all the planning whose end result was the British North America Act of 1867. The Fathers of Confederation openly declared that they proposed to correct the mistakes and remedy the weaknesses of the American federal union. 'The primary error at the formation of their constitution,' John A. Macdonald said at the Quebec Conference, 'was that each state reserved to itself all sovereign rights, save the small portion delegated. We must reverse this process by strengthening the general government and conferring on the provincial bodies only such powers as may be required for local purposes.' While, in the United States, residuary legislative powers were retained by the State, or by the people, in the new Dominion of Canada they were to be held by the federal Parliament. The Provinces and the Dominion were not to be co-ordinate in authority, as a purist definition of federalism would have required them to be; on the contrary, as Macdonald frankly explained, the provincial governments were to be subordinate to the central government. Their responsibilities and functions, it was generally expected, would be relatively small and unimportant; and their legislative authority, even within the field of provincial powers, was not to be absolute. The chief provincial executive officer, the lieutenant-governor, who was to be appointed by the federal government, could reserve provincial bills for the federal government's consideration, and the federal government could disallow provincial acts. 'We thereby strengthen the central parliament,' said Macdonald in the Canadian legislature after he had finished describing federal powers, 'and make the Confederation one people and one government, instead of five peoples and five governments with merely a point of authority connecting us to a limited and insufficient extent.'

The primary aim of Confederation was political – the creation of a great 'new nationality'; and the British North America Act was the result of a political agreement among several provinces, not of a cultural compact of two ethnic groups, English and French. Before 1867, British America still remained, and was still regarded, not as a cultural duality but, in the words of George Cartier, as 'a diversity of races'. 'In our own federation,' Cartier declared, 'we should have Catholic and Protestant, English, French, Irish, and Scotch, and each by his efforts and his success would increase the prosperity and glory of the new confederacy.' Language was only one of the many components that made up the curious cultural medley that was British America before Confederation. National origin and national tradition – Irish, Scotch, and English, as well as French – might be equally influential, and religion, so often sharpened by sectarian bitterness, was perhaps the most important of all. The Fathers of Confederation had to take account of these differences; but their great aim was not the perpetuation of cultural diversity but the establishment of a united nation. At the Quebec and London conferences they gave, on the whole, relatively little time to the discussion of ethnic and cultural questions; and the resolutions they adopted on these matters, though important and essential, were few, precise in their wording, and limited in their scope.

The British North America Act contained no general declaration of principle that Canada was to be a bilingual and bicultural nation – or, for that matter, that it would remain 'a diversity of races'. The Fathers of Confederation were as little inclined to lay down the law about the cultural purpose and future of their new nation as they were to issue a general pronouncement on the nature and probable destiny of mankind. The English and French languages were given equal official status in the Parliament and the courts of Canada, and in the legislature and courts of Quebec. Canada was to establish only two federal courts, the Supreme Court and the Exchequer Court, at Ottawa; and all the other courts in the country were to be provincial courts, constituted and maintained by the provinces. The French language had thus no official standing in the courts of any of the provinces except Quebec; and, perhaps even more important, it was given no protected place in any of the nation's schools. The Fathers of Confederation showed a fair amount of interest in education and its legislative control; but it was very characteristic of these typical British Americans, with their strong denominational affiliations and frequent sectarian biases, that what concerned them was not the role of language, but the place of religion, in the schools. The provinces were given the power to legislate in respect of education; but this authority was limited by some rather complicated provisions designed to protect any rights or privileges concerning separate or denominational schools.

In sum, the distinctive cultural features of French Canada – its language, civil code, and educational system – were confirmed in those parts of the new Dominion in which they had already become established by law or custom. They were not extended in their application to Ontario and the Atlantic provinces. They were given no protected position in the nation as a whole.

⟩⟩⟩ IV ⟨⟨⟨

THE MAKING and inauguration of the new federal constitution, embodied in the British North America Act, was only the first, theoretical stage in the building of the new nation; the far greater task of its territorial completion and integration still lay ahead. The Canada that celebrated the first Dominion Day on the 1st of July, 1867, was composed of only four provinces, Ontario, Quebec (the two former Canadas), New Brunswick, and Nova Scotia; and, in Nova Scotia, Joseph Howe was leading a popular movement for secession from the Dominion. Beyond the restricted boundaries of the original Dominion, the rest of British America, immense, vulnerable, and largely uninhabited, stretched away, east, west, and north, and far into the distance. In the east, the two island provinces, Newfoundland and Prince Edward Island, still held stubbornly aloof from the union. In the far west, the now united province of British Columbia was a likely candidate for admission to Confederation; but she was separated from Canada by Rupert's Land and the North-West Territories, a vast expanse of almost empty country, still owned or controlled by the Hudson's Bay Company.

A formidable task of national expansion and unification confronted the new federal government, appointed on the 1st of July, 1867. The first cabinet was a coalition of former Confederates, drawn from both parties and all four provinces, and representing every important interest – provincial, ethnic, and religious – in nicely graduated numbers. Its leader, the first Prime Minister of the new Canada, was John Alexander Macdonald. At fifty-two, he seemed oddly youthful in appearance. His dark, curly hair was thick, his eyes amused and friendly, his smile genially sardonic. The long oval of his face was spare, and almost as unlined as a young man's; and, unlike most of his contemporaries, who followed the mid-Victorian fashion of beards, whiskers, and moustaches, he was invariably clean-shaven. There was no sign of the heaviness of age in his tall, slight figure, and no hint of the pride of position in the easy, rather jaunty fashion in which he carried himself. He had always been something of a dandy, and he wore his clothes well. He seemed to take life very easily and to find it continually entertaining; and for a long time people had refused to take him very seriously. They had admitted his great expertise in all the devices and stratagems of party politics; but they were inclined to write him down as an accomplished political manipulator, with few ideas and even fewer principles. The events of the past ten years had gradually but effectively altered this early impression; and the movement for federal union had enabled him to reveal his exceptional gifts to the full. The success of Confederation was largely the result of his expert leadership. The British North America Act was, in the main, the expression of his political theory.

Macdonald and his cabinet were anxious to complete the work of union – to appease Nova Scotia, bring Newfoundland and Prince Edward Island into Confederation, and acquire Canada's great inheritance in the north-west. As it chanced, the political circumstances, both hostile and friendly, of the first few years that followed 1867 helped to hasten the completion of their design. The native Canadian drive towards continentalism was strengthened by two external forces – the same forces that had aided the union movement of 1864-7: the urgency of Great Britain and the pressure of the United States. Ever since the beginning of the American Civil War, Great Britain had been moving purposefully towards an honourable withdrawal from British America. It was not that she hoped or intended to cut the imperial connection with Canada, certainly not until Canada was fully prepared to accept separation; but she was anxious to recall her isolated military garrisons, and to escape from her remaining territorial obligation in North America – her ultimate responsibility for the future of the Hudson's Bay Company lands. If Canada took over Rupert's Land and the North-West Territories, not only would England be relieved of an unwanted burden, but Canada would also be better able to endure. Great Britain had supported Confederation because it seemed likely to create a colonial nation strong enough to take over imperial responsibilities. But, so long as Canada remained a mere fragment of a still disunited British America, it would remain vulnerable. If it could acquire all remaining British territory and reach its destined continental limits, it would have its best chance to survive.

The anxious encouragement of Great Britain was the first of the two external forces hastening national expansion; the second was the pressure of a resentful and predatory United States. The Civil War was over; but peace had not brought a settlement of those angry wartime grievances that the North had come to nurse against Great Britain and British America. The triumphant republic could not easily forget or forgive the sympathy which both British and colonials had shown for the Southern cause; and the American government insistently demanded enormous reparations for the losses inflicted by the *Alabama* (a Southern cruiser built in a British shipyard) on American shipping during the war. It was seriously proposed that the whole of Rupert's Land and the North-West Territories should be ceded to the United States in satisfaction of the *Alabama* claims; and both the new American President, Ulysses S. Grant, and his Secretary of State, Hamilton Fish, were expansionists who were prepared to use almost any method, short of armed force, to acquire all or part of British America. In the east, where there were established colonies, the danger was less; but, so long as Nova Scotia was dissatisfied and Newfoundland and Prince Edward Island remained outside the union, there was at least a chance of American intervention. The likelihood was much greater in the west where the politicians and journalists of the frontier state of Minnesota were casting covetous glances upon a vast and almost empty territory which seemed as if it might be theirs for the taking. 'It is quite evident to me,' Macdonald wrote in January 1870, '. . . that the United States government are resolved to do all they can, short of war, to get possession of our western territory, and we must take immediate and vigorous steps to counteract them.'

⇛ V ⇚

THERE WERE DANGERS everywhere. But the pacification of
Nova Scotia was, without any doubt, the immediate and
most urgent task. Joseph Howe and the Nova Scotian Anti-
Confederates had failed to persuade the British government to
exclude their province from the union of 1867; but they refused
to believe that this first rebuff was final. In their eyes, the
sweeping Anti-Confederate successes in both the federal and
provincial elections of 1867 seemed an irrefutable proof, which
even the unwilling British government must recognize, of Nova
Scotia's unanimous determination to escape from Confederation. Howe led a second delegation to England to ask for
repeal of the union; and Charles Tupper, Nova Scotia's leading supporter of Confederation, was dispatched by the Canadian government to counteract his old rival's propaganda. 'Repeal is not even a matter of discussion,' Macdonald declared
bluntly; and this was very much the way in which the British
government looked at it. Neither Conservatives nor Liberals
were willing to undo the work of Confederation. To break up
the newly formed union would simply protract and perhaps perpetuate the fragmentation of British America. It might mean the
indefinite prolongation of Britain's responsibilities in the region
and the indefinite postponement of her military withdrawal from
North America.

This second British refusal meant the end of the repeal movement. What were the Nova Scotian Anti-Confederates to do?
Two extreme, heroic courses – open rebellion or annexation to
the United States – were conceivable; but no Nova Scotian politician, least of all Joseph Howe, could bring himself to advocate such desperate policies. A species of political 'sit-down'
strike, in which the Anti-Confederate majority in the provincial legislature would refuse to govern and prevent their opponents from doing so, was perhaps a more feasible plan; but,
though Howe suggested this course, his Anti-Confederate associates declined to consider it seriously. The movement had
obviously reached a dead end: and Howe came to the conclusion that submission, on the best terms possible, was inevitable.

At first he hoped vaguely that he might obtain some amendments of real substance in the British North America Act; but the Canadian and British governments were adamant in their refusal to consider any constitutional changes. Better financial terms – a larger federal subsidy to the provincial government – was all that Macdonald was willing to grant; and in the end this became the basis of an agreement by which Howe renounced repeal and, in January 1869, entered the federal cabinet.

Long before Howe had made his great renunciation and accepted federal office, two of his new colleagues in the Canadian cabinet, Sir George Cartier and William McDougall, had gone to England to make a start on the next and more ambitious phase of the nationalist programme, the acquisition of Rupert's Land and the North-West Territories. With the help of some heavy persuasion from the British government, the Hudson's Bay Company was induced to cede its lands to Canada in return for a payment of £300,000, and a grant of one-twentieth of the western 'fertile belt'. The Canadian government proceeded very cautiously with the political organization of its nearly empty domain. Rupert's Land was to be governed provisionally as a territory with a small nominated council, rather than as a province; representative institutions and responsible government would come later, when they were warranted by the spread of settlement. William McDougall, the Lieutenant-Governor designate, went west early with the intention of familiarizing himself with the country and its people before the transfer of authority actually took place on the 1st of December, 1869. He never reached his future 'capital', the tiny Red River settlement. On the 30th of October, he was stopped at the Canadian border by a roadblock, held by an armed force of *Métis* or French-speaking half-breeds.

Undoubtedly, a fair number of people at Red River awaited the coming of the Canadians without enthusiasm, or with doubt and misgiving. But it was the initiative of the *Métis* which alone inspired the resistance and gave it force and direction. They were 'a peculiar people', conscious of their distinctive corporate identity and grandiloquently styling themselves 'the new nation'; in fact, their slow ascent from nomadism to civilization was far from complete. Reluctant and indifferent farmers, expert horsemen and hunters, born and bred to a long tradition of direct and violent action, they had built up a semi-military organization through the comradeship of the buffalo hunt. Their uniquely gifted son, Louis Riel, was an able but temperamental and dictatorial man, full of delusions of grandeur, quickly infuriated when his will was crossed, and quite without compunction in the use of force. He and his *Métis* seized Fort Garry, the Hudson's Bay Company's fortified post at Red River, and proclaimed a provisional government for the region.

Riel's immediate object was to prevent the automatic and unconditional transfer of the north-west to Canada; he was determined to obtain safeguards which would ensure the survival of his *Métis* against the peril of Protestant and Anglo-Saxon immigration and settlement. His ultimate aim remains uncertain; he may seriously have considered the alternative of annexation to the United States. Certainly, during the first months of the resistance, the principal advisers of his provisional government were a small group of Americans resident at Red River, one of whom was a government agent and the others avowed annexationists. These men joined forces with the annexationist politicians, journalists, and railway men of Minnesota and the American north-west – 'the Yankee wire-pullers', Macdonald called them; and both groups tried, in their various ways, to persuade the American government to exploit Canada's difficulties, to take advantage of the temporary suspension of British and Canadian authority at Red River, and to press forward the territorial aggrandizement of the United States.

This prospect appalled Macdonald. He was determined that 'the United States should not get behind us by right or by force and intercept our route to the Pacific'; and he realized that, as long as the effective acquisition of Rupert's Land was delayed, the whole of his great design for national expansion was in jeopardy. The resistance at Red River must be appeased as quickly as possible. He knew that he would have to make terms for the union of the north-west with Canada; but he was determined that Canada would negotiate, not with Riel's dictatorship, the provisional government with its American and clerical advisers, but with the Red River community as a whole. Donald Smith, sent west as a federal commissioner, succeeded in calling an assembly or 'convention' of elected delegates from all the parishes of the settlement, French and English; and the 'convention', in its 'list of rights', drew up reasonable terms for the admission of the north-west, as a territory, into Confederation.

This was a sensible settlement; but it was not to be. Riel was resolved to prevent it. The democratically expressed wishes of the Red River community, where they differed from his private plans for his own people, the *Métis*, meant nothing to him; and the very generosity and goodwill of the settlement gave him his chance of thwarting its intentions. The 'convention', in a final gesture of conciliation, had confirmed the provisional government and elected Riel as president. Once back in control, Riel took the negotiations with Canada into his own hands. He appointed the delegates who were to go to Ottawa, and he made short work of the 'list of rights' of the 'convention'. Two new 'lists of rights', drawn up in private by Riel and his clerical advisers, demanded provincial status, which the convention had expressly rejected, and separate or confessional schools, which the convention had not even discussed.

Macdonald was compelled to yield. So long as Riel's provisional government lasted, the threat of American intervention in the north-west remained. A quick settlement was the only solution; but a quick settlement meant, in fact, acceptance of Riel's terms, now strongly backed by French-Canadian influence in the federal government. Macdonald was caught in a squeeze-play with Riel and his clerical and American advisers on the one hand, and Sir George Cartier and the French and Roman Catholic M.P.s at Ottawa on the other. 'The French,' Sir Stafford Northcote, the governor of the Hudson's Bay Company, candidly observed, 'are earnestly bent upon the establishment of a French and Catholic power in the north-west to counteract the great preponderance of Ontario.' 'Manitoba', the name given to the first political division of the north-west, entered Confederation as a province with a top-heavy bicameral legislature, modelled on that of Quebec, two official languages, and confessional schools.

→» VI «←

WITH THE CREATION of Manitoba, the most serious danger threatening Macdonald's expansionist plans had ended. It was now nearly certain that Canada would acquire the whole of the British north-west and that a new transcontinental nation would come into being in North America. It was also fairly clear that the United States, however reluctantly and disapprovingly, was prepared to accept this situation. In the early spring of 1871 a Joint High Commission met at long last in Washington and proceeded to settle all the wartime grievances and controversies – including the dispute over the *Alabama* claims – which had grown up between Great Britain and the United States.

In the meantime, Canada's onward expansionist march had already been resumed. The acquisition of Rupert's Land and the North-West Territories cleared the way for the union with British Columbia. British Columbia had never seriously considered any other destiny; and a petition, circulated in 1869, for annexation to the United States, collected only a few score signatures. The British Columbia Legislative Council, partly elected and partly appointed, agreed to send a delegation to Canada to negotiate for union on terms proposed by the Executive Council; and the three delegates, R. W. Carrall, J. W. Trutch, and J. S. Helmcken, reached Ottawa in June 1870, just after the passage of the Manitoba Act. Their first request was for provincial status with a fully elected legislative assembly and responsible government; they also wanted a generous debt settlement and lavish federal subsidies. But their most interesting – and, as it turned out, their most controversial – proposals had to do with communications with Canada. They asked for the construction of a coach road between Fort Garry and British Columbia, the commencement of a railway within three years, and thereafter an annual expenditure of $1,000,000 on the British Columbia section of the line. The requests were stiff, almost exorbitant; but to the amazement, almost the incredulity, of the delegates, the terms voluntarily offered by the Dominion government vastly exceeded anything they had ever dreamed of asking. The coach road was dropped; instead, Canada offered to begin a railway within two years, and finish it in ten.

In 1873, two years after the entrance of British Columbia, Prince Edward Island followed and became the seventh province in Confederation. Prince Edward Island had rejected 'better terms' in 1869; she might have gone on almost indefinitely considering and declining 'better terms', every few years, in the vague hope of getting a superlative bargain; but in the early 1870s a series of events occurred which stopped this temperamental shilly-shallying. An expensive, badly designed, and corruptly managed railway-building programme ended the Island's state of financial innocence and her proud sense of self-sufficiency. In 1864, at the time of the Quebec Conference, she had had a debt of less than $250,000; in 1874, it had risen to a little over $4,000,000. Canada agreed to assume the debt and to buy up the land of the remaining absentee proprietors; and, reluctantly, through sheer necessity, Prince Edward Island overcame her complacent parochialism and entered Confederation. On the 17th of May, the day S. L. Tilley, the new Minister of Finance, presented the terms of union to the Canadian House of Commons, a daughter was born to Lady Dufferin, the Governor General's wife. 'This, with Prince Edward's Island, makes *twins*,' Dufferin wrote to Macdonald.

In the first six years of its existence, the new Dominion had nearly attained its appointed natural limits. Newfoundland, alone of all the British North American territories, remained outside Confederation. The generous terms of union which the Carter government negotiated with Canada in 1869 were rejected in the Newfoundland general election of the autumn of that year; and the defeat was so decisive that all hope of Newfoundland's admission was abandoned for another quarter-century. Apart from this important limitation, the great work of nation building was complete; but the process of expansion had been troubled and hurried, and Canada had incurred costs, the full extent of which could not then be foreseen. In Manitoba the Dominion had been forced to impose an elaborate, highly unsuitable constitution upon an immature province which had not yet developed its real and permanent character. To British Columbia, the Dominion had promised, on its own initiative, to begin a Pacific railway within two years and to finish it within ten. The burden of the railway was to strain Canada's financial resources to their limit; and the enforced and hasty appeasement of the north-west was to provoke a reaction which would seriously divide the Canadian people.

CHAPTER TWO

National Decisions

IN THE SPRING of 1868, when Confederation was not yet a year old, a group of five young men – Charles Mair, William Alexander Foster, George Taylor Denison, Robert Grant Haliburton, and Henry James Morgan – used to meet and talk for long hours in Morgan's bachelor quarters, one of the 'corner rooms' in the Revere House, a small hotel in Ottawa. Mair was a poet who came from the little village of Lanark. Foster was a Toronto barrister. Denison, also a Toronto lawyer, had become lieutenant-colonel of a militia regiment, the Governor General's Body Guard, and aspired to a professional military career. Haliburton, the son of Thomas Chandler Haliburton, the author of *The Clockmaker*, combined his professional work as a barrister with some rather erudite journalism and the promotion of his family's mining interests in Nova Scotia. Morgan was an Ottawa civil servant who had already begun a second career in the compilation of Canadian biographical dictionaries and the editing of the speeches of such Canadians as Thomas D'Arcy McGee.

With the exception of Haliburton, who was thirty-six years old, they were all under thirty. They were all convinced that Confederation, as it then stood, was a prosaic, humdrum, uninspiring enterprise, resembling nothing so much as a joint stock company which had been put together after a good deal of hard, shrewd bargaining, with immediate and strictly limited purposes in mind. They all agreed that such a soulless form of incorporation, left to itself, would never result in the creation of a great new nationality. A truly Canadian national feeling they felt certain could alone animate Confederation. Canadians must acquire an understanding of their historic origins, a proud realization of the many sources of their strength, an awareness of their national identity, and a confident belief in the unlimited possibilities of their future. 'Canada First' was chosen as the group's motto and soon became its name. At the start, the Canada Firsters professed a very lofty independence of Canadian political parties and party politics; but through Charles Mair, who went west to Fort Garry in 1869 and played a somewhat inglorious part in the Red River insurrection, the group soon became deeply involved in the politics of western expansion, and subsequently in Canadian public affairs in general. Canada First acquired publicity, and with it a number of new adherents. It became a political movement, almost a third party; and, although its members never lost their idealism, they soon became much more interested in practical realities. The Canadian National Association was formed, and early in 1875 it published a programme with planks which dealt with every important aspect of Canadian national life.

The year was significant. The first phase of nation building was over. Canada had attained continental proportions; and, with the exception of the sentinel island of Newfoundland, Confederation was complete. The federal union of nearly the whole of British America was a considerable achievement; but Macdonald himself would have been quite prepared to agree with Canada First that it was a political achievement only. A divided British America had become a united Canada; but the change was a change of constitutional form rather than of economic and social substance. The rudimentary political framework of a nation existed; but the nation itself had yet to become a vital reality. It remained to realize the full potentialities of the enormous half-continent that the Dominion had become – to settle its empty spaces, to develop its resources, to make it the homeland of a prosperous and contented people. These were generally recognized and accepted goals, for all Canadians as well as for the members of Canada First. But how were they to be attained?

The answers to these questions were not found quickly, or

all at once. The Fathers of Confederation and their successors were sure from the beginning about some features of their programme; but about others they were hesitant and divided. It took them some time to decide on certain parts of their plan; and it was not until 1878 that the last great decision in policy, the protective tariff, was taken. By then it had become obvious that Canada had set out on a career of economic nationalism. An economically viable nation was to be established on the northern half of the continent and its development and growth were to be promoted by three major national policies: immigration and western settlement, all-Canadian transcontinental railway transport, and industrialization by means of a protective tariff. The relationship between western settlement and transcontinental transport seemed obvious and most Canadians accepted the ultimate need of a Pacific railway, though they differed about the date of its commencement and the speed of its construction. They disagreed much more seriously about the desirability of the third national policy, the protective tariff; and, as time would show, this became the subject of frequently renewed and almost perennial controversy.

The first and most fundamental of the three national policies, large-scale immigration and western settlement, was accepted by everybody without doubt, misgiving, or disagreement. Immigrants from abroad and settlers in the west were the first essentials. The occupation and development of Rupert's Land and the North-West Territories were basic to the whole design of continental nation building. The west was conceived as the future homeland of millions, as a vast reservoir of new national resources, as a market for eastern commerce and industry, and as the true north-west passage to the Pacific and the Orient. The west would make Canada a nation. Its settlement must be rapid, in the national interest; it should be made as easy and attractive as possible in order to compete with the United States. For all these reasons the federal government should keep control of the whole process in its own hands. By the terms of the British North America Act, lands and natural resources were left to the provinces; but the Fathers of Confederation decided that the management of the great new western domain should remain with the nation in order that it might work out an integrated series of national policies for immigration, settlement, and transcontinental transport.

This the coalition government, led by Sir John Macdonald, proceeded to do. To a large extent, but with some significant deviations, the Canadian westward movement was a planned and directed process. It got under way at least two generations after the American westward movement had started; and it was, in the main, a phenomenon of the railway age. The power of the state preceded rather than followed the westward movement in Canada. Long before any considerable body of settlers reached the west, federal Indian agents, surveyors, engineers, and police had arrived to prepare the way for the newcomers and to protect and control them. During the 1870s, the Canadian government negotiated a series of treaties by which the western Indian tribes surrendered their original title to the land in exchange for reserves. The first detachment of the Royal North-West Mounted Police trekked west in 1874. A uniform and integrated survey of the whole enormous region was begun in 1869, with the Winnipeg Meridian as a base line, and the section of 640 acres as the basic unit. The Dominion Lands Act of 1872, frankly modelled on the American Free Homestead Law of a decade previously, provided that a settler could lay claim to a quarter section of 160 acres on payment of a small registration fee. He could acquire title to his homestead in three years, provided his settlement duties were fulfilled; and, in addition, he could obtain pre-emption rights to a neighbouring quarter section.

The political organization of the North-West Territories came last. It was not until 1875, when Alexander Mackenzie had succeeded Sir John Macdonald as Prime Minister, that the Parliament of Canada completed its western arrangements by providing for organized government in the region beyond Manitoba. Mackenzie then did what Macdonald had tried to do – and had been prevented from doing – in 1869-70; he established a territorial form of government for the north-west, with powers more limited than those of a province. He sought to avoid the mistake that had obviously been made in Manitoba –

the mistake of determining in advance, and in detail, the constitution of a country which could hardly yet be said to exist. His intention was to provide the region with a simple, extremely flexible political system, which would permit the future westerners to make their own decisions and create their own institutions, as changing times and circumstances required. The North-West Territories Act of 1875, which established a nominated council but provided for its gradual evolution into an elected assembly as the growth of settlement warranted, proved on the whole to be a well-conceived measure which was readily adjustable to the growing maturity of the west, and which lasted for thirty years down to the creation of the provinces of Alberta and Saskatchewan in 1905.

In the main, Mackenzie and his ministers attained their object; but in two important respects they failed. A system of separate or confessional schools was added, by amendment, to the original North-West Territories Act of 1875; and, two years later when the statute was amended again, French was given official status in the courts and the legislature. These changes were not the result of a deliberate governmental attempt to promote bilingualism and biculturalism on the prairies. Mackenzie and his ministers never for a moment suggested or implied that they were trying to establish an equal partnership of French and English in the north-west. The Fathers of Confederation, a number of whom were still members of the House of Commons and the Senate, acknowledged no moral commitment to biculturalism, and, during the debate, spoke not one word in support of either the French language or separate schools.

Separate schools, in fact, formed no part of Mackenzie's original draft bill of 1875. The amendment proposing them was moved by Edward Blake, a Liberal M.P. who was not, of course, a Father of Confederation, and not even a member of Mackenzie's cabinet, from which he had resigned a year before. In the Senate, the only Father of Confederation who spoke on the amendment was George Brown, who vigorously opposed it; and it passed the upper house by a majority of only two. Two years later, the grant of legal status to the French language came about in an even stranger and more accidental fashion. Like the proposal of sectarian schools in 1875, it was not a government amendment at all; it was introduced by a private member of the Senate; and when it was brought down to the Commons, David Mills, the responsible minister, greeted it with distinctly less than bicultural fervour. He reminded the members that the dominant language of the region was Cree; he said that he thought the new North-West Council was the only body that could properly settle the question of official languages. He regretted the Senate amendment, and reluctantly accepted it because otherwise it would be impossible to get the revised statute through Parliament before the close of the session.

The federal arrangements for the settlement of the north-west – the first of the great national objects – were thus a mixture of careful, long-term planning and hasty, ill-considered action. The preparations for the actual occupation and exploitation of the land itself had been started long in advance, and carried out deliberately and systematically. On the other hand, some of the west's basic institutions, in the Territories as well as in Manitoba, were established prematurely and haphazardly, not as a result of any careful estimate of future western necessities, but in response to the pressure of immediate circumstances, and the influence of eastern party politics. Some of the mistakes made in Manitoba had been repeated in the north-west.

⇛ II ⇚

THE SECOND of the great national projects – the Pacific railway – never quite gained the unanimous support that had been given to the policy of western settlement. Everybody agreed in principle that communications with the north-west should be improved and that eventually this would mean a railway; but people differed about the timing of such a vast undertaking; and these latent disagreements were brought violently into the open when the terms of the bargain with British Columbia were revealed. Sir George Cartier, who had taken charge of the negotiations during the illness of Macdonald, represented the expansionist spirit of the coalition government in its most aggressive form. He had eclipsed the British Columbian proposals by his magnificent offer to begin the Pacific railway in two years and to finish it in ten. The Conservative caucus in Ottawa, informed of this princely largesse, exploded in doubts and criticisms; in Parliament the Liberal opposition denounced the railway clause of the agreement as an extravagant and ruinously expensive commitment. The resistance, tacit or open, on both sides of the House was so serious that Cartier, though he refused to alter the terms of union, was obliged in the end to introduce a government resolution promising that the rate of taxation would not be increased for railway purposes.

Nevertheless, the Conservatives were determined to honour the bargain with British Columbia. They were convinced that the Pacific railway was essential to the national plan; but at the same time they realized that, in sponsoring such an undertaking, Canada was facing the hideous dilemma which always confronts young peoples and new nations, with vast territories, hopeful prospects, great ambitions, and little money. On the one hand, the national interest plainly required that the railway should be owned and controlled by Canadians. On the other hand, how was it possible for the Canadians to finance such a vast undertaking themselves? The Intercolonial Railway – another national commitment, made at Confederation – had been built as a government work. But, if Cartier and Macdonald had ever believed that the Pacific railway might be constructed in the same direct fashion by the state, the thought did not survive the ominous parliamentary reception of the bargain with British Columbia. Part at least of the enormous burden of this new national enterprise would have to be shifted into private hands. But how could it be done with safety? The Canadians could not supply the necessary capital themselves. They would unquestionably have to seek it outside. How could they get it from England, where interest in investment in Canada had obviously declined? And, if driven to rely largely on American financing, how could they be sure that the railway would remain in Canadian control and serve genuine Canadian interests?

In 1872 and 1873, these hypothetical questions became real questions which urgently demanded answers. Two Canadian syndicates, or 'rings', were organized to compete for the Pacific Charter. One, the Interoceanic Railway Company, had David L. Macpherson as its president; the other, headed by Sir Hugh Allan, was called the Canadian Pacific Railway Company. Macpherson was a substantial Toronto business man, an experienced railway contractor, a good Conservative, and a warm friend and admirer of Macdonald. Allan, on the other hand, had gained his experience and success in transatlantic shipping. In 1852, he and his brother Andrew had formed the Montreal Ocean Steamship Company, and in the past two decades they had made 'Allan' almost as famous a name as 'Cunard'. Sir Hugh – he had been knighted in 1871 for his services to transatlantic transport – was the senior in age and probably the richer of the two men; but, despite the prominence of his position in Canadian business, he knew very little about railways.

It was possibly Allan's awareness of this deficiency in his knowledge and experience that led him to welcome the approaches of a group of New York and Chicago railway promoters. Several of these men were already involved in the Northern Pacific Railway, an American project which, on the face of it, was a potential rival of the Canadian Pacific; and their motives for joining Allan were obscure, if not equivocal. Allan remained the titular head of the Canadian Pacific Railway Company; but, in fact, he was the solitary Canadian in a group of American capitalists with divided interests and loyalties. Macpherson's Interoceanic Company, on the other hand, had no connections with the United States. It drew support chiefly from Toronto, which during the last two decades had been slowly becoming a serious rival of Montreal.

Macdonald, faced with the crucial decision of awarding the charter, viewed the situation anxiously. For party reasons, he did not wish to take sides in the commercial rivalry of Montreal and Toronto; for other and higher political reasons, for vital national interests, he was resolved to prevent an enterprise of such importance falling under the control of foreigners. The problem was complicated and dangerous; but, in Macdonald's eyes, its solution seemed obvious and simple. He must persuade Allan to get rid of his doubtful American colleagues and to unite with Macpherson's reliable Canadians. The result would be a strong national company in which the interests of the two leading commercial centres, Montreal and Toronto, would be reconciled. All during 1872, Macdonald struggled to effect an amalgamation of the two companies.

The plan seemed certain to succeed. Yet, in the end, it completely failed. It failed because of the vehement and assertive personalities of the two principals, Macpherson and Allan; Macpherson's ineradicable jealousy and suspicion were matched and exceeded by the reckless ambition and duplicity of Allan. Macpherson was determined to prevent Allan from becoming president of the amalgamated company; he refused to believe – and with good reason – that Allan would really break with his American colleagues. Allan, on his part, insisted on being president and stuck doggedly to his aim of gaining majority control of the company for himself and his American friends. A strange and violent change had, within a few months, come over the character of this soberly successful Scottish shipowner. The Pacific railway project obsessed him. He now saw himself as the dominating force in a great, amphibious transport system which would encircle more than half the globe; and this grandiose conception drove him into a brief, fantastic career of corruption, duplicity, and intrigue. He spent a small fortune in promoting the public opinion that would force the Macdonald government to meet his terms. He contributed lavishly to the Conservative campaign fund in the general election of 1872, in the vain hope of gaining special favours. He persistently evaded Macdonald's requests that he get rid of his American colleagues. Macdonald, despairing of achieving the amalgamation, proceeded to form a third, completely new, government-sponsored company from which the Americans were to be excluded. Allan was to be president; but this was his only privilege. And he had to pay dearly for it. Casually, even bluntly, he informed his American colleagues that their partnership was at an end.

The Americans, furious at their betrayal, were determined

that Allan should not climb to triumph over their prostrate bodies. They demanded revenge; and they, and the leaders of the Canadian Liberal Party with whom they quickly got in contact, already possessed, or soon acquired, the means of exacting revenge to the full. Allan had left behind him a clear trail of amazingly indiscreet and incriminating documents. His garrulous letters to the American promoters told the full story of his fantastic misrepresentations and shameless double-dealing; the telegrams and memoranda he had received from Cartier and Macdonald revealed the huge total of his contributions to the Conservative campaign fund in the general election of 1872. The Americans simply handed over their letters to the Liberal leaders; and the Liberal leaders, by suborning the chief clerk in the office of Allan's solicitor, got possession of the documents which proved how much Allan had contributed to the Conservative war chest.

On the basis of this evidence, the Liberals charged, in the spring of 1873, that the Canadian Pacific Railway Company was really financed by American capital and that it had been awarded the Pacific Charter in return for election campaign contributions. A long and detailed inquiry by a royal commission left both these specific charges unproved. Allan had spent his own, not American, money in promotion; and the charter had finally been given to a completely new company, in which the Americans had no part. Nevertheless, Macdonald was open to severe censure. He had taken election funds from a man with whom he was negotiating a major contract in the national interest.

The Pacific Scandal, as it was inevitably called, destroyed Allan and the first Canadian Pacific Railway company. It brought the resignation of the Conservative government in November 1873. It nearly closed Macdonald's political career. The first great effort at western expansion had ended in catastrophe.

→≫ III ≪←

THE LIBERALS, or Reformers, had gained office, not on their own merits, but simply as a result of the overwhelming discredit of the Conservatives. A national Liberal Party could scarcely be said to exist; certainly it was not prepared to rule. The Reformers of Ontario and the Rouges of Quebec had not had a good record of co-operation in the past; and they had not established effective links with their potential Maritime colleagues, many of whom were former Anti-Confederates. Alexander Mackenzie, the new Prime Minister, was an honest, sincere, hard-working, and devoted public servant; but his views were not large, and he was neither an inspiring leader nor a good manager of men. He led a disunited and unorganized following in Parliament, and presided uneasily over an ill-assorted, frequently changing group of ministers. Some were plainly unfitted for office, others accepted it reluctantly, and still others showed a regrettable tendency to resign at the first opportunity.

Perhaps the most temperamental member of this unreliable company was Edward Blake. Blake was an able man, with a fine legal mind, a ready and masterful grasp of complex problems, and a superb gift for incisive but prolix argument. His instinctive urge was to direct and control; but he grew restive under the routine of administration, and he joined and left the ministry without the slightest concern for anything but his own convenience. 'Blake,' said his colleague Richard Cartwright, the Minister of Finance, 'was constitutionally incapable of serving loyally under anybody.' Behind him was a discontented radical wing of the Liberal Party which would have liked to see him replace Mackenzie as leader. And there were times when Blake undoubtedly shared their aim.

Mackenzie and his colleagues differed considerably from the Conservatives in their attitude to the questions of national growth. They viewed Canadian nationalism in a quite different light. Their interests lay rather in Canadian constitutional autonomy and political reform than in Canadian economic development. They introduced the ballot – which Macdonald

had opposed – in order to improve the character of Canadian
political life; and for the same reasons they enacted that general
elections, which before had straggled on from constituency to
constituency for a fortnight or more, should be held on a single
day. On Blake's initiative, the Governor General's instructions
were amended so as to bring them into accordance with Canada's new national status. The Supreme Court of Canada, for
which Macdonald had prepared the way, was established; and,
again on Blake's part, a strenuous effort was made to stop
appeals from it to the Judicial Committee of the Privy Council in England. Both Mackenzie and Blake showed a strong
tendency to resist any attempt on the part of the Governor
General or the Colonial Office to intervene in Canadian domestic affairs; and this prickly Canadianism soon got them involved in a long-drawn-out dispute with the Governor General,
Lord Dufferin, over the Pacific railway.

The railway continued to be the central issue of national
expansion. The collapse of Allan's company had flung the Pacific
project back on the Canadian government. What were the
Liberals to do about it? They had vehemently opposed the
terms of the union with British Columbia; Mackenzie had
angrily declared that the agreement was 'a bargain meant to be
broken'. And the disaster of the Pacific Scandal had simply
confirmed the party's firm conviction that Conservative daring
and improvidence were wrong and Liberal prudence and
economy unquestionably right. Even if the economic weather
had remained favourable, Mackenzie and his colleagues would
probably have been very cautious and deliberate in their
approach to the Pacific railway. But, just as they took office, the
whole western world was settling down into what proved to be
a prolonged and serious slump. Inevitably, the depression
increased the already formidable difficulties in the way of
financing a Canadian transcontinental railway. The Mackenzie
government, which was even more eager than the Macdonald
government had been to shift a large part of the burden on to
the shoulders of a commercial company, found that its liberal
invitations to possible railway promoters went completely
unanswered.

What was to be done? If it had not been for the promise to British Columbia, the Liberals might have postponed the Pacific railway indefinitely. But a promise, however mistaken and foolish, had been given; and Mackenzie and at least some of his colleagues believed that a real attempt must be made to honour it. In the end, the government decided to undertake the railway as a public work; but it took for granted that, in the circumstances, it would not be required or expected to comply with the terms of the original agreement. The railway had not been begun within the two years originally prescribed; it was now utterly impossible to complete it within ten. A new, less onerous agreement was essential. But what were its precise terms to be? Over this crucial issue there broke out a prolonged and unseemly row – a row that seriously divided the Liberal Party, embroiled the Liberal government with the Governor General and the Colonial Office, and strained the relations between the Dominion and British Columbia to the breaking point.

Mackenzie confidently hoped and believed that British Columbia would willingly accept a modified version of the terms its own delegates had requested when the negotiations for union had opened in Ottawa in June 1870. He declined to fix a date for the commencement of construction of the railway; but he offered to prosecute the surveys vigorously, to spend $1,500,000 annually on the British Columbia mainland once the route had been finally chosen, and, in the meantime, to build a railway at federal expense from Esquimalt to Nanaimo on Vancouver Island. To his great surprise and chagrin, British Columbia unceremoniously turned down this offer and appealed over the head of the Dominion for the intervention of the imperial government. Carnarvon, the Colonial Secretary, who accepted the role of arbitrator in the dispute, bettered Mackenzie's terms by increasing the annual expenditure on the mainland to $2,000,000, and fixing 1890 as the final date for the completion of the railway. Reluctantly, sullenly, Mackenzie agreed to the Carnarvon compromise, and tried for a while to carry it out. But he had reckoned without Blake and Blake's followers, who regarded Mackenzie's original offer as the extreme limit of concession, and were quite willing to see British Columbia secede from the union if she found it unsatisfactory. The Esquimalt and Nanaimo bill was defeated in the Senate, with prominent Liberal senators concurring in its rejection; and poor Mackenzie realized, with a shock, that he must subordinate the appeasement of British Columbia to the pacification of Edward Blake. Blake entered the cabinet as Minister of Justice; and henceforth, to the disgust of British Columbia and the disapproval of Dufferin and Carnarvon, his 'hard line' dominated Liberal railway policy.

Yet the railway did make progress under Mackenzie. It was pushed forward, not in accordance with some great national plan, but in a piecemeal, provisional fashion, in which the guiding principle was economy. The north-west was to be reached by simply filling in the gaps in the existing water transport and the existing American railways. A section of the main line from Winnipeg to Lake Superior was started. A branch was built from Winnipeg to Pembina on the international border; and this line, connecting with the American railways to St. Paul and Chicago, completed the first unbroken railway route between central Canada and Manitoba. It was a success, one of Mackenzie's few successes; but there was nothing distinctively Canadian about it. It had been achieved in continental, not national, terms.

⇨ IV ⇦

THE THIRD AND LAST of the three great national policies was the protective tariff. It was adopted years after the other two major decisions had been reached, and it provoked the most angry and persistent of all the public debates over the national programme. The eventual need for a railway to the Pacific had been conceded almost from the beginning; and the dispute over the project centred largely on the date of its commencement, and the speed and method of its construction. The controversy over the tariff went somewhat deeper; it concerned a revolutionary change in an old policy, a change advocated on a new and different principle. A frankly protective tariff would, in fact, be a sharp departure from the commercial traditions of both British America and Canada. Up to Confederation, the British American provinces had stuck fairly faithfully to low revenue tariffs. Canada, the most advanced province economically, had gone furthest in the direction of 'incidental protection', though it had never openly avowed acceptance of the protective principle. In the argument over the Quebec scheme of union, the Anti-Confederates in Nova Scotia and New Brunswick had professed great alarm at these high Canadian rates; and Canada, anxious to quiet Maritime fears that commercial policy after Confederation would be fashioned largely in accordance with Canadian interests, voluntarily reduced its tariff in the summer of 1866, leaving 15 per cent on manufactured goods as its highest rate. This reduction brought Canadian customs duties approximately down to the Maritime level; and this was the tariff adopted for the new Dominion by the first Parliament after Confederation.

Despite a limited amount of tinkering, it remained virtually unaltered for the first seven years of the union. But, already, even before the coming of the depression, the forces that threatened its maintenance were gaining in strength. In the last two decades, a small-scale, decentralized manufacturing industry had succeeded in establishing itself in Canada, particularly in Ontario and Quebec. The American Civil War, which compelled American industry to concentrate on wartime production, gave Canadian manufacturers a great opportunity to dominate their own home markets; and for some years this relative immunity from American competition was prolonged by the postwar inflation in the United States. Then, just as American industry was prepared to re-enter the export business vigorously, the depression came; and the depression, which lowered the prices of manufactured goods and consequently lowered the level of Canadian *ad valorem* protection, enabled both American and British manufacturers to dump the low-priced products of their overstocked factories on Canada. Canadian manufacturers, crying indignantly that their own private commercial preserve had become a 'slaughter market' for foreigners, began to organize for increased protection. As 1875 progressed, protectionist views began to appear more frequently in the resolutions of

Boards of Trade, in newspaper editorials, and in candidates' speeches in urban by-elections.

The Canadian manufacturers suffered; so also did the Canadian government. The avowed object of Confederation had been the building of a new transcontinental nation; for this Canada had made ambitious plans, devised bold policies, and committed itself to very large expenditures. The Liberals had distrusted some of these plans and had tried to modify their scope or delay their implementation; but, despite all their efforts, they had been left with a heavy expenditure which had become increasingly difficult to finance. It was impossible at that time to levy an effective income tax in Canada; and the nation's only substantial resource was a low revenue tariff, a tariff which under the falling prices of the depression was bringing in less every year. In 1874, R. J. Cartwright, the new Liberal Minister of Finance, had tried to anticipate his first deficit by raising the rate on manufactured goods to 17½ per cent. But was that enough? Ought the rates to be raised higher, and, if so, on what principle? Or was there some other way in which Canada could revive its sagging economy and gain the revenue necessary for national development?

Early in 1875 it became clear that there were no other alternatives available. The Reciprocity Treaty of 1854-66, which permitted the free exchange of natural products between Canada and the United States, had coincided with sustained good times, broken by only one serious slump; and many Canadians were inclined to look back nostalgically on those twelve good years as a lost golden age. Repeatedly but vainly the Canadian government tried to persuade the United States to accept a broad trade agreement comparable to the vanished treaty; but the post-war American governments, with their hard protectionist views, had only the slightest interest in such a proposal and no interest at all in any arrangement that did not give American manufacturers some advantage in the Canadian market. The draft treaty, which George Brown succeeded in 1874 in negotiating with the American Secretary of State, Hamilton Fish, included two important categories of manufactures; and, since this was likely to hurt the Canadian manufacturers without helping the Canadian treasury, it quickly provoked a loud argument. As it happened, however, the advantages and disadvantages of the draft treaty were never tested; early in 1875 the American Senate unceremoniously rejected it.

The ground for manoeuvre had been sharply narrowed. There were now three choices only. Canada could stick by its existing tariff; or it could raise the duties for revenue purposes only and in strict accordance with free-trade views; or, finally, it could increase the rates, with protection as well as revenue in mind, 'the duties falling', as the Conservatives explained, 'upon the articles we are ourselves capable of producing'. For a time Cartwright, the Minister of Finance, hesitated. A youngish politician of forty who had begun political life as a Conservative and had shifted to Liberalism for no more exalted reason than his failure to obtain the portfolio of Finance from Sir John Macdonald, Cartwright was at first inclined to take the second of his possible choices. But the pressure of the free-trade Liberals, led by the Nova Scotians, was too much for him; and in the decisive budget speech of 1876 he took his stand immovably on the existing tariff. 'This,' he announced pontifically, 'is no time for experiments.' A greater misinterpretation of the feeling of the time could hardly have been made. The depression had put the Canadians in a mood for experiments, and it had hastened the conversion of the Conservatives to protective principles.

For some time before Cartwright's inept and provocative budget speech, Macdonald and Charles Tupper, his principal lieutenant since the death of Cartier, had been cautiously advocating tariff changes; and for the next three years they carried on a strenuous campaign in favour of a 'national policy' of protection, at first prudently described as 'a readjustment of the tariff'. They took whatever advantage they could get from the popularity of this proposal as a depression measure; but, in the main, they concentrated far more on its alleged permanent benefits for the nation. It would, they claimed, increase the size and strength of Canada, and for two principal reasons: it would provide the state with the revenue necessary to finance national expansion, and it would give private enterprise a chance to diversify the national economy. It would create jobs, promote the flow of trade between the industrial east and the agricultural west, and thereby provide business for the Pacific railway.

With this optimistic and aggressive programme, the Conservatives won a smashing victory in the general election of September 1878.

»» V ««

WHEN A TRIUMPHANT and rejuvenated Macdonald formed his new government in the autumn of 1878, the long debate over the national policies had finally ended. The confidence of the Conservatives had grown steadily during the strenuous campaign which ended in the victory of the general election; and in 1879, when the depression began to lift, the return of prosperity seemed to confirm the validity of their nationalist programme and strengthened their belief in it. In those first bold years of the new régime, the note of economic nationalism was sounded loudly and with increasing assurance. In 1879, when the Minister of Finance, the New Brunswicker S. L. Tilley, presented his first budget, the government obviously had abandoned all its reservations and embarked upon a definite attempt to promote industrialism in Canada by means of a protective tariff. Eighteen months later, when a contract was signed with a new syndicate, the future Canadian Pacific Railway Company, Macdonald and his colleagues had in effect returned defiantly to their original railway policy, the policy that had apparently failed so disastrously in 1873.

There were differences, however. The two major principals in the new syndicate were George Stephen and his cousin, Donald A. Smith. Stephen was an easterner, the president of the Bank of Montreal, solidly established in the finance of Canada's chief commercial city; Smith, as Chief Commissioner of the Hudson's Bay Company in Canada, had acquired wealth and an unrivalled knowledge of the Canadian north-west. They were Scotsmen whose families came from Speyside, in the Highlands; their eastern and western experiences complemented each other; and, best of all, they had just scored a dramatic success in a western railway venture which, in some important ways, was very like the far bigger project they now proposed to undertake. At Smith's instigation, they acquired a bankrupt Minnesota railway, the St. Paul and Pacific, and in short order built it into a highly flourishing enterprise which laid the basis of their fortunes. They were now as financially strong as Allan had been, or stronger; they possessed what Allan had conspicuously lacked – practical experience in western railway construction and land settlement. They were Canadians who were dependent neither upon American knowledge nor American support; and they were ready to give up Mackenzie's makeshift devices and to return to the original nationalist strategy of a railway that would run through Canadian territory from sea to sea.

These were solid advantages. Macdonald had to pay dearly for them. The sections of the railway already built as public works by both Liberal and Conservative governments, and valued at over $30 million, were transferred without charge to the new company. It was given a land grant of twenty-five million acres and a subsidy of $25 million, to be earned as the construction of the line progressed; and – most notorious and controversial of all – it was granted a monopoly of western traffic for twenty years. Though these terms were, in fact, less generous than those previously offered by both Conservative and Liberal governments, they were nevertheless large concessions for a new nation to make and a small population to bear. Politically, they were extremely vulnerable terms; and the Liberals leaped upon them with angry enthusiasm. They denounced Stephen and his colleagues as the potential landlords and monopolists of the whole west. They attacked the idea of an all-Canadian railway and insisted that it would be criminal folly to build a line across the rocky, unprofitable country north of Lake Superior.

This dispute between national and continental strategy in railway-building was the final expression of a basic conflict between Conservatives and Liberals over the true nature and proper development of the Canadian economy. The dispute had now been going on for a decade; and with every year of argument the two contrasting views had grown sharper and more distinct. The Conservatives had espoused the National Policy of protection and the national strategy of all-Canadian railways. The Liberals stood by the doctrines of international free trade and the sensible economies of continental transport. The purpose of the Conservatives was a diversified and balanced national economy, a nation state separate from the United States and economically viable in its own right. The aim of the Liberals was a Canada that concentrated on its own specialties, and accepted its proper place in an international trading world. In the eyes of the Conservatives, the tariff was the beneficial means of promoting industry and strengthening the economy; to the Liberals higher duties simply meant increased costs and benefits to the few at the expense of the many. The Liberals believed that Canada was and should remain a low-cost country, a cheap place to live in, whose government should intervene as little as possible in economic matters and stick firmly to retrenchment as its guiding principle in public finance. To the Conservatives this seemed a tame and spiritless programme for a young and vigorous people to adopt. They were convinced that the state ought to use its directing authority and its financial strength to plan and promote the development of the new nation.

The debate was over. The Conservatives had won it. And their plan now faced the uncertain chances of the future.

CHAPTER THREE

Time of Troubles

GRADUALLY A DIFFERENT colonial system is being developed,' Macdonald had declared in the Canadian Assembly, back in the winter of 1865, 'and it will become, year by year, less a case of dependence on our part, and of overruling protection on the part of the Mother Country, and more a case of a healthy and cordial alliance.' That prophetic statement had been made only a few months after the Quebec Conference; and everything that had happened since – Confederation and the transcontinental expansion of the Dominion – seemed to ensure that Macdonald's prediction would come true. Canada, the Canadians insisted, had ceased to be an ordinary possession of the British Crown; she had become a nation, geographically vast, and potentially powerful. Her new stature obviously raised the novel question of her status in the British Empire and her position in the international world; the organization of the Empire might have to be radically altered to accommodate this astonishing phenomenon, a colony of transcontinental proportions. Edward Blake, for a while, had considered imperial federation; and Canada First had demanded 'Consolidation of the Empire; and in the meantime a voice in treaties relating to Canada'.

Macdonald shared their interest in the problem, though he did not agree with their solutions. Like them, he saw Canada, not as a simple colonial 'dependency', but as the first 'auxiliary nation' in what would soon become a new imperial constellation of associated and allied powers. He did not believe – he never would believe – in imperial federation; the changes he wanted

43

were not formal changes in imperial institutions but informal yet significant changes in the conduct of imperial foreign policy. Canada, he argued, had its own responsibilities, interests, and aims, which were in many cases quite distinct from those of Great Britain; and, as a result, the British government, while it adequately represented the United Kingdom, could no longer claim that it stood for the Empire as a whole. In these new circumstances, the British government's monopolistic control of imperial foreign policy had become invalid.

Henceforth, the conduct of the Empire's foreign affairs must become a collective enterprise, in which Canada and the other great British colonies must play the part and exert the influence which their new importance required. Such a necessary reform would not, in Macdonald's opinion, weaken the Empire's diplomatic unity in the slightest; unity, on the contrary, would be strengthened by a frank recognition of the Empire's existing political plurality. A new Canadian representative, with an imposing title, should be sent to England to promote Canada's distinctive interests – to encourage British immigration and investment, and to improve trade relations with foreign powers. In European countries, he could act in association with the diplomats of the foreign office; even in England, his position would be 'quasi-diplomatic' in character. Macdonald pressed the case for such an appointment against the polite but uncomprehending reluctance of the British government, and in the end he triumphed. Alexander Tilloch Galt was appointed High Commissioner for Canada in London; and, in the spring of 1880, he set out for his new post.

The first bold, confident statement of Macdonald's design for Canada had now been set down. It was the primary thesis of the Canadian nation. As time would show, it possessed an extraordinary power to convince and inspire, and an extraordinary capacity to endure and revive. And, in the early promising 1880s, it seemed almost certain of triumphant success. In those first years after his return to power Macdonald was like a veteran conductor at the very top of his form, with a superlatively responsive orchestra before him. For nearly a decade, Canadians had been working at cross purposes, or they had been discouraged by circumstances from working very hard at anything at all. Now came a sudden, magical turn of fortune. The depression of the 1870s was definitely lifting. After five years of steady decline, prices were buoyant once again. Exports, which had remained at a low, dead level throughout the slump, were substantially up; and in 1880 and 1881 export values reached and exceeded totals which had not been recorded for the previous ten years. Under the beneficent effect of Tilley's new tariff, national revenue rose in two years by approximately 50 per cent. There were more immigrants to Canada in 1882 than there had been in any single season for the previous thirty years; and Manitoba's population, 62,260 in 1881, had more than doubled during the first decade of its history. In these encouraging circumstances, the sense of failure and frustration which had haunted the 1870s rapidly dwindled; and the original aims of Confederation – the rapid growth of population, the settlement of the west, the expansion of the nation on a continental scale – began to seem close and attainable goals. The Conservatives had almost performed the miracles they had promised; the Conservatives deserved reward. In the general election of 1882, Macdonald's government was returned to power with a majority as big as that of 1878.

His national plan, in its full detail, had now been approved and accepted with enthusiasm. In all probability, this primary thesis of the Canadian nation would for generations win strong national support. But it was not the only proposition before the Canadians; and, just as its first statement was reaching its assured conclusion, the fundamental antithesis began to find vigorous expression. It had first been voiced, in a confused way, but with gradually increasing clarity, during the debates of the 1870s over the national policies; but now it was heard again, urged by strange voices, and for a variety of new and compelling reasons. A new generation of Canadian politicians, most of whom had risen to prominence after the union of 1867, began to attack the basic principles of Macdonald's system; and, all too soon, the return of adverse economic circumstances led people to doubt and question the expediency of the national policies. The denial of the Macdonald thesis was to reveal itself in a

protean multiplicity of forms – in cultural and religious controversies, political protest movements, constitutional conflicts, and
battles over commercial policy. Macdonald's national design had
many aspects, and provoked many and varied responses. But its
fundamental basis was Macdonald's original constitutional
principle – the idea of a strongly centralized nation state –
which he had tried so hard to embody in the British North
America Act. Historically it was the starting point of his whole
national plan; and, appropriately enough, it was against this
original and central principle that the first attack on the
Macdonald system was launched.

→» II «←

ITS LEADER was Oliver Mowat, the Premier of the province
of Ontario. Mowat had been one of the original three
Liberal members of the Canadian coalition that carried Confederation; but, soon after the conclusion of the Quebec
Conference, he resigned to become Vice-Chancellor of Ontario.
Eight years later, after the Liberals had gained power in
Ontario, he emerged from what Macdonald called 'the legal
monkhood of the bench' and succeeded Edward Blake as
Premier. A short, rotund person, with a bland, bespectacled
countenance and a slightly sanctimonious expression, Mowat
had a high opinion of his own virtues and was fond of describing
himself as a 'Christian statesman'. He was, at least, an intensely
political Christian, who possessed a remarkable talent for
gaining the loyalty, and the votes, of a wide variety of denominations. He never neglected any division of the provincial
community that counted politically; and his quick concern for
Ontario's rights and interests was equally comprehensive. For
the sake of Ontario, he was ready to do battle at any moment
and against all comers. And he brought to his many combats a
remarkable combination of determination, effrontery, and legal
cunning.

In 1878, when Macdonald regained office in Ottawa, Mowat
had been Premier of Ontario for six years. He was solidly

established and very sure of himself at Toronto. And he had developed a new theory of Canadian federalism, exclusively provincial in its bias, which he held with dogmatic assurance. That this theory differed from – and, in fact, completely contradicted – the original conception of Confederation was, of course, well known to Mowat, for he had been a member of the Coalition Government of 1864 and had been present at the Quebec Conference. At the end of his career, in interviews with his prospective biographer, he attempted to explain away at least a part of this contradiction by falsifying the official record of the Quebec Conference concerning the federal power of disallowance. But, while he was Premier, the knowledge that he was repudiating principles which he had previously endorsed and attacking a constitution which was partly his own handi-work apparently did not cause him a moment's concern. In effect, he went back to the Grit tradition, which was older than Confederation and older than the Coalition of 1864 – to the Upper Canadian tradition of sectional grievances, claims, and protests; and, in the context of the federal union, this tradition acquired fresh vitality as the doctrine of 'provincial rights'. Mowat's aim now was to elevate the political status of his province and to enlarge the sphere of its legislative and administrative powers. He utterly denied the tacit assumption of the Quebec Conference that the 'local' governments would decline in importance to virtually municipal levels.

A struggle between Ottawa and Toronto – between federal paramountcy and provincial rights – was inevitable. The fury of the constitutional battles which Mowat and Macdonald waged against each other resounded through the early 1880s. Mowat was determined to prove that the government of Ontario was not subordinate to, but co-ordinate with, the government of Canada. He insisted that the Lieutenant-Governor of Ontario was as fully a representative of the sovereign within the limits of provincial jurisdiction as the Governor General was within the federal sphere. In his confident opinion, the executive authority which the Lieutenant-Governor possessed – and which Mowat and his colleagues exercised as constitutional advisers – was not an authority delegated by Ottawa but the prerogative power of the Crown. He was equally convinced that, on the subjects assigned to it exclusively by the British North America Act, the authority of the provincial legislature was sovereign. Anything in the British North America Act which expressed or implied the constitutional inferiority of the provinces was highly obnoxious to him.

He hated, with a special hatred, the federal power of the disallowance of provincial laws. But to Macdonald disallowance was a vital adjunct of Dominion paramountcy and national leadership. He intended to use it, and to use it not infrequently, to maintain national standards in legislation, to defend collective national interests, and to preserve natural rights and human freedoms throughout the Dominion. To Mowat disallowance was a degrading badge of provincial subordination. He was resolved to defy its use. Three times, in the years 1881-3, on the invitation of his government, the provincial legislature passed an Act for Protecting the Public Interest in Rivers, Streams, and Creeks; and three times Macdonald disallowed it. The determination of the antagonists was certainly not inspired solely by their concern for justice. Macdonald was protecting the property rights of a Conservative lumberman, and Mowat was defending the commercial interests of a Liberal lumberman; but beneath this partisan rivalry a real principle was nevertheless at stake. Mowat intended to make the rivers and streams of the province a common transport system for the entire lumber industry; Macdonald objected that this was a 'flagrant violation' of the private rights of those who had made particular streams navigable at their own expense. It was only after the courts had confirmed the principle of Mowat's Act that Macdonald finally desisted.

In another area, where federal and provincial legislative powers met in potential conflict, a perhaps even more important battle was going on. During the 1870s and early 1880s, both the Parliament of Canada and the provincial legislature of Ontario attempted in various ways to regulate the distribution and sale of beer, wine, and spirits. On the lowest level, this was simply an unedifying scramble for the considerable amount of political patronage involved in licensing; on a higher plane, it became a

serious competition between the provincial concern for municipal decency and order and the federal interest in national
standards of health and welfare. For really the first time since
the union, the enumerated powers of the provinces came into
direct conflict with the federal residuary power to legislate for
'the peace, order, and good government of Canada'. The fate of
the residuary clause – the foundation of Macdonald's whole
federal system – was at stake.

Macdonald fought hard, with everything he had; but he
discovered that the ground on which he hoped to have a solid
legal footing was yielding beneath him. The decisions of the
courts were going in Mowat's favour. Despite the establishment
of a Canadian Supreme Court in 1875, the Judicial Committee
of the Privy Council in Great Britain remained the final
authority for all constitutional cases under the British North
America Act; and the Judicial Committee never even attempted
to repeat for Canada the great work of creative interpretation
which the American Supreme Court had performed for the
United States. In the eyes of the Committee, the British North
America Act was simply an ordinary statute, rather than a
constitutional framework designed for the expanding energies
and requirements of a potentially great nation; and, like an
ordinary statute, it was judged by the narrowest and most
limited canons of interpretation. For a brief while, in the decision in *Russell* v. *the Queen*, the first constitutional case concerning the liquor licensing power, it seemed possible that the
Committee might accept the generous meaning which the Fathers of Confederation had obviously attached to the residuary
clause; but within a year these expectations had grown less
confident. The decision in *Hodge* v. *the Queen*, the second legal
dispute over the licensing power, appeared to place limits on
the wide authority of the residuary clause. And even more
plainly it gave legal authority to Mowat's favourite doctrine
that the provincial governments were not subordinate to, but
co-ordinate with, the Dominion.

→»» III «←

THE DEFEAT in the courts was the first sign of a definite change in Macdonald's fortunes; but it did not long remain the only evidence of the fact that the first, unchallenged phase of his national leadership had come to an end. The losing battle with Mowat was quickly followed by an ominous decline in the prosperity which had favoured the Conservatives ever since they had regained power in 1878; and the return of the depression of the 1870s inevitably meant trouble for the policies of national expansion. The first two of these national policies, western settlement and the Pacific railway, were particularly vulnerable to adverse economic circumstances, for they depended for their success upon external factors – international finance and trans-atlantic migration – over which the government of Canada had almost no control.

Down to the summer of 1883, the enterprise of the Canadian Pacific Railway was driven forward with an easy swiftness which seemed assured and unending. This spectacular advance was the work of a great triumvirate, George Stephen, Donald Smith, and William Cornelius Van Horne. Smith, the eldest of the three, a man of over sixty, with a great, white beard, and calm, assured eyes, brought to the task the wealth of his experience, his for-tune, and the strength of his steady support. Stephen had all his cousin's constancy and determination; but he was, on the surface at least, a much more temperamental and emotional man, who rose quickly to heights of exaltation and fell appar-ently into black despairs. Van Horne, the youngest of the three – he might, so far as age was concerned, have been Donald Smith's son – was a robustious and vehement middle-western American, with a profane and explosive habit of speech, a ruthless determination, and an enormous organizing skill. Stephen and Smith came to rely without question on the driving energy and furious *élan* of their new general manager. Stephen leaned heavily upon the solid wisdom and calm authority of Smith. But both Smith and Van Horne, and everybody in the Canadian Pacific Railway – and indeed everybody in the Cana-dian government – depended upon the financial genius of

George Stephen. Stephen was the author of the Canadian Pacific's grand strategy. He had devised a plan which freed the railway from the heavy burden of fixed debt charges and assured its ultimate financial success, but which, in the short run, exposed it to the hazards of hand-to-mouth financing.

Down to the autumn of 1883, good times had hidden the one vital defect of Stephen's plan; but now it was suddenly disclosed. Obviously the boom which had blessed the first few years of Macdonald's new government was petering out. The New York stock market went into a decline, with railway issues leading the descent; and the shares of the Northern Pacific, the Canadian Pacific's most obvious rival, dropped sharply. This sudden break in public confidence in the new transcontinental railways came, most unfortunately for the Canadian Pacific, at the moment when George Stephen had decided that he must dispose of another large block of his capital stock. From the start, it had been his fixed intention not to resort to the issue of bonds; he was determined to rely solely upon his cash subsidy, the proceeds of his land grant, and the sale of the company's common stock. Now he needed fresh support from London and New York; but, by the autumn of 1883, these markets had become cautious, or indifferent, or hostile. In New York, the American transcontinentals led the attack on the Canadian Pacific. In London, at the headquarters of the Grand Trunk Railway of Canada, the officers worked their hardest to prejudice British investors against this upstart Canadian venture which was insolently attempting to invade their jealously guarded monopoly of traffic in Ontario and Quebec.

Early in the autumn of 1883, Stephen devised an ambitious scheme for the sale at good prices of the $45 million which still remained of his original capital stock. In good times, the plan might have been a complete success; in the actual circumstances of that uneasy, depressed autumn, it was a tragic and costly failure. The shipwreck of his elaborate scheme plunged Stephen and his railway into deeper difficulties than ever. With his own resources strained to their limit and his creditors yelping persistently at his heels, he finally turned back in desperation to the only source of help that still remained, the Canadian government. In January 1884, he asked Macdonald for a government loan of $22.5 million, on the security of a first mortgage on the property of the railway. It was a tremendous total, a total all too ominously close to the subsidy which had been authorized only three years before; and, as he gazed in fascination at the terrible figures, Macdonald was appalled. He knew that it was hazardous in the extreme to risk the national credit at a time of declining revenues and difficult financing; he realized even better that it was politically dangerous to impose on a young nation a burden which was too great for it and which Parliament – and even his own political followers – might refuse to accept.

Yet he could not bring himself to abandon his great design. He was convinced now that Stephen and Smith were the best instruments he could ever find for his purpose. He had never doubted that an all-Canadian transcontinental railway was essential for the expansion and integration of his country; and he knew only too well that the fulfilment of the great national plan, which he had begun to form twenty years ago, was now the only reason for his existence. He delayed, but he never really hesitated. Privately, he gave the assurance of government support which the Bank of Montreal required before it would advance another copper to the Canadian Pacific. In Parliament, despite the clamour of the opposition, the misgivings of some of his own followers, and the political blackmail exacted by the Quebec Conservatives, he and Tupper, the burly Minister of Railways and Canals, drove the loan bill through all stages to its final passage on the 5th of March, 1884.

➔➤➤ IV ➤➤➔

THE PROBLEM of the railway did not come alone. Along with it came another and equally formidable problem, the north-west and its settlement. Only a few short months before, the west, its prospects and hopes uplifted by good grain prices, spreading railway lines, and incoming masses of settlers, had flung itself into a frenzy of speculation in land. Winnipeg, unable to house its mob of new citizens, seemed for a time to have become a city of tents; and all day long, and far into the night, lots on empty streets in hypothetical prairie townsites were sold and resold, at fabulous prices, at every street corner. As early as the spring of 1882, the boom was evidently slackening. By the autumn of 1883, it was definitely over. Prices began to sag. The annual influx of immigrants steadily declined. The years 1883, 1884, and 1885 were marked by dry summers and early autumnal frosts. Nothing was going well. Nothing, it seemed, might ever go well again. The west collapsed into a depression which was all the more intolerable because it meant the frustration of hopes and expectations that only recently had been held so very high.

If these reverses had befallen a mature and settled community, they would have been hard enough to bear. But in the middle 1880s the north-west was not a settled community. It was, in fact, passing through a period of profound changes; and all its three main social groups – the white settlers, the Indians, and the *Métis*, or French half-breeds – were forced to confront major problems of adjustment. The difficulties of the white settlers – collapsing land values, poor harvests, falling prices, and high freight rates and elevator charges – were the familiar difficulties of the first stages of western pioneer settlement and of the ups and downs of the business cycle. They were serious difficulties, but not nearly so disturbing as those faced by the Indians and the *Métis*. The white settlers had to endure the discouragements and abuses of a system to which they were accustomed; the Indians and *Métis* had to come to terms with a strange and alien kind of existence. The old wild, free life of the open prairie was gone, or going. The Indians had exchanged their primordial titles to the vast north-west for the narrow confines of reserves. The *Métis*, fleeing to a far-western sanctuary after the creation of Manitoba, found to their consternation that the rapid tide of white government and settlement was following them inexorably. In their bewildered and hostile eyes, this new encroachment was another usurpation which they were determined to resist; and, in the summer of 1884, they invited Louis Riel, who had become an American citizen and was living in Montana, to return and lead their movement of protest.

The deterioration of Riel's character was very marked. In the fifteen years since he had left Red River, his megalomania had grown greater than ever. His ungovernable rages, delusions of grandeur, messianic claims, and dictatorial impulses had all become more extreme; but these violent excesses were not the only symptoms of his curious mental and moral decline. He had lost his shrewd appreciation of realities. His sense of direction was confused and his purposes were equivocal. He showed, at intervals, a cynical selfishness and a ruthless cupidity. Though the *Métis*'s claim for compensation was based solely on their small fraction of the aboriginal title to the land, he had not the slightest hesitation in demanding the lion's share of the indemnity for his own people, at the expense of the Indians; and, although in public he professed that his sole aim was the redress of the *Métis* grievances, in private he was quite ready to promise that if the government made him a satisfactory personal payment of a few thousand dollars he would induce his credulous followers to accept almost any settlement the federal authorities desired, and would quietly leave Canada for ever.

In private, Riel asked a bribe. In public he demanded a political settlement for the north-west along the lines of the Manitoba Act of 1870. It was impossible for Macdonald to grant either the one or the other. Even if Riel was ready to sell himself, the federal government could not afford to buy him; and, even though the *Métis* were willing to risk everything in the hope of re-enacting their triumph at Red River, Macdonald was determined not to repeat the tragic mistake he had been compelled to make in 1870 with the creation of Manitoba. Provincial status, which was not granted until twenty years later and only after a massive immigration had taken place, would have been even more stupidly and dangerously premature for the north-west in 1885 than it had been for Manitoba fifteen years earlier. In fact, the only important claim in Riel's preposterous programme which could be conceded without danger was the *Métis* demand for a money compensation for their share in the Indian title to the land.

Even this large concession was highly unlikely to have either beneficial or lasting results. All the experts opposed this doubtful method of rewarding an improvident people; everybody expected that the *Métis* would squander this second cash payment as profitlessly as they had the first. But Macdonald was anxious to keep the peace if he could; and, in the end, the government reluctantly consented to appoint a special commission with power to enumerate the half-breeds of the north-west and to make an equitable settlement of their claims. The telegram announcing this important concession, read to the *Métis* assembled in St. Anthony's Church at Batoche, ought to have ended the agitation; but Riel, who presided over the meeting, contrived to ensure that it would not. He had received no answer to his demand for a settlement of his 'private' claims; and he looked back, in fascinated remembrance, to the tremendous days when he and his poor half-breeds had forced the Dominion of Canada to accept the terms which were later embodied in the Manitoba Act. He had done the impossible once. He could do it again! By this time the white settlers had abandoned him, and the major Indian tribes withdrew their support from his doomed cause. But he plunged recklessly forward. And on the 26th of March, 1885, a party of his *Métis* met a detachment of Mounted Police in an armed encounter at Duck Lake.

On the same day, in the room of a friendly M.P. in the Parliament Buildings at Ottawa, George Stephen, the President of the Canadian Pacific Railway, was writing to Prime Minister Macdonald in tones of hopeless and resigned finality. Once again, though a loan had been granted only a little more than a year before, the railway was in desperate financial straits; and once again, after repeated and vain attempts to obtain fresh financing, the frantic Stephen had reached the gloomy conclusion that the company's one hope of survival lay in the Canadian treasury. Financially, a new loan was the only way out; but was a new loan politically possible? On this crucial issue, the cabinet was badly divided; the Minister of Finance, Tilley, was highly dubious. Macdonald, warned of resistance from his own political followers and of newspaper opposition, did not believe that it would be possible to carry a new loan through Parliament. And, if it had not been for the outbreak of foolhardy and meaningless violence in the north-west, he might never have made the attempt.

The crisis of the railway and the crisis of the rebellion coincided. Each solved the other. The rebellion ensured the completion of the railway; the railway accomplished the defeat of the rebellion. The Canadian Pacific had been granted an unexpected but brilliant opportunity of demonstrating its effi-ciency as a transport system and its usefulness in a great national emergency. Inspired and directed by Van Horne's ruthless energy and organizing genius, it rose magnificently to the occasion. Within less than a week the first troops from the east had reached Winnipeg by train; within less than another week the first of the three striking columns of Canadian militia set out northward from the main line of the C.P.R. towards the Saskatchewan River. The rebellion, which might have spread and strengthened with time, was localized and pinned down. Riel, left now with his *Métis* and two small bands of northern Indians, lost the initiative immediately. On the 12th of May, his stronghold at Batoche was captured and the back of the rebellion had been broken.

During the summer and autumn of 1885, the entwined his-tories of the railway and the rebellion drew towards their strangely contrasted conclusions. Everybody realized that the Canadian Pacific had helped greatly in the swift suppression of the revolt; and this public recognition ensured the easy passage of the final loan through Parliament. While Van Horne's con-struction gangs hastened to finish the last gaps in the mountains and north of Lake Superior, Riel was tried, found guilty, and sentenced to hang for treason. On the 7th of November, in Eagle Pass in the Monashee Mountains, at a place Stephen had determined should be called Craigellachie in memory of his clan's meeting-place and battle slogan, Donald Smith drove home the last spike in the completed transcontinental line; and nine days later Louis Riel dropped to his death in the prison at Regina.

⇾⟫ V ⟪⇽

O N THE 22ND OF NOVEMBER, less than a week after the execution of Riel, a great meeting of mourning and protest was held in Montreal. A large crowd assembled in the Champ de Mars. A long succession of speakers denounced the 'hangman's government' at Ottawa, and extolled Riel as a pitiable victim of English oppression and Protestant bigotry. Riel had been a half-breed, a naturalized American citizen, and an apostate to the Roman Catholic faith; but the thousands of French Canadians in the Champ de Mars, whatever their political affiliations, seemed eager to identify themselves with Riel's cause; and, although the majority of the speakers at the meeting were Liberals, some prominent Conservatives sat on the platform and joined in the indignant denunciations. In this apparent unanimity, Honoré Mercier, who had succeeded to the leadership of the provincial Liberal Party two years before, thought he saw his chance. He proposed that, in order to defend French Canada against English injury and oppression, both Liberals and Conservatives in the province of Quebec should unite to form a single '*parti national*'.

Was this appeal likely to succeed? Would the mass protest over the fate of Riel have a tragic ending in the dissolution of the existing Canadian party system and the organization of new parties on strictly 'racial' lines? This was the outcome for which Mercier had long been hoping and planning. A renegade Conservative who had broken with Cartier over the issue of Confederation, Mercier had come to believe that the continuance of political division would be fatal to French Canada and that a single party could alone ensure its survival. In 1871, he had made a first unsuccessful attempt to form a *parti national*; subsequently he tried on several occasions, but in vain, to effect a coalition with the Quebec Conservatives. To him the idea of the *parti national* was not in the least new. The agitation over the death of Riel simply gave him what looked to be a very favourable opportunity of carrying it out.

To Edward Blake, who in 1880 had become leader of the federal Liberal Party, the hubbub over Riel also seemed too good a chance to be missed. Blake piously announced that he did not intend to make a political platform out of the Regina scaffold; but from the beginning he had been keenly aware of Riel's political possibilities, and there was no reason why he should cease to be so now. In 1871, when he had been Leader of the Opposition in the Ontario legislature, he had moved a resolution demanding that the 'murderer' Riel should be brought to justice; and, in the following year, after he had formed the first Liberal government in Ontario, he had introduced the resolution again, adding to it a $5,000 reward for the 'murderer's' arrest and conviction. Undoubtedly he had gained a good deal of political capital from these astute moves. Not only had they embarrassed the federal government; but also – which was more important at the time – they had helped substantially to overthrow the Conservative government in Ontario. Why was it not possible for Blake and the Liberals, with Riel's invaluable aid, to repeat in the Dominion the triumph they had won fifteen years earlier in the province? Blake had gained support in Ontario by attacking Riel. The Liberals began to hope that they could gain support in Quebec by defending him. Quietly, towards the end of the year, they began working to undermine the political allegiance of the Quebec Bleus and to transfer them from the Conservative to the Liberal Party.

This ingenious design miscarried. The Conservative Party simply declined to split into two racial divisions. In the main, Conservative politicians and newspapers in both provinces continued to follow the party line. In Ontario, the one conspicuous exception to this general rule of conduct occurred in the late autumn of 1885, when the Toronto *Mail*, the leading Conservative newspaper in the province, began furiously to reply to French-Canadian abuse and threats with the menace of a war of extermination. This short-lived outburst was the natural Toronto reaction to the sinister rumours that were coming out of Montreal. By that time the Toronto Conservatives had become aware of the Liberal plot against the Quebec wing of the party; and they angrily promised themselves that, if all of French Canada ever dared to unite in a single party of 'race and revenge', English Canada would be strong enough to exact an

appropriate and terrible retribution. These fulminations subsided fairly quickly for the sufficient reason that the French-
Canadian party of 'race and revenge' never materialized.
Langevin, Chapleau, and Caron, the three French-Canadian
leaders in the federal cabinet, stuck by their posts and ably
defended the government decision not to commute Riel's sentence; and the great majority of the Quebec Bleus followed
their leadership.

This did not quite end the matter. A fair number of French-
Canadian M.P.s were still dissatisfied. They felt that government
policy had been mistaken; they knew that many of their constituents deeply resented the execution of Riel. Though they
were ready to remain loyal to the Conservative Party, they
wanted a single opportunity of publicly expressing their disapproval. Macdonald was aware of their discontent and he decided
that they must be given a chance of putting it on the record in a
manner which would do the least harm to the Conservatives and
the most damage to the Liberals. In the House of Commons,
Landry, a Quebec Conservative, introduced a resolution deplor-
ing the fact that the government had permitted Riel's death
sentence to be carried out. As soon as Landry had sat down,
Langevin, at Macdonald's request, rose, made a brief formal
reply, and moved the previous question. The scope of the
debate, and of the vote, was thus narrowed to the question of
Riel's mental state and the commutation of his sentence; and
although Blake was willing to excuse Riel on the score of
insanity, the other English-Canadian Liberal leaders conspicuously refused to follow his example. They were ready enough to
criticize the Conservative policy in the north-west; but a good
many of them believed that Riel was a convicted rebel who
richly deserved his fate. When the vote came, the Landry motion
was defeated by nearly three to one. Seventeen French-Canadian
Conservatives, not quite a third of Macdonald's following from
Quebec, voted for the resolution. Twenty-three of Blake's
English-Canadian Liberals voted against it.

On one occasion, and to a limited extent, traditional political
loyalties had yielded to newly aroused racial feeling. It was
becoming evident that the Riel agitation and the upsurge of

French-Canadian 'nationalism' were likely to have only limited effects in federal politics. But in the province of Quebec, under Honoré Mercier's leadership, the idea of the *parti national* was undeniably making some progress. Mercier was a big, handsome man, with black hair *en brosse*, luxuriant handle-bar moustaches, a bold, impressive manner, and a torrential eloquence. He succeeded in persuading a few Quebec provincial Conservatives, chiefly right-wing Ultramontanes, to join with his Liberals in founding the new party; and for the next six months he and his followers mounted a vigorous nationalist attack against the 'hangman's government' at Ottawa. In the provincial general election of October, the Liberals and Nationalists gained at the expense of the Conservatives; and in January 1887, when the legislature met, Mercier took over power in Quebec.

Only a few weeks later, on the 22nd of February, 1887, came the Canadian general election. Its results indicated clearly that Conservative popularity had suffered a serious but by no means fatal decline. The Conservatives had won 123 seats, the Liberals ninety-two; Macdonald's majority, sixty-eight at the beginning of the previous Parliament, had been reduced to twenty-five. A total of fifteen seats were surrendered to the Liberals in Quebec; but Conservative losses, though most severe in that province, were not confined to it; and the reduction of their Quebec following was not a sudden, precipitate drop from a consistently high level of strength in the past. In the two general elections of 1872 and 1874 they had done as badly, or nearly as badly. This time they would have a comfortable majority, with a strong contingent from every province except, oddly enough, Prince Edward Island.

It was too much for Edward Blake. The strategy of exploiting the Riel affair for the benefit of the Liberal Party in Quebec had been only a very qualified success; and for the second time as Liberal leader he had been defeated in a general election. Ill, defeated, and dejected, he resigned; and, at his own choice, Wilfrid Laurier succeeded him. There was now a new Liberal leader of the Opposition at Ottawa, as well as a new Liberal Premier at Quebec.

CHAPTER FOUR

A Nation on Trial

IN 1887 CONFEDERATION was only twenty years old; but already the young nation had entered what was perhaps the most dangerously critical period of its existence. The last half dozen years had been a troubled sequence of reverses and misfortunes. The project of the Pacific railway had almost collapsed, the settlement of the west had been halted by bad times and rebellion, and the cultural concord of Confederation had been shattered by the agitation over the fate of Riel. The strains and stresses within the community now seemed numerous and serious enough to threaten its cohesion. The attacks on the individual national policies were broadening out into a general assault on Macdonald's whole system. For the last six years the forces opposing his national design had been gathering in strength, and in vigour and quality of leadership; and in 1887, led by Wilfrid Laurier and Honoré Mercier, they moved forward for the final onslaught.

At forty-five – he was only eight years younger than Blake, the disappointed, disillusioned man he was succeeding – Wilfrid Laurier had already left youth for middle age. A tall, slight man, gracious in manner, facile in speech, with a thoughtful, 'bookish', slightly indolent attitude to life, he hardly seemed the stuff of which commanding leaders are made. People had accepted him readily enough as Blake's first lieutenant in the province of Quebec; but people were a little surprised and disconcerted to find him suddenly installed as Blake's successor in the Dominion of Canada. He was not very well known in Ontario, and hardly known in the Atlantic provinces at all. In Quebec, where for a generation a dominating clergy, with strong Conservative and ultramontane sympathies, had been instructing the faithful that liberalism in all its forms was evil, he was naturally regarded with some suspicion and distrust by many of his Roman Catholic countrymen.

His first task – a task which also faced Honoré Mercier in Quebec – was to free the Liberal Party from the clerical censure under which it had been struggling for a generation; but, unlike Mercier who as a former Bleu had no past of his own to live down, Laurier trailed behind him his deplorable youthful record as a Rouge and a member of the notorious Institut Canadien, a literary and scientific society, liberal and anticlerical in character, which had been suppressed by the Roman Catholic hierarchy. Nearly ten years before, he had started the difficult business of restoring himself and his party to respectability. He had sought to distinguish clearly between political liberalism on the one hand and Catholic liberalism on the other. He had tried to dissociate the Canadian Liberal Party from the revolutionary and anticlerical liberalism of Europe and to identify it firmly with the Christian and constitutional liberalism of England – the liberalism of Burke, Grey, and Gladstone. Such a sober Britannic ancestry would, he shrewdly suspected, give him a double advantage. It would reassure fears in Catholic Quebec; it would inspire confidence in British Ontario.

Like Mercier, Laurier had been reasonably successful in this work of rehabilitation. But it was not enough to prove oneself politically respectable. It was also necessary – and particularly necessary for a newly appointed leader – to be original and constructive. Laurier wanted a new policy to mark his rise to the federal leadership, just as Mercier needed a new policy to signalize his succession to power in Quebec. All that Laurier had to guide him in his search was the knowledge that Blake's policy of racial exploitation must be dropped and that something religiously and racially neutral that would likely interest the whole country must be put in its place. His chances of hitting upon a novel and popular idea might have seemed less obviously good than Mercier's; but in fact he discovered and appropriated a new and daring plan of action in a matter of a few months. He found it in a place where Blake, obsessed with Quebec and the Riel affair, had never even thought of looking – in the economic condition of the country. He found it in the depression, in the disappointments, frustrations, and grievances that had been accumulating during the depression, and in the daring scheme that could end it, commercial union with the United States.

On his part, Mercier proved to be equally fertile in invention and expedient. Like Laurier, he realized that everything possible had already been got out of the Riel affair. Riel was dead; but the nationalist passions which his death had aroused still lived on. And Mercier was determined to exploit them. His general aim was to promote the growth, and defend the culture, of French Canada; but unlike either Cartier or Laurier he identified French Canada closely, if not exclusively, with the province of Quebec. Quebec, in his ambitious conception, was to become the strong and prosperous homeland of all the French-speaking peoples of North America. He tried to repatriate the French Canadians who had gone to live in the New England states; he sought, by opening up the frontier regions in the northern part of the province, to make homes for them and for the surplus population of the overcrowded St. Lawrence valley. Development schemes and public works were, of course, an essential part of his programme; and, to prove himself independent of Anglo-Canadian finance, he looked for capital in Paris and New York.

Mercier's heroic nationalist role inevitably required him to adopt a hostile attitude to the federal government at Ottawa. It was politically profitable for him to make a show of asserting Quebec's claims and interests in the federation; it was financially necessary for his government to get larger federal subsidies in aid of Quebec's expensive development schemes. Previous provincial governments, which, of course, had been Conservative in politics, had managed on several occasions by persistent pressure to gain 'better terms' from the not unfriendly Conservative administration at Ottawa. But Mercier, the Liberal-Nationalist who had led the vituperative crusade against the 'hangmen' of the capital, could hardly expect them to yield to persuasion now.

Frontal assault had been his method before. He would have to continue it. But need he continue it alone? Quebec was constitutionally a province of the Dominion, one of seven; and Mowat of Ontario had proved years before that English-speaking provinces could be even more alert and pugnacious than Quebec in asserting provincial rights and resisting federal pretensions. Why should not Mercier exploit and organize this common provincial dislike of federal power and federal policies? Why should he not lead a league of discontented provinces in a general assault against Ottawa?

Early in March 1887, Mercier wrote to Mowat of Ontario, tentatively suggesting that there ought to be a better understanding among the provincial governments 'with a view to the organization of a system of common defence'. Ten days later, when the legislature opened at Quebec, the Speech from the Throne announced that the government proposed to call a conference of the provinces and the Dominion to consider 'their financial and other relations'.

→»» II «←

MERCIER'S SENSE OF TIMING was extraordinarily acute. For a variety of reasons, some political and constitutional, some economic and financial, his proposal awakened an immediate and lively interest. The response to his invitation was good, though, unfortunately for him, by no means unanimous. Macdonald, who from the first regarded the scheme as a barefaced Liberal conspiracy against federal leadership and federal policies, refused to let the Dominion be drawn into such a hostile conclave. British Columbia and Prince Edward Island, both ruled by governments friendly to Macdonald, declined Mercier's invitation. The other provincial administrations, three of which were Liberal and the fourth professedly non-partisan, appeared to be delighted at the prospect of a conference on federal-provincial relations, financial and otherwise. For one thing, they all badly needed money. Manitoba's repeated begging expeditions to Ottawa had given her an unflattering reputation as the chief professional mendicant in the union; but the other provinces, though they were never quite so chronically hard up, chafed under the narrow limitations of the original financial settlement. Even Ontario, the most affluent of them all, found that her superior attitude to increased subsidies was changing. In the past she had denounced 'better terms' as federal bribes to keep discontented provinces within the Conservative fold; but, if all the provinces were to be suborned out of revenues collected largely in Ontario, why should not Ontario get her share?

All the provinces shared in the demand for more money; but, in addition, each had its own special claims or grievances to prefer. As always, Mowat was eager to advance the constitutional status of his province and to free it from the hated federal control of disallowance. Norquay, the Premier of Manitoba, was equally opposed to a veto power which had been used far more frequently against the legislature of his province than it had been against Ontario's. The Norquay government, convinced that high freight rates in the west were directly attributable to the Canadian Pacific Railway's monopoly of western traffic, decided to provide for competition in transport by chartering other railway companies to build to the international border where they could connect with American lines. The federal government, believing equally firmly that the national interest required the maintenance of the Canadian Pacific's chartered rights, disallowed no fewer than thirteen Manitoba railway acts in the years 1882-7. For a long time now Manitoba had been in a high state of indignation over the federal exercise of disallowance and the federal policy of all-Canadian transcontinental railway transport.

In the Atlantic provinces, the grievances were less specific and less directly traceable to federal policies; but this did not prevent the two Maritime premiers, W. S. Fielding of Nova Scotia and A. G. Blair of New Brunswick, from blaming the Dominion for all their provincial misfortunes. In Nova Scotia, the tradition of resistance to the union, which Joseph Howe had established only twenty years before, was still strong; and for many Maritimers the history of those two decades had conclusively proved the truth of Howe's belief that Confederation was a bad bargain for the Atlantic provinces. Undeniably Nova Scotia and New Brunswick were in a depressed, almost stationary condition in the 1880s; but to a very considerable extent this was the result of contemporary economic circumstances over which the Dominion had no control. The shift from wooden to iron shipping, and from sail to steam, meant the slow but inexorable decline of the Maritime shipbuilding business. The shrinking dried-fish markets in the West Indies, and the sudden termination of free trade in fish to the United States – the consequence of the abrogation in 1885 of the fisheries clauses in the Treaty of Washington – led inevitably to widespread distress in the Maritime fishing industry. Obviously it would be political folly to tilt against such amorphous but powerful international forces; and Nova Scotia, which took the lead in the Maritime agitation, preferred wisely to lay the whole charge against the Dominion and to demand its heavy damages from the federal government. In 1886, Fielding had revived Howe's old slogan of secession with the intention of blackmailing Ottawa into granting larger subsidies. Mercier's invitation gave him the chance of achieving the same object with less political risk.

The conference was held in Quebec City where, in October 1864, the original Quebec Conference had laid the bases of the federal union; and the federal union, embodied in the British North America Act of 1867, had now been in operation for a little over twenty years. These were significant circumstances which Mercier emphasized; they helped to give colour to his novel theory of Confederation. The British North America Act, he declared, was not a statute of the imperial Parliament but a compact of the British American provinces. The provinces had made the constitution; the provinces could alter the constitution. After a thorough trial of twenty years, they had come to the conclusion that there were serious defects in their constitutional handiwork; and they were meeting in Quebec City, where the original compact was made, to alter its terms at their discretion.

This theory was Mercier's chief contribution to the proceedings. He did not demand a special position or special powers for

Quebec; but he was an apt pupil of Mowat's constitutional teaching and an eager advocate of Mowat's plans for the constitutional aggrandizement of the provinces in general. The other premiers were ready to endorse the doctrine of provincial rights provided they could lay their hands on a lot more provincial revenue; and the result was a long string of resolutions which coupled an elaborate plan for bigger federal subsidies with a catalogue of all the principal constitutional changes for which Mowat had been fighting. The execrated federal power of disallowance was abolished; and the provinces were given the right to nominate half the members of the Senate.

What followed was the complete and resounding defeat of the compact theory of Confederation. The second 'Quebec Conference' had not been a conference of all the governments of Canada, nor even of all the provincial governments of Canada. The imperial government and Parliament, which alone possessed the power to make formal amendments to the British North America Act, could obviously pay no attention at all to these strange proceedings at Quebec; and the five participating provinces, now revealed in their true light as a league of malcontent Liberal governments, did not know what to do with their precious resolutions. The frontal attack on the constitution had failed, and Macdonald's original conception still stood. But it had been severely shaken. It was no longer possible – and for other and better reasons than the resolutions of the second Quebec Conference – to look on the provinces as subordinate, semi-municipal bodies. The decisions of the Judicial Committee of the Privy Council had favoured them; their responsibilities were great and growing; and they had kept the loyalty of their citizens. The interprovincial conference of 1887 was an impressive indication of their rising importance.

⇶ III ≪≪

ON THE 12TH OF OCTOBER, eight days before Mercier welcomed the delegates to the second Quebec Conference, Sir Richard Cartwright, one of Laurier's chief lieutenants in Ontario, declared his personal support for commercial union with the United States. Formally this declaration was simply a trial balloon which did not commit the Liberal Party. Laurier had not yet spoken; but it was obvious that, in the few short months since his accession to the leadership, the Liberals had gone a long way towards the adoption of commercial union as their new economic policy.

The agitation for complete free trade with the United States was not a great deal older than the Liberal interest in it. The idea of commercial union was a product of the return of the depression and the memory of better times in the past. From the beginning the policy of protection had aroused controversy; but, after 1883, when the brief boom petered out and the downswing of the 1870s was resumed, it became far more vulnerable to attack. To a considerable extent, the tariff had been regarded as a depression measure, and obviously it had not done a great deal to relieve the depression. Was it, after all, the right policy for Canada? Had its adoption been, in fact, a terrible mistake? Would it not be better to go back to the older plan of freer trade relations with the United States? In retrospect, the period of the Reciprocity Treaty, 1854-66, seemed to shine with the lustre of a lost golden age. Why not enlarge the basic principle of the Treaty, and make Canada and the United States a completely free trade area, with a common tariff against all the world, including Great Britain?

In this mixture of disillusionment and hope lay the origins of the Commercial Union movement. Its beginnings, in both Canada and the United States, were quite independent of party politics. The first Commercial Unionists formed a relatively small group of relatively unimportant business men and mining promoters – Canadians who had done well in the United States and Americans who had prospered in Canada – and some not very prominent politicians on both sides of the border. In Canada, the movement aroused the most interest and acquired the strongest support in Ontario. The two Toronto morning papers – the *Globe*, Liberal, and the *Mail*, originally Conservative but now rapidly reading itself out of the party as a result of its maverick course – both became ardent advocates of Commer-

MOTHER BRITANNIA.—" *Take care, my child!* "
UNCLE SAM.—" *Oh! never mind, if she falls I'll catch her!* "

'*Child Canada Takes Her First Steps*'
"The anxious encouragement of Great Britain was the
first of the two external forces hastening national expansion; the second was the pressure of a resentful and predatory United States."

Sir Alexander Mackenzie
". . . an honest, sincere, hard-working, and devoted public servant."

Sir John A. Macdonald by J. W. Bengough
"In those first years after his return to power Macdonald was like a veteran conductor at the very top of his form, with a superlatively responsive orchestra in
front of him."

Riel addressing the jury
". . . Riel was tried, found guilty, and sentenced to hang for treason."

'Let the Big Chief Beware'
"The federal government, believing equally firmly that the national interest required the maintenance of the Canadian Pacific's chartered rights, disallowed no fewer than thirteen Manitoba railway acts in the years 1882-7."

D'Alton McCarthy   *Honoré Mercier*

". . . those two strangely contrasted nationalists, hurled defiance at each other over the twin issues of 'race' and religion."

'Dignified Attitude of the Liberals': 1891 election

". . . the loss of financial independence might be followed swiftly by political annexation to the United States. These doubts and fears counted enough, with enough people, to decide the contest."

SIR ADOLPHE CARON—" Me and Joe Ouimet will now exhibit Sare Mackenzie. Bowell in the act of forming his heroic resolve to protect ze rights of ze menoritee."

'Quebec Gets a Show': 1895
"Under the vacillating and procrastinating Mackenzie Bowell, [the government] ordered Manitoba to remedy the minority's grievances and Manitoba truculently refused."

Farewell to the Manitoba Transvaal Contingent, 1899
"The South African War was another outlet . . . through which Canadian imperial sentiment poured in an irresistible flood."

Emigrants leaving for Western Canada, 1902
"Canada still kept its old resemblance to a busy station on an international railway."

Wheat in Saskatchewan
"Western Canada was well on its way to becoming one of the greatest granaries in the world."

Sir Wilfrid Laurier by H. Julien
". . . Laurier presided with the confident aplomb of a conjurer pulling an endless succession of rabbits out of a magical hat."

cial Union. The widespread and powerful publicity which these two papers gave the movement accounts, largely, but not entirely, for its transient and perhaps superficial popularity. But there was another important reason for its brief success. Commercial Union had a solid intellectual core; its basis was a coherent and plausible body of facts and ideas. And the chief exponent of this basic theory was an extremely skilled controversialist, Goldwin Smith.

Smith was a product of Eton and of Magdalen College, Oxford, and a former Professor of History at Oxford University. A highly eccentric member of the English governing class, who admired the United States and American democratic institutions, he finally emigrated to the republic, found it not entirely to his liking, and moved north to settle down comfortably in Toronto. He became, in the end, perhaps the greatest exponent of the idea that Canadian Confederation was unnatural, could not endure, and that Canada's ultimate destiny lay in a continental union with the United States. His fundamental loyalty was given to what he himself called 'Anglo-Saxonry'; and his ultimate aim was 'the moral, diplomatic, and commercial union of the English-speaking race throughout the world'. For a time after his arrival in Canada, during his uneasy association with Canada First, Smith apparently believed that Canada, along with the United States, might become a second successful experiment in North American democracy; but soon he became convinced that a strong Canadian nation was impossible of achievement. Canada's continued membership in the British Empire, Smith considered, stunted the growth of a genuine Canadian national feeling; the persistent solidarity of French Canada hindered the development of national unity; and, perhaps most important of all, the geography of North America divided Canada into a series of regions, more closely connected with similar regions in the United States than with themselves. The American and Canadian economies, in Smith's view, were complementary, not competitive; he had not the slightest doubt that the idea of founding a separate Canadian nation on an east-west axis was a huge mistake. With greater force, cogency, and wit than anybody else, he set out the fundamental antithesis to Macdonald's primary thesis of the Canadian nation. He was Macdonald's arch-enemy.

For these reasons Laurier and the Liberals saw in Smith a useful ally, and in his ideas a valuable ammunition dump. For them the appearance of the Commercial Union movement was clearly a godsend. As recently as the general election of February 1887, the Liberals had not taken up any decidedly hostile stand to the national policy of protection; Blake had declared that fairly high duties were a necessity for Canada's revenue. But the election had been lost, and Blake's policies discredited, and Blake himself had retired. It was time, not only for a new leader, but also for a new policy. A new policy was surely the likeliest way to bring success to the new leader. It must differ sharply from Blake's racial appeal; it ought perhaps to be something neutral, economic, emotionally unexciting – something likely to appeal to the commercially minded English of Ontario and the Maritimes, as the Riel affair had never done. Commercial Union seemed to fill the bill exactly.

Yet the Liberals inspected this gift horse very carefully. There were tremors of apprehension about its political implications. It would certainly mean commercial discrimination against England and ominously closer relations with the United States; it might conceivably result in the loss of Canada's fiscal – and even of its political – independence. Apparently these possibilities did not perturb Laurier in the slightest. In a vague and general way, he was, like Cartwright, a continentalist; and, above all, he wanted a 'bold' policy. On the other hand, the two previous Liberal leaders, Alexander Mackenzie and Edward Blake, were opposed to the daring proposal, and they still wielded an important influence in the party. In these circumstances, J. D. Edgar suggested a compromise called Unrestricted Reciprocity, which was supposed to mean free trade in all articles of the growth or production of the two countries, but separate tariffs against the goods of the rest of the world. The phrase caught on; and at the beginning of the session of 1888 the Liberal canons adopted Unrestricted Reciprocity with the United States as its official policy.

≫ IV ≪

H ONORÉ MERCIER was entering the second year of his prime-ministership just as the federal Liberals made this radical change in their commercial platform. He needed a new policy, a policy in which the crusading ardour of his administration could be fittingly expressed. And there were not many choices. He stood really for only two things: the new Quebec Liberalism, cleansed of the anticlerical and irreligious taints of its Rouge past; and the new Quebec 'nationalism', vigorously aroused by the north-west rebellion and the execution of Louis Riel. With the second of these, Mercier had gone about as far as his invention would carry him. He had tried to make Quebec strong and prosperous, and to rally the Frenchmen of North America to its support; but he had never conceived of the idea of a separate position for Quebec in Confederation. The most he had been able to suggest was a protest movement of all the provinces, in which Quebec would play a fairly prominent part; and with the calling of the interprovincial conference in Quebec in the autumn of 1887, that notion had been exhausted, with no very striking results.

Mercier fixed the second string on his bow. He turned back to the meritorious task of re-investing Quebec Liberalism with the odour of sanctity. And fortunately again he discovered that an opportunity for faithful service was awaiting him. A controversy had arisen in Quebec over the compensation which Roman Catholics had come to believe should be paid for the properties of the Society of Jesus – properties which had been escheated to the Crown at the time of the conquest; and both the Jesuits and the bishops were urging their rival claims to the indemnity. With the approval of the Pope, who acted as final arbitrator in the dispute, Mercier arranged a settlement and imposed it in his Jesuits' Estates Bill. On the surface, the bill seemed a pacific rather than a provocative measure; but any public bill that mixed money and religion was likely to prove an irritant to the sectarian spirit of the nineteenth century. The Jesuits' Estates Bill seemed to depend for its validity upon the authority of the

Pope rather than that of the provincial legislature; it irrepressibly awakened memories of a dreaded and hated society which
the Pope himself had at one time suppressed; and it could be
claimed that indirectly it endowed an organized religion and
therefore contravened the principle of no clerical endowments –
a principle which most Protestants believed had been settled for
ever at the time of the secularization of the Clergy Reserves.

Inevitably a clamour arose in Ontario for the disallowance of
the act. A new and fighting body, the Equal Rights Association,
was formed to organize public pressure in favour of disallowance; and in March 1889 the 'Noble Thirteen' (or the 'Devil's
Dozen') staged a formidable attack on the act in the House of
Commons. The most important consequence of the agitation,
however, was the emergence of D'Alton McCarthy as the
English-Canadian nationalist antithesis of Honoré Mercier and
his Quebec 'nationalism'. A warm-hearted, impulsive, vigorous
Irishman, with crisp hair, searching eyes, and a moustache curl-
ing over a full-lipped mouth, McCarthy was a natural platform
orator with a talent for eloquent but also incisive and well-
argued oratory. He entered politics as a protégé of Macdonald's;
he had come to be regarded as the hope of the Conservative
Party; and he had been offered, and had declined, the senior
portfolio of Minister of Justice. He was too ambitious to be
content with a small ministerial salary, and too high-spirited
and independent-minded to remain amenable to the discipline
of party politics. The events that followed the execution of Riel
– the sudden rise of Mercier and his 'Nationalistes' – had convinced him that English-Canadian supremacy and Canadian
national unity were threatened. French Canada, he believed,
had become a far too distinctive, exclusive, and powerful *bloc*
in Canadian life. He had attacked the Jesuits' Estates Bill, not
so much because he disliked the Roman Catholic Church and
its institutions, as because he regarded them suspiciously as
manifestations of a separate and impermeable French-Canadian
culture. He was closer to Lord Durham than he was to George
Brown. He refused to accept dualism as a principle of Canadian
life. He wanted unity achieved and maintained through English-
Canadian supremacy.

The fundamental question in Canadian politics, he told Macdonald, was not whether Canada was to be annexed to the United States or not 'but whether this country is to be English or French'. He urged his old leader to abandon the historic Anglo-French alliance which, ever since 1854, had been the foundation of the Conservative Party. Macdonald's refusal even to consider such a course drove McCarthy further along in his own defiantly independent attempt to awaken English Canada to a sense of its extreme peril. In a speech at Stayner, Ontario, in July 1889, he prophesied that the problem of French Canada would be settled by ballots in that generation or by bullets in the next. He had already done his best to arouse the English-speaking majority of his native province to a realization of the dangers inherent in French-Canadian claims, pretensions, and special privileges; and now he decided to extend his crusade to Manitoba and the North-West Territories.

There he found a land which seemed almost to be waiting, in eager anticipation, for his arrival. The institutions of the prairie country, including sectarian schools and official bilingualism, had been imposed prematurely under heavy pressure and without much forethought in the 1870s; but by the end of the next decade, English-speaking and Protestant immigration had overwhelmed the bilingual culture of fur-trading days and determined the permanent character of the west. The use of French died out completely in the Manitoba legislature; and in 1889, when Joseph Royal, the new Lieutenant-Governor of the North-West Territories, ventured to open the Territorial Council with a speech in English and French, he evoked astonishment and annoyance. In both Manitoba and the Territories, Roman Catholic schools decreased in number while the so-called Protestant schools multiplied and took on a largely non-sectarian character. In the summer of 1889, before the arrival of McCarthy, ministers in the new Greenway government of Manitoba announced that they intended to establish a single, uniform, non-denominational system of education in the province.

McCarthy's western visit was therefore the occasion, not the cause, of the controversy that followed. When, at Portage la Prairie and Calgary, he reminded the westerners that they were living under unsuitable and objectionable constitutions in whose making they had had no influence whatever, he awakened an instant response. At Portage la Prairie, Joseph Martin, who was Attorney General in Greenway's provincial government, rose immediately after McCarthy had finished speaking and identified himself with McCarthy's attack on the separate schools and bilingualism. A few months later the Territorial Council petitioned Parliament for the repeal of clause 110 of the North-West Territories Act, the clause which gave official status to the French language. And, in January 1890, basing his resolution on the principle that 'it was expedient in the interest of national unity that there should be community of language', McCarthy moved in the House of Commons for the deletion of clause 110.

⇾⟫ V ⟪⇽

DURING TWO YEARS, 1888-90, while Mercier and McCarthy, those two strangely contrasted nationalists, hurled defiance at each other over the twin issues of 'race' and religion, an ominous change in leadership and commercial policy had taken place in the United States. The new President, Benjamin Harrison, was a Republican; and it could hardly be expected that he, and his Secretary of State, James G. Blaine, would welcome the reduction of trade barriers. Unfortunately, the probability that the American tariff would not be lowered was soon changed into the alarming certainty that it was about to be raised. A new tariff act, the McKinley Act, which lifted American protection to the highest level in history, imposed prohibitive duties on a number of agricultural products, including the coarse grains which were one of Canada's few export specialties to the United States; and, in particular, it was certain to end for ever the lucrative trade in barley which had grown up between southern Ontario and New York State.

The McKinley bill passed Congress successfully and was to go into operation in October 1890. In Canada, this prospect created a feeling of anxiety close enough to desperation. People assumed, almost frantically, that efforts must and would be made to avert or mitigate this approaching disaster; and both Liberals and Conservatives reached the conclusion that the negotiation of a new trade agreement with the United States offered the only sure way of escape. Here the agreement of the two parties ended; they differed profoundly over the scope and character of the proposed agreement. The Liberal policy, Unrestricted Reciprocity, implied a continental common market; the Conservative proposals could not go beyond the limits imposed by their design of a separate Canadian economy. The National Policy, however, still left a good deal of room for manoeuvre; and, in fact, the Conservatives had included a standing offer of a reciprocal trade agreement with the United States in every budget since that of 1879.

Macdonald decided that these offers should be renewed. The worst results of the McKinley Act would not likely appear, he expected, before the harvest of 1891; and he realized that, if his government was to have any chance of survival, a general election must be held within that brief respite. Probably his best hope of success at the polls lay in the reality, or the prospect, of some new trade agreement with the United States; and late in the autumn of 1890, he tried, through the Colonial Office and the British Minister at Washington, to open trade discussions with the American government. These approaches were at first tolerated, and then abruptly and openly repudiated; and Blaine announced that no negotiations for a 'partial' reciprocity were being carried on. Obviously the Conservatives would have no promising trade agreement to display to the voters in the winter of 1891; but Macdonald decided that further delay was dangerous and that a winter election was unavoidable. As a result, the main issue of the election was simplified and sharpened. The Conservatives could do no more than take their stand on their old platform, the National Policy, now weather-beaten and battered by long years of economic adversity.

What they now faced was a mounting mass of apparently irrefutable evidence which seemed clearly to imply that the National Policy was a failure or, at best, a very qualified success. The Dominion of Canada was now nearly a quarter of a century old; and the goals which it had originally set for itself – large-scale immigration, the settlement of the west, and the creation of a diversified and prosperous national economy – seemed as far away as ever. The immigrants who were expected to settle the prairies and swell the nation's population never came – or came and frequently left again for the United States; and scores of thousands of native Canadians followed them annually across the international boundary. During the two decades from 1871 to 1891, Canada was, in fact, what has been called 'a huge demographic railway station' where thousands of men, women, and children were constantly going and coming, and where the number of departures invariably exceeded that of arrivals. An estimated 1,256,000 people came to Canada in those twenty years; and an estimated 1,546,000 left it, most of them presumably for the United States. There was a net loss of nearly 300,000 through migration; Canada was not even holding its natural increase; and in two decades Canadians added only about 1,150,000 to their number, reaching a total population in 1891 of 4,833,000. Enormous areas of the north-west were empty, or nearly empty, yet; after twenty years, the inhabitants of Manitoba and the North-West Territories numbered barely a quarter of a million. And in certain parts of the Atlantic provinces, the population was almost stationary.

The Canadian Pacific Railway had been built, but at a great cost. In a decade nearly $75 million had been added to the national debt. In 1891, with about half a million more population, the total value of exports was almost exactly what it had been in 1881; and the national revenue for 1891 exceeded that of ten years earlier by barely a million. It was true that in the same decade the number of persons employed in manufacturing had increased by 40 per cent and the gross value of production, in a time of falling prices, had risen by nearly 50 per cent. Undoubtedly the protective tariff had enlarged the Canadian economy and reduced the net loss of population through emigration to the United States. It had helped to maintain a fair rate of growth both in the gross national product and in the *per capita* gross national product; but nevertheless the personal income of the individual Canadian was falling slowly but steadily behind that of the individual American.

This gloomy record, in most of its discouraging details, could not be denied. It could only be explained; and part of the explanation could certainly be found in the circumstances of the depression – in the falling prices and contracting international trade which had undoubtedly slowed down Canada's progress. Her ambitious experiment in economic nationalism had admittedly been launched at a most unpropitious time; but was this the only reason for its apparent failure? Had the disappointments and frustrations of Confederation a deeper origin? Was there some fatal defect in the national design itself, and in the policies that the Conservatives had adopted to achieve it? Was the whole idea of a separate national economy north of the international boundary a huge and terrible mistake? Would it not be far better for Canada to take her humble place as a useful member of a great continental commercial union?

The two rival conceptions of Canada's destiny – now fully developed and complete – faced each other in immediate and absolute contradiction. The issue was vital for the future; and Canadians, realizing this, were quickly caught up in a breathless, continuous whirl of lively discussion and emotional excitement. The brief, hectic winter election campaign was marked both by the high intellectual level of its debates and the defamatory excesses of its flag-waving patriotism. In his *Canada and the Canadian Question,* Goldwin Smith published the fullest and best statement of his belief in Canada's inevitable absorption in a continental union. The most effective rejoinder to Smith's book appeared in a review by G. M. Grant, the Principal of Queen's University, who defended Canadian independence on moral grounds and prophesied a great and beneficial future for Canada within the British Empire. Edward Blake, the former Liberal leader, who had never believed in Unrestricted Reciprocity and who declined to run in the election, provided, in his address to his former constituents of West Durham, an elaborate, acute, and highly damaging analysis of the disadvantages and dangers of Liberal trade policy.

Some of these disadvantages and dangers were immediately obvious; others could be glimpsed only obscurely in an uncertain but threatening future. Canada was financially dependent upon its tariff; and under free trade with the United States it would at once lose at least half of its national revenue. It would also be forced to discriminate commercially against England, the Mother Country upon which it still depended for military and diplomatic protection and financial support. In all probability Canadian fiscal autonomy would not long survive a trading association which so closely resembled a complete commercial union; and the loss of financial independence might be followed swiftly by political annexation to the United States. These doubts and fears counted enough, with enough people, to decide the contest. 'The Old Man, the Old Flag, and the Old Policy' won in the March election of 1891, and won it, Macdonald thought, on 'the loyalty cry'. It was loyalty in part to England, with which Canada was closely associated and consciously dependent; but it was loyalty mainly – predominantly – to Canada and the idea of a transcontinental nation in northern North America.

->>> VI <<<-

MACDONALD DIED on the 6th of June, 1891. The general election killed him; but it saved his national system from destruction. It was the culmination of his difficulties, the climax of a long series of trials and conflicts which had begun far back in the autumn of 1883 and which had affected every level – political, constitutional, economic, and cultural – of Canadian life. The time of troubles was not yet ended; but the danger of any drastic alteration in the national plan, of any radical change in the historic national policies, was now over. The country had survived its long ordeal without serious loss of faith and without any noticeable change in direction; and, despite the continuance of the depression and the outbreak of another struggle over religion and education, Canadians began to look towards the future with increasing confidence as the decade of the 1890s continued.

The Conservative party was on its way to a substantial recovery. It had won the general election of 1891 by the same majority as that of 1887; but it had lost seats in the central provinces of Ontario and Quebec. These losses had been made good by gains in the Maritime provinces; but electoral successes in what Sir Richard Cartwright flatteringly described as 'the shreds and patches of the Dominion' never counted for much with the Liberals. The Liberals, in fact, were so convinced that they had been cheated out of their rightful victory in the election that they disputed many returns and an unusually large number of by-elections were held as a result. They rushed into these contests with confidence and eager expectancy, only to meet defeat after defeat in prolonged succession. At the end of 1894, the Conservatives had made a net gain of eighteen seats in Ontario, three in Quebec, and one in the Atlantic provinces. On the morrow of the general election, the Conservative majority had been thirty-one; in the session of 1894 it was over seventy.

The downfall of the Conservatives was not gradual and inevitable; it was sudden and fortuitous. And it came about as the final result of the unexpected twists and turns – the strange chances and mischances – of the long-drawn-out controversy over Manitoba's schools. As Joseph Martin had virtually promised on the platform of Portage la Prairie, the Greenway government had abolished the official status of the French language and had established a new provincial system of non-sectarian public schools, to which all citizens, irrespective of their religious beliefs, were obliged to contribute, and to which alone provincial grants would be made. The Roman Catholics of Manitoba naturally disliked this measure, and tried – and failed – to have it set aside in the courts on the ground that it prejudicially affected the rights and privileges concerning denominational schools which they had enjoyed at the time of the union. In effect, the Judicial Committee of the Privy Council ruled that the minority's educational rights and privileges had been acquired by law not before, but after, the union of 1870. Such rights were much less strongly protected by the constitution; but there was a provision in the British North America Act by which a religious minority might appeal to the federal government against any provincial statute which adversely affected educational rights acquired after union, and the federal government might intervene to provide a remedy even to the extent of enacting remedial legislation.

Did this provision apply to Manitoba? The wording of the relevant clause in the Manitoba Act differed from that of the British North America Act, and the decisions of the courts were twice reversed. Finally, in January 1895, the Judicial Committee of the Privy Council decided that Manitoba's school legislation did prejudicially affect minority educational rights acquired after 1870, that the minority could appeal to the federal government to protect these rights, and that the federal government might intervene to redress the minority's grievances. Up until that point, the Dominion had postponed all thought of intervention, waiting until its authority in the matter had been established in the courts, and secretly hoping that no obligation to act would be laid upon it. Now all possibility of delay and evasion was over. The Dominion was confronted with the appalling political necessity of action. Like Parliament, and like the country as a whole, the Conservative government at Ottawa was badly divided on the issue. Roman Catholics – and particularly French-Canadian Roman Catholics – demanded instant federal intervention; English-speaking Protestants protested vehemently against the 'coercion' of Manitoba. Slowly, unhappily, rent by periodic cabinet crises, the Conservative government moved towards its doom. Under the vacillating and procrastinating Mackenzie Bowell, it ordered Manitoba to remedy the minority's grievances and Manitoba truculently refused. The veteran Sir Charles Tupper, the Canadian High Commissioner to the United Kingdom, returned to Canada, and, in an attempt to strengthen the administration, joined the cabinet as Secretary of State and government leader in the Commons. Tupper sincerely believed that the Dominion had a moral and constitutional obligation to provide redress; and it was he who presented the government's remedial legislation to the House of Commons. Led by Laurier, the Liberals blocked it with a sustained filibuster, and before the remedial bill could be passed, the seventh Parliament expired by the effluxion of time.

The Manitoba schools question, which was the central, but by no means the only, issue in the general election of 1896, has often been misrepresented as a straight conflict between Conservatives upholding confessional schools and federal authority and Liberals defending non-sectarian education and provincial rights. In reality, the Conservatives were never united in support of Tupper's straightforward stand. In Quebec, of course, the Bleus paraded their willingness to defend the educational privileges of the Manitoba minority; but in Ontario, despite Tupper's repeated declarations of policy, Conservative candidates in large numbers announced firmly that they would not vote for remedial legislation. The party was openly and hopelessly divided. The denials of the back-benchers cast serious doubts on the validity of the leader's promises; and as a result the Conservatives lost seats in Ontario as well as many more in Quebec.

Laurier enjoyed a distinct advantage. He could, and did, remain evasive and non-committal throughout the entire controversy. At no point did the Liberal Party commit itself to a frank advocacy of provincial autonomy in education. Laurier never went further than to suggest that the actual state of Manitoba's schools should be investigated and that the Dominion should attempt to conciliate, rather than coerce, the government of Manitoba. Liberal newspaper editors in Ontario shouted 'hands off Manitoba' to their approving readers; but Liberal candidates in Quebec promised French-Canadian voters that their party could get a far better settlement for the Manitoba Roman Catholics – and, if necessary, by federal intervention – than the Tories could. The Roman Catholic hierarchy in Quebec, which is often wrongly alleged to have opposed the Laurier Liberals officially, enabled them, in fact, to maintain their equivocal attitude with easy impunity. The Bishops' *mandement* simply required electors to vote for candidates who would solemnly promise to support remedial legislation in Parliament, should it ultimately become necessary to do so. The great majority of the Liberal candidates in Quebec took the oath in good faith and without the slightest hesitation.

The main difference between the two parties was that one was politically vulnerable and the other was not. The Conservatives could be punished by defeat for the evasions and contradictions of which both parties were guilty. And a Conservative defeat could mean only a Liberal victory. A Liberal victory it was, but a lucky victory, not fully deserved. For the first time in a federal general election, three third parties – McCarthyites, Patrons of Industry, and the Protestant Protective Association – ran a number of candidates; and they complicated the issues and results of the campaign. 46.3 per cent of the popular vote went to the Conservatives, and 45 per cent to the Liberals; but the Liberals gained 117 seats to the Conservatives' eighty-nine, and that was what really counted.

CHAPTER FIVE

The End of Colonial Security

WでそのHAT DID the Liberal victory portend? What, in particular, would Liberal rule mean for the national policies on which Macdonald had relied to promote the country's development? Nobody could be very sure, for the Liberals had been eighteen years in the wilderness of opposition; but their record, on the face of it, was not very reassuring. They had denounced the Canadian Pacific Railway as an insane and ruinous defiance of North America's natural transport routes. They had expatiated upon the evils of Canadian protectionism and proclaimed at enormous length the advantages of the North American common market. If they had won the general election of 1891 they would at least have tried to carry out what would have amounted to a revolution in Canadian commercial policy. Yet now, only five years later, the revolution was apparently neither feared nor eagerly awaited. Nobody really expected drastic change. Everybody quietly assumed that the Liberal Party itself had altered.

One of the principal reasons for this alteration was Wilfrid Laurier himself. The man who, ten years before, had looked as if he would remain a capable French-Canadian subordinate under an English-speaking chief had in fact become an accepted and unquestioned party leader. The control he exercised differed radically from that of either of his predecessors. He belonged to the tradition of Macdonald, not to the tradition of Mackenzie and Blake. Mackenzie had been well meaning and honest, but ineffectual; Blake had been intellectually able but politically inept. Laurier could not rival Mackenzie's simple virtues or Blake's mental gifts; but as a political leader he was superior to both of them. He was a quietly, insistently dominating man, with a shrewd sense of political realities, a flexible, empirical approach to problems, and an alert appreciation of the sources of power. In the past, the Liberal Party had had a history of doctrinaire intellectualism and voluble virtue. Laurier obviously intended to change all this.

His first act was to end the quarrel over Manitoba's schools. During the election campaign, he had preached the virtues of 'investigation' and 'conciliation'; and, in Quebec at least, his candidates had certainly implied that a victorious Liberal Party would provide a better remedy for the distressed Manitoba minority than the Conservative Remedial Bill would have done. Once in power, Laurier dropped the idea of an investigation completely; instead, he pursued a policy of conciliation to the apparent point of appeasement. By the terms of an agreement which was quickly concluded with Manitoba, religious instruction was permitted, but not made compulsory, during the last half hour of school; and Roman Catholic teachers might be employed when requested by a required number of Roman Catholic parents. A third important clause was clearly meant to encourage French-Canadian 'nationalist' pretensions rather than to protect Roman Catholic educational privileges; it provided that teaching might be carried on in 'the bilingual system', in French, or other mother tongue of the pupils, as well as in English. In all other respects, Manitoba's new non-denominational schools, to which alone government grants were made and citizens' taxes paid, continued exactly as before.

Laurier had declared that the Conservative Remedial Bill gave the Roman Catholics of Manitoba 'the minimum of relief'. His own settlement gave them a great deal less; and, with considerable justification, the bishops came to the angry conclusion that he had betrayed them. They launched such a sustained and furious attack on the agreement and its author that Laurier felt obliged to appeal to Rome, and an apostolic delegate was sent out to Canada to investigate. The Pope finally issued an encyclical enjoining acceptance of the Laurier settlement as a partial satisfaction of the educational needs of the Roman Catholic

Church; and the episcopal thunders subsided into a low growl. Laurier had shown flexibility and resourcefulness in meeting the demands of Manitoba and outmanoeuvring the opposition of the episcopacy; but these signs of a liberal and independent spirit in religious and educational affairs by no means implied that he was going back to the anticlericalism of his youth. He placed, in fact, little reliance on his old Rouge friends. His principal ally and confidant in Quebec in the 1890s was Israel Tarte, a renegade Bleu. Laurier had no intention of letting old party ideology and history prevent him from getting the lion's share of popular support in a Catholic and Conservative province such as Quebec.

In Ontario, he showed himself equally ready to drop old encumbrances and to escape from old embarrassments. When he had become leader in 1887, the powerful Ontario division of the party was dominated by Edward Blake and Sir Richard Cartwright, veterans who were inclined to treat their protégé with a certain avuncular condescension. By 1896, when Laurier took office as Prime Minister, he had put Cartwright very firmly in his place, and had successfully got rid of Blake. Blake, who had always opposed Unrestricted Reciprocity and who had tried in vain to persuade the Liberals to give it up after their defeat in the election of 1891, finally retired from Canadian politics and in 1892 left for Great Britain. So long as Blake remained in Canada, Laurier seemed to cling tenaciously to his belief in continentalism and North American free trade; but, once Blake was safely out of the country, Laurier began, with dispatch but without acknowledgement, to follow his old leader's wise advice. In 1893, one year after Blake's departure, the Liberal Party, meeting in convention at Ottawa, unostentatiously dropped Unrestricted Reciprocity in favour of an innocuous resolution advocating greater freedom of trade. Three years later, on the eve of the election of 1896, Laurier made public a carefully worded correspondence between himself and a Liberal manufacturer, which went far to prove that the Liberal Party took a very responsible view of Canadian industry and was most unlikely to lay irreverent hands on the tariff.

Laurier's treatment of Sir Richard Cartwright, his old Ontario mentor, was a pledge that these promises would be made good. Cartwright had become objectionable, not because, like Blake, he had opposed Unrestricted Reciprocity, but because he had been too closely associated with it. As the 'Blue Ruin Knight', who had made a pleasurable hobby and a serious profession out of denouncing the national policy of protection, Cartwright had become notorious to the Canadian business community. Although an acknowledged party liability, he could not be completely written off; he would have to be carried, but carried in a less significant, less conspicuous position. He was given the secondary portfolio of Trade and Commerce; and his old post at the Ministry of Finance went to the Nova Scotian, William Stevens Fielding. In April 1897, when Fielding brought down his first budget, George E. Foster, the tall, thin, lugubrious Conservative who had been Finance Minister in the previous administration, observed derisively but accurately in the House of Commons that there was now no difference in the fiscal policies of the two parties. To those old, unconverted Grit free-traders who still believed fondly in past Liberal professions, Fielding made only two concessions. The duties on agricultural machinery and farm equipment, which had already been reduced by the Conservatives, were cut a little lower; and – what was much more important – a new minimum tariff, 25 per cent lower than the general level, was offered to all countries which would treat Canadian trade as favourably. Great Britain, though she could grant no equivalent preference, for she admitted goods freely whatever their country of origin, was declared to have qualified for the minimum tariff immediately.

The British, or imperial, preference, the most striking feature of Fielding's budget, was also the feature most diametrically opposed to the economic continentalism which Laurier and his colleagues had been so earnestly advocating only six years before. The preference was intended to increase trade with the United Kingdom and thus to strengthen the east-west axis of the Canadian economy. It was a far more imperially minded device than any that the Conservatives had ever introduced. And if further proof was needed to confirm the new Liberal approach to Canada's fiscal and commercial policies, it was amply provided by the conduct of the Laurier government at the sittings of the Canadian-American Joint High Commission of 1898-9. The Commission had been established to settle a number of outstanding problems, including the Alaska boundary and trade relations; and in the past the Liberals had always claimed that, since they believed in freer trade relations with the United States, they could negotiate a reciprocal trade treaty much more easily and successfully than the supposedly anti-American Conservatives. Yet now they mysteriously failed to create an amicable atmosphere of mutual concession. Lower duties were seriously discussed for only a few items – coal, flour, and lumber; and the unregenerate Cartwright was the only Canadian representative who showed any enthusiasm for free trade. 'There has been a great deal of misconception,' Laurier wrote to Principal Grant of Queen's University, 'as to the character of the negotiations at Washington. The impression was that we were struggling with might and main to obtain a wide measure of reciprocity. The reverse is the truth.'

By what it failed to do, as well as by what it did, the 'New Liberalism' served to promote transcontinental and transatlantic trade, and thus to strengthen the east-west axis of the Canadian economy.

→» II «←

THE OLD NATIONAL POLICIES apparently could not be bettered at home. But abroad, Laurier began to face strange and novel problems for which the traditional solutions would obviously not suffice. Up until virtually the end of the nineteenth century, the Canadians had regarded the outside world mainly as a market for their staple products and a source of manufactures, capital, and population. They had never been obliged to concern themselves seriously with international affairs. There were few occasions in which they had felt any real apprehension about world politics. Apart from the American Civil War, which they had watched from terrifying ringside seats, the great powers of the English-speaking world had not been involved in serious conflict for nearly half a century; and the American Civil War was already a generation away. Canada had been able to give all its energies to the business of internal development. The world was being looked after by somebody else, though the Canadians not unnaturally assumed that the process of maintaining the peace was almost automatic. After 1895, the mechanism ceased to work so smoothly. The long Britannic peace was finally reaching its conclusion. And Canadians awoke to the realization that the world was becoming a dangerous place.

The first manifestation of this new state of affairs was the sudden, vigorous rise of American imperialism during the 1890s. For Canada, the most dangerous feature of this powerful outward thrust was the accompanying assertion by the United States of its primacy in the politics of the western hemisphere. 'Today the United States is practically sovereign on this continent,' Richard Olney, President Cleveland's Secretary of State, declared in 1895 at the time of the boundary dispute between Venezuela and British Guiana, 'and its fiat is law upon the subjects to which it confines its interposition.' Olney's and Cleveland's immediate object was to compel Great Britain to accept the arbitration of the disputed boundary; but they justified this demand by an enormous enlargement of the Monroe Doctrine. Any 'permanent political union' between a European and an American state was condemned as 'unnatural and inexpedient'; and any European power which attempted to intervene on behalf of its remaining 'temporary' American possessions could do so only by methods which the United States considered acceptable. Canada was the only nation in the two American continents which was still linked with a European power; and Great Britain, though she showed no signs of abandoning the Dominion, was obviously surrendering her other remaining interests in the New World to the demands of the preponderant republic. After President Cleveland had backed up Olney's contention in a truculent message to Congress, Great Britain hastily agreed to arbitrate the Venezuela boundary. And only a few years later, under heavy and repeated pressure from the United States, cunningly exerted at the moment of deepest British involvement in the South African War, the United Kingdom gave up the equal rights in the Panama Canal which she had acquired by treaty half a century earlier.

The increasing weakness of Great Britain in the Americas might expose Canada to the heavy weight of American hegemony. And, at the same time, Great Britain's increasing involvement in Europe might implicate her most important dependency in the power politics of the Old World. The growth of imperial Germany paralleled the rise of an imperialistic United States. After 1896 Great Britain occupied an obviously dangerous position; and, emerging quickly from her isolation and evident unpopularity, she set out to win friends and cultivate good relations. The settlement of her outstanding disputes with France and Russia made her an uneasy member of the European alliance system. Her retreat in the Venezuela dispute and the abandonment of her rights in the Panama Canal earned her the grudging friendliness of the United States. These diplomatic manoeuvres on both sides of the Atlantic vaguely threatened Canada; she might be involved in Great Britain's imperial interests or European commitments; she might be injured by British appeasement of the United States.

In 1896, Canada's role in imperial defence and foreign policy was still very much what it had been fifteen years before, when the office of High Commissioner to the United Kingdom had been established. At that time, Macdonald had repeatedly declared that he had no wish to break up the diplomatic unity of the Empire; he had simply insisted that the conduct of imperial foreign policy must become a co-operative enterprise, in which Canada would have a voice. Since then the High Commissioner had represented Canadian commercial interests at several European capitals; the Canadian share in the settlement of Canadian-American problems had grown steadily larger, and four out of the five British representatives on the Joint High Commission of 1898-9 had been Canadians. Yet no other missions had been set up abroad, even in the United States where Canadian interests were so important; the High Commissioner to the United Kingdom was still Canada's only permanent external representative; and not even the semblance of a Foreign Office or Department of External Affairs had been created at Ottawa. Imperial diplomacy was centred at London; it was an elaborate organization in which Canadian politicians and civil servants merely performed occasional or minor functions. Treaties were signed by Great Britain on her own responsibility; her decisions made peace or war for the whole Empire; and correspondingly she bore the main burden of imperial defence. Canada had only a small permanent force, a neglected and inefficient militia, and no navy at all. The Empire was, in fact, an unequal partnership in which the chief authority and the main obligations lay with the United Kingdom.

→≫ III ≪←

THIS WAS THE POSITION in law and custom; but, at the end of the nineteenth century, the law and custom of the past no longer satisfied the Canadians. They identified themselves more closely and intimately than ever before with the British Empire; but it was this very sense of partnership and common purpose which revealed the inadequacy of the old imperial constitution. Canadian national feeling had grown perceptibly stronger and more conscious. The doubts, the uncertainty, the infirmity of purpose which had characterized the late 1880s had dwindled steadily ever since the election of 1891; and Canadians now believed, with a renewed and strengthened conviction, that the hopes and intentions of Confederation could be realized, and that in the very near future. Canada, they felt certain, would unquestionably be a great nation; it would be great, partly because of its own potential strength, but partly also because of its membership in the British Empire. The imperial connection was not an outworn and tenuous constitutional tie, shrunken and brittle with age, kept feebly alive by feelings of tutelage and obligation; it was a strong emotional attachment, glowing with new pride and fresh hopes and aims, vitalized by important national interests and national ambitions. In the nineteenth century, Great Britain had kept the balance of power in the English-speaking world and had thus enabled Canada to survive the perils of American continental imperialism. The Anglo-Canadian alliance had done great things for Canada in the past. Would it not certainly do equally great things in the future? It had made Canada a nation. Might it not also enable her to become a world influence, almost a world power?

The narrow provincialism and dependent security of colonial days was gone or going. Among Canadians there was now a greater sense of responsibility, a wider knowledge and stronger interest in world affairs, and, above all, a greater consciousness of their own energy, power, and ambition. This expanding national outlook, this irrepressible impulse to play some part in international politics, was eager to find an outlet. The imperial connection was not only its historic and instinctive form of expression; it was also the channel which reason and ambition would choose. The British Empire was a great world-wide collective organization in which Canada could maintain and strengthen her own national autonomy and, at the same time, exert a real and positive influence on the fortunes of mankind. Left by herself, cut off from the Empire, a little independent North American country, submerged in the deep shadow of its colossal neighbour, the United States, Canada could lead only a meagre, tributary, and subservient existence. Nearly twenty years before, G. M. Grant, in his book *Ocean to Ocean*, had contemptuously dismissed 'independence' as a possible course for Canada; 'only dreamers or emasculated intellects,' he declared, 'would seriously propose "independence" to four million people face to face with thirty-eight million.' Grant's population figures were those of the census of 1871; but in the meantime the disparity between the human resources of the two nations had grown far more intimidating and hopeless. In 1901, only 5,371,315 Canadians were confronted by seventy-six million Americans!

No, 'independence' was not the road to real autonomy and real influence. The greatness of the future would be realized, not by the break of the imperial tie, but by its steady continuity and progressive development. In Canada, as the century drew towards its close, the imperial idea became at once a popular enthusiasm and a reasoned political and ethical philosophy. Canadians were finding a fresh, exciting satisfaction in the power, pomp, and prestige of the Empire; and, at the same time, they were also elaborating a new moral and social justification for its existence and continuation. Queen Victoria's Diamond Jubilee, which was a much more imperial affair than its predecessor ten years earlier, was the first great public occasion in which they could join, as recognized if junior partners, in celebrating the glories and achievements of the Empire. That these glories lay, not simply in the acquisition of wealth and power, but also, and more particularly, in the successful dissemination of civilized standards of private morality and public conduct among the backward peoples of the world, was a doctrine which G. M. Grant and George Parkin had been preaching, with persuasive eloquence, in a long series of lectures, reviews, articles, and books. In their view, the British Empire was the greatest secular instrument for the betterment of the world that then existed. It was Canada's great privilege to participate in such a noble enterprise; through the Empire she could realize her own personality to the full and at the same time take her place in a great providential mission for the elevation of mankind. To play her part adequately, she would need more influence and authority within Empire; but in exchange for more power she must be willing to accept more responsibility. Inevitably these exchanges and adjustments within the Empire would require a reform of its constitution, a re-allocation of its duties and prerogatives. Was it not time to make a living reality of that 'different colonial system' of which Macdonald had spoken more than a generation ago?

Laurier was sensitively alive to the winds of public opinion. Now he felt them stir, and shift, and freshen. Continentalism and commercial independence from Great Britain were as discarded and forgotten as the fashions of ten years ago. Imperialism, imperial preferences, and imperial recognition were all the mode. In 1887, Macdonald had been too preoccupied with domestic affairs to attend the first Colonial Conference; but Laurier had not the slightest intention of missing the celebrations and discussions of the Jubilee. It was a curious indication of his own provincialism that he had never yet crossed the ocean to Europe. Now he was bound for the greatest ceremonial occasion and the first truly intergovernmental council in British imperial history. The conference of 1897 was to be a gathering of the senior governments of the Empire; only the self-governing colonies were present, in the persons of their premiers; and of these Sir Wilfrid Laurier – the knighthood was a jubilee honour – was obviously the most prominent and distinguished. The other premiers represented only individual South African or Australasian colonies; he spoke for a united and transcontinental Canada. In manner, he was easy, gracious, charming. His fluent rhetoric matched the grandeur of the ceremonies; his sentiments echoed the prevailing feeling of Empire solidarity. He told an audience at the National Liberal Club that 'it would be the proudest moment of my life if I could see a Canadian of French descent affirming the principles of freedom in the Parliament of Great Britain'. To a group in a House of Commons committee room he declared that Canadian national feeling would soon demand expression through some form of representation in the Imperial Parliament or in some grand imperial council or federal legislative body.

These reflections were offered in the early summer months of 1897, when the Empire was at peace. Only a little more than two years later, it was at war. The South African War was another outlet, wider and more inviting than the Jubilee itself, through which Canadian imperial sentiment poured in an irresistible flood. The War, and the Alaska boundary dispute which quickly followed it, were the two episodes through which Canada first came into direct contact with the exciting and dangerous international politics of the twentieth century.

→»» IV ««

LIKE THE CANADIAN imperialists, the British imperialists believed that the reorganization of the Empire would have to mean the sharing, not only of powers and privileges, but also of responsibilities and burdens. At the Colonial Conference of 1897, Joseph Chamberlain, the British Colonial Secretary, had proposed a federal imperial council and an imperial common market; but he had also invited colonial contributions to imperial defence. And obviously the South African War gave the mature, self-governing Dominions and colonies their first great chance to respond. There is no doubt that Chamberlain and Lord Minto, the new Canadian Governor General who arrived in Ottawa in the autumn of 1898, hoped for an official contingent from Canada, and would have been very pleased if the Canadian government had offered one in the early days of the dispute with the Boer republics. But these British suggestions and requests came to Laurier privately, and through a Governor General who genuinely sympathized with the Prime Minister's reluctance to commit himself to action in advance; and their total effect was negligible in comparison with the compelling pressure of Canadian public opinion, which from the first had shown itself to be independently and spontaneously on the side of Great Britain in its quarrel with the Transvaal and the Orange Free State. On the 31st of July, 1899, on Laurier's own motion, the House of Commons passed a resolution expressing sympathy with the 'Uitlanders', the British subjects who had come to the Transvaal to mine the gold of the Witwatersrand and who had been denied political rights by the Kruger government. And, as war drew closer, this firm belief in the essential justice of the British cause began to take the form of a demand for active Canadian participation. On the 18th of September, Colonel Sam Hughes, a prominent member of the militia, wrote to a number of Canadian newspapers inviting applications from all who were prepared to go and fight in South Africa. He received about 1,200 replies.

Early in October, the British imperialists made their only open attempt to persuade the Canadian government to take action. On the 3rd of October, the British government sent a circular telegram to all the colonies expressing its thanks for the offers of troops from the Dominions and giving detailed instructions as to how the units were to be organized. On the same day, in a new issue of the *Canadian Military Gazette*, there appeared an article confidently predicting that Canada would send a contingent to South Africa; and this was thought to have been inspired by the new General Officer Commanding the Canadian Militia, Major-General Edward T. Hutton, who had come to Canada with the hope of reforming the militia and making Canadians more conscious of the needs of defence. It was not clear on the surface whether the circular telegram of the 3rd of October referred to an official promise of troops, or to unofficial and voluntary offers from individuals; but from Chamberlain's private correspondence it is perfectly obvious that he hoped the Canadian government would send an official contingent.

This stirred Laurier to quick action. On the 4th of October, he bluntly and categorically denied the rumour in the *Canadian Military Gazette*. He admitted that Canadian troops could be sent overseas if the defence of Canada required it; but he insisted that there was no danger for Canada in South Africa, and that, since Parliament was not in session, no appropriation could be made for the dispatch of a contingent. This sounded conclusive and final; but it was not. Exactly ten days later, on the 14th of October, Laurier completely reversed his stand and offered an official contingent. This was not the result of pressure from the British imperialists, for they had already shot their bolt, in vain. The pressure came from Canadian public opinion, aroused by the British declaration of war on the 11th of October, and by the inflammatory propaganda of such papers as Hugh Graham's *Montreal Star*. When Laurier got back to Ottawa from a speaking engagement in Chicago, he found that the cabinet, with the exception of the French-Canadian members, was solidly in favour of some form of participation. In an order in council of the 14th of October, the government undertook to equip and transport a force of not more than one thousand men to South Africa. This, it was explained, was not a precedent for the future, and not a departure from the principles of constitutional government, since parliamentary approval was not necessary for the small sum required.

The dispatch of the contingent to South Africa was Canada's first response to the international tensions and dangers of the new age. The second response was the struggle to defend Canadian rights in the dispute over the boundary of the Alaskan 'panhandle', the long, narrow strip of land jutting down the coast from the main body of Alaska. According to the terms of the Anglo-Russian Treaty of 1825, the boundary, from the Portland Channel north, was to 'follow the summit of the mountains situated parallel to the coast', so long as this summit was to be found within ten marine leagues of the sea; and in case, at any point, it exceeded this limit, the boundary was to be 'formed by a line parallel to the windings of the coast and which shall never exceed the distance of ten marine leagues therefrom'. In fact, the coast was extremely jagged and irregular, with a number of deep inlets or fiords, the chief of which was called the Lynn Canal; and it was the possession of the Lynn Canal, the easiest entrance to the Yukon goldfields, that was the main issue in the dispute. The Canadian contention was that there was a mountain chain fairly close to the coast, but that, if the alternative boundary had to be followed, the line should be drawn ten leagues from the mouths of the inlets, the inlets themselves being regarded as territorial waters. The American claim was that there was no distinct and recognizable chain of mountains and that the boundary should be drawn ten leagues inland from the heads of the inlets. The first interpretation would give Canada access to the sea; the second would assure the United States an unbroken strip or *lisière* around the heads of the inlets and would shut Canada completely out from the ocean.

Undoubtedly, the arguments in favour of the American case were extremely strong. Until fairly recently, nobody had vigorously contested the Russian and American contention that the *lisière* was unbroken; British as well as Russian and American maps showed the boundary running around the heads of the inlets; and Americans occupied the ports on the Lynn Canal by squatters' rights, if not by legal title. Historically, if not legally, the Canadian case was weak; and it was still more seriously weakened by the diplomatic circumstances in which the Empire found itself. Great Britain's withdrawal from the New World, a process hastened by her prolonged involvement in South Africa, had left her with no real basis of authority or influence in

North America. The surrender of her treaty rights in the Panama Canal meant that she had literally nothing to bargain with. In the United States, William McKinley had been succeeded as President by Theodore Roosevelt, a convinced and truculent champion of the new American imperialism; and Roosevelt pugnaciously insisted that the Canadian case in Alaska was 'trumped up' and utterly worthless. Great Britain and Canada proposed arbitration; but the United States, which had imposed arbitration in the Venezuela dispute, declined to accept it herself, and instead demanded a purely judicial tribunal, with an equal number of representatives on each side. Great Britain was prepared to support Canada up to a point, but not to the extent of seriously compromising her relations with the United States; and at length she reluctantly accepted the American proposal. The terms of the Treaty of January, 1903, which established the judicial tribunal emphasized in every word the purely judicial nature of the inquiry; but, in fact, the tribunal, when it met in the following autumn, was subjected to intense and persistent political pressure through every form of persuasion, compulsion, and menace which Roosevelt and his diplomatic agents could employ. In the end, the British representative on the Anglo-Canadian team, Lord Alverstone, deserted his two colleagues to vote with the Americans; and this broke the deadlock and gave a purely political award to the United States.

⫸ V ⫷

AT THE END OF JULY 1903, a little over a month before the Joint High Commission was to meet in the rooms of the Foreign Office in London, Laurier revealed to the Canadian Parliament his plans for the last phase, the transport phase, of the new Liberal nationalism. Here also, as in the case of the manufacturers and the tariff, it was obvious that the Liberals had been going through an intensive process of re-education along modern commercial lines. They flung to the winds their old prudent and parsimonious misgivings about transcontinental railway enterprises; and, with a swiftness and a completeness acquired through frequent practice, they paid the last of the Conservative national policies – the policy of all-Canadian transport – the supreme compliment of adoption. Against all their grave warnings and gloomy predictions, the Canadian Pacific Railway had proved itself a tremendous success. The line that would never pay for its axle grease was now overtaxed with traffic; and this deficiency in the great national east-west route gave the Liberals the justification they needed to repeat the triumph the Conservatives had scored a generation earlier. They too would become railway builders, on a greater and gaudier scale than ever before.

But how? The answer was Laurier's, reached independently of the views of the rest of his cabinet and in opposition to the wishes of the principal ministers concerned, including the Minister of Railways and Canals, A. G. Blair. Laurier knew nothing whatever about railways; all he had ever done in the past was to travel on them. He did, however, know a great deal about Canadian politics; and in his mind the political advantages which a new transcontinental railway would bring to the Liberal Party were scarcely less important than the economic advantages it would confer on the Canadian people. A general election would probably be held in 1904, and he knew that he ought to have something material to give to Ontario and the Maritime provinces, as well as to the west. Above all, he must have something very impressive to offer to his native province of Quebec. What better could it be than a railway in the barren highlands to the north? Honoré Mercier, the first great advocate of northern settlement, had been driven out of office by a scandal as malodorous as any in the history of his not very politically squeamish province; and he, and his deputy minister of agriculture and colonization, François Xavier Labelle, 'the apostle of colonization' as he was reverently called, were both dead. But their expansionist and missionary spirit lived on. The clergy, politicians, and business men of Quebec were still united in a pious endeavour to colonize the northern parts of the province with the surplus French-Canadian population which had long showed an alarming disposition to emigrate to the United States.

As early as 1895, a group of local Quebec promoters had planned a northern railway project which would help to carry the French language and the Roman Catholic faith into a region which had remarkably few attractions except its remoteness from the contagion of English-speaking Protestantism.

Laurier dreamed of a new transcontinental. Two existing railways – the Canadian Northern Railway and the Grand Trunk Railway of Canada – cherished exactly the same dream. The Grand Trunk, a venerable and debt-ridden organization, which had recently come under the direction of a new and energetic general manager, Charles M. Hays, was a central Canadian railway, with terminals at Portland, Maine, and Chicago. The Canadian Northern was primarily a network of western lines, centred in Winnipeg, and controlled by William Mackenzie and Donald Mann, two of the most ingenious, daring, and successful railway promoters in Canadian history. By 1902, the Canadian Northern had been extended as far eastward as Port Arthur, while the north-western terminus of the Grand Trunk was at North Bay, on Lake Nipissing. In retrospect, it seems obvious that the most efficient and economical solution that the government could possibly have devised would have been to persuade or compel the Canadian Northern and the Grand Trunk to amalgamate or co-operate in a joint system.

This was the arrangement which Clifford Sifton, the Minister of the Interior, favoured and which Laurier tried for a while to press upon the principals, Hays, Mackenzie, and Mann, during the winter of 1903. But two major obstacles prevented the adoption of this sensible solution of the problem. The first was the overweening ambitions of the Grand Trunk and the Canadian Northern, both of which ardently desired to repeat independently the success of the Canadian Pacific, and to capture a satisfactory share of the nation's transcontinental traffic. The second and perhaps equally important obstacle was the political plans of Laurier and the political hopes and demands of his followers across the country. The amalgamation, or collaboration, of two existing railways, one eastern and one western, would have few beneficial side effects for Ontario and none at all for the Maritime provinces. Above all, it would do nothing to promote the colonization of northern Quebec and thus to satisfy the pious aspirations of the clerics and 'nationalists' of the province.

No, the co-operative plan would not do, politically. Unable – or unwilling – to impose it, the government proceeded, as a result, to authorize not one, but two, new transcontinental railways. In 1902, apparently without expecting that Mackenzie and Mann would ever take advantage of their chartered rights, it empowered the Canadian Northern to extend its lines eastward to Ottawa and Montreal; and in the following year it began negotiations with the Grand Trunk. At first, the Grand Trunk proposed that it would build from North Bay, on Lake Nipissing, its existing northern terminus, westward across Canada to the Pacific; but this practical and relatively inexpensive proposal was rejected by the government, ostensibly on the nationalist ground that the Grand Trunk's eastern terminus was Portland, in the United States. A transcontinental Grand Trunk could not qualify as an all-Canadian railway, the government patriotically explained; what it failed to point out was the equally important fact that a transcontinental Grand Trunk, like an amalgamated Grand Trunk–Canadian Northern, would do nothing to satisfy Maritime economic ambitions or to aid French-Canadian colonizing endeavours in the north. The Grand Trunk plan, in short, was economically sensible, but politically valueless. It was turned down, and in its place a much more ambitious and costly scheme was substituted. The government negotiated a highly complicated agreement with the Grand Trunk for the construction, in two great divisions, of still a third railway from coast to coast. The eastern division, called the National Transcontinental, which ran from Moncton to Quebec, and then in a wide northern arc through Quebec and Ontario to Winnipeg, was to be built by the government and subsequently leased to the Grand Trunk. The western division, which took a northerly route across the prairies and through the Yellowhead Pass, was to be built by the Grand Trunk, and called the Grand Trunk Pacific.

⇢⇢⇢ VI ⇚⇚⇚

IN NOVEMBER 1904, when Laurier fought and won his third general election, the nature and meaning of the new Liberal nationalism had been fully revealed. There was nothing at all novel in its familiar features. The Liberals had not devised new national policies; they had simply appropriated the national policies of their Conservative predecessors. It was not in the well-known ways of domestic affairs but in the strange and rather frightening world of external relations that Laurier had been forced to make novel and unwelcome decisions. At first, as in the grant of the imperial preference to Great Britain and in the speeches delivered at the time of Queen Victoria's Diamond Jubilee, he had seemed to show an interest in a more formal imperial collaboration; but this phase was over almost before it had begun. Laurier could indulge in daydreams about Canadian representation in a grand imperial council, or paint romantic pictures of himself, 'a Canadian of French descent affirming the principles of freedom in the Parliament of Great Britain'; but when it came to the practical business of running the Empire, of which Canada was a part, on a co-operative basis – with military co-operation necessarily involved – his enthusiasm quickly cooled. He had assumed that the Empire meant peace; but apparently it could also mean war. Imperial reorganization, he had supposed, might include the further exchange of trade privileges, or even the creation of an imperial council or federal legislature; but that it would also entail active and constant participation in imperial defence and foreign policy he had never for a moment imagined. Diplomacy was a sinister game, and war a monstrous enterprise, to which European nations, including, unfortunately, Great Britain, seemed to be incurably addicted. Laurier shrank from this foreign and dangerous world with an aversion compounded of inexperience, apprehension, and moral disapproval – feelings which had their origin, not only in his genuine idealism, but also in his mental habit of colonial detachment and North American sense of self-righteous isolation.

The South African War gave him an opportunity of insisting

that the corollary of colonial contributions to imperial wars was colonial participation in the making of imperial policy. But this was an argument which he apparently did not even think of using. The dispatch of the Canadian contingent to the Boer War seemed to have no purpose whatever beyond the satisfaction of English Canada's demand for action. Laurier wanted no share in the post-war settlement in South Africa; he apparently made no attempt to take advantage of Canada's war effort in order to obtain benefits at home or to influence imperial policy abroad. A year later, at the Colonial Conference of 1902, his detachment became more obvious and more evidently deliberate. Chamberlain voluntarily offered, what Laurier had never requested, a voice in imperial foreign policy in exchange for a share in the burden of imperial defence. The offer was politely but firmly refused. Laurier would not help to make a co-operative commonwealth out of the Empire; he showed no sign of wanting to use the Empire as a vehicle by which Canada could promote her own interests and realize her potential influence in the world at large; and soon his disinclination to take any real part in imperial organization seemed to change into an anxious desire to escape from its trammels completely. On the morrow of the Alaskan boundary award, he clearly implied in Parliament that Canada had best take the conduct of her foreign policy into her own hands. Was this the separate path that he was likely to take in the future? Would the final goal of Liberal nationalism be an independent Canada?

CHAPTER SIX

The Consequences of Success

I T WAS NOT a change in policies, but a change in circumstances, which brought Canada its rapidly increasing prosperity during the fifteen years of Laurier's rule. Down
until nearly the end of the nineteenth century almost everything
had conspired to ensure the failure of Confederation. After the
beginning of the twentieth century almost everything combined
to bring about its success. Canada was still a staple-producing
country, exporting raw materials in large quantities to more
mature industrial nations; and this type of economy could
hardly have been more indulgently favoured by the fortunate
combination of circumstances that prevailed in the first decade
of the new century. The long decline of prices, which had
dropped about 35 per cent in the last quarter century, was
finally arrested; and though all commodities shared in the increase, the prices of raw materials, and particularly foodstuffs,
rose more rapidly than the prices of manufactured goods. At the
same time, transportation charges in general, and notably ocean
freight rates, were falling; and thus the costs of production,
particularly of agricultural production, were steadily dropping,
while revenue was sharply up.

A second and perhaps even more important factor in the
Laurier prosperity was the decline in interest rates and the
ready availability of capital at extremely low cost. For the first
time in half a century Canada enjoyed a real investment boom;
money, about two-thirds of it coming from Great Britain,
poured in to help finance all the varied undertakings of a new
and rapidly expanding nation. The construction of farm build-

ings, the purchase of farm machinery and livestock, the enlargement of industrial plant and equipment, the provision of urban
facilities – roads, street railways, waterworks, sewage and electric
light systems – and, above everything else, the enormous expansion of railways, all came out of this huge capital expenditure.
Between $4,500 and $5,000 million, about one-half of which was
obtained from borrowing abroad, was invested in capital goods
in the period 1896-1910; and rapid and ubiquitous construction
consumed quantities of materials and created quantities of jobs.
The investment boom was one of the solidest bases of the
prosperity of the period.

A final favourable circumstance of Liberal prosperity was the
sudden resumption of immigration on a grand scale. For over
thirty years, Canada had tried, and tried in vain, to capture the
imagination of the intending immigrants of the Old World. For
thirty years she had utterly failed to shake the fixed assumption
of Britishers and Europeans that the United States represented,
in the purest and most complete form, the freedom and opportunity that America meant to the world. It was not until very
late in the nineteenth century that the glowing myth of the
American west began to fade in European eyes, and then only
because the free land of the United States had finally run out.
The only remaining frontier in North America lay in the Canadian prairies; and the westward-marching column of pioneers at
last swerved north-westward to occupy it. Canada was the 'last
west' – 'the last, best west', as Sifton and his propagandists in
the Department of the Interior insisted; and he appealed successfully not only to Britishers and central and eastern Europeans but also to Canadians, Americans, and Canadians who had
previously emigrated to the United States. Canada still kept its
old resemblance to a busy station on an international railway;
and Canadians, native-born or migrant, were its potential or
real passengers, some of them merely making a night's stop-over
before going on in the morning train. An estimated 1,782,000
people arrived in Canada in the decade 1901-11; and, in the
same period, 1,066,000 left it. The numbers, both coming and
going, were larger than ever before; but now, for the first time
in three decades, there was a net gain of over 700,000 people.

It had happened, as Canadians had always hoped and believed it would; but in a generous, lavish fashion which far exceeded the most romantic flights of the imagination. New men, new capital, and new and more capacious markets had vindicated the hopes and plans of Confederation. Its first two great aims, large-scale immigration and western settlement, were being realized with results that bettered expectations. It had always been assumed, as an article of faith, that immigration and western settlement would ultimately make the nation; and now, to the immense pride and satisfaction of everybody, this was happening, literally before their eyes. The lone and empty north-west, which the restless peoples of the world had avoided for so long, had now become one of the main goals of twentieth-century migration. In 1901, homestead entries in the north-west had numbered only 8,157; ten years later they reached a total of 44,479. By 1911, over 57,500,000 acres of land had been occupied in the three prairie provinces and nearly 23,000,000 acres, or 40 per cent of this total, had been improved. The nation's production of wheat, which had been only 55,572,000 bushels in 1901, rose to 231,237,000 in 1912. Western Canada was well on its way to becoming one of the greatest granaries in the world.

The occupation and rapid development of the west was the most striking and famous feature of the great upswing in the first decade of the twentieth century. But western settlement had been only one of the national policies and its successful realization was only a part, though a most important part, of Canada's spectacular success. In 1879, over twenty years earlier, the nation had embarked upon an ambitious and controversial attempt to build up a native Canadian manufacturing industry by means of protective tariffs. During those twenty years the pace of growth had been deliberate; now it was suddenly and enormously accelerated. During the first decade of the century, about $800 million of new capital was invested in manufacturing plant and equipment; and by 1910 the labour force in manufacturing numbered a little over half a million people. The census value added by manufacturing had more than doubled in ten years; and in 1910 the contribution it made to the gross national product equalled that of agriculture. The value added by agriculture had increased by 80 per cent during the decade; the contribution of manufacturing had jumped by 128 per cent.

The Fathers of Confederation had had two great aims: through the national policies they had sought to build a transcontinental Canadian economy, and to strengthen it by the better balance of economic diversification. During the first decade of the century, both these objects seemed to have been attained. The simple British North America of pre-Confederation days, with its largely rural population and virtually complete dependence upon the export of a few primary staple products, had been substantially modified, and a much more complex industrial system had come into being. In a decade, construction of all kinds had given the nation a magnificent endowment of modern capital equipment. A vastly expanded system of services now catered to the sophisticated needs of a stratified industrial society. And Canada, equipped and ready, was proving to be one of the twentieth century's earliest and most dazzling successes. In ten years, its gross national product had increased by 64 per cent. The Canadian economy was growing faster and the Canadian standard of living was rising more rapidly than were those of its huge and envied rival, the United States.

↠ II ↞

THE POPULATION of Canada, which had been 5,371,315 in 1901, rose to 7,206,643 in 1911. It was an impressive increase of nearly 35 per cent, and its most spectacular feature was, of course, the settlement of the western plains. Of the gain of nearly two million people, well over a million were distributed throughout the three prairie provinces and British Columbia. In a single decade the increase of population in Alberta was over 400 per cent and in Saskatchewan nearly 440 per cent. In comparison with these startling advances, growth in other parts of the country seemed relatively much more modest. Prince Edward Island suffered an absolute loss of population during the period. Nova Scotia and New Brunswick made only slight gains. Quebec and Ontario did considerably better with increases of 22 per cent and 16 per cent, respectively, within the decade. The two central provinces, with over 4,500,000 inhabitants in 1911, still made up the great bulk of the Canadian people. It was true that their combined share of the total population, which had been 75 per cent in 1881 and 70 per cent as late as 1901, had now fallen to about 63 per cent; and obviously the nation's centre of gravity had shifted slightly west. But it had not shifted a great deal. The western movement was accompanied and modified by another significant demographic current, the drift from the countryside to the cities and towns.

The rise of the cities was the social expression of the growth of the new industrial Canada. Industrialism meant the slow decline of the primary economic activity of the farm, and the development of an increasingly complex and sophisticated division of urban labour. In 1871, only about 20 per cent of the Canadian people had lived in towns and cities; by 1911, this proportion had more than doubled. The largest increase in the urban population, an increase of about 17 per cent, came in the first decade of the century, and, as the urban labour force grew in size, its organization became more elaborate, with more numerous gradations, and greater differentials of reward. As might have been expected, the number of Canadians employed in manufacturing, construction, transportation, and communications rose substantially during the ten years from 1901 to 1911; but there were equally significant advances in the growth of more skilled and influential occupations, from which the managers and directors – the patricians of the new industrial society – would most likely emerge. The ranks of the professions increased by about a third, clerical workers nearly doubled their numbers, and bankers and merchants more than doubled theirs.

One important feature of the industrial expansion of the first decade of the century was its concentration in Ontario and Quebec. In Nova Scotia, the iron and steel industry benefited from the railway building and construction boom of the period; but, in the main, Maritime small industries and handicrafts lost ground; and in 1911 Ontario and Quebec together accounted for four-fifths of the total value of manufacturing production in

Canada. It was in the central provinces that the rise of the towns and cities and the development of the new stratified urban society became most conspicuous. Winnipeg with 136,000 inhabitants and Vancouver with 100,400 were two important developments of western expansion; but the urban manifestations of the new industrial order in central Canada were more numerous and far bigger. In the first decade after Confederation, only one town, Montreal, had a population of over 100,000; now Montreal was a city of nearly half a million people, and Toronto, its rapidly growing rival, was approaching 400,000. Here, in these two metropolitan centres, were concentrated the technical and professional skills, the expert knowledge and experience, the economic power and social influence that dominated the country. It was an increasingly affluent society, and at its top stood the chief beneficiaries of the Laurier boom, the Laurier plutocracy, made up of bankers, engineers, corporation lawyers, railway builders, mining promoters, pulp and paper producers, and public utility entrepreneurs.

The great majority of the immigrants who helped to settle the western prairies and swelled the crowds in the cities of central Canada were English-speaking in origin; but for the first time a significant minority of newcomers from central and eastern Europe introduced a novel element into the composition of the Canadian people. In 1871, British and French had together made up about 92 per cent of the population; other European stocks, of which the Germans were the most important, accounted for less than 7 per cent of the whole. These proportions lasted without much change down until nearly the end of the nineteenth century; but in 1911, as a result of the great immigration of the previous decade, a very different state of affairs had come into being. The British and French, it was true, still stood in very much their old relationship with each other. There had been approximately twice as many British as French in 1871; in 1911, the ratio was about the same. Together, British and French still retained their old predominance; but it was not as absolute as it had been. Their combined share of the total population had fallen to about 83 per cent; and the proportion of other European stocks had risen to about 13 per cent.

The largest increases, in the decade 1901-11, were among the Germans, Scandinavians, and Ukrainians; but there were also small minorities of Russians, Austrians, Italians, and Poles, as well as over 40,000 Asiatics, mostly Chinese.

The chance that many of these new groups would resist cultural assimilation and retain a large measure of ethnic separateness, at least for a long time, was very great. History and ideology prevented Canada from becoming a second North American melting pot. The Canadian cultural mosaic, the tessellated ethnic pavement of the first half of the nineteenth century, was firmly based on Canada's experience, both as a colony of Great Britain, and as a separate North American community. Canada had not rejected Europe; unlike the United States, she had clung to Great Britain; and, along with the British political connection, she retained the British cultural differences which, for centuries, had separated English from Scotch and Ulstermen from southern Irish. This inheritance of British cultural diversity was immensely strengthened in British America by the presence and persistent separateness of the French. A tradition of cultural pluralism was well established in British America during the middle decades of the nineteenth century; and, although its strength had declined in English Canada since Confederation, the French fact still kept it alive. In Canada, the new immigrants found a country that was prepared historically to tolerate their various ethnic identities. The privileges granted to confessional schools were a great advantage. Laurier's settlement of the Manitoba school question which permitted bilingual instruction, in French or another language as well as in English, helped to preserve the speech of the homeland; and compact ethnic communities discovered in the very isolation of the immense prairies a strong protection for their distinctive ways of life.

In Canada, the first dozen years of the new century were marked by restless human mobility and social confusion, as well as by rapid economic expansion and great prosperity. Immigrants, in huge and increasing numbers, were arriving in Canada; others were departing for the United States. Canadians themselves were emigrating to the republic; other Canadians, expatriates in the United States, were returning to Canada; and still other Canadians, from rural areas throughout the country, were crowding into the swiftly rising towns and cities of Ontario and Quebec. It was an agitated but energetic and hopeful period, and out of its strenuous but creative turmoil a new and very different Canada was coming into being.

⟫ III ⟪

OVER THIS WHOLE vast transformation, Laurier presided with the confident aplomb of a conjurer pulling an endless succession of rabbits out of a magical hat. It was only too natural for him to assume that he had done it all himself with a few magnificent passes of his enchanter's wand. Everything now was so delightfully easy, where before it had been so painfully difficult. For years that seemed endless in retrospect, Canadian government had been a dreary round of grinding poverty, cheese-paring economies, and frightening indebtedness; now it had suddenly changed into a gay parade of continuous affluence, careless extravagance, and unlimited credit. Capital was readily available, in large quantities, and at ridiculously low rates of interest; and it no longer seemed risky to borrow when a few years of Canada's buoyant revenues would pay off the nation's entire net debt. Goods were pouring into the country, and the customs tariff, which was the main source of federal moneys, was working wonders such as had never been seen before. It was true, of course, that expenditures were also rising steeply; in 1911 they were more than three times what they had been in 1896. But, despite the fact that a large part of the heavy capital expenditures for national development were charged to current account, the deficits were not large; and frequently there were comforting surpluses.

In these easy, prosperous circumstances Laurier and his colleagues naturally viewed the future with boundless optimism and unqualified confidence. The great aims of Confederation were on the point of achievement. The industrialization of central Canada was a vital reality; the settlement of the west had proceeded so far that the political maturity of the North-West Territories would soon have to be recognized by the grant of provincial status. All that really remained to do was to complete the projected transcontinental railways, to triple the means of all-Canadian transport, and thus to give the east-west axis an unbreakable solidity. At Confederation, the federal government had assumed the task of promoting national expansion and development. Often in the past, it had played its part under great difficulties and embarrassments; then it had been necessary to scrimp and save, to delay and to be cautious. But now, when the way was so easy, and final success so near, there must be no holding back – no silly inhibitions, no self-defeating parsimony, no over-scrupulous concern with petty details. The huge expenditures and contingent liabilities of the present would be merely a trifle to the populous and prosperous Canada of tomorrow. And, in the meantime, of course, they would make the political fortunes of the Liberal Party.

Nowhere was this prevailing mood shown more exuberantly than in Laurier's railway policy. A. G. Blair, his first Minister of Railways and Canals, had criticized and opposed this policy in its early stages; but Blair was not the first, or the last, of Laurier's colleagues to realize that they were expected to take the Prime Minister's orders obediently and that, if they showed signs of unseemly independence, they would be kept in the dark until he had finished making their decisions for them. Blair objected to accepting political responsibility for a *fait accompli* of which he disapproved, and he resigned. His successor, H. R. Emmerson, another New Brunswicker, understood more clearly than Blair had done that his success in office depended largely upon his submission to a shrewd and powerful leader, who always wanted his own way and was prepared to use almost any means to get it. In a few years, to be sure, Emmerson also was obliged to resign; but his resignation was the result of a scandal in his private life, and not the consequence of any attempted insubordination to the Prime Minister. The Prime Minister's control of railway policy was absolute; and his great new railway enterprises moved steadily forward, as lavish in execution as they had been grandiose in conception. It was true, of course, and the Laurier government took a great deal of credit for the fact, that direct subsidies of land and money were not given to the Canadian Northern and the Grand Trunk Pacific as they had been to the Canadian Pacific; but, in ample compensation, Laurier discovered, and exploited to the full, the magical device of the government guarantee, by which a deserving railway, such as the Grand Trunk or the Canadian Northern, could dispose of quantities of its bonds to the investing public on the strength of a federal guarantee of principal and interest. Here the Laurier government displayed a trusting generosity, and it began to pile up contingent liabilities for the benefit of both railways.

But this was not all by any means. The bounty available for railways was far from exhausted. There remained the unlimited requirements of the eastern or government division of the new system, the National Transcontinental, winding its lonely way through the unknown hinterland of northern Quebec and Ontario. The National Transcontinental was the realized ideal of every practical politician, a completely political railway. It had been planned, section after inconsequential section, in response to political pressures and with an eye to political advantages; and it was built with undeviating consistency according to the same principles. The supervision of its construction was ostensibly entrusted by Laurier to a special National Transcontinental Railway Commission, composed of commissioners who knew nothing about railways, and chaired by an ousted Liberal premier of Quebec, Simon Napoléon Parent, who regarded his appointment as a well-merited opportunity of serving the Liberal Party and rewarding its political friends. Under Laurier's ultimate authority and control, Parent and Emmerson presided over a treasury of political patronage more copious than any group of Canadian politicians had ever had at their disposal before.

Before the gluttonous eyes of railway promoters, engineers, and contractors there was now spread a luscious barbecue beside which the meagre opportunities of the Canadian Pacific Railway syndicate must have looked like the lenten supper of a particularly ascetic and frugal order of monks. The huge expenditures mounted; the charges of fraud, and waste, and inefficiency grew. But Laurier remained unperturbed and unabashed. When critics brought accusations of corruption, he referred their complaints to Parent or Emmerson, with the comfortable knowledge that nothing would be done about them. When other critics grew alarmed at the growing expense, he explained that, since the National Transcontinental on completion was to be leased to the Grand Trunk Pacific, its total cost to the nation would be no more than a few years' interest on the required capital. Who could be so unpatriotic as to insinuate that the actual cost of construction would so vastly exceed the estimate that the Grand Trunk would in the end repudiate the agreement? Who could be so pessimistic as to suggest that the government guarantee, given so prodigally to the Grand Trunk Pacific and Canadian Northern railway bonds, would eventually have to be honoured?

Only the future would disclose the truth of these rumours and suspicions; but, in the meantime, in another part of his programme of national expansion, Laurier found himself confronted by open and determined resistance. Suddenly, in one of the chief government measures of the session of 1905, the bills establishing the two new prairie provinces, his authority as Prime Minister was challenged. It was not, of course, that there was any serious dispute over the main purpose of the Autonomy Bills, as they were called. Everybody agreed that the North-West Territories had made good their claim to the institutions of political maturity; and between them the federal cabinet and the territorial government quickly settled most of the details of the transition from territorial to provincial status. There were to be two new provinces, Saskatchewan and Alberta; each was to have its own provincial legislature, a specified representation in the federal Senate and House of Commons, and generous financial terms, which foreshadowed the general revision of the subsidy system two years later. The only question that remained to be decided was, in fact, the question of education.

Laurier was well aware of the strong, instinctive French-Canadian belief in sectarian or confessional schools; and he knew that the educational clauses in the Autonomy Bills offered the last chance of providing constitutional safeguards for this kind of education in Alberta and Saskatchewan. He also realized that Clifford Sifton, his Minister of the Interior, the great defender of Manitoba's new educational system in the 1890s, would be strongly opposed to confessional schools; and he had no reason whatever to be ignorant of the dislike which the people of the North-West Territories had repeatedly shown for sectarian education. By two ordinances of the Territorial Legislature, passed in 1891 and 1902, they had virtually swept away the educational clauses of the North-West Territories Act of 1875 and in their place had established a provincial system of public schools, under the control of a department of government, with a common programme of studies, a common inspection of schools, and common qualifications for teachers – a system which, while it permitted minority Roman Catholic schools, reduced their privileges to a minimum.

The obstacles to a return to the old order might have seemed formidable, even insurmountable. But Laurier, with the advice and encouragement of his Roman Catholic colleagues and friends – Charles Fitzpatrick, the Minister of Justice, Senator Sir Richard Scott, and Henri Bourassa – decided, in complete disregard of the known wishes of the inhabitants of the Territories, to restore the educational clauses of 1875 in their original, unaltered form. The two cabinet ministers most likely to oppose this revolutionary reversal, W. S. Fielding and Clifford Sifton, were both fortunately out of the country at the time. During their absence, the Autonomy Bills, including the controversial clauses, would be pushed through Parliament; and on the return of the Ministers to Ottawa, they could be confronted with one of Laurier's political specialties, the accomplished fact.

The essence of the plot was its simplicity and boldness. It might have succeeded with the new, subservient kind of colleague that Laurier now preferred to have about him. But men of any independence of mind and strength of character were not likely to give in to such a shabby and impudent stratagem. Friends and sympathizers warned Sifton and Fielding of what was going on in Ottawa in their absence, and they quickly responded. Fielding let it be known that he was opposed to the

educational clauses. Sifton hurried back from the United States
and, after a single interview with the Prime Minister, resigned
his portfolio as Minister of the Interior. This decisive action
helped to rouse such a storm of opposition that Laurier found it
prudent to yield; and the original educational clauses of the
Autonomy Bills were drastically revised. The authority of the
legislatures of Alberta and Saskatchewan to deal with education
was not to be unlimited. But the educational rights and privileges guaranteed to the Roman Catholic minority by the revised
Autonomy Bills were not those set out in the federal statute of
1875, but those only which had survived the territorial legislation of 1892 and 1901.

≫≫ IV ≪≪

IN THE AUTUMN of 1908 another general election returned
the Laurier government for the fourth time, though on this
occasion with a majority reduced by nearly twenty. Laurier had
now been Prime Minister for twelve years, and those twelve
years had shown him to be an extremely successful, but not a
particularly inventive or innovating, nation builder. He had not
made any serious changes in the national design of his Conservative predecessors, and prosperity had apparently vindicated it.
He had coped, one by one, in a piecemeal, extempore, empirical
fashion, with the pressures that came from outside; but he had
never attempted to devise a plan which would prepare Canada
for her place in the dangerous external world, in the same way
as the domestic national policies had enabled her to survive and
prosper as a separate nation in North America. Years earlier,
Chamberlain's proposals for imperial collaboration had been
rejected in a series of bland and unilluminating negatives. But
the promises – and the threats – which had seemed to fore-
shadow an independent Canadian initiative in defence and
foreign policy had never been followed up or made good. A
Department of External Affairs was indeed established five years
after Laurier had argued that Canada ought to conduct its own
diplomacy; but the new office was simply a distributing centre

for correspondence from the United Kingdom; and no new Canadian missions were established abroad. Obviously the Laurier government had no intention of undertaking a separate Canadian foreign policy; and it showed not the slightest sign of an awakening sense of independent responsibility for Canadian defence. Laurier informed Lord Dundonald, the General Officer Commanding the Canadian Militia, that he must not take the militia seriously, since Canada was protected by the Monroe Doctrine. He failed to give the same instruction to a Canadian admiral for the sufficient reason that there was no Canadian navy. The promise, made solemnly more than six years before in the Colonial Conference of 1902, that Canada would assume its just share of the burden of defence, had never been honoured.

This serene mood of detachment and inaction was suddenly ended in the spring of 1909 by the German naval scare. Everybody who read the newspapers knew that imperial Germany was rapidly building warships, including a number of the new super-type of battleship called 'dreadnought', after the first of its class in England. But, until the spring of 1909, very few people seriously suspected that this new German navy was ever likely to threaten British naval supremacy, admittedly the first defence of the Empire. On the 16th of March, 1909, British subjects all over the world were disagreeably enlightened when Reginald McKenna, the First Lord of the Admiralty, frankly admitted in Parliament that British supremacy on the high seas was endangered, and called for a greatly increased programme of naval construction. Extreme concern, amounting almost to panic, swept over England; and this state of excitement and anxiety was quickly communicated to Canada.

One member of the Canadian House of Commons, George E. Foster, a former minister of finance and a prominent member of the Opposition, had not needed McKenna's dramatic warning to awaken his apprehensions. Over a month before the naval scare began in Great Britain, he had given notice of motion concerning Canadian naval defence. It was a modest, uncontroversial resolution that he submitted, a resolution that simply laid down the general principle that Canada was now strong enough to assume her proper share of the burden of the defence of 'her exposed coastline and great seaports'. If it had been debated in February, the resolution might have had little effect, and Laurier would have been able once again to dodge the whole issue of a Canadian naval service just as he had been successfully dodging it ever since the Colonial Conference of 1902. In fact, however, Foster's motion did not come up until nearly a fortnight after McKenna's speech in London and its significance was transformed out of all recognition by the naval scare.

In the end, it became the basis of a government resolution, proposed by Laurier and amended by Robert Borden, the Leader of the Opposition, which passed the House unanimously. This apparent unanimity has served to conceal the important differences of opinion brought out during the debate and has misled historians into believing that at this stage Laurier and Borden were in complete agreement about naval defence policy. Borden did indeed accept Laurier's contention that Canadian national autonomy and Canadian national dignity required a Canadian naval service. But he saw Canadian defence within the context of imperial defence; and for him the Canadian navy was essentially a fleet unit within the world-wide organization of the imperial navy. Moreover, he was far more deeply impressed than Laurier by the imminence of danger; and, although he agreed that 'regular and periodical' contributions of money or ships to the imperial navy were not an entirely satisfactory way of providing for Canadian defence, he also insisted that in certain circumstances an emergency contribution might become absolutely essential. The day might come, he argued prophetically, 'when the only thing we could do in the absence of preparation in this country would be to make some kind of contribution'.

In the summer of 1909, the two Liberal ministers concerned, L. P. Brodeur, Minister of Marine and Fisheries, and Sir Frederick Borden, Minister of Militia, went to England for a conference on defence. The British officials suggested a fleet unit based on Canada's west coast which would be an integral part of the imperial navy in Pacific waters. Brodeur and Borden would have none of this. They wanted a 'two-ocean' navy, and protection for both Canadian coasts rather than a place in a world-wide system of naval defence. They came back to Canada with plans for a force of five cruisers and six destroyers; and next year, in the session of 1910, the Prime Minister presented this scheme to Parliament in the Naval Service Bill. The purpose and functions of the proposed force were not very clearly defined. In an emergency, and at the discretion of the Canadian government, it could be put at the disposal of the British navy; but such action would require confirmation by the Canadian Parliament, which must be called within fifteen days, if it was not already in session. Laurier, in short, declined to say definitely what Canada would do in the case of a European war in which Great Britain was involved. He admitted that legally Canada was at war when Great Britain was at war; but he insisted that this did not necessarily mean participation in actual hostilities. He conceded the liability; but he was anxious to narrow its scope as much as possible.

Laurier's Naval Service Act did not end the naval controversy. Defence, naval and military, was an integral and vital part of the far more general question of Canada's future position in the British Empire; and, over this fundamental issue, Canadians were still uncertain and deeply divided. Laurier had attempted to occupy middle ground between two passionately opposed and apparently irreconcilable schools of thought. On the one hand were those Canadians who believed that Canada now had interests and responsibilities in the external world and could play her new international role most effectively through the British Empire. On the other hand were those very different Canadians who felt secure in the peaceful isolation of North America, hoped to escape entanglement in the incorrigible rivalries of Europe, and looked with suspicion and distrust on all schemes for armed co-operation inside the British Empire. These 'nationalists', as they liked to call themselves, insisted that Canada had no need of a navy for her own protection and would simply be giving assistance to British imperialistic designs if she established a Canadian naval service. The imperialists, on their part, either called loudly for an outright, unconditional contribution to the Royal Navy, or argued in favour of a fundamental reorganization of the structure of the Empire which would divide power and responsibility in defence and foreign policy among Great Britain and the Dominions. The members of the first Round Table group, which was formed in Toronto in 1908-9, began to discuss, clarify, and expound the new ideas of imperial collaboration. At the same time distrust of British imperialism and fear of British defence policies found a fluent and forceful spokesman in Henri Bourassa, who in 1910 started publication of the new French-language newspaper, *Le Devoir*.

Bourassa's wide political and social interests, combined with his clerical sympathies and ultramontane views, had already won him a considerable following in Quebec; but he now extended and deepened his influence in French Canada by the advocacy of a peculiarly narrow and isolationist nationalism. Though at some points he seemed to agree with such typical English-Canadian nationalists as J. S. Ewart, the Ottawa lawyer and pamphleteer, and J. W. Dafoe, the editor of the *Winnipeg Free Press*, he in fact differed from them profoundly. He never shared Dafoe's belief that Canada must be prepared to move into the larger sphere of external affairs; he utterly rejected Ewart's contention that Canada was a virtually independent nation which should now take the last step towards separate sovereignty under the British Crown. Independence for Canada was the last thing Bourassa really wanted. His defiant nationalist gestures barely concealed a deep feeling of insecurity and an instinctive sense of dependence. He did not trust the English-Canadian majority in Canada, and he feared the external pressure of an imperialistic United States. At bottom, he still wanted others to supply protection to French Canada; and, as long as Canada formally remained a part of the British Empire, he retained the colonial assumption that Great Britain should supply protection free of charge. In Quebec, these views were extraordinarily pervasive, and, apart from the orthodox Liberals, who remained loyal to Lauricr's Naval Service Act, they won the support of most French Canadians, including the Quebec Conservatives, led by F. D. Monk.

Borden's position was acutely difficult. He was pulled this way and that by two diametrically opposed divisions of his party.

On the one hand were the colonially minded Conservatives of Ontario, who jeered at Laurier's 'tin-pot' navy and clamoured for an immediate contribution to the British fleet. On the other were the equally colonially minded Quebec Conservatives, who hated the thought of expenditure for naval armaments, feared any change in the existing imperial relationship, and insisted that before Canada accepted any new and strange obligations the consent of the Canadian people through a plebiscite must be obtained. Faced by these contradictory demands, Borden tried to devise a naval policy which would keep his party united, reconcile its two extreme, divergent wings, and at the same time provide for the present and future needs of the defence of Canada as a nation within the British Empire. All the main elements in his plan had been present, in a rudimentary form, in the speech he had delivered a year earlier, on the Foster resolution; but they were now developed and combined in an elaborate design in two parts, an emergency policy to meet the urgent necessities of the moment and a permanent policy to satisfy the long-term requirements of the future.

Borden remained true to the major decision taken in 1909. He was at one with Laurier in believing that Canada must ultimately have its own navy, a navy under Canadian control, and, as far as possible, built and manned by Canadians. He was equally convinced that this navy would be essentially a fleet unit of the Royal Navy, and automatically associated with it if a war broke out in which the Empire was involved. Such an important contribution to imperial defence, he believed, could be requited only by the grant of a share in the determination of imperial foreign policy. A change of this drastic nature in the organization of the Empire would have to be worked out in detail by Great Britain and Canada; and, when the arrangement was complete, it should be submitted, he argued, to the Canadian people for ratification. This was his permanent policy, his long-range solution of the problem of naval defence; but obviously the Anglo-Canadian agreement would take some time to arrange, and the Canadian fleet unit a much longer time to build. The permanent policy, the policy of the future, could not possibly meet the urgent needs of the terrifying present. A crisis in

Europe was imminent, he now felt certain; and, at this dangerously late stage, the only effective contribution Canada could
make to naval defence was an emergency gift of capital ships to
the Royal Navy.

Borden believed that the emergency part of his programme
would amply satisfy the Ontario Conservatives. His permanent
policy, and particularly the provision which required its approval by the Canadian people, would, he hoped, go far to meet
the demands of the Conservatives from French Canada. These
hopeful expectations were only partly fulfilled. Monk declined
to join in Borden's amendment to the government naval
resolutions and submitted a separate resolution expressing the
distinctive French-Canadian point of view. Yet Borden did not
abandon his scheme. He believed that Canada must take her
place in world affairs and that she could do so effectively only
through the British Empire, whose authority and responsibility
must now be shared on a co-operative basis. He had brought the
Britannic design of John A. Macdonald and G. M. Grant close to
practical realization.

⟶≫ V ⟪⟪⟵

THE ATTACK on the Naval Service Bill, which had been
carried forward with determination on two quite different
fronts, was a serious threat to Liberal power; but that troubled
year 1910 was to bring other ominous signs of Laurier's declining prestige and increasing vulnerability. In the summer, after
the passage of the Naval Act, he went west to see the land which
he could almost claim had sprung into being under the magic
passes of his sorcerer's wand. The west had experienced a period
of rapid and phenomenal growth which had been crowned by
the grant of provincial autonomy; and the new prairie provinces, in their swift passage towards economic and political
maturity, had soon begun to acquire their own distinctive outlook on national affairs. Already they had come to feel restive
within the established Canadian parties and critical of traditional Canadian national policies. For years now, western grain-

growers had been founding co-operative associations to defend and promote their special interests; and Laurier's western tour, which had been conceived as something approaching a triumphal progress, was periodically interrupted by organized deputations of determined farmers who came to present petitions, expound grievances, and demand reforms. A drastic reduction of the tariff, a sharp increase in the British preference, reciprocity with the United States, and government acquisition of terminal elevators were some of the large items on their formidable list of demands.

By the time autumn came, Laurier had become a very sober Prime Minister. In November 1910, a Bourassa 'nationalist' candidate defeated a Laurier Liberal in an important by-election in Drummond-Arthabaska; and, in December, a large gathering of western grain-growers, reinforced by a considerable body of Ontario farmers, descended upon Ottawa and repeated, with emphasis, their demands of the previous summer. The Liberal government badly needed a new and striking policy which would distract public attention from old controversies and regain popular support in doubtful areas. And, in the winter of 1910-11, Laurier suddenly began to hope that he had found it. In 1907 the Canadian Parliament had established a new intermediate tariff, midway between the preferential and maximum rates, and this was granted to France for reciprocal concessions. The French treaty provoked American charges of commercial discrimination and threatened American tariff reprisals, which William Howard Taft, the new President of the United States, was just as anxious as Laurier to avoid. The two governments met and arranged a face-saving compromise; and these agreeable talks formed the prelude to more ambitious negotiations. Taft suggested a general trade treaty. Laurier and Fielding accepted the idea eagerly. By January 1911, they had reached a broad trade agreement which removed the duties on a wide range of natural products and lowered them on a number of manufactured and semi-finished products as well.

This agreement, the so-called 'Reciprocity Treaty' of 1911 – which, in fact, was to come into operation by concurrent legislation of the two countries – was Laurier's undoing. His followers from the manufacturing regions of Ontario warned him repeatedly that the agreement was highly dangerous politically; but he went confidently ahead, apparently believing that, as in the past, his possible losses in Ontario would be more than made good by gains in the west and by the steady support of Quebec and the Atlantic provinces. A general election was due in the not very distant future and he might have gone to the country immediately; but he was sure he had a certain winner and that he risked nothing in a parliamentary battle. The resulting debate dragged on through the winter and into spring; and by degrees the Liberals lost the initiative and their own confidence. Taft had to call a special session of Congress in order to get the agreement accepted in the United States; and the Canadian Parliament adjourned so that Laurier could go to England to attend the coronation of George V. It was not until the middle of the summer that Laurier realized that he must dissolve Parliament and face an election. By that time, the Opposition had had a solid six months in which to marshal its forces.

The Reciprocity Agreement of 1911 and the proposal of Unrestricted Reciprocity in 1891 both implied an untried and ambiguous economic relationship with the United States; and both were defeated for that reason. Like Macdonald, Borden claimed that he was defending Canadian national autonomy against the perils of American continentalism; like Macdonald, he industriously waved the old flag and beat loudly on the patriotic drum. He used Macdonald's methods, but with considerably greater effect. The Reciprocity Agreement of 1911 was a much more moderate proposal, a far less dangerous modification of the Canadian national policy than Unrestricted Reciprocity had been twenty years before; but Borden's victory was nevertheless much more conclusive than Macdonald's. His task, which outwardly might have seemed a good deal more onerous, was in fact easier, and chiefly as a result of the great changes that the two intervening decades had brought. Macdonald had to contend with the pessimism and defeatism which had been ground into the Canadian people by over ten years of depression. Borden could take advantage of the enthusiasm and national self-confidence that had been inspired by a decade of prosperity. In 1891, the national policy had been a suspected failure; in 1911 it was an acknowledged success.

In 1911, Laurier was defeated by the Laurier boom. Laurier prosperity had hastened the industrialization of central Canada, and the industrialization of central Canada meant the ruin of the Reciprocity Agreement. In the rapidly growing towns and cities of Ontario and Quebec, a new industrial society, its numbers constantly swollen by migrants from the countryside, was busy with an intricate variety of occupations, most of which were ultimately dependent upon the success of the Canadian national policies. It was in the minds of these people that the collective image of Canada as a separate, competitive economy in North America had taken on the greatest clarity and appeal. They were numerous and politically powerful, and they were superbly led by the new Liberal plutocracy, the chief beneficiaries of Laurier policies and Laurier prosperity, a class far better organized and influential than it had ever been in Macdonald's day. In three general elections, most prominent members of the plutocracy had voted Liberal as instinctively as they breathed and as successfully as they made money; but now, led by the notorious 'Eighteen Liberals' of Toronto – a group including bankers, corporation lawyers, manufacturers, and merchandisers – they broke their Liberal allegiance. In their eyes, Laurier had betrayed them. They had come to identify the national policies with Liberalism; and to them Laurier appeared as an apostate who had abandoned his own established religion. They could not understand why he had revived a half-forgotten heresy which the Liberals themselves had repudiated nearly twenty years before and which had lain in deserved oblivion ever since. It was Laurier who had a new doctrine to preach to the Canadians. It was Laurier who was driven to propaganda.

It was unsuccessful propaganda. In the Atlantic provinces and the west, the Liberals did little better than break even with the Conservatives. In Quebec, Monk and the other Conservative candidates followed the line they had already laid down in Parliament, and, with the help of the Nationalists, increased their holdings in the province to twenty-seven seats. In Ontario, industrialism had had perhaps its strongest and most pervasive effects; and there the provincial Conservatives, led by the Premier, James P. Whitney, had succeeded, through such popular measures as the establishment of the Ontario Hydro Electric Power Commission, in gaining a reputation as the progressive champions of the people's needs and interests in a modern industrial society. The Conservatives had cultivated the new Ontario of the twentieth century; the Liberals had neglected and disregarded it. But Ontario was in no mood to be disregarded and now it took its revenge. It gave seventy-two seats to Borden and only thirteen to Laurier.

CHAPTER SEVEN

The Great Divide

IN OCTOBER 1911, when he formed his government, Robert Laird Borden had been fifteen years in politics and leader of the Conservative Party for ten. His square, rugged countenance, with its heavy eyebrows, drooping, rather melancholy moustache, and hair parted in the middle with a little quiff on either side, was handsome in a sober, almost solemn fashion; and his deep, lugubrious voice and measured delivery matched the gravity of his appearance. At fifty-seven, two years older than Laurier had been when he gained power in 1896, Borden had reached the further side of middle age and had had lots of time to acquire political experience. Yet, in comparison with that dextrous and highly sophisticated political veteran, Laurier, he often seemed to behave with something of the clumsy earnestness of a novice. In 1901, he had accepted the leadership of the party with reluctance; and the next ten years had failed to prove him a particularly successful politician. His complex naval policy, designed to reconcile the open disagreements among his followers, had proved to be only a very qualified success; and the party that he led into the general election of 1911 seemed to be composed of two separate divisions, fighting two entirely unrelated engagements. Discontented Conservatives had worked, with little or no concealment, to depose him; and the conspiracies against his leadership lasted down to the early spring of 1911, when the campaign against the Reciprocity Agreement was already well under way.

Borden had survived these plots and had won the election of 1911; but he was soon to find that success, no more than failure, could ensure loyalty. Obviously, the most serious threat to party unity lay in his elaborate naval defence scheme; but, obviously also, and by his own repeated assurance, the first emergency phase of his naval policy was an urgent task which must be carried out at once. In domestic affairs, there was nothing of great national importance that he had promised or wished to undertake; the national policies, he and his ministers assumed, would simply continue on their triumphant way. The defeat of the Reciprocity Agreement had settled the question of the tariff; the annually increasing influx of immigrants would soon complete the settlement of the west. Laurier's pet project, the National Transcontinental, was, to be sure, a monstrous perversion of the Conservative policy of all-Canadian transport; and the rumours of fraud and inefficiency in its construction seemed so authentic that early in 1912 Borden sacked S. N. Parent and appointed a Royal Commission of investigation. Otherwise, the ambitious programme of railway expansion proceeded in its grandiose way, encouraged by a boom that showed no sign of slackening.

At home everything seemed well; but abroad there was still no real ray of light in a dark and threatening prospect. As a senior nation of the Empire, second only to Great Britain herself, Canada, in Borden's view, was inescapably involved in the outcome of the approaching international crisis. Her best defence, both of her own particular interests and of the world order in which she believed, lay in the unified imperial association; but, in order that she might play to the full the mature part to which she was now entitled, the centralized Empire of the past must become the co-operative British Commonwealth of the future. The guiding principle of this great imperial reorganization, he believed, was that Dominion participation in imperial defence must be matched by a Dominion share in the determination of imperial foreign policy. His task was to persuade both the British government and the Canadian people, including particularly his own party, that this principle must be accepted. He would have to convince the British that power must be shared. He would have to satisfy the Canadians that responsibilities and burdens must be borne.

In the early summer of 1912, when Borden sailed for England on the first phase of his mission, he had a contribution of capital ships to offer, and a voice in foreign policy to ask in return. He found the British Prime Minister, H. H. Asquith, and the First Lord of the Admiralty, Winston Churchill, ready and eager to accept a free gift of dreadnoughts for the Royal Navy, but somewhat unprepared for a change in the conduct of policy, and unhelpful about ways and means of carrying it out. Only the year before, at the Colonial Conference of 1911, Asquith had declared firmly that British responsibility in foreign affairs could not be shared. The prospect of a bonus of two or three battleships made a judicious qualification of this blunt language necessary; and he now permitted himself the cautious admission that Great Britain ought to respond, as far as possible, to the reasonable Canadian request for a voice in the determination of policy. Where this 'voice' was to be heard, and what influence it might expect to carry, were questions which received no very precise answers. The only practical suggestion which the British ministers could think of to satisfy Canada's 'reasonable request' was the proposal that a Canadian representative should regularly attend meetings of the Committee of Imperial Defence. Borden replied that this was all very well, but that it did not go nearly far enough. The Committee of Imperial Defence was a purely advisory body. What he wanted was a voice in policy decisions.

Borden came back to Canada determined, at all events, to fill in his side of the modern imperial equation; and in October the government decided as an emergency measure to make a contribution of three capital ships to the Royal Navy. At once Borden began to run into obstacles. F. D. Monk, the senior French-Canadian minister in the cabinet, had declined, despite Borden's entreaties, to accompany him to England in the summer. He had obviously wished to have nothing whatever to do with combined operations in imperial defence; and now he resigned his portfolio on the ground that the proposed offer of dreadnoughts had not been submitted to the Canadian people for approval. The French-speaking section of the Conservative cabinet was growing weaker, and less truly representative of opinion in French Canada; but Borden, conscious of his strength in Parliament and the country, pushed ahead, and in December 1912, his Naval Aid Bill was introduced in the House of Commons. With the help of the new closure rules, largely devised by an extremely promising Conservative back-bencher, Arthur Meighen, the Bill was forced through the Commons, despite a pertinacious Liberal filibuster. It was even hoped that it might pass the Upper House, for, though fifteen years of Laurier rule had built up a formidable Liberal majority in the Senate, a number of English-speaking Liberal senators believed strongly in Canadian aid to imperial defence. A compromise arrangement might have been possible; but at this point Laurier characteristically intervened. He produced what was to become the favourite weapon of this last phase of his career – the delicate insinuation, the subtle hint, of resignation. The mere thought of this dreadful possibility drove his senatorial followers back to their rigid party loyalty; and, at the end of May 1913, the Naval Aid Bill was defeated.

This was a hard, but not entirely unexpected, check. It was quickly followed by another serious reversal – the sudden collapse of the boom – which jarred Borden and his ministers with the shock of an unpleasant surprise. For a dozen years Canadian prosperity had depended upon a vast inrush of new capital, a sustained orgy of construction of all kinds, and a profitable exploitation of Canada's wheatlands and other natural resources. Now this genial combination of favourable circumstances suddenly disappeared. The price of money rose sharply; the broad stream of investment began to dwindle into a thin trickle; and the prices of all Canada's major export specialties – wheat, lumber, newsprint, and base metals – were steadily dropping. The continuous hum of construction – the characteristic sound of the previous decade – rapidly subsided. For ten feverish years it had seemed as if there never could be enough houses, public buildings, factories, municipal improvements, public utilities, harbours, and canals; and then, all of a sudden, there were too many. They had all helped to sustain the boom; but, without any doubt, the greatest contribution to the national prosperity had been made by those mammoth undertakings, the new railways; and it was now painfully clear that the new railways were in trouble.

Sir William Mackenzie and Sir Donald Mann – they had been knighted in 1911 by a grateful and admiring Liberal government – were the first to feel the pressure of the tight money market. In London, where so many millions of Canadian Northern bonds had been successfully negotiated in the past, there was heard a sinister whisper that 'Canadians' had been oversold. Mackenzie and Mann turned to Brussels, Amsterdam, and Geneva; they switched to New York; and finally, in desperation, they came back to Ottawa, where the federal government, now under Borden, agreed to give them aid, but only in return for the transfer of large blocks of the Canadian Northern common stock which so far they had managed to keep in their own hands. In the session of 1914, the government of Canada became more than ever directly and deeply involved in the fortunes of Mackenzie's and Mann's giant enterprises; and, at the same time, it was unpleasantly reminded of its ultimate responsibility in the fate of the eastern, government-built division of the National Transcontinental Railway. In midwinter of 1914, George Lynch-Staunton and F. P. Gutelius, appointed two years before to investigate all aspects of the construction of the eastern division, issued a report that was a shocking recital of fraud, duplicity, collusion, incompetence, and mismanagement. Would the Grand Trunk, which, after all, was in business to make money not waste it, honour its engagement to lease a railway that had been built at such a vastly inflated cost? Or would the National Transcontinental, eastern division, 'the railway designed to carry elections rather than passengers', be returned to the care of its legitimate parents, the politicians?

It was summer, 1914, and time had run out. Borden was faced with two failures, his own and his predecessor's. War was about to break, but effective imperial co-operation in defence and foreign policy was as far away as ever. The boom was over, and Laurier's grandiose railway-building projects threatened to collapse in ruins about him.

⫸ II ⫷

UP TO THE VERY LAST moment almost nobody believed that war would really come. Its outbreak was greeted with stunned incredulity; but, once the incredible had happened, there was no doubt or uncertainty about the course Canada ought to take. The Canadian government had had no part whatever in the British diplomacy of the previous decade or in the last-minute British efforts to avert the catastrophe. Borden and his ministers were ignorant of the nature and extent of the British commitments in Europe; but, now that a life-and-death struggle was at hand, they assumed, almost as a matter of course, that those commitments must be honoured by the whole Empire-Commonwealth, including Canada. In 1899, at the opening of the South African War, there had been hesitation, reluctance, indecision; now Canada's mind was made up at once. She was not merely legally at war; she was morally at war as well; and the great majority of Canadians felt an urgent need of participation in the approaching struggle and a deep sense of responsibility in its outcome. On the 2nd of August, Borden offered to send an expeditionary force overseas, if it was needed, and on the 6th the cabinet ordered the mobilization of the first Canadian contingent. Parliament, meeting hurriedly in emergency session on the 18th of August, repeated and confirmed these engagements. 'As to our duty,' Borden said, 'all are agreed, we stand shoulder to shoulder with Britain and the other British Dominions in this quarrel.' 'When the call comes our answer goes at once,' Laurier declared eloquently, 'and it goes in the classical language of the British answer to the call of duty: "Ready, aye, ready!" '

The real truth was, of course, that Canada was not 'ready' at all. The Canadian naval service did not exist; no capital ships had been contributed to the Royal Navy. There was, on paper, a small permanent military force of a little over three thousand men, and a non-permanent active militia of nearly seventy-five thousand. The mobilization of the First Canadian Division was an extraordinary feat of improvisation, enthusiasm, and energy; and on the 3rd of October, the thirty-three thousand men of the

First Division, the largest force that had yet crossed the Atlantic, sailed from Gaspé harbour. In 1915, when the Second Division reached Europe, the Canadian Expeditionary Force was organized as a corps; and, during the next year, its strength was increased by two additional divisions. At the outbreak of the war, many informed observers would probably have assumed that a force of 50,000 men was the utmost that Canada could, or would, contribute to a war in Europe. But on the last day of December 1915, in a special New Year's message to the Canadian people, Borden announced that the Canadian government had as its object an army of 500,000 men. By this he seems to have meant, not simply the total of enlistments, but the actual strength at which the Canadian Expeditionary Force was to be maintained. It was a formidable promise, made apparently without any serious study of what was involved in such a huge commitment of manpower, and with only some perfunctory consultation with a few cabinet ministers. Borden believed that he expressed the national conviction that Canada was in the war as a principal and must fight with everything she had. Privately some of his colleagues and associates doubted the wisdom of his enormous undertaking; but publicly it was greeted with a general clamour of approval.

The Canadian Expeditionary Force was the greatest collective enterprise that Canada had ever attempted. The War of 1914-18 was the greatest experience that the Canadian people had ever known, or would ever know. The first decade of the century had brought tremendous changes to Canada; but a single decade, even a decade of tumultuous expansion, could not entirely alter the settled habits of generations of slow growth. It was the war that completed the great transformation and demonstrated its reality for all to see; and, for both those Canadians who went away to fight, and those who stayed at home to work and wait, those four crowded years meant the end of the old, familiar Canada they had known so long. In 1914, the nation resembled an overgrown, awkward adolescent who had not quite reached manhood, a country boy still largely unaccustomed to city ways, a colonial who had only recently ceased to call the Motherland 'home'. Canadian life was a curious mixture of the old and the very new, of established routines and modish innovations, of traditional restraint and novel wilfulness and violence. The strange presence of the twentieth century was most clearly visible in the cities and towns. Yet the majority of the townsmen and city-dwellers were only a few years, or a decade, or a generation, away from the farm; and on the farm, in eastern and central Canada, if not in the west, Canadians carried on the business of living in much the same way as their fathers and grandfathers had done in late-Victorian or mid-Victorian times.

Motor cars, bearing a strong resemblance to the carriages from which they were descended, rattled about the city streets; they numbered nearly 75,000 in 1914, and a little less than half of the total were registered in Ontario. But street railways still carried the great majority of urban workers to their occupations; waggons rumbled and buggies sped along the narrow country roads as they had done for generations; and the hundreds of millions that Canadians kept putting into transcontinental railways was in itself a sufficient sign of their comfortable assumption that trains would remain for ever the only way of travelling distances. Concrete and asphalt pavements had been laid in the cities; but the familiar plank sidewalks and wood-block roads still did duty in smaller places; and hard street surfaces, of whatever composition, ended with the suburbs; and dirt gravel roads, muddy in spring, dusty in summer, quiet and rarely travelled at all times, stretched tranquilly away into the green distance.

The amenities provided by the new technology were only gradually altering people's habits. In 1914, 542,000 telephones, business and residential, had been installed in Canada; but Canadians still relied heavily on older and more familiar forms of communication. Relatively, they wrote far more letters and sent far more telegrams than they were to do later; and in 1913 there were more post offices in Canada than there have ever been since. In cities and towns, gas was replacing coal and wood for cookery, just as electricity was replacing gas for lighting; but, in the country, except in Ontario where the new Hydro Electric Power Commission had begun a 'rural electrification programme', most farmhouses were still lit by lamps. In winter, farmhouse bedrooms were chilly places, for the great kitchen stove could not diffuse its warmth everywhere; but central heating systems fed by coal or coke had been installed in the majority of town houses; and, in those most recently constructed, hot-water radiators had superseded the old 'registers' with their fitful gusts of warm air.

There was slightly less formality in daily life than there had been; but men and women differed almost as much in their vocations as they had done in Victorian times, and the heavy influx of poor European immigrants probably strengthened rather than lessened class distinctions. The long-skirted frock coat had gone out of fashion for ordinary day attire; but prominent citizens in business or politics still wore it frequently on formal or public occasions. The 'business' or lounge suit, which was the common workaday costume of most men except those in overalls, had a much shortened jacket, but kept the traditional vest or waistcoat. Women laced themselves in stiff boned corsets, and, although their skirts had narrowed to a more tubular shape, they were still nearly ankle-length. In the open, in both good weather and bad, men and women invariably wore hats; they usually addressed each other, including acquaintances of long standing, by their surnames, prefixed by Mr., Mrs., or Miss. Women accepted their traditional roles as housewives or ladies of leisure with apparent equanimity. In 1911, they constituted only about 10 per cent of the labour force, and a large number of those gainfully employed were in domestic service. As yet, they could not vote either in provincial or federal elections; and the Canadian women's suffrage movement was a feeble, apathetic imitation of its militant British original.

It was a Christian, or, at least, a church-going, society. The rancorous sectarianism of mid-Victorian days had largely died away; and the co-operation which, ten years later, was to lead to the establishment of the United Church of Canada was already in effective existence in the new western provinces. The churches probably did their best work in pioneer prairie settlements and found it hardest to cope with the novel spiritual and moral problems of industrialism and city life. There were clergymen, chiefly within the Methodist Church, who were concerned with urban social welfare, and, in a few cases, took a particular interest in the immigrant communities in the suburbs of the growing cities. But all too often the churches, like the police magistrates and the municipal authorities, judged prostitution, promiscuity, drunkenness, and juvenile delinquency by strict, old-fashioned moral standards. A very large part of the enthusiasm and energy of the churches was still put into foreign missions; and the domestic reform causes which they supported, such as the crusade for the prohibition of intoxicating liquors, often had their origin in puritanism. Mid-Victorian standards of personal conduct and private morality were still taught and preached as a living faith in homes, and schools, and churches; but Edwardian affluence, urban growth, and heavy foreign immigration had undeniably weakened their authority and influence. There were over six times as many divorces in 1911 as there had been in 1901; and, in the period from 1901 to 1914, court convictions for indictable offences of persons over sixteen years increased by over 400 per cent.

The Canadian economy and the Canadian people had changed and were changing; the Canadian state seemed scarcely to have changed at all. Canadian government, at both provincial and federal levels, remained very much what it had been at Confederation – remote, detached, undemanding, and, at the same time, very unconcerned. The provinces imposed corporation taxes and succession duties at modest rates; the Dominion relied almost entirely, as it had done since Confederation, on customs and excise duties; there was as yet no federal income tax or sales tax. The Militia Act, continuing an old requirement of pre-Confederation days, provided that all males between eighteen and sixty were liable for military service; but this provision had, of course, never been enforced; and, since conscription for defence was so completely alien to British experience, everybody assumed that it never would be. The state, in short, made few demands and imposed few obligations; but, in compensation, it performed few services and gave very little assistance. There were no mothers' or children's allowances, and no pensions for the blind or the aged. The maimed, the mentally retarded, the very old, the unemployed, and the unemployable had to find their support within the still surviving solidarity of the family. Free public schools and hospitals and asylums, which were supported mainly by the municipalities, with some help from the provinces, remained the principal social and welfare services of the period. The construction or the financial support of railways and canals were still the most important economic activities in which the state had become involved; but the western provinces, with their provincial telephone systems, and Ontario, with its popular Hydro Electric Power Commission, had brought government into the control and operation of important public utilities.

→≫ III ≪←

THE FIRST WORLD WAR brought this old Canada to the close of its existence. Already, in the first dozen years of the new century, the nation's character, occupations, and interest had radically altered; and now the war renewed and quickened these trends of development. The economic stimulus, which had helped so much to encourage them, had languished in 1913-15; but in the first year of hostilities it returned, re-invigorated and intensified by the demands of wartime. The special requirements of the war were foodstuffs, which Canada was superbly equipped to produce in huge volume, and munitions of war, chiefly shells and explosives, which Canadian factories could quickly learn to manufacture. The sharply rising prices of agricultural products brought about a second vast expanse of improved farmland and lifted Canadian exports of wheat and flour, coarse grains, and cattle and meat to record heights. The industrial plant and equipment, and the experienced labour which had been left idle by the sudden cessation of the railway and building construction boom, and the drop in consumer demand, were now quickly adapted to the production of munitions. Manufactures of iron and steel more than tripled in value during the period 1910-17. The value of non-ferrous metal products more than doubled in the same years.

The war was not only the first great war that Canada had ever fought; it was also the first of the total wars of modern times. Very rapidly it would involve the whole Canadian economy, affect the entire Canadian community, and profoundly alter the mental and moral outlook of millions of Canadians. In 1914, these revolutionary changes were just over the horizon; but nobody had glimpsed them yet, and nobody even suspected their approach. The liberal, free-enterprise system, it was assumed, would continue to give general satisfaction. The state, it was taken for granted, would get along well with its old, few, and primitive pieces of regulatory machinery. Reliance was still placed on the individual, on individual effort and voluntary sacrifice; and, with powerful economic inducements and equally powerful patriotic stimuli, success was achieved for some time. Contracts for munitions and other military supplies were lavishly distributed; a vast expansion of bank credit stimulated production; and voluntary enlistments in the armed services, encouraged by Borden's dramatic 'pledge' of an army of half a million men, held up well into the spring of 1916. Then the ominous signs of trouble began to appear. Enlistments, which had totalled 34,913 in March 1916, dropped to 8,389 in July. Suddenly there were shortages of foodstuffs and important raw materials; popular complaints against hoarding and profiteering became vociferous; and the cost of living began to rise steeply. Beginning in 1916, the federal government was besieged with entreaties to allocate and ration scarce commodities, curb hoarders, fix prices, and conscript wealth. The provinces felt the mounting pressure of those two oddly associated crusades – the women's suffrage movement and the agitation for the prohibition of intoxicating liquors – both of which had drawn new strength from the idealism of wartime and the instinct for self-denial.

The real revolution in the nature and functions of the Canadian state began in 1916. In 1916-17, the three prairie provinces, followed by British Columbia and Ontario, gave votes to women in provincial elections; and, in the same two years, all the provinces, with the exception of Quebec, proscribed the sale of spirits, wine, and beer, except for medicinal and scientific purposes. At Ottawa, a harassed but determined federal government found itself exercising strange economic controls and experimenting with novel methods of financing. In the past, Canada had borrowed abroad, chiefly in England; but by the summer of 1915 it became obvious that Great Britain could do no more than meet the cost of its own war effort and of Canadian expenditures abroad. The closure of the London money market drove Canada back on her own resources; and in order to pay her domestic wartime costs and to finance British purchases in Canada, the federal government began to appeal to the Canadian investor on a scale utterly unknown before. The first domestic loan, for $100 million, was offered in the autumn of 1915; and by the end of the war Canada had borrowed over $2 billion from its own citizens.

In the meantime, the federal government was rapidly regaining the paramount position which the Fathers of Confederation had intended it to have and which it had gradually lost during the long years of *laissez faire* and peace. The trend towards decentralization, which had been largely decreed by the legal decisions of the Judicial Committee of the Privy Council, was now reversed; and the Dominion took over the complete and undisputed mastery of all the major activities of the nation at war. A Business Profits Tax was imposed early in 1916 and made retroactive to the beginning of the war; and in November an order in council was passed to prevent hoarding, profiteering, and unjustified increases in the cost of living. The next year saw the imposition of a corporation and personal income tax, the appointment of a Food Controller and a Fuel Controller, and the establishment of the Board of Grain Supervisors, with authority to market the entire Canadian wheat crop. Finally, in February 1918, came the creation of the War Trade Board, a body armed with exceptional powers of regulation, which, if the war had continued, would have enabled it to exercise complete supervision over the national economy. In the main, these boards and agencies dealt with procurement, allocation, and rationing of scarce materials, and here their greatest successes were scored. Their greatest failure lay in the feeble attempt to control prices, which, in large measure because of the government's own inflationary policies, kept irrepressibly rising.

Along with this increasing reliance on government regulation, there began, slowly and reluctantly, a great experiment in public ownership. The Conservatives had never been fanatical believers in the doctrines of economic liberalism and individual enterprise. Unlike the Liberals, they had, from the start, been perfectly ready to use the power and resources of the state to develop and protect the national economy; and in 1904 Borden had proposed a single new transcontinental railway, built and controlled by the federal government. But it was no longer possible, as it would have been in 1904, to design a new, integrated national transport system. Two rival transcontinental railways, their planning bedevilled rather than regulated by government, and their cost inflated by ambition, corruption, and mismanagement, had actually been built. Public ownership was not a first choice, but a last resort; and the hesitating steps with which the federal government took over the Canadian Northern, the Grand Trunk Pacific, and the Grand Trunk Railway were simply the inescapable consequences of the complete collapse of the ambitious Liberal railway-building programme of the previous decade. Already, during the brief pre-war depression, the railways had been tottering; the war hastened their final downfall. The London money market was now closed to all further borrowing; and the soaring costs of wartime operation leaped far above the revenue from increased traffic. Mackenzie and Mann were at the end of their tether. Early in 1915, the Grand Trunk Pacific evaded its engagement to lease the eastern division, the National Transcontinental; and, before the year was out, the Grand Trunk Railway, staggering under the crushing burden of its unlucky subsidiary, actually had the audacity to invite the Canadian government to take over the Grand Trunk Pacific and assume all its liabilities including its debts to its own parent! 'I said I would personally prefer to resign,' Borden angrily recorded in his diary, 'and let the Grits clean up their own mess.' Short of this heroic but impossible solution, what was the Conservative government to do? On the one hand, the ministers feared that to let the railways go into receivership would have a shattering effect on Canadian credit abroad; and, on the other, they knew very well that it was politically impossible to go on for ever pouring public money into what were virtually insolvent private companies. All Borden could think of – and, in his extremity, he regarded the notion as a positive flash of inspiration – was to propose that the government should keep the railways going by means of small, temporary advances, a species of railway 'dole', and that in the meantime a thorough and impartial investigation of the whole complex problem should be undertaken. Then, he could only hope, a practicable and permanent solution would emerge. In July 1916, a Royal Commission of Inquiry was appointed consisting of A. H. Smith, vice-president of the New York Central Railroad, Sir Henry Drayton, head of the Canadian Board of Railway Commissioners, and W. M. Acworth, a British railway statistician.

->>> IV <<<-

IN A PIECEMEAL, experimental, uncertain fashion, the government coped with the problems inherited from the past as well as with the strange difficulties of total war. But, behind all these worries over government controls, wartime finance, and insolvent railways – and, indeed, the prime cause of most of them – was the nation's greatest anxiety and burden, the war. The war was by now well into its second year; and already two important facts about Canada's part in it had become obvious. Abroad, Canada had made a major contribution to the war effort of the British Empire, without receiving any share in its direction; and, at home, the unity with which the Canadian people had entered the war was becoming seriously impaired. The gradual disintegration of the national concord of August 1914 was apparent to everybody. But it was Borden, as Prime Minister, who was most concerned over the contradictions implicit in Canada's wartime role.

In the summer of 1915 he had spent nearly two months in England. Among British politicians he found a curious lack of urgency and some signs of inefficiency, indecision, and neglect. He was repeatedly frustrated in his attempts to get definite answers to his questions; and he came to the angry conclusion that the British were simply muddling through without settled objectives or time-tables. His impatience with the conduct of the war strengthened his conviction that Canada must be given a share in its direction. Years before 1914 he had conceived the idea of a co-operative Empire-Commonwealth in defence and foreign policy; but the defeat of his Naval Aid Bill had virtually destroyed his case for a voice in the making of policy. Now the magnitude of the Canadian war effort supplied a justification which the pre-war gift of three dreadnoughts could never have equalled. The Canadian Corps in France had been regularly increased in size; the famous pledge of an army of half a million men gave firm assurance that Canada intended to play a principal's part in the conflict. Yet, so completely was she excluded from British councils of war and so largely denied all confidential information concerning their decisions, that the Canadian Corps might have been an army of mercenaries offered for nothing to a foreign power. This state of affairs, in Borden's eyes, had now become intolerable. He began to urge Canada's right to be informed and consulted. By mid-winter of 1916, his efforts had had at least some results. In February, Bonar Law, Colonial Secretary in the British Coalition government, sent out a group of important war documents under strict security provisions. But, if something had been done to supply information, no attempt at all had been made to arrange for consultation.

Even this was not all. Canada had not yet gained her rightful place in the conduct of the war; and – what was far worse – she was rapidly losing the unity of purpose with which she had entered it. It was true, of course, that, right from the beginning, Canadians had differed significantly in their attitudes to the war, and in their understanding of its nature and obligations. A nation which had so recently gained such a vast increase of its population from so many different national sources could hardly be expected to make a uniform response. Fewer than 30 per cent of the enlisted men in the First Canadian Division were Canadian-born. The young, unmarried immigrants from the British Isles were the quickest to volunteer in August and September of 1914; but this original discrepancy in the rate of enlistment was soon followed by others as the native Canadians came forward in growing numbers. City-dwellers were more ready to join than countrymen; the prairies showed more eagerness than the Atlantic seaboard. Above all, and beyond any real doubt or question, French Canada began to lag farther and farther behind the rest of the nation. And this continued and stubborn non-conformity was at once a symptom and a cause of the growing estrangement of English Canadians and French Canadians.

There were several valid reasons, as well as some specious excuses, for the progressive alienation of French Canada. In the early months of the war, the Canadian military authorities failed to create a sufficient number of distinctive French-speaking battalions and passed over capable French-Canadian officers who deserved promotion. They blundered badly when they appointed an English-speaking Protestant clergyman as director of recruiting in the Montreal district, though in fact the appointment was made only after a number of suitable French Canadians had declined the post. These slights and mistakes, this unthinking ineptitude, helped to arouse a feeling of injury and resentment; but such specific grievances were not the real cause of French Canada's mounting antagonism. The real cause was a fundamental difference of opinion over the purpose of the war and the nature of Canada's part in it. For English Canadians the war was undoubtedly the most important event in their history. They believed that it was a great moral struggle for the future peace and happiness of mankind; they were convinced that Canada was engaged in it, not as an assistant or a subordinate, but as a principal. Neither one of these two basic assumptions was generally accepted in French Canada. French Canadians were colonials and isolationists who saw no reason why Canada should try to play a major part in world affairs. They were local patriots whose first loyalty went to the province of Quebec rather than to the Dominion of Canada. Their dominating purpose was the defence of their own provincial culture, not the establishment of world peace and security.

At this particular time, moreover, a real and serious danger to this provincial culture seemed to be impending. The vital heart of French Canada was its language and its educational system; and in the early years of the war both Manitoba and Ontario began to limit the use of French, as a subject of study and as a language of instruction in their provincial schools. At bottom, these new restrictions were the determined expression of an aroused English-Canadian nationalism which had awakened to the realization that, after a decade of massive immigration, Canada was only too likely to become a jumbled cultural mosaic and a babel of strange tongues. In 1915, a report of the Manitoba Department of Education made it plain that the Laurier educational compromise of 1896 was likely to perpetuate the use of German, Polish, and Ukrainian, as well as French, in the province. Three years earlier, the Merchant investigation in Ontario revealed the fact that the great majority of the teachers in the bilingual schools in the eastern part of the province were badly trained and inefficient, and a large proportion of their pupils barely literate. Both Ontario and Manitoba now decided on drastic remedies. Manitoba simply repealed the clause providing for bilingual teaching; in Ontario, the Department of Education issued Regulation 17 which sharply limited the use of French, both as a subject of study and as a language of instruction.

Manitoba's action was much the harsher and more conclusive of the two; but Ontario adjoined Quebec, the Franco-Ontarians were strongest along the interprovincial boundary, and it was Regulation 17, rather than the repeal of the Laurier compromise in Manitoba, that aroused the passionate indignation of French Canada. The French-speaking citizens of Ottawa, who provided the intellectual leadership for the Franco-Ontarians, defied Regulation 17, and turned the capital into an educational chaos. They lost their case in the courts; the judges, in trial after trial, reached the only possible conclusion – that the educational guarantees of the British North America Act applied to religion, not language. But, though the legal battle went against them, they succeeded in making Regulation 17 a political issue in which the whole of French Canada became involved. It was denounced everywhere as an example of Prussian tyranny as atrocious as anything in Germany; the struggle over the schools of Ottawa was raised to a level of moral significance far higher than that of the war in Europe. The Quebec Nationalists, led by Bourassa, who used every incitement to exacerbate the controversy, were its principal beneficiaries politically; and Laurier, who regarded Bourassa with fear and jealousy, was determined that his dangerous rival should not walk off with all the new accumulation of political capital in an aroused Quebec. He insisted upon the introduction, in the House of Commons, of a resolution appealing to the legislature of Ontario to respect the privileges hitherto enjoyed by children of French-Canadian parentage of being educated in their mother tongue. The Liberal members from the western provinces and Ontario protested that this resolution was ill-timed, out of place, and dangerously provocative; but Laurier was adamant. The well-worn threat 'to step down and out' of the leadership of the party was pressed so far that the Ontario Liberals capitulated; but the westerners, digging their heels in, joined the large Conservative majority which rejected the resolution.

⇥ V ⇤

THE RANCOROUS cultural conflict continued unchecked during the last six months of 1916. Here there could be no easy appeasement or reconciliation; but elsewhere Borden's problems were finding unexpected solutions. Before the troubled year drew to its close, his hopes for a more energetic war effort, in the direction of which Canada would have a greater influence, were realized more completely than perhaps he had ever imagined they could be. Early in December, a major political crisis in England ended in the downfall of Asquith and the reorganization of the Coalition government under David Lloyd George as Prime Minister. The great distinguishing feature of the new ministry was an inner War Cabinet of five members, headed by the Prime Minister, of which Bonar Law, Chancellor of the Exchequer, and Lord Milner, Minister without Portfolio, were both members. These men – the Welsh village solicitor, the Glasgow ironmaster, and the imperial proconsul who had inspired the Round Table movement – differed from the leisurely patricians whom they had displaced, not only in the energy and determination with which they wanted to carry on the war, but also in their appreciation of the contribution which the Dominions had made, and could make, to the final victory. In all probability it was Milner who first suggested that they should be called into consultation on the conduct of the war; but his proposal found a ready acceptance. 'The more I think about it,' Lloyd George wrote to Walter Long, the new Colonial Secretary, only a few days after the new cabinet had been formed, 'the more I am convinced that we should take the Dominions into our counsel in a much larger measure than we have hitherto done in our prosecution of the war. They have made enormous sacrifices, but we have held no conference with them as to either the objects of the war, or the methods of carrying it out. They hardly feel that they have been consulted. As we must receive even more substantial help from them before we can hope to pull through, it is important that they should feel that they have a share in our councils as well as in our burdens.' On the 25th of December, Long cabled Ottawa, announcing the calling of an Imperial Conference; and, a few days later, in another message, he explained that what was intended was not 'a session of the ordinary Imperial Conference, but a special War Conference of the Empire'.

Borden sailed for England on the 14th of February, 1917, and returned to Ottawa on the 15th of May. He came back convinced that the Allied position in the war was still dangerously critical and that only a prolonged and desperate effort on the part of the whole Empire-Commonwealth would achieve victory. He was determined that Canada should have its full share in this endeavour. Until then, his government had relied upon the voluntary system of recruitment; but in December 1916 he had frankly warned a group of labour representatives that he could give no assurance that conscription would not be introduced; and, by the time he returned to Canada, he had reached the definite conclusion that the voluntary system would not suffice to honour Canada's commitment. A National Service Board, established in the autumn, with R. B. Bennett as its director, tried, during the winter months of 1917, to take an inventory of Canadian manpower; but this very incomplete registration yielded only a negligible number of volunteers. In April 1917 – the month of the Battle of Vimy Ridge, in which 10,602 Canadians were lost – enlistments in Canada numbered only 4,761. Other Commonwealth countries, Borden knew, had already faced the dwindling returns of the voluntary system, and Great Britain and New Zealand, though not Australia, had decided that conscription was the only answer. The United States, which had entered the war early in April 1917, was to base its army upon compulsory selective service.

'Upon my return,' Borden wrote later, 'quick decision was necessary.' Within ten days of his arrival in Ottawa, he had settled upon two major policies. On the 18th, he announced in the House that the government proposed to introduce conscription for military service; on the 25th, he invited Laurier to join with him in forming a coalition or union government. From the beginning, the two proposals, conscription and union government, had been inextricably linked together. There were now coalition governments in both England and France; and, to many Canadians on both sides of the political fence, it seemed clear that party politics were out of place in wartime and that the war effort could be carried on successfully only by a national, bi-partisan government. The Conservative cabinet, however, was still seriously divided on the question; and the final decision, in favour of coalition, was Borden's own. He was convinced that such a momentous national policy as conscription could best be undertaken and carried out by a union of parties. For him, the fulfilment of Canada's contribution to the war was the supreme consideration. But there was another impending national decision – the permanent settlement of the railway question, which almost equally needed a broad base of political support. In April, the Royal Commission of Inquiry on the railways brought down its findings, rather unhelpfully, in two reports. The chairman, A. H. Smith, proposed an elaborate plan which maintained the principle of private enterprise. The majority, Sir Henry Drayton and W. M. Acworth, recommended that the Canadian Northern, the Grand Trunk Pacific, and the Grand Trunk Railway should all be taken over 'by the people

of Canada' and, along with the government lines, the Intercolonial and the National Transcontinental, united in a single
system. But how could any Canadian government, except a
government literally entitled to call itself 'national', undertake
such a gigantic venture in public ownership?

In three interviews with Laurier, Borden made the Leader of
the Opposition a proposal of remarkable – and indeed astonishing – generosity. Though the Conservatives had, at that time, a
majority of more than forty in the House of Commons, he proposed a coalition in which each party 'should be represented by
an equal number of members outside the office of Prime Minister'. He even undertook to make the Conservative wing of the
coalition acceptable to Laurier, which, as he said himself, was
practically entrusting the nomination of the government members to the Leader of the Opposition. Finally, in response to
Laurier's argument that so drastic a policy as conscription could
not be introduced without an appeal to the people, Borden
went so far as to agree that the new Military Service Act, though
passed in the existing session of Parliament, would not be proclaimed until a general election had given the coalition government a mandate for its enforcement.

It was all in vain. In a final interview, on the 6th of June,
Laurier declined the proposal. Borden's purpose had been
single and his conduct straightforward. Laurier's motives were
mixed and his behaviour ambivalent. He repeatedly declared
his belief that conscription was wrong in principle and unnecessary and inexpedient in practice; but, if his views were as fixed
and uncompromising as this, his negotiations with the Prime
Minister ought to have ended conclusively at their first interview. The fact that they did not, and that, instead, the talks
continued for nearly a fortnight, strongly implies that Laurier's
decision was taken, not simply on principle, but as the result of
a number of considerations. For Borden, the Canadian Corps's
need for reinforcements was, in itself, a completely sufficient
argument for both conscription and coalition. He believed that
the whole strength of the nation ought to be put into the struggle for victory; and it seemed right and, indeed, essential to him
that, in the supreme crisis of the war, both Liberals and Conser-

vatives 'should rise above all considerations of party interest or advantage'. To Laurier the idea that the conduct of the war should transcend party politics was a preposterous and, indeed, an incomprehensible notion. A war in which, so he firmly believed, Canada was fighting, not for her own sake, but in a junior capacity as Britain's assistant, was not a transcendent enterprise, but an ordinary government undertaking, and, like all other government undertakings, well within the scope of party politics. Compulsory military service might very well turn out to be a terrible political blunder for the Conservatives. Why should he not take advantage of their mistakes? It would be sound party tactics to decline joining the coalition and to refuse to extend the life of Parliament for another year. A general election, in which conscription would be the central issue, would therefore be inevitable. In that contest, Laurier hoped and believed he might regain power at Ottawa. He was certain, at any rate, that he would recover the allegiance of his fellow French Canadians in Quebec.

Laurier's decision was crucial for Canada. In 1917 a division of opinion among Canadians over the policy of conscription for military service was inevitable. By uniting with Borden in a coalition, Laurier might have minimized this division and helped to ensure that its unfortunate consequences would not be too serious or lasting. By refusing Borden's magnanimous offer, he deepened and widened the division to the proportions of a chasm, and prolonged, if he did not perpetuate, its evil results.

CHAPTER EIGHT

Unrest and Dissent

IT WAS A NOISY, fractious, argumentative summer. The debate on the Military Service Bill, in which Arthur Meighen took a conspicuous part for the Conservatives, came to a weary close towards the end of July. The whole of August was taken up by an equally vehement and protracted debate on the Canadian Northern Acquisition Bill. The government had decided that it would accept, and carry out, with some important modifications, the principal recommendation of the Drayton-Acworth majority report of the Royal Commission of Inquiry on the railways; and the first stage in this involved and cumbrous move towards nationalization was the acquisition of that almost fabulous enterprise, the Canadian Northern Railway. Four hundred thousand shares of the railway's capital stock, of the par value of $40 million, were already held in trust for the Crown; the government proposed to complete the national control of the property by the purchase of the remaining six hundred thousand shares at a price to be determined by a three-man board of arbitration. It was not, of course, a question of giving compensation to a large, unhappy company of Canadian, British, and foreign investors who had mistakenly put their money into the Canadian Northern; 51 per cent of the non-government shares were still owned by those monopolizing buccaneers, Mackenzie and Mann, themselves. But they had pledged their entire holdings to the Canadian Bank of Commerce in return for the cash advances that had alone kept the railway going.

For four long weeks, in the shrillest tones of outraged morality, the Liberal opposition denounced the bill. The Canadian Northern stock, they repeatedly insisted, was utterly worthless; to pay compensation for it was simply to give an undeserved gratuity to the friends of government in Toronto who controlled the Canadian Northern, the National Trust, and the Canadian Bank of Commerce. To the Liberals, this group of political favourites was all the more objectionable inasmuch as it included several of those despicable renegades, the perfidious 'eighteen' Torontonians who had betrayed the Liberal Party in 1911; and, indeed, among its members was Sir Thomas White, the Conservative Minister of Finance, who had actually had the effrontery to sponsor the bill in the Commons! This imaginary conspiracy to provide a belated reward for Liberal traitors had no real basis in fact, as White could readily show; but it was harder to prove that compensation for the Canadian Northern stock was in the public interest than that it was not for the private advantage of a few political friends. White and Meighen tried to argue that outright confiscation of the stock would do just as serious an injury to Canadian credit abroad as the bankruptcy of the railway would have done two years earlier, and that the total loss of its enormous loan might bring about the collapse of the Canadian Bank of Commerce and a widespread financial panic as a result.

The passage of the Canadian Northern Acquisition Bill hastened a curious and important realignment of political forces in Canada. Liberals, in or out of Parliament, were not the only adversaries of the bill. It was also harshly criticized by the two principal English-speaking newspapers in Montreal, the *Gazette* and the *Star*, both of which were traditionally Conservative in their political affiliations; and it was privately but bitterly opposed by those two venerable and potent friends of the Conservative Party, the Bank of Montreal and the Canadian Pacific Railway. Lord Shaughnessy, the president of the Canadian Pacific, had his own ideas about railway reorganization in Canada, and he had confidently proposed to Borden that all Canadian railways, including his own, should be united in a single gigantic national system under the existing management of the Canadian Pacific. According to this extraordinary and one-sided proposal, the Canadian government would merely be obliged to pay the bond holders, guarantee an annual dividend to the shareholders, and meet all deficits! Canada, however, was to have no control whatever over the operation of its own national railway system; that was to be the exclusive responsibility of the directorate of the Canadian Pacific, which, according to the plan, was to be completely independent and endlessly self-perpetuating. The cold reception which this fantastic scheme received in Ottawa convinced Shaughnessy that government policy was nationalization in the literal sense of the word and that his railway would have to compete with a publicly supported rival. At this the Canadian Pacific turned angrily upon the party which had created and preserved it through long years of adversity; and, along with the Bank of Montreal, and the major financial interests of Montreal, it went into strenuous opposition.

French Canada had been lost to the Conservatives through conscription. The Canadian Northern Bill had alienated financial Montreal. Could the Conservative government recoup in Ontario and the prairie provinces the terrible losses it had suffered in Quebec? Its only hope lay in the support of the unhappy but hesitating conscriptionist Liberals. Some of these were already in Parliament and available; but others – such as N. W. Rowell of Ontario, and A. L. Sifton, J. A. Calder, and T. A. Crerar of the western provinces – were deeply engaged in provincial politics or business. Could they be persuaded to come to Ottawa and join a coalition? For weeks, for months, they seemed totally incapable of making up their own minds. A real belief in the need of political union for the successful prosecution of the war impelled them forward; the prestige of their old leader and the potent example of his refusal to unite with Borden held them back. They shyly advanced; they coyly retreated. All summer and into the early autumn, they behaved like a bevy of fluttering and coquettish girls, alternately accepting and rejecting the advances of an undeniably attractive group of suitors against whom their mothers had solemnly warned them.

In the end, it was the action of the Conservative government that made up their minds for them. In September, towards the end of the interminable session, Meighen introduced a measure which almost seemed to imply that if the Liberals, even including the conscriptionist Liberals, persisted in playing party politics in wartime, the Conservatives could play party politics also, and far more effectively. The Wartime Elections Bill – the first bill to give women the vote in federal elections – enfranchised the wives, widows, mothers, sisters, and daughters of men in the armed forces serving overseas; it disfranchised enemy aliens who had become naturalized Canadians after the 31st of March, 1902. Meighen's main justification for this very partial and discriminatory bill was that 'war service should be the basis of war franchise': this was a feeble excuse for a measure which violated all the accepted canons of liberal democracy, and the outraged Liberals attacked it eloquently on principle. But for them its most appalling feature lay in the fiendish ingenuity with which it enfranchised women who would probably vote Conservative and disfranchised western farmers who almost certainly would vote Liberal. For all Liberal M.P.s, and particularly for westerners, the electoral prospects looked extremely dismal. When the session ended late in September, the conscriptionist Liberals were still hesitating; but finally, on the 12th of October, a Union government was formed, with ten Liberal or Labour members, and thirteen Conservatives, including the Prime Minister, Sir Robert Borden.

Barely two months later, on the 17th of December, the general election gave the Union government a smashing victory; the Unionists elected 153 members, the Laurier Liberals only 82. It was the greatest majority that had ever sat in the Canadian House of Commons; but, as usual in an electoral system of single-member constituencies, the popular vote was a good deal less conclusive; and it went far to prove Laurier's belief that there was a strong latent opposition to the government's programme. The Laurier Liberals received less than 8 per cent of the soldier vote, but very nearly 47 per cent of the civilian vote. Quebec accounted for nearly a third of this large total; but in other provinces as well there was significant evidence of dissent. In both Nova Scotia and Prince Edward Island, the Liberals won a small popular majority; and, even in Ontario, 38 per cent of the voters cast their ballots for Laurier. Liberal strength was spread fairly evenly across the whole of English-speaking Canada; but sixty-two of the eighty-two Liberal seats were won in the province of Quebec. Quebec stood out in emphatic isolation from the rest of the country and in united opposition to the policies it had endorsed. Laurier had argued that he must defeat Bourassa; but, in fact, Bourassa supported him in the election. The Nationalists ran no independent candidates and, in effect, the Laurier Liberals identified themselves with the Nationalist cause.

The election had revealed the potential strength of the protest against the Military Service Act; and, as the last eight months of the war dragged grimly along, resistance, either spontaneous or organized, began openly to show itself. The anti-draft riots which had long been feared in turbulent Montreal broke out unexpectedly in the more sedate Quebec City on the night of Good Friday, the 29th of March, 1918. Armed resistance was to be confined to the province of Quebec; but the opposition to conscription and the Union government was by no means solely cultural or 'racial' in character. Organized labour, which was growing rapidly during the war years, yielded a grudging acquiescence in both registration and conscription, though only against an emphatic protest from a militant minority of its members. Much of rural Ontario accepted the Military Service Act doubtfully, resentfully, and on the strength of a promise of generous exemptions to farmers' sons; but this policy of limited enforcement was summarily abandoned when the German offensive of March and the collapse of the Fifth British Army brought on the last great crisis of the war. On the 19th of April, Borden moved and carried a resolution cancelling the exemptions and lowering the draft limit from twenty to nineteen years. The results of this decisive action were ominous for the future. In May, the United Farmers of Ontario, with the help of representatives from Quebec and a few delegates from the west and the Atlantic provinces, organized a mass protest in Ottawa against the cancellation. In September, the annual convention of the Trades and Labour Congress denounced the enforcement of the Military Service Act and demanded the conscription of wealth.

→»> II «←

THE CONSEQUENCES of the Military Service Act were to be many, varied, and pervasive; but it had been enacted for a particular and definite purpose, and that purpose, despite a good deal of misrepresentation then and since, was achieved. Subsequently, it was argued that conscription had 'failed absolutely in the ostensible aim of providing greater reinforcements than the voluntary system'. Laurier had prophesied that it would fail; and obviously Laurier must have been right. But, in fact, Laurier was wrong; and the apologists and hagiographers who tried to justify his stand have simply falsified the record. After October 1917, enlistments increased at an average monthly rate which the voluntary system, if it had been continued, could not possibly have equalled, or even remotely approached. From January to October 1918 the monthly totals rivalled those achieved by the voluntary system during its most successful period – now two years in the past – from the autumn of 1915 to the summer of 1916. The aim of the Military Service Act was the dispatch of 100,000 reinforcements overseas. Between 96,000 and 100,000 were enlisted under the act, and more than 47,000 were sent overseas before the war ended. If it had continued, there can be no doubt that Borden's declared purpose would have been fulfilled.

The Canadian contribution had been assured. The last great German offensive had failed and the triumph of the allied arms seemed certain. During that final summer of the struggle, a second series of meetings of the Imperial War Cabinet and the Imperial War Conference, which Borden attended throughout, seemed to establish more securely than before both the theory and practice of the new co-operative Empire-Commonwealth. Were these two wartime bodies likely to become the models for that post-war imperial reorganization which Borden and the other Commonwealth leaders now believed was inevitable? In

1917, the Imperial War Conference had decided that the imperial organization of the future was too important and intricate a subject to be settled in detail during the war; but, at the same time, it had solemnly recorded its belief that the post-war Empire-Commonwealth must give the autonomous Dominions an adequate voice in foreign policy and must provide for continuous consultation as a necessary basis for common action. The declaration of these general – though very vaguely general – principles was now followed by some significant changes in practice. The traditional connection between the Colonial Secretary and the Governor General, which ever since Confederation had been the only official channel of communication between the Dominions and Great Britain, was now by-passed by a new method which placed the various governments of the Commonwealth on a level of equality. Henceforth the Dominions' Prime Ministers could consult directly with the Prime Minister of Great Britain. Henceforth also, they could appoint ministers to represent them at the meetings of the Imperial War Cabinet during the intervals between its plenary sessions.

Borden left England on the 17th of August and reached Ottawa one week later. He had been back barely two months when, on the 28th of October, a message from Lloyd George informed him that the surrender of Germany was imminent and that it would be well for him to prepare to return for the peace negotiations. On the following day Borden replied that the Canadian press and people, as well as the Canadian government, expected confidently that Canada would be represented in her own right at the peace conference. In London, when the Imperial War Cabinet met on the 20th of November, the question of what form Dominions representation would take was still undecided. Despite his cable of the 29th of October, Borden, as well as General Smuts of South Africa, might have been willing to settle for the inclusion of Canada, through a panel system, in a single British Empire delegation; but, in Ottawa, the Canadian cabinet showed plainly that it preferred the earlier decision in favour of 'special' representation; and, in the Imperial War Cabinet, W. M. Hughes, the pugnacious and vehement Prime Minister of Australia, was determined that his country's voice must have independent means of expression. In the end the War Cabinet decided to combine both ideas and to press for the representation of the Dominions at Paris in their own right as well as through their membership on a panel from which part of the British Empire delegation would be chosen. The Dominions and India, the cabinet urged, should be placed on an equal footing at the conference with Belgium and the lesser Allied powers. In the end, this aim was not realized, for Belgium and Serbia were allotted three representatives each, and the senior Dominions, as well as the other smaller powers, only two. This reduction was formally a diplomatic defeat, but, in fact, not an important setback. The real work of the conference was done, not in its plenary sessions, in which all the nations participated, but in the Supreme Council which was dominated exclusively by the great powers. Canada's dual position at the conference saved her from the virtual exclusion to which the other smaller countries had to submit. She was admitted to the counsels of one of the 'Big Three' nations which in the end made the settlement; and, as members of the British Empire delegation, the Canadians played a part in the work of the conference which it would have been utterly impossible for them to do as the representatives of a small, unattached nation.

At Paris, Canada's chief interest lay in the public recognition of her new status. The Canadians were painfully aware that their country was not yet generally accepted as a sovereign state. They were equally convinced that Canada's contribution to the winning of the war had entitled her to a standing equivalent to sovereignty. Only a great international gathering could endorse such a lofty claim; and, for Canadians, the supreme importance of the Paris Peace Conference lay in its unquestioned authority to validate their country's credentials and admit it to the rank of statehood. Two great new world institutions, the League of Nations and the International Labour Organization, were to be created at Paris; and to Borden and his colleagues it seemed essential that Canada's new status should be publicly recognized by its admission to these bodies on exactly the same basis as sovereign states. Somewhat belatedly, they discovered that the language of international diplomacy, with its use of such traditional words as 'state' and 'empire', was ill-suited to express the existing constitutional relationships of the British Commonwealth. They also found, to their dismay and increasing anger, that members of the American delegation, and particularly its labour experts, were strongly opposed to the verbal changes which would concede the Canadian claim. With their ingrained suspicion of the sinister power of British imperialism, the Americans automatically assumed that separate places for the Dominions and India would simply mean six British Empire votes; and they stubbornly insisted that the American people would not accept this overwhelming preponderance. In April and May 1919, Borden had to battle hard for what he believed to be Canadian rights; and it was not until the 6th of May, the day before the treaty was presented to the Germans in a final, formal session of the conference at Versailles, that he secured from Clemenceau, Wilson, and Lloyd George an explanatory memorandum, confirming the status of the Dominions, which fully satisfied him. Canada was recognized as an original member of the new world order, the League of Nations, with separate representation, in her own right, in both the League Assembly and the International Labour Organization, and with the possibility of election to one of the non-permanent seats on the League Council.

In 1919, the League of Nations was an international club, of great repute and portentous respectability, into which it was highly desirable for a young nation like Canada to gain admission. All the best nations belonged to the new club; only colonies, dependencies, protectorates, and other constitutionally inferior territories had been excluded. Canada in 1919 was an eager 'joiner' in part, but by no means wholly, for reasons of status. Borden and his closest associates believed firmly in the central idea of the League. They did, indeed, object to Article X of the Covenant which bound the members of the League 'to respect and preserve as against external aggression the territorial integrity and existing political independence' of all member states. As Borden said, this article seemed to assume, without any investigation whatever, the justice and expediency of all existing political boundaries. The unwisdom of this comprehen-

sive endorsation frightened him; but it did not weaken his conviction, held now for over a decade, that Canada must take her
place in the international community and accept the duties and
responsibilities of mature nationhood. He approved strongly
of the League's role in the settlement of disputes and the
preservation of the peace.

→» III «←

LONG BEFORE Borden had finished his congenial work in
Paris, his worried colleagues in Ottawa were begging him
to come home. In a puzzled fashion, they realized that the
country was full of strange unrest, and noisy with extraordinary
complaints. They found themselves in the midst of the confusing
economic and social turmoil which the war had pent up and the
peace had now released. The losses, the privations, the unequal
sacrifices of war, the grossly contrasted benefits of wartime prosperity and inflation had awakened a sullen feeling of injustice
in many Canadians. The example of the Russian Revolution,
the brave new worlds and peaceful utopias of wartime oratory
and idealism, had bred in many others an unquestioning belief
that peace would bring a different and a far better Canada in
which government would do vastly more for them than it had
ever done before. The great debate over the nature and functions of the state, which had begun during the war, became
more general and more passionate. Did not the national interest
mean something quite different now from what it had meant
before the war? Should the old national policies of the past be
drastically changed or abandoned? Would the old political
parties be broken up and new parties take their place?

The most searching of these questions were being asked by
occupational groups or classes. Trade union membership, rising
from 166,000 in 1914 to 378,000 in 1919, had more than doubled
itself; and trade union activity had increased even more rapidly
in the same five years, and had acquired a new militant spirit.
In 1909, at the height of Laurier prosperity, there had been
only ninety strikes and lockouts involving only a little over

18,000 workers; ten years later, in 1919, with the wartime boom still in the ascendant, the number of strikes and lockouts had risen to 336, and nearly 150,000 workers were affected by them. A relatively large number of these struggles had been fought in Winnipeg and the towns of the Pacific coast; and already a significant difference of opinion over aims and methods had divided eastern and western labour. In the main, eastern labour was organized along craft lines and was strongly influenced by the example of the American Federation of Labor and its president, Samuel Gompers. Western labour was largely led by a skilled group of British socialist immigrants who brought with them the idea of organization along industrial lines culminating in a single immense union of all workers. In Ontario labour leaders based their hopes on independent political action within the existing parliamentary system; and the Independent Labour Party of Ontario, founded during the summer of 1917 to fight the oncoming federal general election, remained labour's strongest political organization in Canada. In Manitoba and British Columbia, there was more scepticism about the value of parliamentary representation, a good deal more talk about the class conflict and the struggle for power, and a far greater inclination towards direct action through the general strike. In September 1918, at the meeting of the Canadian Trades and Labour Congress in Quebec City, the two opposing labour philosophies met in a resounding clash. The radical westerners completely failed to persuade the Congress to endorse a re-organization of the Canadian labour movement by industry instead of by craft; but this defeat, far from dampening their ardour, simply drove them into independent action. In March 1919, they held an Interprovincial Western Labour Conference at Calgary. There the delegates talked in spacious Marxist terms about the socialist future of Canada. They proclaimed the great principle of the industrial organization of all workers. They organized the One Big Union – the 'O.B.U.'.

A few weeks later, in May 1919, the Trades and Labour Council of Winnipeg called a general strike in support of the metal and building trades, who had gone out over their demand for better wages and the right of collective bargaining. The

general strike was not inspired by the Calgary conference or
directed by the O.B.U.; but public opinion regarded it as a
presumptuous and illegitimate weapon in an industrial dispute;
and, in the excited imaginations of many Canadians, the crisis
in Winnipeg foreshadowed a general attempt to gain political
control of the country by revolutionary means. The federal
government, with Meighen as Acting Minister of Justice, intervened quickly and decisively. It amended the Criminal Code by
drastically enlarging the definition of sedition and seditious
conspiracy, and severely increasing their penalties. It hastily introduced retroactive amendments to the Immigration Act which
permitted the deportation of British-born immigrants. In the
early morning of the 17th of June, eight strike leaders were
rounded up and sent to Stony Mountain Prison; and on the 21st
of June, 'Bloody Saturday', when the strikers and their sympathizers assembled in front of the City Hall to protest against the
arrests, mounted police galloped down Main Street with drawn
pistols and, in two charges, broke up the crowd and ended all
resistance.

The Union government became more than ever a hated name
to organized labour; but by the summer of 1919 organized
labour still counted far less politically than its leaders had hoped
and believed it would only a few months earlier. It had failed
utterly in its two attempts to make effective use of its novel
radical ideas and its newly gained wartime strength. The Winnipeg strike, the great effort to win the class struggle by direct
action, had ended in a bloody defeat; the Independent Labour
Party, though it still remained in being, had not succeeded in
electing a single one of its candidates in the general election of
1917. Apparently labour, for the time being, had shot its bolt;
but this failure did not mean that post-war dissent had exhausted its force. The decline of militant labour was accompanied by the rise of another new political movement – the
Progressive Party, which came quickly into prominence as the
political expression of the agrarian protest movement in Ontario
and the west. Its origins, of course, went back to the first decade
of the century; but the war had temporarily deflected it from its
original aims. Organized agriculture accepted conscription and

supported the Union government – the Ontario farmers until the cancellation of exemptions and the westerners as long as the war lasted. Once it ended, however, they returned to the determined defence of their own class and regional interests and their own special needs. They had become convinced that the national policies of Canada benefited commerce and industry to the marked disadvantage of agriculture, and promoted urban growth at the expense of the countryside. Their belief that these rural needs and values could not be adequately served by either of the old political parties, and must be promoted by an independent political movement, grew out of a curious mixture of regret for the past and disappointment in its achievements and of hope and apprehension for the future. Rural Ontario, which looked back vainly and longingly on its old dominance of the province, had reached the almost desperate conclusion that it must make a final effort to repel the creeping inroads of industrialism and the depopulation of the countryside. The west, which had always felt certain that ultimately it would transform the whole character of Canadian political life, had at last decided that it must try to do by itself what it had repeatedly failed to accomplish in uneasy co-operation with eastern Canada.

Late in November 1918, barely a fortnight after the Armistice, the Canadian Council of Agriculture published a newly revised edition of its Farmers' Platform, which was promptly popularized under the challenging title of the 'New National Policy'. It demanded an immediate and substantial reduction of the tariff, complete free trade with Great Britain within five years, and reciprocal free trade with the United States along the lines of the Reciprocity Agreement of 1911. It was a collectivist document in so far as it advocated the nationalization of all types of transportation and communication; but it had nothing to say about labour, or social security and welfare. Its most unusual feature was a series of democratic political proposals – the initiative, the referendum, and the recall – which were designed to permit the constituencies to take part in the legislative process and to control their members of Parliament. As a whole, the New National Policy offered a broader, more 'national' platform than any of its predecessors; but, as before, the

162 ➤➤ CANADA'S FIRST CENTURY

farmers' tariff proposals formed the hard essential core of their programme. It soon became clear that the Union government could retain its western support only by tariff concessions; and in the spring of 1919, when the changes offered in Sir Thomas White's budget seemed quite inadequate, the break came. T. A. Crerar resigned his post as Minister of Agriculture in the coalition; and he and eight western Unionists voted against the government in the final budget division.

➤➤ IV ⬅⬅

ALL THIS CAUSED the Union government grave concern. It also roused the lively interest of the Liberal Party. And, by the spring of 1919, the Liberals were moving, in a cautious but purposeful fashion, towards the great reconciliation of their party. The winning of the war had made conscription – the main cause of their disruption – an issue of the past. The death of Laurier, who had personified the resistance to conscription, removed the most important obstacle to the return of the conscriptionist Liberals to their old allegiance. Immediately after the Armistice, Laurier had announced that a national convention – the first since 1893 – would be held the following year to determine the post-war programme of the Liberal Party. Now the convention would have an even more serious duty to perform: it would have to elect a new leader. And for this crucially important post there were really only two candidates, the veteran, W. S. Fielding, who had supported conscription but had not joined the Union government, and William Lyon Mackenzie King.

At forty-four – one year younger than Laurier had been when he took over the leadership of the party – King differed from his former chieftain in many important ways. Laurier belonged to Canada's colonial pre-industrial past; King had deliberately trained himself to play a great role in Canada's industrial future. An earnest, puritanical, sanctimonious young man, at once intensely self-centred and ostentatiously public-spirited, King was moved by the two driving ambitions, which he always contrived to reconcile, of serving suffering humanity and advancing his own career. A grandson of William Lyon Mackenzie, the excitable and highly incompetent 'little rebel' of 1837, King believed piously that it was his mission to carry forward his grandfather's great work for the common people. Almost from the start, he had had a political career in mind; he regarded his first post in the federal civil service mainly as a useful preparation for an active role in Liberal Party politics. The adroitness with which he ingratiated himself with the Governor General, Earl Grey, was only exceeded by the complacent effrontery with which he urged his promotion on Laurier. In 1909, Laurier finally gave him the portfolio of the new Department of Labour; but two years later the general election of 1911 brought defeat to the Liberals and cost King his seat in the Commons. It might have seemed that his triumphant progress towards the prime-ministership had been abruptly stopped; but temporary reverses never shook King's intimate conviction that divine providence was guiding his entire career towards some great and useful end. He bided his time. He would yet be recognized as the Messiah who would reign over modern Canada in the industrial age.

For the next half-dozen years, King lived mainly in the United States, where he busied himself setting up company unions for the Rockefellers, solving labour problems for other powerful American corporations, and writing his political and social testament, a diffuse dissertation called *Industry and Humanity*, in which a small number of unexceptionable general principles and moral platitudes were set out with a great show of earnest goodwill and scholarly authority. During all this time he had carefully kept in touch with Canadian politics; and, in 1917, despite discouragements and frequent misgivings, he decided to run, as a Laurier Liberal, in the general election. He was one of the very few prominent English-speaking Liberals who remained faithful to Laurier; and it was this conspicuous loyalty, as he shrewdly suspected at the time, which ensured his election as the leader of the Liberal Party in the August convention. He had comparative youth on his side, and something of a reputation as a social and industrial reformer with progressive views; but, apart from his distinction as Laurier's steadfast follower, he was almost unknown to the delegates. Their ignorance of his qualities and defects hardly mattered. He personified the resistance to conscription. He was Laurier's avenger. He was surely Laurier's only legitimate successor. And by a well-organized manoeuvre, in which King's French-Canadian supporters, if not King himself, must have taken an active part, the convention was led to believe that Laurier himself had intended King to succeed him. In fact, Lady Laurier had informed several prominent Liberals, including King, that her husband would have preferred to have Fielding follow him as leader. King flatly refused to believe this incredible report. He *knew* it was Sir Wilfrid's wish that he should have the succession! He believed, too, that a Higher Power even than Sir Wilfrid had providentially arranged his inheritance of the leadership. 'Look ye who doubt, and say whether or not ye believe there is a God who rules the world.' Such was the appropriate biblical message for the 7th of August, the day of the election, in King's faithful companion and guide, *Daily Strength for Daily Needs*. King himself never doubted. He won on the third ballot by the small majority of thirty-eight in a vote of over 900. How fully had his faith been justified!

The other great work of the convention was the framing of a new Liberal platform for the post-war world. The drafting committees were very conscious of the social and political unrest that had been mounting steadily ever since the Armistice. They were much less interested in Liberal tradition than in popular contemporary appeal. The resolution on the tariff reproduced, in all essentials, the proposals which had been put forward in the Farmers' Platform, the New National Policy of the previous autumn; and the long, detailed resolution on labour, which was plainly King's handiwork, promised a new code for industry, as well as unemployment insurance, old-age pensions, and the other benefits of the future welfare state. Obviously the new Liberal programme was aimed in large part at the farmer and labour protest groups; but there were complicating circumstances which made the appeal sound less than convincing. Everybody was aware that the tariff resolution had met serious opposition in the convention, and that Mackenzie King owed

'*The Real Emergency*'
"Borden's position was acutely difficult. He was pulled this way and that by two diametrically opposed divisions of his party."

Henri Bourassa by J. H. Lemay
"Independence for Canada was the last thing Bourassa really wanted. His defiant nationalist gestures barely concealed a deep feeling of insecurity and an instinctive sense of dependence."

'Looking Our Way': August 1911
"The Reciprocity Agreement of 1911 and the proposal of Unrestricted Reciprocity
in 1891 both implied an untried and ambiguous economic relationship with the
United States."

'Don't Be Scared': 1914
"The real truth was, of course, that Canada was not 'ready' at all."

'How Laurier Leads Quebec': 1917 election
"The Nationalists ran no independent candidates and, in effect, the Laurier Liberals identified themselves with the Nationalist cause."

Imperial War Conference, May 1, 1917
Front row, left to right: Arthur Henderson, Viscount Milner, Lord Curzon, Andrew Bonar Law, David Lloyd George, Sir Robert Borden, W. F. Massey (Prime Minister of New Zealand), J. C. Smuts (Minister for Defence, Union of South Africa).

Borden addressing Canadian troops, July 1918
"The Canadian contribution had been assured. The last great German offensive had failed and the triumph of the allied arms seemed certain."

Winnipeg riots, June 21, 1919
". . . mounted police galloped down Main Street with drawn pistols and, in two charges, broke up the crowd and ended all resistance."

Imperial Conference, 1926: Ernest Lapointe, Mackenzie King, Vincent Massey, Peter Larkin (Canadian High Commissioner in London)
"The high degree of . . . self-satisfaction became obvious . . . when King arrived in London for his second Imperial Conference."

Arthur Meighen
'. . . nothing could seriously disturb his firm belief that most of humanity's problems could be solved by hard work and plain living."

R. B. Bennett
". . . he never lost the simple tastes, the severe moral standards, and the evangelical fervour of his Methodist upbringing . . . his impressive presence radiated the confidence of wealth, professional success, and political power."

The depression
". . . the humiliated and hopeless crowds of unemployed in the cities."

A 'Bennett Buggy' containing Mackenzie King (right), Saskatchewan 1934
". . . steadily depreciating equipment . . ."

Mitchell Hepburn and Maurice Duplessis, 1937
'It was only natural that Duplessis of Quebec and Hepburn of Ontario should become close friends and joint enemies of King and his Royal Commission on Dominion-Provincial Relations."

'Adrift on a Stormy Sea'
"Late in November 1937, the Royal Commission set out to conduct a series of public hearings across the country. One by one, its three mortal enemies, Aberhart, Hepburn, and Duplessis, declared their uncompromising opposition."

Prime Minister King with the German foreign minister,
Baron von Neurath, 1937
"At that time 'appeasement' was used, not ironically and
pejoratively, but sincerely and approvingly, to indicate a
general but definite approach to European politics. . . . No
contemporary politician held this view more strongly or clung
to it more tenaciously than Mackenzie King."

his election as leader to the support of the Quebec delegates, the most conservative, if not reactionary, division of the Liberal Party.

Rural Ontario and the west had very good reasons for suspecting that the Liberals, once safely in power, would never carry out their low tariff policy; and the farmers' movement, despite the blandishments of the Liberal convention, continued confidently on its separate way, quite unconnected with either of the old parties and opposed to both. Its first electoral success came unexpectedly in Ontario. There the Independent Labour Party, which had maintained its wartime organization, joined the United Farmers of Ontario in their attack on the Conservative provincial government. In the provincial general election of October 1919, the U.F.O. emerged as the strongest single group; and, with the help of a dozen Labour members and a few Independents, it formed a government with E. C. Drury as Premier. In January 1920, a conference at Winnipeg, summoned by the Canadian Council of Agriculture, established the National Progressive Party; and late in February, immediately after the session opened, the small agrarian representation in the House of Commons adopted the same title and elected T. A. Crerar as their parliamentary leader.

->>> V «-

CONFRONTED by a militant farmers' group and a reorganized Liberal Party, the Union government continued, somewhat uncertainly, on its way. The future looked dark. The existing situation was extremely puzzling. The natural inclination of the Unionists was to move cautiously forward along familiar lines, to complete important tasks already undertaken, and to wind up the special governmental activities of four years of war. Most of the wartime economic controls were abandoned; but the continuance of the inflation and the unsettlement of the overseas grain markets seemed to require at least another year of the Wheat Board's control, and the establishment of a Board of Commerce with price-fixing powers. In September 1919, at the opening of the special session of Parliament, the Peace Treaty and the Covenant of the League of Nations – the triumphant rewards of four years of endeavour – were presented for approval. Canada's new role in the Commonwealth and her recognized status in the new world order of the League were, in Borden's view, two of the greatest achievements of his government; but, although the Treaty and the Covenant were approved without a division, the debate revealed a disturbing amount of confusion and uncertainty about Canada's position, and fear for her future in a dangerous world. An obstinately lingering colonial feeling and a growing sense of North American isolation combined to revive all the old apprehensions of the perils involved in either a co-operative Empire or an international security system. Canada, Liberal speakers kept on insisting, was not yet a sovereign nation, despite Borden's claim; as a subordinate part of the British Empire, she had still no standing in international law; and her acceptance of the Covenant would simply saddle her with all the responsibilities of nationhood before she had fully gained its powers and privileges.

The second major measure of the special autumn session of 1919 was the nationalization of the Grand Trunk and the Grand Trunk Pacific railways. The two systems were inseparably connected, for not only had the Grand Trunk Pacific been planned as an extension of the Grand Trunk Railway, but also the Grand Trunk Railway had advanced its subsidiary large sums of money and guaranteed a considerable part of its bonded indebtedness. For three years, pending a final settlement, the Borden cabinet had gone on paying an advance to keep the Grand Trunk Pacific going; but, in January 1918, the new Union government decided that this apparently endless expenditure of public money must stop, and that a suitable final settlement could only be the nationalization of both the Grand Trunk and the Grand Trunk Pacific. The justification for this decision lay in the undoubted fact that the Grand Trunk Pacific was a bankrupt speculation which would soon bring about its parent's insolvency and ruin; but the government's case for the nationalization of both railways was strengthened by the equally obvious fact that both were essential to a successful national system. Borden now proposed that the Canadian government would take over the Grand Trunk Railway and all its subsidiaries, assume all their liabilities and fixed charges, and in addition pay an annuity for the benefit of the shareholders. The officers of Grand Trunk fondly imagined that they could go on quarrelling indefinitely with Borden and Meighen over the amount of this annuity; but Borden and Meighen, tiring of this interminable argument, ended it abruptly by the simple method of withholding all further financial aid. On the 1st of February, 1919, the Grand Trunk Pacific defaulted on one of its debenture payments; one week later, the government placed it in receivership under the War Measures Act; and, early in November, the Grand Trunk Acquisition Bill, which provided for the arbitration of the shareholders' equity, became law. Its opponents, the determined adversaries of public ownership, were the Quebec Liberal M.P.s, and, outside Parliament, the press and the big corporations of Montreal, including, of course, the Canadian Pacific Railway. On the issue of railway nationalization, the western agrarian members voted with the government, but for other purposes their support was gone. And now the loss of Quebec, both French-speaking and English-speaking, was confirmed.

In addition, in the very near future, the Unionists were likely to lose their wartime leader, Sir Robert Borden. The anxieties of office had plainly worn Borden out, but the question of the leadership was postponed in the vain hope that he might recover; and it was not until July 1920 that he finally resigned. Who was to succeed him? If it had been left to the back-benchers at Ottawa to decide, their first choice unquestionably would have been Arthur Meighen. Meighen's obvious intellectual ability, his enormous capacity for hard work, his accomplished skill as a debater were only too obvious in the Commons; and back-bench Conservative and Unionist members had often watched with admiration and delight the easy, masterly fashion in which he presented a complicated government bill, or tore an opposition argument into meaningless tatters, or reduced a quaking Liberal member to inarticulate fury. His talents had, in fact, made him a commanding figure in the

House, and a monopolizing force in the Union government. But this very pre-eminence, which in the eyes of the back-benchers seemed to justify his promotion to the leadership, was viewed with jealous doubts and questionings by his colleagues in the cabinet. Their genuine fear that Meighen would hope-lessly alienate Quebec gave strength and substance to their natural feelings of resentment. If Sir Thomas White, the affable former Liberal, who had been Borden's Minister of Finance, could have been persuaded to accept the leadership, they would much have preferred him. But White absolutely refused to return to public life. Reluctantly, the ministers agreed to serve under Meighen.

It was an inevitable and yet, in some ways, an unfortunate choice. Meighen had been born on a farm in south-western Ontario, of Ulster Presbyterian stock. His was a brilliant intelli-gence, but it never completely freed him from the strong clutch of his origins. Tall, slight, austere, severely simple in his tastes, and endlessly hard-working, he kept to the end the mental out-look of his farming boyhood, with all its sharp clarity and some of its narrow limitations. Nobody believed more firmly than he that man is a rational animal whose conduct should be governed by reason; no political career was ever based more completely on the assumption that the electorate could be won only by solid evidence and logical argument. His intellectual honesty was unqualified; his logical grasp of a difficult practical subject was masterly. But it was within a comparatively narrow range of familiar, concrete issues that the strength of his critical and analytical mind was most clearly revealed. He had never as-sumed that the Conservative policies of the nineteenth century were a sufficient answer to the problems of the twentieth. As the principal author of the Canadian National Railways, he was strongly committed to state ownership; he had been a member of the wartime governments which had regulated the national economy and marketed the nation's wheat. But he still believed that the tariff was the central issue in Canadian politics. He regarded the post-war intellectual ferment with old-fashioned disapproval. In his view, the theorists and idealists who saw the war as a prelude to a better world and a richer life were simply 'chasing rainbows'. There was contempt in his attitude to the abstract speculations of universities; and nothing could seriously disturb his firm belief that most of humanity's problems could be solved by hard work and plain living.

⟶⟫⟫ VI ⟪⟪⟵

ONE OF THE twentieth-century Conservative policies that Meighen was ready to continue was Borden's plan for a co-operative Empire-Commonwealth, with a common front in defence and foreign affairs. Already, before Borden's retirement, another significant step had been taken to bring this scheme into practical operation. In May 1920, it was announced, in both Ottawa and London, that Canada would appoint her own diplomatic representative in Washington. This new external officer – the first to be named since the appointment of the Canadian High Commissioner in London forty years earlier – was to be established physically in the British embassy in Washington, and, during the ambassador's absence, he was to act on his behalf concerning British affairs. But his main business was the independent conduct of all Canadian relations with the United States. He was to act on instructions from the Canadian government; but this was by no means meant to imply that the policies he pursued would be separate from, or at variance with, those of Great Britain. It was explicitly stated in the announcement that the new appointment did not denote any departure from the diplomatic unity of the Empire.

But how was the diplomatic unity of the Empire to be maintained? In 1918 the Imperial War Cabinet had made arrangements for more rapid communication between Great Britain and the Dominions; but the general question of the reconstitution of the new Empire-Commonwealth had been postponed until after the peace. Nobody was in a hurry to take up this formidable task; and, in June 1921, when the Dominions' Prime Ministers finally assembled again in London, their thoughts were running less on constitutional generalities and much more on particular problems and solutions. The constitutional conference on which Borden had set his heart was put off indefinitely; and instead the Prime Ministers plunged into a practical discussion of how the means of communication among the governments of the Empire could be improved and agreement on foreign policy achieved. Here Meighen was in his element, and he took the initiative. He suggested that imperial conferences ought to be as nearly continuous as possible, and certainly more frequent than before the war. He admitted the final constitutional responsibility of the United Kingdom in the making of imperial foreign policy; but he argued forcefully that, in any aspect of policy in which a Dominion was vitally interested, its opinion ought to be given special weight, and, indeed, accepted as decisive.

As usual, Meighen was talking, not in abstract, general terms, but with a concrete and particular issue in mind. The aspect of imperial foreign policy which was of paramount concern for him was the Empire's relations with the United States; and the particular problem that bothered him at the moment was the renewal of the Anglo-Japanese alliance. This alliance, designed to protect British and Japanese interests in India and the Far East, had been first negotiated in 1902, when Russia seemed to be the most serious threat to those interests, and revised in 1905, when Germany had taken Russia's place as the principal danger to the far-eastern *status quo*. Since then, the menace from both of these countries had vanished; and the United States had become an important Pacific power, with a growing tendency to regard Japan and Japanese interests with suspicion and dislike. It was inevitable that the United States would criticize and resent the renewal of the Anglo-Japanese treaty; and it was only too possible that she, and her new far-eastern friend, China, would draw closer in opposition to what they both would regard as an attempt to perpetrate an Anglo-Japanese hegemony in the Far East.

Meighen was very conscious of the strength of this American disapproval. He was convinced that Canada would suffer most from any serious breach between the British Empire and the United States; and he believed accordingly that here was an aspect of imperial foreign policy in which Canadian opinion ought to be conclusive. A completely new state of affairs, he told the Prime Ministers, had arisen in the Far East and must be recognized. Great Britain should give up the Anglo-Japanese alliance, and press instead for a multilateral agreement among the principal powers in the Pacific and the Far East, including China and the United States. Gradually, against the vociferous opposition of W. M. Hughes of Australia, Meighen won the other Prime Ministers over to his point of view; and in the end it was agreed that Great Britain should propose a general conference on Pacific affairs, and only if that failed would the alliance with Japan be renewed. This British proposal coincided nearly enough with the American interest in an international agreement for the limitation of armaments; and the result was the Washington Conference of November 1921.

Meighen had made a reality of Borden's ideal of the co-operative Empire-Commonwealth. He had exercised a decisive influence upon an aspect of imperial policy which was of paramount importance to Canada. It was perhaps the greatest success of his brief prime-ministership; and it was ironical that it had been achieved in the realm of external relations in which he was obviously a novice. In domestic politics, where he could claim to be a seasoned veteran, the whole trend of events was running strongly against him; and he had not been back in Canada very long before he realized that his government could not face another session of the existing Parliament and that an election would have to be held before the year was out. Some of his advisers suggested that the party needed bold, new policies and that he must look, not to the past, but to the future. He paid little attention to this advice. The radical innovator in imperial affairs became the arch-conservative of Canadian politics. His gospel was the gospel of hard work, 'old high standards of living and character', and no 'isms' or theories. His chief policy – virtually his only policy – was the defence of the protective system. He tried to make the tariff the principal issue of the election in the hope that the protectionist Liberals, frightened by the free-trade views of Crerar and Mackenzie King, would join with the Conservatives to save the National Policy.

This hope proved to be completely vain. Meighen's simple strategy miscarried. It miscarried in part because Mackenzie King, who realized just as well as Meighen how seriously the tariff could divide the Liberals, simply refused to accept it as the principal issue of the campaign. Instead, he announced in grandiloquent tones that the real issue was Meighen and Meighen's government. He presented himself as the godlike avenger of the Canadian people's wrongs; he worked himself into a lather of moral indignation over the iniquities and abominations of the Unionist cabinet; he denounced Meighen and his colleagues as a corrupt, extravagant, militaristic, and autocratic government, which had ruled by order in council and in defiance of Parliament. These vague, grandiose charges diverted public attention from Meighen's practical issue; and his strategy, even where it had a chance to operate, failed to produce the effects for which he had hoped. His insistence on the tariff lost him the west and did not win Quebec. In Quebec as a whole, Meighen was hated as the principal author of conscription. In Montreal he was angrily regarded as the architect of the Canadian National Railways and the opponent of the Canadian Pacific Railway and St. James Street finance. The 'big interests', which Mackenzie King loved to identify with the Conservative Party, were solidly Liberal in Montreal; and the French-Canadian electorate was exhorted, in a campaign of deliberate vilification unique in Canadian history, to stamp Meighen out of political existence.

The campaign very nearly succeeded. In the general election of December 1921, the Conservatives won only fifty seats, the lowest number to which the party had ever been reduced since Confederation. The Liberals took a total of 117 seats; and there were sixty-four Progressives, three Labour members, and one Independent.

CHAPTER NINE

The Mackenzie King Millennium

THE HALF-DOZEN YEARS that followed the general election of 1921 were years of increasing spiritual and political deflation, and of rising material prosperity. Like other North Americans and West Europeans, the Canadians had conceived of the war as a struggle for the future of mankind; they had viewed victory as the necessary prelude to a better world and a richer life. Henceforward, they hoped and believed, the concept of the national interest would have a different and a far more ample meaning. As a result, the historic national policies had come under attack; the old national political parties – first the Liberals and then the Conservatives – had gone down to defeat and ruin; and for a while it seemed likely that new political parties, more appropriate vehicles for the ideals of a new age, would take their place. This revolutionary movement reached its climax in 1921, just at the moment when the inflationary wartime boom finally collapsed. The beginning of the brief post-war depression coincided with the defeat of the Conservatives in the general election. Then, slowly at first, but with increasing feebleness and uncertainty, the current of political and social dissent began to lose its force and direction. The dreams and visions of wartime faded away in the grey morning of familiar activities. The 'fit country for heroes to live in' receded indefinitely into the future; and, as it vanished over the horizon, a prosaic but comfortable sense of affluence gradually took its place.

Most appropriately, Mackenzie King became the presiding genius of this new era in Canadian history. He could hardly

173

be called its author, but he personified its spirit better than anybody else could possibly have done. At forty-seven, a short, stoutish man, with a torso like a barrel, and already, when in full voice, an audible wheeze, King had outgrown the beliefs of his humanitarian and reformist youth, but clung sentimentally to their vocabulary. At one and the same time, he could talk the elevated language of wartime idealism and practise the mean devices of post-war realpolitik. His verbal currency was invariably tendered in the highest denominations; but in practical politics he always dealt in very small change. He dignified ordinary and commonplace actions with sanctimonious moralizing; he loved to justify doubtful conduct by unimpeachable moral principles; he extolled the free and independent judgment of the people, and, in fact, relied on the calculated manoeuvres of partisanship. He made both big words and small deeds serve his turn. There was at once more in him than met the eye, and a great deal less than filled the ear.

The making of Mackenzie King's first cabinet was a brilliant illustration of the practical application of his political principles. He confided to his brother that 'the people' were his only real concern and that he was not content to rely upon 'the big and powerful interests of the country'. In the new House of Commons, with its curious balance of forces, this pious aspiration was difficult to carry out. The sixty-five Progressives from Ontario and the west, who presumably stood for 'the people', did no more than equal the sixty-five Quebec Liberals, who certainly included among their number some choice representatives of 'the big and powerful interests of the country'. King had usually treated the Progressives in a fatherly fashion as Liberals in a hurry, and he fully intended, in the end, to bring them back into a united party; but, at the moment, he needed them far less than he needed the Quebec reactionaries. Over one-half of his total following of 117 members – only one fewer than a majority of the House – was made up of the Quebec Liberals; and, if his own party remained united and steadfast in its allegiance, he might only occasionally need Progressive support. Inevitably, his devotion to 'the people' was modified by a sense of his very real dependence on 'the big and powerful interests'. He told the Progressive leaders that there could be a 'coalescence', but no formal 'coalition' of parties, and that they and their friends could be offered no more than three places in the cabinet. No definite and precise commitments could be made about policy.

In the end, the Progressive leaders declined King's offer; but only after a prolonged argument within their party which revealed much of its character and limitations. Obviously the Progressives had not done as well in the general election as they had hoped. With sixty-five seats instead of the seventy-five which some observers had predicted, they just failed to dominate the House of Commons; and, what was equally important, their full strength was weakened by serious internal divisions. Within the Progressive movement as a whole there were two separate groups, each with its own leaders, and its own distinct conception of the meaning and purpose of Progressivism. The first, a 'Manitoban' group led by Crerar, Hudson, and Drury, were essentially reformers; the second, an 'Albertan' division, of which J. C. Morrison of Ontario and H. W. Wood of Alberta were the principal spokesmen, were radicals if not revolutionaries. Wood, Morrison, and their followers hoped to rid the country of the two-party system and to replace it with group government based on the twin principles of occupational representation and constituency autonomy. Crerar, Hudson, Drury, and their followers wished not to destroy but to revitalize the old party system; they hoped for a new reformed party, in which all the progressive forces in the country would find a place, and from which 'the big and powerful interests' would be excluded. It was a vague and general aim which might be attained through the rise of the new Progressive Party to truly national proportions. But it might equally well be realized by the reforms of the existing Liberal Party, a reform brought about by the expulsion of its protectionist elements in Ontario and Quebec, and their replacement by the progressive forces of the west.

The 'Manitobans' and the 'Albertans' could unite in denouncing tariffs and high freight rates. They were equally disinclined, though for very different reasons, to take on the role of official opposition in the House of Commons. The Manitoba moderates, who were still attracted by the idea of a coalition with the reforming Liberals, could scarcely put themselves in formal opposition to Mackenzie King; and the Albertan radicals, who believed in the complete independence of each individual member of Parliament, looked on the whole elaborate business of parliamentary parties, caucuses, and whips as a denial of true democracy. The radicals could not possibly realize their ideal of group government; but they succeeded only too well in preventing Crerar and his moderates from coming to some arrangement with the Liberals; and their devotion to the doctrine of the absolute autonomy of the individual member precluded that disciplined unity of action by which alone the Progressive Party as a whole could have held the balance of power in the House. Rapidly the party sank deeper and deeper into the mire of frustration and futility. Two more attempts to bring Liberals and Progressives together failed during the summer and autumn of 1922; and by this time Crerar had had enough. He resigned the leadership.

→»» II «←

As the fortunes of the Progressive Party declined, the first signs of an economic recovery became apparent. The post-war slump was to be relatively brief, but its initial impact was sudden and shattering. In 1921 the vast wartime expansion of credit and the all too frequently uncontrolled inflation ended in a general liquidation. The wartime boom collapsed, and commodity prices moved steeply downwards. Canada's export specialties were particularly hard hit; in two years, the price of wheat declined by nearly 45 per cent and Canadian export prices in general were down by 40 per cent. The demand for Canadian products abroad fell off; and the value of trade to the United States, where new prohibitive duties had been imposed on the import of livestock and meats, dropped disastrously by over 40 per cent from 1920 to 1921. The west, which had come to concentrate so heavily upon the production of wheat, and the Atlantic provinces, which had to accustom themselves to the total stoppage of war orders, suffered more seriously than other parts of the nation; but the decline of income on the prairies and of purchasing power in the Maritime provinces had its inevitable effect upon central Canadian industry. The demand for consumer goods was sharply curtailed; and in 1920-22 the cities and towns of Ontario and Quebec were troubled by unemployment.

Then, in 1923, the swing upward was resumed once more, and the nation soon found itself deeply involved in that almost fabulous episode in the economic history of western Europe and the Americas, the great boom of the 1920s. For Canada these half-dozen rich, exciting years had their own special significance. In the end they were to lead to a reckless, speculative abandonment which was new and strange in Canadian experience; but, for some time, returning prosperity developed in the accustomed Canadian fashion and ran along very familiar lines. At first, all the traditional, wholesome ingredients of Canadian economic success appeared to be present in reassuring abundance, just as they had been in that model period of national prosperity, the Laurier boom, and just as the Fathers of Confederation would have been overjoyed to see them. Export prices were moving up again, while shipping and railway freight rates, interest charges, and prices of manufactured goods had either remained stationary or had dropped. Wheat, the golden hoard which had made Canada's fortunes two decades earlier, was once again endowing the whole nation with its riches. During the peak years of the 1920s the annual exports of wheat and flour exceeded by a wide margin the highest levels attained during the war; and Canada's share of the world wheat market was over three times what it had been at the end of the Laurier boom. Immigration had started up again, in numbers which were encouraging, though, of course, they could not rival the huge totals of the five pre-war years; and Canadian, British, and American capital was once more pouring into a wide variety of construction projects.

On the surface, the new boom bore a remarkable and reassuring resemblance to the old. Yet it differed from the experience of the past, in ways which were significant for the future. The continued primacy of wheat seemed assured; but a few ominous signs of weakness were beginning to appear in its solid foundations. European agriculture, after a long period of ruin and desolation, was gradually regaining its old productivity, and European governments, anxious to hasten its recovery, began to give it protection against the import of foreign foodstuffs. Beginning in 1925, Italy, Germany, Austria, and Czechoslovakia all imposed high duties on imported cereals. In 1925, the price of No. 1 Northern wheat, after a splendid ascent from the low point of the brief post-war depression, began to flatten out, slump, and then slide slowly downwards. In 1929, with exports of 407,000,000 bushels, more than 40 per cent of the world's trade in grain, Canada was undoubtedly the pre-eminent exporter of wheat; but, despite the great rejoicings over the bumper crop of 1928, the awkward, depressing fact remained that there was an unsold carry-over of more than 100,000,000 bushels.

In the 1920s, as in the first decade of the century, a second principal feature of the economic upswing was the investment boom. Both periods saw the same huge capital expenditures on construction, machinery, and equipment; but the total for the third decade of the century, over $6 billion, was higher than that for the first, and, what was still more significant, its distribution was very different. Railways – particularly western branch lines – canals, and harbours, those three standard expressions of Canada's original national policies, profited, of course, from this vast new outlay of funds, though relatively less than during the Laurier prosperity; and once again money was expended on housing, public buildings, and manufacturing plant and equipment in very much the same lavish way as it had been in the first decade of the century. All these expenditures ran along very familiar lines; but here the resemblance to the past ended. In the new period, very little was invested in those traditional instruments of advancing settlements, farm buildings, farm equipment, and livestock; but, on the other hand, capital was pouring into the pulp and paper mills, the metal smelters and refineries which were busy producing the newsprint, woodpulp, and base metals – nickel, copper, lead, and zinc – the new twentieth-century staple products which were rapidly gaining a place of central importance in Canada's export trade.

The costly promotion of the new staple industries was one major feature of the investment boom of the 1920s; but it was marked with equal emphasis by the huge capital outlays required for the development of the new kinds of energy, and the new forms of transport and communication. The telephone, the automobile, electric light, and electric power were signs, which everybody knew and appreciated, of the easy and expansive life of the 1920s; and everybody assumed that the great sums necessary to provide them, and to increase their use and enjoyment, must, and would, be expended by government and private enterprise. The nearly 530,000 new telephones that were installed during the 1920s required a capital expenditure of $150 million; and, in the same decade, the majestic total of $607 million was invested in new hydro-electric power installations. The number of motor vehicles registered in Canada had quadrupled in the five years from 1915 to 1920, and tripled again in the decade from 1920 to 1930. In 1930, 1,232,500 passenger cars and trucks were running about the streets and roads of Canada; and this vast and continuously moving transport army had already compelled a radical and extremely expensive transformation of the extent and character of the nation's highways. Municipalities and provinces had, among them, spent nearly $380 million on highways during the 1920s.

The great expansion of the 1920s effected a significant change in the orientation of the Canadian economy and in the direction of its development. Laurier prosperity had been firmly based on the east-west axis, both transcontinental and transatlantic, the main line of Canada's future as the Fathers of Confederation had conceived it. Western agriculture had expanded to provide British and foreign markets with wheat and flour; eastern and central Canadian industry had developed in order to serve the prairie provinces with manufactured goods. In an endless variety of ways, almost the whole of Canada had taken part in the successful settlement of the west. Western settlement had been the first aim of the Fathers of Confederation, the greatest of all national enterprises. But now, at last, it was an accomplished fact; and, for the new generation of enterprisers, the great economic attractions of the 1920s lay not in the west but in the north, in the water power, minerals, and pulpwood forests of the Precambrian Shield. The empty western plains had been the patrimony of the entire Canadian people; but the lion's share of the riches of the Precambrian Shield belonged to Ontario and Quebec, and the much smaller remainder to Manitoba. The Maritime provinces, which had had their fair share of the profits of western expansion and wartime construction, failed, unlike the rest of Canada, to recover from the brief post-war slump and subsided into a seemingly chronic depression. British Columbia, which had before been so closely associated with the national transcontinental system, found, through the opening of the Panama Canal, a new and cheaper trade route to world markets and a new prosperity for her mines and lumber industry.

The trend of economic exploitation had veered sharply from west to north; the direction of export trade was shifting more slowly, but with growing conviction, from east to south. During the years of Laurier prosperity, the value of exports to the United Kingdom had exceeded the value of exports to the United States by a substantial margin, amounting to as much as 100 per cent in the first years of the century, and to 50 per cent or more thereafter. Throughout the great economic expansion of wartime, trade to Great Britain retained and, in 1916-17, enormously increased its old superiority. But meanwhile exports to the United States had been steadily growing; and in 1920, for the first time in decades, their total value exceeded that of exports to the United Kingdom. For the next five years, the two markets, British and American, were almost equally valuable to Canadian exporters; but after 1925, total export values began to show, with increasing emphasis, the evidently superior attractions of trade to the Republic. Canadians were finding new and profitable sales openings in the United States; and, at the same time, Americans were discovering new and promising opportunities for investment in Canada.

During the decade 1920-1930, about $2.5 billion of American money was invested in Canadian enterprises. The American stake in the Canadian economy was steadily increasing, just as the British was steadily declining. In 1900, British investment had amounted to 85 per cent, and American to only 14 per cent, of all non-resident capital invested in Canada. Thirty years later the position, though not reversed, had been radically altered. British investment had declined to 36 per cent of the whole; American had risen to 61 per cent.

This shift in relative proportions was striking; but equally significant was the fundamental difference between British and American investment. British investors had put their money mainly into Canadian railway, industrial, and government bonds; and Canadians had used these funds to promote independent Canadian enterprises. American entrepreneurs, in sharp contrast, had concentrated on direct investment, and had thus already acquired ownership or control of a large number of Canadian businesses. The Canadians owed debts to the British; to the Americans they had conceded an ever-increasing equity in Canada. The basic principle of the nineteenth-century British Empire, in economics as well as in politics, had been devolution – the encouragement of local initiative and the grant of local autonomy. The hard foundation of the twentieth-century American empire was to be centralized control.

⇢⟫ III ⟪⟵

THE GROWING IMPORTANCE of Canada's North American environment as a force in her development as a nation was a significant feature of the decade of the 1920s. It was plainly revealed, not only in the increasing concentration on American markets and the increasing dependence on American capital, but also, and equally, in a declining concern for the world beyond the limits of the North American continent. Borden had won for Canada a voice in Commonwealth policy and a place in the League of Nations; but the value of these gains depended almost wholly upon the extent to which the

Canadian government was prepared to make use of them. Membership in the League would be almost meaningless unless Canada took its new international role seriously; and an effective co-operative Commonwealth could be maintained only if both Canada and Great Britain continued to believe in it, to respect its conventions, and keep up its customary practices. None of these things happened. In England, the post-war governments neglected the new methods of imperial communication and consultation; and, in Canada, control of external affairs fell into the hands of William Lyon Mackenzie King, a man who was completely indifferent to the League, and hostile to the very idea of a common imperial foreign policy. Lloyd George and Winston Churchill may have been forgetful or contemptuous of the new machinery of Empire; but King hated it.

King's career anticipated and exemplified, to a remarkable degree, Canada's new orientation to world affairs. In 1919, when he took over the leadership of the Liberal Party, he was essentially a North American, rather than a Canadian, citizen. More of his life had, of course, been spent in Canada than in the United States; but he had gained a very significant part of his training and adult experience in the Republic. After he had obtained his bachelor's degree at the University of Toronto, he might, with the aid of a fellowship, have taken up graduate studies there; but he preferred to go on to the University of Chicago and then to Harvard. In August 1914, when thousands of Canadians, many his own contemporaries, were volunteering for service overseas in the Canadian Expeditionary Force, King was setting out on what proved to be five years of extremely interesting and highly lucrative work as an adviser in labour relations to the Rockefeller Corporation and other large American firms. He had acquired an expert knowledge of American capitalist enterprise and a sympathetic interest in American industrial society. His long absences from Canada, his almost total absorption in American problems, confirmed his detachment from England as well as from Europe. Sir Wilfrid Laurier's isolationist political legacy could not have descended to a more appropriate heir.

Laurier had bravely resisted Joseph Chamberlain's sinister attempt to create a new 'centralized' imperial system. King was certain to continue Laurier's imperial policy; but his North American training and experience naturally inclined him to push it one important stage further. Laurier, a neo-colonial to the last, had accepted the legal liabilities of membership in the Empire-Commonwealth. He had argued, it was true, that Canada had no obligation to participate actively in all imperial wars; but he had not tried to exempt her from any of the commitments of imperial foreign policy. What Laurier had never attempted, King now set out to do. The co-operative Commonwealth of wartime, which in his eyes was simply a revival of the old, hateful 'imperial centralization', must be ended as quickly as possible, and Canada must withdraw from any new commitments that Great Britain might accept in the post-war world.

Towards the League of Nations, King's attitude was outwardly more deferential and sympathetic, but, at bottom, equally negative. His criticism of the League cut much deeper than Borden's. Borden had objected to the sweeping guarantees of Article X of the Covenant; but he had believed firmly in the idea of international organization and collective security. King had no confidence in the League's fundamental purposes and principles; and he could not escape the fear that Canada's membership would sooner or later involve her in dangerous foreign complications. It was impossible, of course, publicly to withdraw from the League; that would create a scandal, and scandal must be avoided. But the League could be – and was – treated with indifference and neglect, and its obligations explained away. As for the hated 'imperial centralization' in foreign affairs, more drastic action would probably be required. And King waited for an opportunity to declare himself.

The test case came suddenly and without warning. The Treaty of Sèvres, to which Canada, as well as Great Britain and the other allied powers, was a party, had provided for a demilitarized zone on both sides of the Dardanelles and the Bosporus. In September 1922, this strip was suddenly threatened at Chanak in Asia Minor by the forces of the nationalist

Turkish leader, Mustapha Kemal Pasha; and Great Britain determined to uphold the Treaty and defend the Straits, even if she had to do it alone. Churchill cabled the Dominion governments inquiring whether they 'wish to associate themselves with the action we are taking and whether they would desire to be represented by a contingent'. There had been no previous official consultation about the Near East crisis, although, of course, the papers were full of it. Churchill's cable was sent in the old-fashioned roundabout way, through the Governor General; and, before it reached King, the news of its dispatch had been made public by the British government in a strongly propagandist press release. King was justifiably annoyed by this exhibition of mingled carelessness and presumption; but his reproach that he had not been kept informed and consulted about British policy was spurious. He did not want to be consulted. Like Laurier, he believed that consultation involved the consultant in responsibility. He simply wished to keep Canada out of the trouble in the Near East; and the fact that she was a signatory of the Treaty of Sèvres, and presumably ought to feel some concern about the violation of its terms, meant nothing whatever to him. He could not, of course, answer Churchill's inquiry with a blunt refusal. Instead, he temporized. Parliament, he replied, could alone sanction the sending of a contingent, and he would be glad to have further information in order to decide whether Parliament should be called.

This pointed withdrawal from a collective commitment in the Near East represented the negative side of King's pragmatic approach to a separate Canadian foreign policy. The positive aspect appeared soon after in the signing of the Halibut Treaty, which provided for the regulation of the Halibut Fishery in the North Pacific. By this time the legal limitations on Canada's right to negotiate, sign, and ratify her own treaties had become slight; and the chief remaining tokens of her formal inferiority in international law lay in the fact that Great Britain, not Canada, appeared as the contracting party in the title of a treaty, and that the signature of a British as well as of a Canadian representative was required. King determined that these practices must now be changed. The Halibut Treaty, he argued, did not affect any British or imperial interest; and Great Britain therefore should not appear as a contracting party in its preamble, or participate in its signature. King's aim was clear enough; but he approached it in a characteristically dilatory, evasive, and mystifying fashion. In the end he got most of what he wanted. The preamble of the Treaty simply declared its purpose without any mention of contracting powers; and Ernest Lapointe, who had negotiated it, signed alone. But Sir Auckland Geddes, the British Ambassador to Washington, was not made aware, until almost the last moment, that his signature was not wanted; and, in his understandable annoyance, he treated Lapointe with petulant rudeness.

In the autumn of 1923 when Mackenzie King arrived in London for his first Imperial Conference, the point had been reached, he felt, when some general statement of his position was necessary. His diplomatic successes of the previous twelve months had encouraged him; and a major change in the staff of the Department of External Affairs had provided expert and sympathetic support for his views. In 1921, when King took office, the most important senior official in the Department had been its legal adviser, Loring C. Christie. Christie was an extremely able man; but he had been closely associated with Borden and Meighen in the development of the common imperial policy, and he was naturally antipathetic to the separatist and isolationist bias of King's approach to foreign affairs. In such an important matter, King had no use for civil servants with opinions of their own; and Christie was so effectively disregarded and snubbed that early in 1923 he resigned. His place in the department was taken by Dr. O. D. Skelton, a former Professor of Political and Economic Science at Queen's University, who had just proved his devotion to the Liberal Party by writing a biography of Sir Wilfrid Laurier, which, with its tone of sustained and fulsome eulogy, must have satisfied even King. At an earlier period of his career, Skelton had failed to obtain a post in the British Indian Civil Service; and a resentful grudge against the exclusiveness of the British governing class lay at the bottom of his deep distrust of the devious schemes and devices of the British Foreign Office. Skelton was an isolationist and separatist after King's own heart. He had 'the right point of view', King observed with immense satisfaction.

At London, King might have demanded a formal declaration of Canada's new separate and independent status; but this was not his way. Instead of asking for an explicit repudiation of the co-operative Commonwealth in defence and foreign policy, he simply kept on insisting, at every opportunity, that it no longer had any validity. Lord Curzon, the British Foreign Secretary, opened proceedings with a long review of foreign policy 'not of these islands alone, but of the Empire'. In his first general statement to the conference, King explicitly denied this assumption; and he was determined that no hint or suggestion of it could be permitted in the *Report*. The draft resolution on foreign policy which Curzon prepared seemed to King to commit Canada to the support of British foreign and defence policies, present as well as past. He demanded that the resolution be revised; and, when the conference proved unwilling, he announced that, in that case, he would have to insist on the inclusion of a special clause, exempting Canada. This ultimatum was decisive. The *Report* became a colourless and non-committal review of general problems in foreign affairs. It did not lay down policy, and it closed, as King wished, with the statement that the conference was not an imperial peace cabinet, but a conference of separate governments, each responsible to its own parliament.

⇥ IV ⇤

AT HOME, as the fourteenth Parliament drew towards its end, the dwindling flame of post-war radicalism flickered uncertainly. Its chief political manifestations in Canada had been the Progressive Party and the Independent Labour Party; but these protest movements had failed to attract much popular support and had been weakened by serious internal disagreements. Labour had managed to elect only two socialists to the House of Commons. The Progressives were divided between reforming moderates who simply hoped to give farmers a larger share of the benefits of free enterprise, and radical doctrinaires who wanted drastic political reforms and economic and social changes. In 1924, a half-dozen of the Albertan radicals, thereafter familiarly known as the 'Ginger Group', withdrew from the Progressive caucus; and next year, during the budget debate, a larger number of Manitoban moderates defied party policy, and voted with the government. In the Commons, the party had lost all discipline and coherence. In the country, the membership of the provincial farmers' organizations rapidly declined; and, in the Ontario general election of 1923, the Drury government was defeated by the Conservatives.

In the next few years a series of surprising electoral victories put the Conservatives in power in all three of the Atlantic provinces. In the east, the revival of the Conservative Party seemed to herald the triumphant return of the old party system; and, even in the west, the grain-growers were putting into a giant new co-operative marketing venture, the Wheat Pool, the enthusiasm and energy which only a few years before they had given to political action. The Wheat Board, which had marketed the entire Canadian crop during the war, had apparently proved, to the farmers' complete satisfaction, that a single selling agency could do better for them than they could do individually for themselves, in competition with each other, through ordinary commercial channels. But the post-war decisions in the Judicial Committee of the Privy Council indicated clearly that the re-establishment of the Wheat Board in times of peace would be beyond the legislative powers of the federal Parliament. And the grain-growers, despairing once again of political remedies, set out to replace the vanished government monopoly with a voluntary, co-operative pool.

The federal general election of 1925 came close to restoring the old two-party system, but failed to do so by a crucial margin. In the new Parliament, there were 116 Conservatives, 101 Liberals, 24 Progressives, two Labour members, and one Independent. The Conservatives had made an impressive recovery, but they had not gained a majority; and the Progressives, though reduced to little more than a third of their former strength, held the balance of power much more effectively in the new Parliament than they had in the old. Mackenzie King claimed a dictator's choice of three possible courses; he could, he announced, either resign at once, or let Parliament decide the issue, or advise an immediate dissolution. The first two courses were constitutionally legitimate; the third course was quite unconstitutional, and Lord Byng warned King that he could not grant him another dissolution. In the end, King decided to remain in office and meet Parliament. His government survived precariously until June 1926; but, on the 18th of that month, the report of the special committee on the scandals in the Department of Customs and Excise disclosed a shocking state of venality and corruption in the public service, and confronted King with the most serious danger he had yet faced. The committee's majority report, which provided evidence without imputing blame, gave the Conservatives an obvious opportunity; and H. H. Stevens moved an amendment censuring the government. Around this amendment, and two sub-amendments, debate raged violently for a week; and late in the evening of the 25th of June, the Woodsworth sub-amendment, which King supported because it removed the censure from the Stevens amendment, was defeated by two votes. King faced the menacing spectre of defeat; but he was determined to avoid the fatal encounter. He asked the Governor General to grant him a dissolution. The man who had affirmed the pious principle that Parliament must decide now wanted to prevent Parliament from reaching its decision. The man whose trial was still proceeding in the High Court of Parliament tried to escape its verdict by appealing, over its head, to the higher tribunal of the electorate.

Lord Byng declined to grant the dissolution on the ground that Meighen had not yet been given a chance to govern and that all expedients should be tried before another general election. For two days King fought doggedly to get his way; he even suggested that the Governor General should cable the Secretary of State for the Dominions and ask for his instructions on the constitutionality of a dissolution. King had always posed as the paladin of Canadian autonomy; but he now assumed that the British government would side with him against Lord Byng, and he was all eagerness for the intervention of Downing Street. The principle which he was perfectly ready to betray was upheld by the Governor General; Byng refused to evade his own responsibility as representative of the Crown in Canada by appealing to England. He held firmly to his decision not to grant a dissolution. And, in an access of vindictive fury, King resigned, refusing even to continue in office until his successor was appointed, and rejecting Meighen's request for a conference on the remaining work of the session. He had violated still another principle of parliamentary government – the principle that His Majesty's government must be carried on; but later, when he was taunted with this constitutional offence, he retorted virtuously that he had offered to hold his resignation 'in abeyance' until the Governor General had made other arrangements. This statement, as his correspondence with Lord Byng proves, was false. He had offered to wait, not until a new government was formed, but until the Governor General could get the advice of the Dominions Office on the constitutionality of a dissolution.

Lord Byng then invited Meighen to form a government; and Meighen, for whom no other course was open, accepted. His position was one of extreme difficulty. He could not appoint his cabinet in the usual way, for at that time a member of the House of Commons who accepted a salaried office under the Crown had to vacate his seat and seek re-election; and the absence of the principal Conservatives from the House would have exposed their leaderless followers to quick defeat. In these circumstances, and for the brief remainder of the session only, Meighen decided to form a temporary government; he appointed six ministers without portfolio, who accepted responsibility for the various departments of government as 'acting ministers' only. This method of appointment was perfectly constitutional, with ample precedent; but, two days later, Mackenzie King, in a paroxysm of moral indignation, attacked Meighen's government as an arbitrary assumption of power. He contended that the Conservative acting ministers were not ministers at all, but simply private members, who had no authority to carry on the business of government. Lapointe, his French-Canadian lieutenant, argued that the acting ministers were regularly appointed ministers who had accepted offices of profit and must therefore vacate their seats. These two completely contradictory and equally false assertions were ingeniously combined in a single motion which declared that, if the acting ministers were legally administering their departments, they ought to have vacated their seats, and that, if they did not hold office legally, they had no right to govern. This fraudulent resolution, with its spurious air of posing a logical dilemma from which there was no escape, proved too much for the muddled and gullible Progressives; and Meighen's government was defeated by one vote.

In the general election which followed in September, Meighen tried to make the corrupt Liberal administration the central issue of the campaign; but King succeeded in imposing on the electorate the grandiose humbug of a 'constitutional crisis' which had no existence outside his own injured vanity. His evangelical earnestness, if not his sham arguments, may have won him some converts; but the real explanation of his success in the election lies in the return of the former Progressives, whom he had wooed so long, to the Liberal fold. The Liberals won 116 seats, and, with the ten Liberal Progressives upon whose support they could count, their majority in the Commons was assured. The Conservative following declined to 91; and the Progressives, though representatives of both their moderate and radical divisions were returned, virtually ceased to exist as a third party.

-》》 V 《《-

S TABLE GOVERNMENT had been restored; Mackenzie King's last important political aim had been achieved. Canada had been saved from the hideous vortex of European militarism and had withdrawn to the invulnerable citadel of North America. The obligations of the League of Nations had been explained away and the sinister machinations of the British Foreign Office had been foiled. Those misguided political pilgrims, the Progressives, who had knelt at false shrines and worshipped strange gods, had at last returned to the faith of their Liberal forefathers. A presumptuous British Governor General, who had mistakenly supposed that the Crown exercised prerogatives independently of the Prime Minister of the moment, had suffered the humiliation of a well-merited public rebuke. Virtue had triumphed in the end. The return of economic prosperity was a golden proof that the nation's troubles were over. The Canadians, that chosen people, were already tasting the joys of the Mackenzie King millennium in their history. There was virtually nothing for government to do, except stay in power. Power became an end in itself. And, apart from a vigilant concern for its own indefinite survival, the Mackenzie King government settled down into a state of satisfied immobility.

The high degree of this self-satisfaction became obvious in October 1926, when King arrived in London for his second Imperial Conference. In the past, his Commonwealth policies had been his strongest policies; but his supreme aim, to detach Canada from British foreign policy, had been successfully achieved, and in 1926 the diplomatic unity of the Empire had become a thing of the past. The final break in that old unity had been made by Great Britain herself. In the League of Nations, all attempts, including the Geneva Protocol, to remedy the weaknesses of the Covenant and to create a system of guarantees which would satisfy western Europe's demand for security, had ended in failure; and Great Britain finally accepted the alternative of the Locarno Agreements, a series of treaties independent of and supplementary to the Covenant of the League. Canada was not, and did not want to be, represented at Locarno; she was not consulted about the Rhineland pact; and a special clause exempted her, and the other Dominions, from its provisions, unless they formally signified acceptance. Canada never ratified the treaties. She had compelled Great Britain to acknowledge publicly the plurality of the Commonwealth in foreign policy.

Yet, though Mackenzie King was complacently satisfied with Commonwealth relations in general, he did have one specific proposal to make to the conference. He was determined to exact the last ounce of his triumph over Lord Byng. Byng had been an imperial officer, an agent of the British government, and his refusal to grant King a dissolution meant, according to the King version, that the British government had interfered in Canada's domestic affairs. This interpretation of the events of that June weekend in Ottawa was, of course, utterly false. It was King who had begged the Governor General to ask for orders from Downing Street, and the Governor General who had properly refused. But, in Mackenzie King's view, the truth as he saw it and the truth laid up in the mind of God were absolutely identical. Henceforth, he decided, the Governor General must be publicly declared to be a representative of the Crown, and not an agent of the British government, or any of its departments.

Apart from this – and it was important enough – King had little to propose. And it was General Hertzog of South Africa who forced the pace at the Conference of 1926. Hertzog wanted a public statement of the independent status of the Dominions. At the word 'independent' King drew back uneasily. He loved cloudy, imposing words and phrases; but definitions always disquieted him. And, although it was all very well to take part, as he himself had done, in a watered-down version of the American Revolution, it was quite another thing to put one's name to such an uncompromising document as a Declaration of Independence. He opposed Hertzog's demand for virtual independence; equal status seemed to him to be an entirely satisfactory alternative. But, at the same time, he declined to join the British and Australian delegates in their emphasis on imperial unity. The Earl of Balfour's draft definition, which combined the two principles of equality of status and association within the Commonwealth, was a compromise that exactly suited him.

The conference removed what remained of the old colonial limitations on the sovereignty of the Dominions; but its chief innovations were concerned with the conduct of foreign policy. The *Report* recognized that the Dominions were already conducting foreign relations, particularly with their nearest neighbours, and that this practice was certain to grow. It was also clearly implied that the change in the position of the Governor General, who up to then had been the chief channel of imperial communication, would have to be followed by the creation of some new machinery for consultation among the governments of the Commonwealth. In the next three years, the Canadian government established legations at Washington, Paris, and Tokyo. There had been a High Commissioner for Canada in England since 1881; and now, in 1928, a British High Commissioner was appointed to Canada. At Ottawa, the Department of External Affairs began to recruit the personnel of an expanded professional foreign service.

⋙ VI ⋘

THE YEAR 1926 had been a hectic and exhausting period in King's life. The next three years were years of not very dignified inertia. The federal government moved forward sluggishly on its unenterprising, inactive way. It was as if the Dominion, having done its part to fight and win the war, had completed the last of its great undertakings, and found no further purpose or meaning in continued political existence. No new national enterprises were launched; and the historic national policies of Macdonald's day were wound up or simply allowed to continue of their own momentum. Despite all the post-war clamour, no substantial changes were made in the tariff. Western lands and natural resources, which the federal government had controlled in order to carry out its great plans for immigration and western settlement, were now returned to the jurisdiction of the prairie provinces; and the transference clearly implied that the first object of Confederation had been attained and that there was no further need of federal leadership. The Canadian National Railways system, under the direction of its active new president, Sir Henry Thornton, was extended and consolidated; but the great days of railway-building were over; and the St. Lawrence Deep Waterway, the only transport project comparable to Laurier's National Transcontinental, never awakened any creative enthusiasm in King. He repeatedly postponed serious consideration of the scheme, and, under pressure from the provinces, virtually abandoned federal claims to the control of water power in navigable rivers.

In the platform adopted at their 1919 convention, the Liberals had committed themselves to an extensive programme of labour legislation and social security; but in these fields, where Mackenzie King had always claimed to be an expert and an earnest reformer, extremely little was accomplished. The one positive achievement was the introduction of old-age pensions; but this was not so much the result of King's zeal for the welfare state as of the strong bargaining position occupied by the two Labour members, J. S. Woodsworth and A. A. Heaps, in the crucial session of 1926. With forces evenly balanced on either side of the House, the votes of these two independent members might prove decisive; and they used their power to extort from King a promise to introduce old-age pensions. The Old Age Pensions Bill, which was vetoed by the Senate in 1926, was passed in the following year; but at this point the social security legislation of the Liberal government came to an abrupt stop. King even went so far as to terminate the grants which the Union and Conservative governments had been giving the provinces in aid of their expenditure for paved highways, technical education, public health, and unemployment offices. The governing aim of the Liberal administration was to avoid new commitments, reduce the burden of old obligations, and return, as far as possible, to pre-war finance. The wartime debt was steadily paid off. The corporation tax disappeared; the personal income tax and the sales tax were both lightened; and the tariff once again approached its accustomed place as the chief source of Canadian revenue.

While the federal government behaved as if it had exhausted its usefulness, the provinces plunged eagerly into a wide range of government activities. The aggressive provinces represented the enterprise and affluence of the 1920s far better than the cautious Dominion. The economic developments and the social pressures of the decade, as well as the emphatic trend of constitutional decisions, all favoured the growth of provincial jurisdiction. The recent judgments of the Judicial Committee of the

Privy Council in the Board of Commerce case and the Toronto Electric Commissioners *v.* Snider case reduced the federal residuary power, upon which the Fathers of Confederation had relied so heavily, to an exceptional authority, exercisable only in emergencies; and the rapidly growing functions of the modern state – economic controls, labour legislation, social security – seemed to have fallen definitely into the hands of the provinces. The provinces began to expand their health and welfare services; the mounting burden of technical and occupational education was carried on their shoulders. They were strenuously engaged in promoting the growth of their forest and mining frontiers, in laying down a costly network of paved highways, and in sponsoring great hydro-electric power utilities. While federal annual expenditures declined during the 1920s, provincial expenditures doubled. Provincial indebtedness doubled also. The provinces were spending and borrowing freely on the comfortable assumption that an endless prosperity would continue to supply all the revenue necessary for their vastly expanded services. New and lucrative sources of provincial income had been discovered. The wartime prohibition of wine and spirits lasted only a few years; and during the 1920s most of the provinces made the sale of liquor a highly profitable government monopoly. The proceeds of the sale of motor licences and of the new provincial gasoline tax increased rapidly with the growth of automobile traffic. The rich yields of these 'consumption' taxes depended, of course, upon a fairly opulent style of living. But had not the North American continent attained a new and permanent level of economic good fortune?

And then, on Thursday, the 24th of October, 1929, the bottom dropped out of the New York stock market.

CHAPTER TEN

The Crash

THE COLLAPSE of the stock market meant nothing to Mackenzie King; he was not even aware that anything of the slightest importance had happened. He only dimly and gradually began to realize that the crash might result in a depression and that the depression might become a serious political problem. Even when the unpleasant truth could no longer be disregarded, he failed to comprehend that special remedial efforts would certainly be expected of the federal government. He never dreamed that new and extraordinary methods might be required. Thrift seemed to him to be a wise practice in both his own affairs and the nation's finances; and he could not conceive of a situation in which this old-fashioned virtue might actually prove harmful. Even if he could have anticipated the economic theories which Keynes was soon to make so fashionable, he would have found it difficult, as well as distasteful, to carry them out. In Canada, there was no central bank through which the government might have sought to stimulate investment by a national expansion of credit. King might, of course, have stepped up government spending; but this possibility never even occurred to him. For ten years, his government had been practising economies, reducing taxation, and paying off debt. In his eyes, this was a proud record. He nursed the comfortable delusion that all Canadians were – and would continue to be – impressed by it.

He was still in a complacent frame of mind when the session opened in 1930. He had no special measures to propose for the depression. The Speech from the Throne boasted that employment had reached record heights in 1929, failed to mention that it had since declined appallingly, and merely referred to a little 'seasonal slackness'. A. A. Heaps, the Labour member, began a debate on unemployment insurance; and the Conservatives, joining in, attacked the government for its lack of concern for the unemployed and its failure to help the provincial governments in the heavy task of providing relief. King, drawing once more on his copious store of hackneyed precepts, replied righteously that if a province wished to spend money, it ought to collect it itself and not expect the federal government to pay for its extravagance. He admitted that, if the cost of unemployment relief ever threatened provincial or municipal solvency, the Dominion would, of course, come to the rescue; but, he insisted irritably, there was no sign of such an emergency at the moment. It was factious and irresponsible of the Opposition, he claimed, getting angrier every minute, to ask him to subsidize provincial governments, particularly Tory provincial governments. He would not, he concluded furiously, give a five-cent piece to any Conservative government for 'alleged' unemployment relief purposes.

This blazing indiscretion was hardly a suitable prelude to a general election; and a general election in 1930 was what King now decided upon. Hesitating for a while between 1930 and 1931, he had gravely asked the advice of a Kingston fortune-teller, Mrs. Bleaney. Mrs. Bleaney replied, somewhat darkly, that there were forces favouring 1930, and other forces favouring 1931, but that, on the whole, the omens for 1930 were more propitious. King, she predicted, would win a great triumph in the west, from which he would emerge more powerful than ever. This sounded agreeably conclusive and reassuring, and King fixed the 28th of July, 1930, as the date of the election. He confidently expected to win; but there were two bad mistakes in his calculations. He seriously underestimated both the effects of the depression and the impact of the new Leader of the Opposition, Richard Bedford Bennett.

In 1930, Bennett was sixty; he had reached the summit late in life. He had been born in a little New Brunswick village, the son of poor, deeply religious parents, who were devoted adherents of the Methodist Church; and, to the end of his life, he never lost the simple tastes, the severe moral standards, and the evangelical fervour of his Methodist upbringing. When he was twenty-six, he went west, built up a highly successful law practice in Calgary, and, with the help of some profitable investments and two magnificent bequests, became an extremely rich man. The luck that had so consistently blessed his professional and business career deserted him capriciously for a time in public life. He was not made a member of the Union government, declined nomination in the 1917 general election, and, four years later, when he decided to run again, was defeated. It was not until 1925 that he finally won in the Calgary constituency; and after that his progress upward was swift and uninterrupted. The disaster of 1926 seemed to require the sacrifice of Meighen's retirement. Bennett succeeded him as leader of the Conservative Party.

He had reached the heights. Now his impressive presence radiated the confidence of wealth, professional success, and political power. He was a big, portly man, formal in dress, and pompous in manner, 'with a touch', as his friend Max Aitken, Lord Beaverbrook, said, of 'a London Lord Mayor' about him. He looked at colleagues, and other subordinates, with cold, penetrating, and censorious eyes; his manner was abrupt and imperious; he had a domineering will and, despite his sixty years, an unbounded vitality. He spoke rapidly and vigorously, usually without notes, and often his ready flow of words became a torrential eloquence. His industry was tireless, his mastery of the details of any subject astonishingly swift. He liked quick decisions, and believed in positive action. He was the lawyer turned business executive, turned politician, who had succeeded spectacularly in all roles and expected others to follow where he led.

He put all his enormous self-confidence and his evangelical fervour into the general election of 1930. Mackenzie King had disregarded and depreciated the depression; Bennett made it the central issue of his campaign. Only the Conservative Party, he shouted, could save Canada from the disaster into which Mackenzie King and the Liberals had permitted it to flounder.

He promised an imposing list of public works. He denied passionately that tariffs benefited only manufacturers; he would make them fight for the primary producers as well. He would, he declared with savage emphasis, use tariffs to 'blast his way into the markets' of the world or 'perish in the attempt'.

Mackenzie King contemptuously called it demagoguery; but the electoral results were as dramatic as Bennett's electoral methods. The Conservative strength rose in the new Parliament from 91 to 137; the Liberal following fell from 116 to 88. Bennett had a comfortable majority of thirty over all parties in the House.

→⟫ II ⦗⦗

THE NEW PRIME MINISTER faced a truly formidable set of problems. One of the chief features of the depression was an abrupt and terrible decline in the total value of world trade; and this, for a nation that obtained over a third of its national income from the sale of its products abroad, was bound to be tragic. The drop in prices and the contraction of foreign demand were certain to affect all of Canada's export specialties; but, for two of them, wheat and newsprint, the consequences were particularly sudden and severe. Wheat and flour accounted for 32 per cent and newsprint, woodpulp, and pulp wood for another 15 per cent of the total value of Canadian exports; but, even before the advent of the depression, these two staples, which together made up nearly 50 per cent of Canada's export trade, were in serious trouble. Newsprint capacity had been, and continued to be, lavishly over-extended, though prices had been steadily falling since 1924. The bumper wheat crop of 1928 had left a huge carry-over which not even the thin harvest of 1929 had succeeded in reducing. The price of No. 1 Northern wheat at Fort William had been sliding slowly downward since 1925; now it began to drop precipitously. In December 1932, it reached an all-time low of forty-two cents. And, in the four years 1929-32, the total value of newsprint exports to the United States, which was, of course, Canada's chief market, had fallen by nearly 45 per cent.

Upon these two weakened staple industries and trades the depression fell with shattering force. By 1932, the newsprint industry was operating at only 53 per cent of its capacity; and, within another year, half a dozen of the largest companies in the business were bankrupt. The collapse of wheat prices brought about the failure of the Wheat Pool's central selling agency, the organization which was the most ambitious creation of the western grain-growers, and the one on which their hopes for prosperity and security had been chiefly based. As early as the winter of 1930, the Wheat Pool, which had unwisely set too high an interim payment for its producers, was compelled by falling prices and declining sales to appeal to the three prairie governments to guarantee its heavy loans at the banks. When autumn came, prices were still sagging downwards, and a large part of the crop of 1929 was yet unsold. The provincial governments, as well as the Pool and the banks, had now reached their limits. They appealed to the federal government for help; and the federal government, as the price of its assistance, appointed a man in whom it had confidence, John I. McFarland, as the new manager of the central selling agency. The western grain-growers' great attempt at self-help in marketing had ended in complete failure.

The collapse of wheat and newsprint was quickly followed by a decline in the price of the other staples and a steep drop in the volume of their export sales. As in 1921-2, the United States hastened to protect its farmers at the first sign of a slump in agricultural prices; and the Hawley-Smoot tariff of 1930 virtually stopped the Canadian export trade in cattle and dairy products to the Republic. Canada enjoyed an effective monopoly of the supply of nickel, and was able to maintain a fixed price; but the prices for copper, lead, and zinc broke sharply; and the decline in the volume of trade was so great that in the four years from 1929 to 1932, the total value of the exports of non-ferrous metals dropped by over 60 per cent. Undoubtedly, it was the fall of export prices in general which first set Canada off down the steep decline of the depression;

but the contraction of export trade was accompanied by an even more drastic curtailment of investment. A very large part of the boom of the 1920s had been the direct result of heavy capital expenditures in the development of the new staple industries and the new sources of power. Smelters, metal refineries, pulp-and-paper mills, hydro-electric power installations – all with their huge and costly machinery and equipment – had put their ponderous weight into the upward thrust of prosperity. Now these huge outlays ended; and, in the period 1929-32, capital expenditures on new construction, machinery, and equipment declined by over 70 per cent.

It took three years to reveal the true depth of the disaster; but, even in the summer of 1930, the prospect looked desperate enough. Bennett had promised rapid and decisive action. He now made good his word. Parliament met in special session early in September, barely six weeks after the general election; and the new Prime Minister was ready with his cures for the depression. Twenty million dollars – a stupendous sum for the time – was voted for public works and unemployment relief. The tariff was increased more steeply than it had ever been since the inauguration of Sir John Macdonald's National Policy in 1879; and a variety of administrative devices were adopted to prevent dumping and to preserve the home market for the domestic manufacturers. Every important secondary industry in the country was given increased protection. This was simply the first dose of what, for the next two years, became Bennett's standard prescription for the depression. The Unemployment and Farm Relief Bill of 1931 authorized the expenditure of an unlimited amount of money for vaguely defined relief purposes; and, even more strangely – for Bennett, the company chairman, had begun to fear social unrest – it gave the government special powers to combat the spread of 'pernicious' revolutionary doctrines.

On all counts, this was an outrageous measure in Mackenzie King's eyes; but, on this occasion, his customary flow of sanctimonious rebuke, if not exactly stopped, was at least slightly reduced. A House of Commons committee had been investigating the profits and public relations of the Beauharnois syndicate, a group of Montreal promoters who had been authorized by King's government to divert water on the Beauharnois section of the St. Lawrence River for what was expected to be an extremely lucrative hydro-electric power development. Unhappily, the Commons committee discovered that Mackenzie King himself, as well as two of his close friends and political associates, had all benefited, in varying degrees, from the friendly generosity of the Beauharnois syndicate. King's good friend, Senator W. L. McDougald, chairman of the board of the Beauharnois Power Corporation, who was a frequent and welcome guest at Laurier House in Ottawa – though, oddly enough, he never seemed to be able to get into the best Montreal clubs – had obligingly offered to pay the expenses of a little holiday that King took in Bermuda; and King, who hated spending money on anything but his Kingsmere estate, had gratefully accepted. Unfortunately, the little Bermuda hotel bill, which King confidingly assumed would be paid by McDougald himself, was in fact charged to the Beauharnois Corporation; and this awkward fact emerged subsequently in the Commons committee's review of the Corporation's accounts. King was subdued with mortification. He and the Liberal Party, he told the House, were walking in 'the valley of humiliation'.

In the meantime, the new Prime Minister, R. B. Bennett, had walked on to the flood-lit stage of the Imperial Conference of 1930 in London. This conference, as its principal formal achievement, completed the constitution of the Empire-Commonwealth, and paved the way for the Statute of Westminster, passed during the following year. Bennett made no attempt to alter or delay the conclusion of these formalities; but, although he accepted the principle of Dominion status readily enough, he had other and more positive ideas about the Commonwealth. He 'believed fervently', Beaverbrook declared later, 'that Canada's future lay with the Founderland across the ocean'; but there were fairly strict limits to the application of this principle. With heavy financial burdens at home and the prospect of continuing peace abroad, Bennett showed no inclination to regard the Commonwealth as a great co-operative system of defence and foreign policy. King had destroyed the diplomatic unity of the Empire, and Bennett made no conspicuous effort to restore it.

Instead, he concentrated upon imperial trade and tariffs. And, as things stood in the autumn of 1930, he seemed to have both the incentive and the opportunity for immediate action. In England, Beaverbrook was using the editorial columns of the highly successful *Daily Express* to spread the gospel of Empire Free Trade; and, in Canada, the swift decline of wheat prices had raised the question of government assistance to the western grain-growers. Bennett had promised that he could, and would, use the tariff to benefit the primary producer, as well as the manufacturer and industrial worker. Obviously, the conference was the destined place for him to begin; and he now offered, in exchange for reciprocal privileges in the British market, to increase the British preference in Canada, not by lowering the duties on British imports, but by raising the general tariff 10 per cent. The members of Ramsay MacDonald's minority Labour government were distinctly unimpressed by this proposal. J. H. Thomas, the Dominions Secretary, called it 'humbug'. All that Bennett was able to obtain was an agreement to hold an Imperial Economic Conference at Ottawa in the near future.

When the conference finally met in the summer of 1932, political and economic circumstances throughout the world had radically altered, and for the worse. The Japanese invasion of Manchuria had ended the brief decade of post-war peace; and the international financial crisis, beginning in central and eastern Europe, had swept across the continent to Great Britain. England went off the gold standard; a National government, under Ramsay MacDonald, was formed; and the general election of October 1931 gave the Conservatives a dominant place in its counsels. The new Chancellor of the Exchequer was Neville Chamberlain, Joseph Chamberlain's youngest son, 'the hereditary high priest of the Empire faith' and a firm believer in tariff protection. Already, in February 1932, he had imposed a 10 per cent duty on imports, raw materials and foodstuffs exempted; and Beaverbrook and his 'Empire Crusaders' confidently expected that when Chamberlain met that other 'devoted Empire leader', Bennett, in Ottawa the long-awaited day of Empire economic unity would dawn.

But it was not to be. Bennett's belief in both the Commonwealth and the League of Nations was far stronger than King's; but he had no intention of endangering the depressed Canadian economy by the rigid application of an economic dogma, and no inclination to take risks for collective security which none of the great powers showed the slightest sign of proposing. In the House of Commons, he was vague and evasive about Canadian policy with respect to the Japanese invasion of Manchuria; and in the League Assembly, C. H. Cahan, the Canadian delegate, was coldly realistic in his appraisal of Chinese misrule and Japanese grievances in the region. The ends which Bennett and Chamberlain sought at Ottawa were equally limited and sensible. Neither believed that Empire Free Trade was feasible in principle. The most they hoped to do was to exchange specific preferences; and, when it came to the point, these were extremely hard to negotiate. Bennett had already shown very clearly that he was determined to protect most of the shrinking home market for the Canadian manufacturers; and the British delegates, led by Baldwin, still nursed their old fears of the political dangers of duties on food, 'stomach taxes'. The results of four weeks of hard and somewhat acrimonious bargaining were meagre. Canada gained a preference in the British market for her wheat, lumber, apples, and bacon. And, in return, as Bennett had originally proposed, she increased the preference for British manufactures by the simple method of raising the level of the general tariff.

At this point, Bennett had run through his original stock of remedies. Like Meighen and Mackenzie King, he had always regarded the tariff as the central issue of Canadian politics, and the major instrument of government policy; and everything he could think of to do with the tariff had now been done. He kept hoping, and insisting, that he would balance the budget; and when, in the 1932 budget debate, the 'Ginger Group' proposed currency depreciation and controlled inflation, he was just as horrified as King. He profoundly distrusted

novel monetary cures. But at the moment he himself had
nothing further to propose.

→≫≫ III ≪≪←

B Y THE END OF 1932, the depression had reached its nadir.
The national income had fallen by nearly 45 per cent
since 1929. The whole country suffered; but, from region to
region, there were obviously degrees of distress. If the decline
was relatively less in the Atlantic provinces, it was only because
they had enjoyed so little of the prosperity of the 1920s, and,
as a result, had not so far to fall. In Ontario and Quebec, where
manufacturing and the services were concentrated, and where
salaries and wages were more secure, the drop in income was
somewhat less than the national average; but in the western
provinces, and particularly Saskatchewan and Alberta, where
drought and wheat rust combined with falling prices to beggar
whole communities, the fall was tragically precipitous. The
primary producers, who had to sell in world markets, had no
defences against the slump of export prices; but wage-earners
and salaried officials in manufacturing industries were protected
by Bennett's new prohibitive tariffs; and the basic operations
and essential requirements of a nation of ten millions sheltered
the jobs of some professional people, as well as those of
executive administrators and service personnel. If they could
hold their positions, these Canadians were often better off
than they had been, as a result of the decline in the cost of
living; but, like the wage-earners in manufacturing, they were
more than likely to be laid off in the wholesale reduction of
all kinds of gainful employment. In 1933, 826,000 persons –
nearly a quarter of the labour force – were out of work and
seeking jobs.

The 1920s, like the 1900s, had been a decade of purposeful
mobility; the depression years were years of hopeless inertness.
Ever since Confederation people had been coming to Canada
and leaving it in scores and hundreds of thousands. They had
pushed into the remote frontiers of the west and north; they

had drifted back to the cities and towns of the south and centre. For thirty years the currents of hope and ambition had kept up a continuous human agitation; but now the depression brought the restless pursuit of fresh opportunities to a dead end. Immigrant arrivals dropped off to levels which had not been seen since the 1860s, seventy years earlier. Emigration also declined, for the Canadians who had always in the past been welcomed in the United States now found their entry restricted. Even so, and for the first time in four decades, there was a net loss by migration during the 1930s. For the first time also since Confederation, the inconspicuous trek to the cities waned to a narrow file and almost stopped. For most farmers, particularly in eastern and central Canada, it was far better to stay on the land and endure the rigours of a bare subsistence than to join the humiliated and hopeless crowds of unemployed in the cities. For the defeated grain-growers in drought-stricken southern Saskatchewan, the only possible course was to abandon their parched, wind-blown, ash-grey farms and, like refugees from an annihilating pestilence, drive off with all they could carry to the green parklands in the prairie north. Human movement, inspired more by despair than by hope, continued feebly during the depression. Saskatchewan lost more than 25,000 people in the 1930s; and, despite the fact that the municipal authorities tried to restrict relief to their own local jobless, men roamed about the country on the tops of freight cars, searching vainly for work.

In the cities, salaried people and wage-earners accepted pay cuts of 10 per cent and 20 per cent with submissive resignation, and clung apprehensively to their jobs. Farmers eked out a primitive existence and struggled to meet the interest on bank loans for steadily depreciating equipment. Skilled tradesmen, who could pick up odd jobs more easily than others, worked at cut rates and endured long periods of enforced idleness; workers in shops, offices, and factories lived in dread of the periodical lay-offs – weekly, monthly, or seasonal – which occurred whenever their companies' operations ran into a slack period. All these people could preserve some dignity in the midst of degradation, and nurse some hope despite the insistent pressure of fear. But, for wage-earners who had lost their jobs and could get no work, and farmers whose lean cattle starved on burnt-out fields, the only means of survival lay in direct unemployment relief. Relief, distributed mainly by the municipalities, was given, not in cash, but in kind or in vouchers. There were vouchers for bread, meat, milk, fuel, and rent; there was even, in the end, provision for an ugly and shapeless suit of clothes which the recipients called derisively a 'relief uniform'. Within and without the makeshift and invariably inadequate quarters in which these coupons were distributed, people waited patiently for long hours in apparently endless queues.

In the seven years from 1930 to 1937, the total cost of direct relief and relief works approached the staggering sum of a billion dollars. The financial burden varied from region to region, and even from province to province; but, whether it was relatively greater or relatively smaller, it was far too big for the traditional authorities to bear. By section 92 of the British North America Act, the care of 'charities and eleemosynary institutions' had been entrusted to the provinces; but, until the 1920s, the role of the state in the maintenance of public welfare had never been great, and, in the main, 'poor relief' was assumed to be the responsibility of the municipalities. But 'poor relief', in an age when the farm was still relatively self-sufficient and the family offered some protection against adversity, differed profoundly from mass unemployment in a modern society dominated by industry and large-scale commercial agriculture. The municipalities derived their entire revenue from taxes on real property; and it was utterly impossible for them, without the ruin of real estate values, to raise property taxes to the point at which they could bear the mounting charges of relief. It was equally beyond the power of the provinces, despite their recent growth in prestige and affluence, to bear the whole weight of these massive and unprecedented responsibilities. For ten prosperous years the provinces had been expanding their welfare services and paying for them with buoyant revenues drawn from such novel sources as automobile licences, gasoline taxes, and government liquor monopolies; but now, with dismaying swiftness, these fickle revenues shrank, while welfare costs enormously expanded. The burden of unemployment relief was too great for the joint resources of municipalities and provinces; it could only be borne if all three governments, including the Dominion, agreed to bear their share. The $20 million voted in the emergency session of September 1930 was merely the first token instalment of the massive sums transferred by the federal government to the provinces in aid of direct relief and relief works during the period 1930-7. In the end the Dominion assumed about 40 per cent of the total of nearly one billion dollars expended by all governments on relief; and, in addition, she loaned over $100 million to the four western provinces in order to enable them to meet their share of the cost. All these payments were emergency payments, outside the statutory subsidies given by the Dominion to the provinces.

Plainly, the division of functions and revenues between the Dominion and the provinces had broken down. The depression had apparently brought about the failure of Canadian federalism. It had also exposed, for all but the wilfully blind to see, the vital defects of the free enterprise system.

→≫ IV ≪←

THE GREAT DEBATE over the purpose and functions of the Canadian state had begun during the war. It was renewed during the depression with equal intensity and at a deeper level of argument. A fairly large and increasing number of Canadians were rapidly reaching the conclusion that positive action by the state must remedy the admitted weaknesses of economic liberalism or that it must be replaced by a democratic socialist system. The apparent refusal of the two old national parties to consider any measures that were not pure palliatives could not silence these new radicals; their demands simply found alternative outlets in the more drastic programmes of a variety of left-wing movements. The socialist solution, an existing body of ideas, readily available on the British model, was the first to be invoked. It found systematic expression and organized support in the new party, the Co-operative Commonwealth Federation.

The parliamentary origins of the new party lay in the activities of the so-called 'Ginger Group', the association, formed during the 1920s, of the radical Progressives from Alberta and the labour members led by J. S. Woodsworth. This working union of agrarian radicals and urban labour leaders was very largely a western phenomenon; but it became the model from which the new national party was built. The post-war Progressive movement had been based exclusively upon rural Ontario and the agrarian west; but, from the start, the C.C.F. tried to win a broader and more diversified support. The origins of the new party were as much in British socialism as they were in Canadian Progressivism. The League for Social Reconstruction, frankly planned as the Canadian equivalent of the Fabian Society in England, provided the C.C.F. with its basic body of ideas; and the League drew a great deal of inspiration and guidance from the history of British socialism. From the beginning the primary aim of the leaders of the C.C.F. was to unite farmers, industrial workers, and middle class in a genuine democratic socialist party on a national scale.

On the 26th of May, 1932, in William Irvine's room in the Parliament Buildings in Ottawa, the 'co-operating independent' members of the House of Commons, together with some representatives of the League for Social Reconstruction and a few others, met and took the first steps to organize what was first called the 'Commonwealth Party'. In August, a varied assortment of western farmer and labour groups, with some representatives, including a solitary labour leader, from Ontario, assembled in the Labour Temple in Calgary, decided that the name of the new organization would be the Co-operative Commonwealth Federation, and elected J. S. Woodsworth as its first president. A provisional platform, with planks for social welfare, economic planning, and the public ownership and control of financial institutions, utilities, and natural resources, was adopted; but the main work of organization was left until the following year. In August 1933, the new party held its first annual convention at Regina. A democratic, fairly decentralized constitution was agreed upon; and the C.C.F. programme, henceforth called the 'Regina Manifesto', set out the principles of the 'new social order' in fourteen points.

A number of oddly assorted and, indeed, incongruous groups joined the C.C.F.; but it fell far short of winning the support of the three broad social divisions to which it had appealed. The western agrarian parties naturally endorsed its programme; but the United Farmers of Ontario, who decided at first to affiliate with the new party, left it abruptly early in 1934. In Ontario, the C.C.F. drew its main strength from the cities and towns; but even there it was much more successful with the urban middle class than with the industrial workers. Protestants deeply affected by the ideals of the social gospel, teachers and university professors, other professional people and white-collar workers made up the bulk of the party's membership and helped to give it its earnest, slightly sanctimonious air. Organized labour, on a national scale, remained severely aloof. The Trades and Labour Congress, disillusioned by the relative failure of the provincial Independent Labour parties which it had sponsored during the First World War, declined to commit itself to the C.C.F., though it did not disavow its earlier belief that political action was desirable in principle. The All-Canadian Congress of Labour and its only large member union, the Canadian Brotherhood of Railway Employees, were somewhat more friendly; but this favourable attitude did not result in a formal affiliation.

The C.C.F. was the only new party to challenge the existing economic and social order on the federal level of politics; but it was by no means the only political manifestation of the restless and impatient current of discontent that pulsed through Canadian affairs in the early years of the depression. During the 1920s, the provinces had grown enormously in power and political consequence; and it was in the provinces that the first fumbling attempts were made to promote economic recovery and social welfare by policies that stopped short of the socialist remedies advocated by the C.C.F., but were designed to correct the inequities and abuses of *laissez-faire* capitalism by state regulation and public services. In the summer and autumn of 1933, the Liberals won the provincial general elections in both Nova Scotia and British Columbia. Mackenzie King was suitably gratified by these triumphs; but the elections were something more than promising local signs of the revival of the old national Liberal Party. A. L. Macdonald was still strongly influenced by the Nova Scotian tradition of 'Maritime Rights' and opposition to federal commercial policies; but in his first year of office he set up a Royal Commission of Inquiry into the economic condition of the province as a preliminary to reform. In British Columbia, T. D. Pattullo escaped much more completely from conventional Liberal philosophy. In 1932, his party adopted a new platform which called for an expansion of credit, a broad public works programme, and a drastic enlargement of health and welfare services. In the provincial election of 1933 he campaigned with the slogan 'Work and Wages', which, he explained, meant 'the complete overhaul of the nation's economic system'. The election wiped out the Conservative Party, gave the Liberals a handsome majority, and made the C.C.F., though with only seven seats, the official opposition in the legislature.

The Liberal victories that followed in 1934 in both Ontario and Saskatchewan were more orthodox in character; but in both provinces there were signs of a definite shift to the left. In Saskatchewan, as in British Columbia, the Conservatives simply disappeared from the legislature; and the C.C.F., with a mere five seats, found itself suddenly elevated to the post of official opposition. In Ontario, the Conservatives dropped the appalling total of seventy-four seats; but the C.C.F., seriously weakened by internal disputes and the defection of the United Farmers of Ontario, failed completely to compete with the cocky and aggressive election tactics of the new Liberal leader, Mitchell F. Hepburn, and managed to elect only a single member in the new House. Hepburn appropriated Franklin Delano Roosevelt's catch phrase, the 'New Deal', and with it the implied promise of a provincial recovery administration. His cheeky gibes at the affluent and powerful seemed to imply an impatient defiance of the established order; but his main attack was against the corruption and extravagance of the Conservatives and his main promises were drastic economies and a balanced budget.

In the meantime, in both Alberta and Quebec, other protest movements, more radical, at least in theory, than Hepburn's rejuvenated Liberalism, were gaining confidence and popular acclaim. In Alberta, the United Farmers of Alberta government, which was attempting to meet the depression with a tight-fisted programme of economy, had obviously ceased to express prairie radicalism; and the Taschereau administration in Quebec, which had promoted the industrialization of the province through the lavish encouragement of private enterprise, was now faced with the indignant French-Canadian nationalist charge that it had sold the provincial natural resources to English-Canadian and American capitalists. In both provinces a sullen and disillusioned electorate waited hungrily for a new man and a new doctrine; and, by a strange coincidence, both made their appearances simultaneously in west and east. William Aberhart, the Calgary high-school mathematics teacher and fundamentalist preacher, who had attracted a radio audience of hundreds of thousands of eager listeners, became converted to the simple mathematical equations of Major C. H. Douglas's Social Credit. At almost the same time, a group of young left-wing Quebec Liberals, led by Paul Gouin, and calling themselves 'L'Action Libérale Nationale', began a revolt inside the well-disciplined ranks of the provincial Liberal Party; and Maurice Duplessis, who had been elected leader of the Conservative Party in 1933, joined the Liberal insurgents in a united front, the 'Union Nationale', against the Taschereau régime.

In both Alberta and Quebec, a new political and economic philosophy was readily available. Aberhart's followers put their trust in the simple propositions of the national dividend and the just price. In Quebec, Pope Pius XII's new encyclical on social and economic questions had substantially changed the Roman Catholic hierarchy's attitude to socialization and government ownership; and the Liberal members of Union Nationale could now reconcile their nationalist aspirations with their desire for economic and social reform.

≫ V ≪

A T THE END OF 1933, the seventeenth Parliament of Canada was considerably less than two years away from its extreme statutory limit. 'So far,' R. J. Manion, the Conservative Minister of Railways and Canals wrote early in January 1934, 'this great Conservative Party, which is supposed to be the friend of big business, has not one dollar in its treasury.' What was worse, it seemed even more bankrupt of ideas than it was of funds. Bennett had apparently run through all his constructive policies and he could think of nothing better than the continuation of existing palliatives. The new men, the new doctrines, the new programmes kept dramatically appearing, not in Ottawa, but in the provincial capitals. It looked as if the provinces, despite the reverses of the depression, had somehow managed to retain the leadership which they had wrenched away from the federal government during the 1920s.

Yet these appearances were curiously misleading. There were equally strong, though less showy, forces fighting on the nationalist side. Mackenzie King's surrender of the initiative and the assertive rise of the provinces during the 1920s had occurred very largely on the political and economic side of Canadian life; but in the social, cultural, and intellectual sphere the national interest seemed dominant. The 1920s and 1930s saw the birth and rapid growth of an astonishing number of voluntary, non-political, national associations. The Canadian Clubs, founded thirty years before in the 1890s, expanded enormously. The Canadian Authors' Association, the Dominion Drama Festival, and the Canadian Radio League were designed to awaken interest in Canadian literature, Canadian theatre, and Canadian broadcasting. The League of Nations Society and the Canadian Institute of International Affairs provided opportunities for a Canadian approach to foreign affairs. The Canadian Historical Association, the Canadian Political Science Association, and the Canadian Federation of Teachers enabled university scholars and schoolteachers to come together for the discussion of their distinctively Canadian problems. If Canadians desired the benefit of association for any purpose, if they wished to promote any cause, interest, or vocation, it was organization, not on a local or provincial basis, but on a national scale, that they instinctively adopted.

In the early 1930s, this powerful national urge was strengthened, for the first time since the war, by certain highly important political and constitutional circumstances. During the previous decade, the provinces had had it all their own way. The decisions in the Judicial Committee of the Privy Council had consistently favoured them; the new resource industries, the new sources of energy, the new kinds of transportation, and the quickly expanding social services, all came under their jurisdiction. Their rise to prominence and power had been rapid and assured; but it was suddenly arrested by the depression; and the serious weaknesses behind the imposing provincial façade were revealed. Without the financial help of the Dominion, the provinces could never have fulfilled even their constitutional responsibility for unemployment relief; and, despite the brave words of Pattullo, Aberhart, and Gouin, how was it possible for even the strongest provincial administration to devise real remedies for an economic disaster that affected the entire Canadian economy? From the first, the C.C.F. had insisted that only a national attack on the depression could possibly succeed; and among informed people there was a growing belief that the depression, like the war, was a national crisis that demanded and justified federal action. This conviction was powerfully strengthened by the two most recent constitutional decisions in the Judicial Committee of the Privy Council. In 1931-2, it gave exclusive control of both aviation and radio broadcasting to the federal government.

As the decade of the 1930s advanced, the federal government found itself invested with a novel, highly contemporary usefulness and authority. It had gained control of the two newest and potentially most powerful and popular forms of transport and communications; it alone could create the central bank which the depression had proved was necessary for carrying out a national monetary policy. These modern federal responsibilities and opportunities seemed to awaken a new, more flexible, experimental Bennett. He still preferred private enterprise to government ownership; but, if the private enterprisers were Americans who threatened Canadian autonomy, he was quite ready to use the power of the state to resist their encroachments. Like Macdonald, Borden, and Meighen, he was a strong nationalist; and it was national feeling that first impelled him along the path towards state regulation and control. The Bank of Canada, established in 1934, could safely be left in private ownership, as the Macmillan Commission had recommended; but Canadian airways and Canadian broadcasting were obviously vulnerable to the penetration of American airlines, and American radio and electrical companies. Neither government nor private capital was yet prepared to meet the huge cost of a trans-Canada airline; but in the meantime Bennett agreed firmly that American intrusion must be prevented; 'the Americans can fly on their side of the line,' he was heard to say bluntly, 'but we are quite capable of doing all the flying in or over Canada.' This instinctive hostility to American economic imperialism undoubtedly lay behind his sympathetic response to the growing demand for Canadian broadcasting for Canadian radio listeners. The Aird Commission had recommended public ownership; the Canadian Radio League, with Alan Plaunt as chairman and Graham Spry as secretary, successfully popularized the fact that in broadcasting it was either 'the State or the United States'. And, in 1932, Parliament established the Canadian Radio Broadcasting Commission, with Hector Charlesworth as its first chairman.

The next stage in Bennett's course in adult education had an unexpected and curious beginning in the indiscretions of one of his cabinet colleagues, H. H. (Harry) Stevens, the Minister of Trade and Commerce. Along with R. J. Manion, Stevens stood out somewhat incongruously from the little group of corporation lawyers and company directors who occupied most of the senior posts in the Conservative cabinet. A self-taught accountant who had tried a number of employments without notably succeeding in any, Stevens was a sensitive and prickly person with a grudge against the rich and great, and an unabashed readiness for controversy. The human distresses of the depression had moved him to propose certain positive courses of action to the Prime Minister; but these suggestions were apparently received, as Bennett often received other people's notions, with dead silence and a freezing stare, or a contemptuous rejection. Stevens's great chance came in January 1934, when he addressed a convention of boot and shoe manufacturers in Toronto. He had armed himself in advance with detailed information about working conditions in the clothing trades and meat-packing firms. He now charged that the big departmental and chain stores abused their buying power by compelling manufacturers to sell at drastically reduced prices, and that this relentless pressure forced wages down and produced sweatshop conditions in industry.

Three days later, Bennett informed Stevens that he had gone too far in deciding government policy, and must stop. Stevens refused and sent in his resignation. Bennett's erratic intellectual pilgrimage might have ended abruptly at this point; but, strangely enough, it did not. He disregarded Stevens's letter of resignation. He agreed that the charges made by his Minister of Trade and Commerce ought to be investigated; and, early in February, Stevens found himself the chairman of a Select Committee on Price Spreads and Mass Buying, a committee empowered to investigate the causes and consequences of the large spread between commodity and consumer prices. For the next few months, he enjoyed politics as never before. He subjected a long series of manufacturing and merchandising corporations to a persistent and pitiless cross-examination. He brought out the startling contrast between the healthy profits of Canada Packers Limited and the pitiful prices they paid for cattle; he revealed the glaring disparity between the generous salaries enjoyed by the executives of the T. Eaton Company and the mean wages earned by their clerks. Suddenly, through the efforts of Harry Stevens, the Conservative Party had become the friend and protector of the shop assistant, the industrial worker, the farmer, and the small, independent merchant.

The new image did not displease Bennett. By this time, the shift in his own mental outlook was nearly complete. The disclosures of the Price Spreads Committee had dealt a second heavy blow to his liberal individualism. A strong national feeling had convinced him that the power of the state was necessary to defend the autonomy of the Canadian nation; a troubled social conscience, Christian in its origin and nature, now led him to the belief that regulation and control could alone protect the basic human needs of the Canadian people. He was not a patrician with a hereditary paternal concern for the welfare of his dependants. He was a self-made man who seemed the very embodiment of the North American thrust towards personal achievement and success. But, throughout his ascending financial and political good fortune, he had kept intact the severe moral standards of his Methodist boyhood; and now, under the impact of the revelations of the Price Spreads Committee, this evangelical puritanism became a social gospel. He believed in private enterprise; but he was shocked and troubled by the accumulating evidence of its sharp practices, its harsh pressures, its grossly unequal rewards. And the younger men whom he now liked to have about him and whose advice he seemed increasingly to value – R. K. Finlayson, his personal assistant, and his brother-in-law, W. D. Herridge, the Canadian Minister to the United States – were urging him that the evils of Canadian capitalism could be cured by new government controls and government services.

⇛ VI ≪

RADIO HAD PLAYED some part in the general election of 1930; but the succeeding five years had far more fully demonstrated its vast potential value in politics. In the United States, Roosevelt had used it, with enormous success, to explain and justify his New Deal. In Canada, it was the chief means by which Aberhart was successfully converting the province of Alberta to the fundamentalist dogmas of Social Credit. Like Aberhart, Bennett had a new and thrilling message to deliver to Canada; he was a preacher who saw in radio the best means of immediate personal communication with the entire nation. He disregarded Parliament; he ignored the possible constitutional limitations of federal legislative powers; and in five radio broadcasts, beginning on the 2nd of January, 1935, he appealed directly for the support of the Canadian people. His language, frequently borrowed from W. D. Herridge's long personal letters, was the language of a convinced and radical reformer. The capitalist system had been proved to be defective; it must be reformed; and reform meant government intervention, government regulation and control. The state must establish minimum wages, maximum hours of work, and a weekly rest for industry. It must provide unemployment, health, and accident insurance, and an improved old-age pension. For the benefit of the primary producer, the Wheat Board was to be re-established and marketing in other natural products regulated. There were to be amendments to the Combines Act, the Companies Act, and the Criminal Code. And, finally, a Trade and Industry Commission was to continue the work of investigation and reform which the Price Spreads Committee had begun.

Among the electorate in general, these revolutionary proposals raised doubts of Bennett's sincerity and left him open to charges of opportunism. But the most serious result of his apparent last-minute conversion was a deep division in the Conservative Party. His best plan was to minimize the differences among his followers as much as possible and to present a confident and united front in support of the reform programme. But he failed to realize how essential Stevens was to the political success of the new movement; and he took too little pains, and showed too little patience, in dealing with his temperamental and difficult Minister of Trade and Commerce. When the right-wing ministers, led by C. H. Cahan, attacked Stevens in a cabinet meeting, Bennett made no attempt to come to his rescue; and Stevens resigned. If the two men could have resumed their old relations, and if Bennett had called a spring election for a mandate to complete his New Deal, he might have won; but all efforts at a reconciliation failed, and in July, immediately after the prorogation, Stevens announced the formation of a new Reconstruction Party with himself as leader. The division among the Conservatives had now become open and irremediable.

In the general election of October 1935, the Conservative, Reconstruction, C.C.F., and Social Credit parties all had programmes of a sort. The Liberal Party had none – only an empty slogan, 'King or Chaos'. Yet, with only 45 per cent of the popular vote, it piled up the amazing total of 171 seats, and reduced the Conservatives to thirty-nine, eleven less than they had held in the electoral rout of 1921.

CHAPTER ELEVEN

The Politics of Evasion

THE MEANING of the general election of 1935 was purely negative. Two plans for the reform of Canadian capitalism, one offered by Bennett in the solid measures of the New Deal, and the other vaguely indicated in windy generalizations by H. H. Stevens, had both gone down to defeat. The socialist solution, presented for the first time in a Canadian general election, was even more decisively rejected. The C.C.F., which for three years had been instructing the electorate in the virtues of state socialism and centralized planning, got only a few thousand more votes than the hastily improvised, ramshackle party that Stevens put together in the summer of 1935, barely three months before the election. Political victory came to the party that had the least to offer – the party that, so far as the central issue of the welfare state was concerned, had no proposals at all. In his campaign speeches King concentrated on the quarrel between Bennett and Stevens, on the probable unconstitutionality of Bennett's New Deal, and on the security which the Liberal Party alone offered a divided and uncertain Canada. The chief positive policy which the Liberals put forward was that venerable project, so often reaffirmed, so frequently forgotten, the liberalization of trade.

There were some new men in King's cabinet, and some who were still young, though they were not new to politics. But the majority of the ministers were veterans, old and fairly complacent political warhorses whose outlook had been focused so firmly and narrowly by their own experience, as well as by the history of the Liberal Party, that they found it very difficult to comprehend the approach of a new and very different age. The Liberals had always preached a highly decentralized Canadian federalism; they had opposed Macdonald's national policies during the nineteenth century; and they had resisted most Conservative attempts to use the power of the state to carry out the characteristic national purposes of the twentieth. The wartime regulation of the national economy, the Canadian National Railways, the Canadian Radio Broadcasting Commission, and the Bennett New Deal were all Conservative achievements. The Liberals had regarded the process of postwar decentralization and the surrender of wartime controls as natural and proper; they had left the political initiative to the provinces during the 1920s; and throughout that prosperous decade this federal negativism had seemed completely justified by circumstances. Free enterprise was luxuriating in what proved to be a last golden sunset of affluence; the war to end wars had apparently established a durable peace. The veterans of the Liberal Party came to the conclusion that this state of affairs was normal and that it would continue indefinitely, with only relatively unimportant interruptions or changes.

They failed to perceive that a series of significant events, following each other in increasingly rapid succession, were in fact announcing the appearance of a strange new world in both domestic and external affairs. In 1931 came the international financial crisis and the Japanese invasion of Manchuria; in 1933 Hitler gained power in Germany, the New Deal was inaugurated in the United States, and the World Economic Conference failed in London; in 1934, the Disarmament Conference came to an end without result, Germany withdrew from the League of Nations, and, in Canada, the Price Spreads Committee began a hit-and-miss but very popular investigation into the iniquities of unregulated Canadian capitalism. It became obvious that world peace was in serious danger and that, in Canada as elsewhere, free enterprise was likely in future to be limited by government regulation and modified by government welfare services. In 1935 the truth of these serious conclusions was driven home by two further dramatic events; Bennett's New Deal abruptly threatened to bring the interventionist welfare state to Canada, and Mussolini's attack on Abyssinia was a concrete and unquestionable attack on the security system of the League of Nations.

These were the disturbing circumstances which the Liberals faced when they acquired power in October 1935. Fortunately, they did not have to make up their minds in a hurry about the welfare state. Bennett's New Deal had been rejected by the voters and would possibly be declared unconstitutional by the courts. These domestic problems could be approached deliberately; but the question of Italy, Abyssinia, and the League was different. Here a decision might have to be made quickly, for despite the advice of O. D. Skelton, the Permanent Undersecretary, who had tried hard to keep Canada completely detached from the Abyssinian affair, Bennett had gone far to commit the Canadian government to a positive course of support for the League's condemnation of Italy, even if it meant acceptance of the use of sanctions. 'We went into League, took benefits, must assume responsibilities, or get out, not try to hornswoggle ourselves out,' he barked over the telephone to Skelton, contemptuously rejecting the latter's disingenuous evasions. In the League assembly, G. Howard Ferguson, the Canadian representative at Geneva, was talking and acting in an equally forthright manner. Canada concurred in the League's declaration against Italian aggression, and accepted membership in the committee that was to recommend the steps necessary to carry it out.

It was the last time that the government of Canada ever gave its open and unqualified support to the League of Nations. On the 23rd of October, King was back in office once again; and, in their attitudes to collective security and sanctions, he and Skelton were two hearts that beat as one. There was not the slightest doubt now that Canadian policy in the Abyssinian crisis would be modified; but the change came later than might have been expected, partly because the new government's instructions were not too prompt or explicit, and partly because W. A. Riddell, Ferguson's successor at Geneva, was eager to play a leading role in the committee on sanctions. On the 2nd of November, he proposed that coal, oil, iron, and steel should be added to the list of products which members of the League would not export to Italy. For this he was at once privately reprimanded, but not publicly disavowed. It was not until his recommendation had acquired a terrifying notoriety as the 'Canadian proposal' that the frightened Canadian government decided on a public repudiation. On the 2nd of December, Ernest Lapointe announced, in a blunt, clumsily worded statement, that the Riddell proposal 'represented only his personal opinion, and his views as a member of the committee, and not the views of the Canadian government'.

A few days later, the Hoare-Laval plan for the partition of Abyssinia revealed to an astounded world that both France and Great Britain were just as intent as Canada on escaping from their obligations to collective security, and that they were jointly prepared to use methods even more objectionable than those Canada had employed. The outcry in Canada against the repudiation of Riddell was lost in a vast explosion of wrath throughout the western world over the Hoare-Laval plan. Its British author, Sir Samuel Hoare, was forced to resign; the plan itself was discarded. But its abandonment was the last victory for collective security. Great Britain and France were no more ready than Canada to enlarge the embargo against Italy by the inclusion of such a vital necessity as oil. The powers hesitated and delayed; and, while they dithered, Hitler took advantage of European disunion to dispatch a token force to occupy the Rhineland, and Marshal Badoglio's Italian army drove hard towards the capital of Abyssinia. Mussolini proclaimed the new Roman Empire; and all sanctions against Italy were lifted. The Locarno Pact and the Versailles Treaty were no more. The League of Nations was dead. And, in a long speech in Parliament on the 18th of June, 1936, Mackenzie King complacently pronounced its Canadian funeral oration.

⇒⟫ II ⟪⟸

O N DECEMBER 9TH, a week after Lapointe had published his sweeping repudiation of W. A. Riddell, a Dominion-Provincial Conference met in Ottawa. In King's mind, this conference was to be the platform from which a new and cautious experiment in Canadian federalism was to be launched. The old division of functions and revenues between the provinces and the nation had broken down during the depression; and Bennett's New Deal had raised the whole controversial issue of federal initiative in the provision of social services and economic controls. Bennett had arrogantly asserted federal jurisdiction; but his attempt to 'blast his way through' the British North America Act had apparently failed. Mackenzie King characteristically assumed that constitutional amendment was the only way in which Canada could fit herself for her new tasks as an industrialized nation. A new amending process, an amending process in harmony with the Dominion's new sovereign status, was essential. The Liberals had always contended, at least in theory, that the provinces should approve amendments to the British North America Act; and Mackenzie King was faithfully following Liberal precedent when he introduced the subject of constitutional amendment at the first Dominion-Provincial Conference of his new régime. By that very act, he implicitly conceded the principle that a new amending process must be the outcome of negotiation between the provinces and the federal government.

The conference set up a Continuing Committee on Constitutional Questions; and during the winter of 1936 this committee worked out a method of amendment which could be completed in Canada without recourse, as in the past, to the Parliament of the United Kingdom. The Parliament of Canada was to be empowered to enact a new Canadian constitution which would not itself amend the existing federal-provincial relationships of the British North America Act, but would contain a new section setting out a procedure by which they could be amended. According to the terms of this new section, the clauses of the British North America Act were to be divided into four distinct classes, with a different method of amendment for each class, in an ascending order of difficulty. In matters concerning the federal government only, the Parliament of Canada could itself amend; in matters concerning some but not all the provinces, as well as the federal government, amendment would be by act of Parliament and the assent of the legislatures of all the provinces affected. Finally, for general questions, which interested all ten Canadian governments, two further classes were proposed; in the first, amendments could be made by act of Parliament and the assent of two-thirds of the provinces representing at least 55 per cent of the population of Canada; in the second and most fundamental class, the 'entrenched clauses' of the constitution, which were numerous, the concurrence of Parliament and of the legislatures of all the provinces would be necessary. Admittedly this was a complicated arrangement; but it avoided the difficulties which a single rigid formula for all amendments was bound to create. The Continuing Committee, in a relatively short space of time, had produced a practical solution; but its achievement was vain nevertheless. Obviously the rule of unanimity must apply to the amending procedure itself; and a solitary province, New Brunswick, rejected it.

Less than a year later, in January 1937, the Judicial Committee of the Privy Council conclusively settled the fate of the Bennett New Deal. All three labour statutes, as well as the Social Insurance Act and the Natural Products Marketing Act, were declared *ultra vires* of the Parliament of Canada, on the ground chiefly that they affected the exclusive provincial power to legislate in respect of property and civil rights in the province. In vain the Dominion appealed to its residuary authority to make laws for the peace, order, and good government of Canada, and to its enumerated powers to regulate trade and commerce, and to raise revenue by any mode or system of taxation. In vain the federal government called upon the jurisdiction granted by Section 132 of the British North America Act, which empowered it to carry out 'the obligations of Canada or of any province thereof, as part of the British Empire, towards Foreign Countries, arising under Treaties between the Empire and such Foreign Countries'. The three labour statutes – Maximum Hours, Minimum Wages, and Weekly Rest in Industry – were all based on certain draft conventions of the International Labour Organization, the ratification of which, it was argued, was an obligation of Canada arising out of the Treaty of Versailles. Section 132 had helped to give the federal government the victory in the Aeronautics case of 1931, but now it was ruled out as inapplicable. The Judicial Committee decided that the obligations which Canada had accepted in ratifying the labour conventions were new obligations, not obligations under the peace treaty. They were not obligations of Canada as part of the British Empire, but of Canada in virtue of her new status as an international person; and they therefore did not come within the scope of Section 132, which applied to 'British Empire' treaties only. With a strange irony, the new, sovereign Canada would have far less power to implement treaties than the old, colonial Canada had possessed.

Both Bennett's direct attack on the British North America Act and King's circuitous approach to its amendment had failed. In these frustrating circumstances, the intractable problems of the welfare state were dropped for the time being; and King turned back to subjects which were safely within federal jurisdiction. Here he had committed himself to little during the election; his most important promise was to seek a reduction in the forbidding tariffs of the depression years. The Bennett government had begun trade negotiations with the United States; King quickly completed them in the autumn of 1935; and two years later, when the Ottawa Agreements of 1932 came up for renewal, their terms were substantially revised. By the Canadian-American agreement, Canada gave the United States its intermediate or treaty tariff rates, and the United States responded by ending the restrictions which the Fordney-McCumber and Hawley-Smoot tariffs had imposed on Canadian exports. The principle of the imperial preference was retained in the new agreement between Canada and the United Kingdom; but the preferences were no longer created by the simple device of raising the tariff levels against foreign countries; and the preferential margins were narrowed. The King government had made a beginning, but only a beginning, in the liberalization of international trade. In 1935, Canada's treaty rates were higher than her general rates had been in 1929, and the level of protection in all three countries was still considerable.

In domestic affairs, King's advance was similarly cautious. During the Bennett administration Parliament had managed to get over the constitutional objection to the establishment of a national wheat board by the ingenious device of declaring the western grain elevators to be works 'for the general advantage of Canada'. King did not change the wheat board legislation; he altered Bennett's Bank of Canada Act only so far as was necessary to ensure public ownership of the new institution. The administrative weaknesses of the Conservative government's broadcasting commission were corrected, and its powers extended by a new statute which set up the Canadian Broadcasting Corporation. Finally, under the direction of C. D. Howe, now Minister of the new Department of Transport, the long and difficult advance towards a national airline – an advance which had begun years before when the Bennett government built a string of landing fields as a depression measure – ended at last, in the spring of 1937, in the establishment of the publicly owned corporation Trans-Canada Air Lines.

Then, in August 1937, Mackenzie King made a move which, though characteristic of his cautious approach to difficult issues, was at once more original and more courageous than anything he had done since taking office nearly two years before. He appointed a royal commission empowered to carry out 'a re-examination of the economic and financial basis of Confederation in the light of the economic and social developments of the last seventy years'. The members of the Royal Commission on Dominion-Provincial Relations, as it came to be called, were N. W. Rowell, an old 'conscriptionist' Liberal with whom King now made his final peace, Joseph Sirois, a Quebec lawyer and a professor in the Faculty of Law at Laval University, J. W. Dafoe, editor of the *Winnipeg Free Press*, R. A. MacKay, Professor of Government at Dalhousie University, and H. F.

Angus, Professor of Economics at the University of British Columbia. When ill-health compelled Rowell's resignation, Sirois succeeded him as chairman of the commission. Its secretary, whose appointment was a reminder of the strength of the hereditary principle in the Canadian civil service, was Alexander Skelton, O. D. Skelton's son.

The Liberal government had publicly acknowledged that the twentieth century had burdened Canadian governments with social responsibilities and regulatory functions which had not been dreamed of at Confederation. And, by the very act of constituting the Royal Commission, Mackenzie King had asserted the right of federal leadership in the work of constitutional reform. It remained to be seen whether the provinces would dutifully accept federal precedence and follow federal guidance in the amendment of the British North America Act.

→» III «←

TWO NEW NAMES, Alberta and Quebec, had been added to the growing list of provinces in which new governments, with avowedly reforming programmes, had recently gained power. In August 1935, two months before the federal general election, Aberhart and the Social Credit Party had won a smashing victory in Alberta. A year later, the Union Nationale, the coalition of the insurgent Liberal Paul Gouin and the Conservative Maurice Duplessis, piled up a majority in Quebec that nearly equalled Aberhart's in Alberta. It seemed certain that Aberhart, with his beguiling promise of a monthly dividend of twenty-five dollars for every citizen of Alberta, would quickly clash with the federal government and its orthodox monetary views; but there was no apparent reason why the more conventional platform of Union Nationale should bring it into conflict with Ottawa. And, on the surface at least, there was even less likelihood that Mitch Hepburn, the Liberal premier of Ontario, whose highly conservative social and economic outlook was imperfectly concealed by his demagogic populism, should get into controversy with that cautious, circumspect, middle-of-the-road Liberal, Mackenzie King. Yet, by the autumn of 1937, all three provincial leaders were regarding the federal government with resentment or hostility, and all three found in the Rowell-Sirois Commission a new and superabundant cause for open opposition.

Somewhat suprisingly, Aberhart was not the first of the three premiers to fall out with Mackenzie King. He had prudently warned the Albertans that the payment of the monthly dividend could not begin until a year and a half after he came to power; but time went by and he made no obvious preparations for the great day. In fact, he seemed to concentrate exclusively upon the conventional aim of providing cheap, honest, and efficient government for Alberta. He managed to hold off the growing restiveness within his party until the session of 1937, when the disappointed and disgusted backbenchers, who really believed in the principles of Social Credit, revolted against the cautious leadership of the cabinet; and, although they failed to dislodge Aberhart from the premiership, they compelled his government to make a real and determined effort to introduce the 'new economic order'. At this point, the inevitable collision with the federal government took place, with a resounding crash. Early in the spring of 1937, when the backbenchers' revolt was already under way at Edmonton, Ernest Lapointe, the federal Minister of Justice, piously reaffirming traditional Liberal principles of Canadian federalism, declared that he did not think that 'in a federation such as this the power of disallowance could easily be exercised by the federal government'. No man was ever forced by circumstances to eat his words more quickly or more completely than Ernest Lapointe. He soon found that, if necessary, he could exercise the power of disallowance very 'easily' indeed. In 1937-8 no fewer than six Alberta statutes were disallowed; three more were reserved by the lieutenant-governor of the province and subsequently declared *ultra vires* by the Supreme Court.

Aberhart had been held, in the end, to his election promises. Duplessis succeeded in escaping almost completely from his. Union Nationale was a coalition based on Liberal and Conservative equality, but Duplessis very quickly revealed that he was intent on seizing control. Paul Gouin left the coalition in disgust even before the election of August 1936; and when the victorious Duplessis formed a highly Conservative cabinet, from which all the former leaders of Action Libérale Nationale were excluded, these disillusioned and angry radicals also broke away from the new party. Union Nationale was weakened but not too seriously. Duplessis kept the support of the majority of the insurgent Liberals in the assembly. He tightened his hold on the party and its policies. The whole elaborate programme of economic change and social reform with which Union Nationale had wooed the voters in two elections was now cynically and ruthlessly discarded. The hydro-electric utilities remained in private ownership; the English-controlled 'trusts' went their accustomed ways untouched. Duplessis's labour legislation favoured management at the expense of the trade unions; and his notorious 'Padlock Law' of 1937, which permitted the government to close or 'padlock' any premises suspected of propagating 'Communism' or 'Bolshevism' (terms not defined in the Act) revealed a curiously morbid horror of socialist principles. The original radicalism of Union Nationale had vanished. Only its nationalism remained. And this was directed, not against the English control of the Quebec economy, but against the federal government at Ottawa.

It was only natural that Duplessis of Quebec and Hepburn of Ontario should become close friends and joint enemies of King and his Royal Commission on Dominion-Provincial Relations. By this time the appealing image of Hepburn as the friend of the 'little man' and the foe of the 'protected interests' had lost much of its sparkle; but it was darkened beyond hope of restoration in 1937 when the Oshawa local of the United Auto Workers, an affiliate of the newly formed Committee for Industrial Organization (C.I.O.) in the United States, began a strike in the General Motors plant. Hepburn's frantic efforts to expel the 'professional foreign agitators' from Ontario, and to recruit a provincial army for the maintenance of law and order, which had not for a moment been endangered, naturally earned him the warm commendation of Duplessis; and Hepburn responded generously that he would give Duplessis and his policies 'a blanket endorsement'. The Toronto-Quebec axis had been formed; and it was soon turned in defiance against Ottawa.

Temperamentally, Hepburn and King were an utter contrast. Their sharp disagreements had begun very soon after Hepburn was installed in office; but the appointment of the Rowell-Sirois Commission was certain to widen the scope and deepen the significance of this running feud. Hepburn was bound, in the end, to take a pugnacious provincial stand; but at first, pre-occupied with other matters, he hardly seemed to realize the implications of this new federal inquiry. King, without waiting for his commission's report, had already gone so far as to ask the provinces to agree to an amendment of the British North America Act which would empower the federal Parliament to enact a national scheme of unemployment insurance. At first Hepburn handsomely concurred in this proposal; but soon he began to have serious doubts. A national system of unemploy-ment insurance, with equal benefits across the country, would, he argued, result in an appalling financial burden, a burden certain to be largely borne by Ontario and Quebec. 'Equaliza-tion' was a dangerous fallacy; and the appointment of the Rowell-Sirois Commission implied that this vicious principle would be extended over a wide range of social services. Hep-burn and Duplessis began to meet and correspond with the frequency and cordiality of old friends and fellow believers. Together, they planned determined resistance to 'federal en-croachment'.

Late in November 1937, the Royal Commission set out to conduct a series of public hearings across the country. One by one, its three mortal enemies, Aberhart, Hepburn, and Duples-sis, declared their uncompromising opposition. In March, when the commission arrived in Edmonton, the government and legislature of Alberta simply refused to have anything to do with it. At Toronto, in a petulant and ill-mannered harangue, Hepburn attacked federal centralization as a threat to Canadian democracy and denounced the economic unsoundness and financial inequity of 'equalized' non-contributary social services. Neither Duplessis nor any of his ministers greeted the commission officially when it reached Quebec; counsel representing the province appeared merely to state that it denied the federal government's right to appoint such a commission and would not be bound by any of its recommendations. This frigid public reception was not in the slightest improved by the boisterous hospitality which Duplessis offered the commissioners in private. He invited them to a dinner at the Château Frontenac, arrived late and drunk for his own party, subjected the commissioners to a good deal of vulgar banter, and ended the evening by throwing champagne glasses at the electric lights with such accuracy that the restaurant was soon in semi-darkness and the floor and tables littered with broken glass.

⇥ IV ⇤

IN MARCH 1938, just as the members of the Rowell-Sirois Commission were on their way westward to visit British Columbia, the two-year *détente* in the affairs of Europe came to an abrupt close. It had begun with the reluctant acceptance, by all the principal powers concerned, of Mussolini's conquest of Abyssinia and Hitler's occupation of the Rhineland; and it ended, the 12th of March, 1938, with the *Anschluss*, the incorporation of Austria in Germany. The chief feature of the diplomacy of these two years, and of the tense and anxious eighteen months that followed, was summed up in a word that became notorious to later generations, appeasement. At the time, 'appeasement' was used, not ironically and pejoratively, but sincerely and approvingly, to indicate a general but definite approach to European politics. It meant that the peace of Europe could be kept best, not by coercion, sanctions, and force, but by conciliation, concession, and compromise. It meant that the injustices of the Treaty of Versailles must be recognized and rectified, and that Germany had legitimate grievances, claims, and aspirations that deserved to be satisfied.

No contemporary politician held this view more strongly or clung to it more tenaciously than Mackenzie King. Canada, of course, was not directly involved in the politics of European pacification, and King took very good care to maintain her complete detachment; but, though he watched the process of appeasement from afar, he watched it with unbroken and unqualified approval. In September 1936, he bluntly told the assembly of the League of Nations that collective security through sanctions had utterly failed, and that only a world organization with a truly universal membership, using the methods of mediation and conciliation, could possibly save the peace. At the Imperial Conference of 1937, he showed himself ready and eager to support a collective Commonwealth endorsation of appeasement, despite the fact that, throughout his entire career, he had consistently opposed a common imperial policy in defence and foreign affairs. It was at the Imperial Conference that he acquired his unbounded admiration for Neville Chamberlain's wise statesmanship; and, a fortnight later, a two-hour interview with Hitler left him with the firm impression that the German Führer was a man of 'deep sincerity', determined 'not to permit any resort to war'. Thus Chamberlain's programme of positive appeasement seemed, practically as well as ideally, the only right policy; and King welcomed each British attempt to satisfy Germany's demands with steadily rising enthusiasm. His firm belief that private personal discussions could solve almost anything was dramatically confirmed when Chamberlain flew to Berchtesgaden for his interview with Hitler; and he greeted this 'far-seeing and noble action' almost rapturously. Two weeks later, when appeasement reached its culmination in the settlement of Munich, he was moved to positive transports of gratitude and praise. Even the shocking events of the 15th of March, 1939 – the German occupation of Prague and the final dismemberment of Czechoslovakia – did not shake his unalterable faith in the wisdom of conciliation. He was much more disappointed in Chamberlain for abandoning appeasement than he was in Hitler for declaring Bohemia and Moravia protectorates of Germany.

All that Mackenzie King had offered to the politics of appeasement was moral support. All that he was likely to contribute to the politics of resistance was appeal and exhortation. What he would do if resistance ended in war remained an impenetrable mystery. At Berlin in June 1937, he had told Hitler that Canada would join the rest of the Empire in a fight against aggression; but only a month earlier, in the Imperial Conference in London, he had declared that he 'would not venture to predict' what Canada would do if war broke out in Europe. In a speech in January 1939, he repeated Laurier's famous aphorism: 'If England is at war, we are at war and liable to attack'; and he opposed all proposals that Canada claim a right to declare its neutrality. He seemed to acknowledge a constitutional liability; but at the same time he implied that it might mean nothing more than a passive belligerence. On the 20th of March, five days after the German invasion of Czechoslovakia, he went so far as to declare that if an aggressor launched an attack on Great Britain, 'with bombers raining death on London', he had no doubt what the decision of the Canadian people and Parliament would be. This was his strongest statement of purpose; but it was quickly followed by an elaborate qualification. On the 30th of March, he repeated his familiar refusal 'to say here and now that Canada is prepared to support whatever may be proposed by the government at Westminster . . .'

These utterances implied an unwilling and inactive belligerency; and the extent and nature of Canadian rearmament pointed to the same conclusion. In September 1936, the Liberal cabinet had reached the reluctant conclusion that the languishing armed forces of Canada could be rescued from total extinction only by increased expenditures; but the appropriations for 1937-8 were only 20 per cent higher than those of the previous year, and less than half of what the service chiefs had requested. It was not until 1939-40 that the prewar estimates reached the totals which the staff officers had asked three years before; and throughout the whole period the navy and air force were consistently favoured at the expense of the army. Planes and ships suggested a modest 'police force' on the Atlantic and Pacific coasts; a larger army conjured up the horrible spectre of an overseas expeditionary force. 'I think that is now wholly out of the question,' King confided to his diary. Equally out of the question was all co-operation with the United Kingdom in defence. There was to be no Canadian representative on the Committee of Imperial Defence in London. Canadian airmen were not to be transferred for service in the Royal Air Force; and, in the spring of 1938, when the British government proposed that the Royal Air Force be permitted to establish training schools in Canada, this request was turned down. In reply to persistent questions by Meighen, Raoul Dandurand, the government leader in the Senate, tried to disguise the ugly fact of this refusal by replies which were disingenuous and misleading. The proposal had been put forward by Sir Francis Floud, the British High Commissioner to Canada, who insisted that he had made a definite request on behalf of the United Kingdom government; but Mackenzie King – and Dandurand on King's instructions – continued to create the false impression that only informal, exploratory, and inconclusive conversations had taken place. In the end, though he never admitted the fact of the British request, King sought refuge from his critics in the nationalist principle that, in peacetime, there could be no military establishments in Canada except those maintained and controlled by the Canadian government.

On the 23rd of August, 1939, Ribbentrop and Molotov signed the Nazi-Soviet Non-Aggression Pact. Mackenzie King occupied the next few days in sending earnest appeals for peace to Hitler, Mussolini, and the President of the Polish Republic. Strangely enough these exhortations proved unavailing, and on the 1st of September Hitler's armies invaded Poland. The Canadian Parliament was summoned, and King announced that if the United Kingdom became involved in a war to resist aggression, the government would seek parliamentary authority 'for effective co-operation by Canada at the side of Britain'. On the 3rd of September, Great Britain and France declared war on Germany, and four days later the Canadian Parliament met. King left the meaning of the phrase 'effective co-operation' largely unexplained; but he was very explicit about some of its limitations. Home defence was to come first; no decision had yet been made to send an expeditionary force overseas; and, in any case, there would be no conscription for overseas military service. The government's policy, presented in these carefully guarded terms, was accepted by the House of Commons without a division; and, on the 10th of September, King George VI declared a state of war between Canada and the German Reich.

Mackenzie King was essentially a peacetime prime minister, and the declaration of war did not alter his character in the slightest; he simply remained a peacetime prime minister in wartime. Canada had flung the gauntlet down before one of the mightiest military states in the world; but the Canadian government behaved as if it was engaged in a tussle with a native African state or a third-rate South American republic. Despite official discouragement of recruiting, voluntary enlistment in the army was high; and, on the 16th of September, evidently under the pressure of public opinion, the government decided to send one division to England, though at the same time it reaffirmed the principle that there was to be no large expeditionary force. Ten days later, when Hitler's campaign against Poland had already demonstrated the appalling effectiveness of air power, the British government proposed that a giant British Commonwealth Air Training Plan should be carried out in Canada. To the Canadian government, one of the main attractions of this plan lay in the fact that it was essentially a training scheme, of which Great Britain and the other Dominions, as well as Canada, could take advantage, and not a proposal for a large Canadian air force. Mackenzie King liked the scheme so well that he only regretted that it had not been suggested early enough to enable the government to avoid its commitment to dispatch a division overseas; and he insisted that the British provide a formal acknowledgement, which the Canadian government could publish if it chose, that the Air Training Plan had priority over every other part of the Canadian war effort. On the 17th of December, after nearly two months of argument, misunderstanding, bickering, and recrimination, the Air Training Agreement was finally signed.

⟶》》 V 《《⟵

K ING'S REVISED VERSION of the Laurier 'limited liability' policy had now been presented to the Canadian people. As might have been expected, it was attacked from two diametrically opposed quarters, by those who thought it had gone too far and those who thought it had not gone far enough, by Maurice Duplessis on the one hand, and Mitchell Hepburn on the other. With the opening of the war, the Toronto-Quebec axis broke. Hepburn and Duplessis had nothing in common now but their hatred of Mackenzie King, and each had completely different reasons for his animosity. Two weeks after the declaration of war, the Quebec legislature was dissolved and a general election called on the pretext that the federal government, under the sweeping powers of the War Measures Act, was seriously invading provincial jurisdiction. In the circumstances of the moment, Duplessis's appeal for support against the federal 'campaign of assimilation and centralization' was nothing less than a defiance of the Canadian war effort. The King cabinet, including the French-Canadian ministers led by Lapointe, decided that Duplessis must be beaten and that his rival, the provincial Liberal leader, Adélard Godbout, should be given all possible aid. The Quebec ministers made Godbout's cause literally their own by announcing that, if he lost the election, they themselves would resign, leaving the province without representation in the federal cabinet. A completely English-speaking or coalition government would, they prophesied, quickly introduce compulsory military service. 'We', declared the bulky Lapointe fervently, 'are the rampart' between French Canada and conscription.

On the 25th of October, Godbout triumphed by a majority nearly as big as Duplessis's had been three years before. The attack from the left flank on King's middle position had failed; but, in the meantime, a scarcely less formidable onslaught was about to be launched from the right. All during the autumn of 1939, Hepburn kept up a running fire of criticism against the confusion and 'scandalous apathy' of the Canadian war effort; and, when the provincial legislature opened in

January 1940, he could not resist the temptation of a formal vote of censure on the national government's inertia. On the 18th of January, he angrily moved a resolution 'regretting that the Federal Government at Ottawa has made so little effort to prosecute Canada's duty in the war in the vigorous manner the people of Canada desire to see'. King was, of course, deeply offended that such a resolution could be proposed by a supposedly Liberal premier and passed by a legislature in which Liberals had a majority; but his annoyance did not blind him to the fact that Hepburn's provocative action had given him an unexpected but superlative opportunity. He had promised that there would be another session of Parliament. Parliament was, in fact, to meet one week later, on the 25th of January. He dreaded a contentious pre-election session; but he saw now that Hepburn had unwittingly provided him with a means of escape from the ordeal. He could dissolve Parliament and go to the country on the plea that the Premier of Ontario's gratuitous attack on the federal war effort justified an appeal to the Canadian people for its verdict. At first he intended a very short session; but, on the morning of the 25th, he decided to dissolve that very day. It was well past twelve o'clock, with Parliament due to open at three, before his own ministers learnt the amazing secret. All the other M.P.s, including Robert Manion, the recently elected leader of the Conservative opposition, arrived in the Senate Chamber in the confident expectation of a full session of Parliament. It barely began. 'My advisers,' said Lord Tweedsmuir, the Governor General, reading the brief Speech from the Throne, 'have decided on an immediate appeal to the country.' Manion furiously denounced the incredible doctrine that the federal government had the duty or the right to appeal to the national electorate from a vote of censure in a provincial legislature. The Prime Minister, he insisted, must give an account of his stewardship to Parliament; he was responsible to the people of Canada through Parliament. 'No,' King retorted, 'by direct appeal to the people themselves.' Once again, to suit his own convenience, he had substituted plebiscitary democracy for parliamentary government. At 7.07 p.m. on the night of the 25th of January, 1940, the eighteenth Parliament was dissolved. Its final session had lasted a little over four hours.

Mackenzie King had chosen his moment better than even he could then have realized. The 'phoney war' had now lasted five months; it seemed as if it might continue indefinitely. Hitler, who hoped to negotiate a peace after his conquest of Poland, did nothing to provoke the British and French; and the British and French were led to believe that, in two or three years, economic blockade and defensive strategy would win them a cheap victory over Germany. After the fear of air raids gradually subsided, the burden of war rested fairly lightly on the British people; the Canadians were scarcely aware that they were at war at all. King's 'moderate' policies made good sense in such circumstances; and poor Manion's demand for a 'national government' in which 'the best brains' from all parties would unite for a more vigorous war effort seemed a melodramatic extravagance. King expected to win the general election; but the extent of his victory surprised him. The Liberals gained 178 seats in a House of 245. The Conservative strength, 39, was exactly what it had been in the previous Parliament. The Social Crediters lost 7 seats, and the C.C.F. gained only 1.

Mackenzie King's luck had stood by him. The general election was held on the 26th of March. Exactly two weeks later, on the 9th of April, the phoney war ended and the real war began. In a few hours Hitler's forces overran Denmark and Norway; on the 10th of May they attacked the Netherlands and Belgium with efficient and terrific violence. The Dutch and Belgian governments capitulated, and on the 17th of June France sued for an armistice. The British Expeditionary Force was evacuated from Dunkirk; and England faced the prospect of imminent invasion. The nations of the Commonwealth – Great Britain, Canada, Australia, South Africa, and New Zealand – stood alone in their resistance to Hitler.

→≫ VI ≪←

IN ENGLAND, the crisis produced a new War Cabinet and Ministry, with Labour and Liberal representatives included, and Churchill as Prime Minister and Minister of Defence. Nothing of the sort happened in Canada; the Canadian government declined to follow the British example or its own precedent of 1917. King, an inflexible party man who had just scored a huge success in a general election, was in no mood to listen seriously to talk of a national government. What he did was to reshuffle his cabinet, and to pick a strong team for the vigorous conduct of the war. The Defence Ministry was now divided into three departments, with C. G. Power as Minister of National Defence for Air, Angus L. Macdonald as Minister of National Defence for Naval Services, and J. L. Ralston, the acknowledged senior of the triumvirate, retaining the old title of Minister of National Defence. J. L. Ilsley took over Ralston's former portfolio of Finance, and the dynamic C. D. Howe became head of the new Department of Munitions and Supply. The unreal conception of 'limited liability' had been invalidated by events; economy and domestic Canadian politics ceased to be the major considerations determining the size and character of the Canadian war effort. The government introduced the National Resources Mobilization Act, conscripting men for home defence though not for service abroad; and every available Canadian ship and plane was hurriedly dispatched to take part in the Battle of Britain.

The crisis of the spring and summer of 1940 changed the organization and decisively altered the spirit of the Canadian government; but it did not bring any increase whatever in the Canadian government's influence on the conduct of the war. With the defeat and withdrawal of France, the war had become a war between the British Commonwealth and Germany; but the direction of Commonwealth strategy never became a co-operative Commonwealth enterprise. After June 1940, the British War Cabinet, and particularly Churchill and the service Chiefs of Staff, monopolized the authority which up to then they had shared with the French High Command; but

King made no attempt to challenge this exclusively British control. He remained the mental prisoner of Canada's isolationist colonial past. At a time when the nation had completely committed herself to the united Commonwealth defiance of Hitler, he still retained his primitive irrational fear of 'imperial consultation'. In the spring of 1940, when Chamberlain had proposed an Imperial Conference, King had successfully discouraged the idea; and he was just as obstinately opposed to it a year later when Robert Menzies of Australia and Peter Fraser of New Zealand, both of whom wanted their Dominions to exercise some influence on the conduct of the war, brought up the subject of an imperial war cabinet or an Empire council. The war was nearly two years old when, in August 1941, King made his first wartime visit to England; and even then the journey was undertaken, not because he intended to claim a share in the direction of the war, but because he was jealous of Roosevelt's meeting with Churchill at Placentia Bay, Newfoundland, and because he realized that his continued seclusion in Ottawa was arousing serious criticism among the Canadian people.

The crisis of 1940 did little to change Canada's relations with Britain; but it had a profound effect upon her relations with the United States. Mackenzie King disliked consultation and joint planning with a comrade-in-arms; but he welcomed them with a neutral. In 1938, President Roosevelt had paid a popular and much discussed visit to Canada; and in the spring of 1940, when King travelled south for a brief holiday, he had several long, confidential talks with Roosevelt and his Secretary of State, Cordell Hull. A friendly acquaintanceship had already developed, but it was the crisis of 1940 that hurried it into a close association. A sudden, anxious concern for the security of North America was awakened in Washington. The collapse of France, the Americans confidently assumed, would soon be followed by the fall of Britain; and for a time Roosevelt and Hull actually tried to ensure that, if the British government were compelled to sue for peace, the Royal Navy would be dispatched across the Atlantic to North America. Churchill's refusal even to consider such a possibility forced the Americans to turn from thoughts of acquiring the salvage of an Empire to plans for preventing its wreck. Aid, Roosevelt decided, might be given to Britain, but only on hard bargaining terms which would directly strengthen North American defence. The United States had fifty over-age destroyers that she was willing to dispose of; and Roosevelt now proposed that these be exchanged for air and naval bases in Newfoundland, Bermuda, and the British West Indies. This kind of Yankee horse-trading, to which Roosevelt took so naturally, offended Churchill; and in the end he signed ninety-nine-year leases for bases in Newfoundland and Bermuda without any mention of the destroyers. Mackenzie King was kept informed and heartily approved of the destroyers-for-bases deal, even though one of the bases was to be in Newfoundland, the island which Canada had always hoped would eventually become a Canadian province.

A few days before this Anglo-American exchange was made public, Roosevelt succeeded in fitting Canada even more firmly into his plans for the defence of North America. Mackenzie King was extraordinarily susceptible to the President's easy charm, and when Roosevelt telephoned and invited him down to Ogdensburg, on the American side of the St. Lawrence, for a private talk on the defence question, he instantly accepted. He drove down the next day, accompanied only by the American Minister to Canada, and spent the night of the 17th of August in the President's private railway car. Roosevelt proposed the creation of a permanent joint board, composed of an equal number of Canadians and Americans, to study the common defence problems of the two countries and make recommendations to their governments. In the past, King had repeatedly and solemnly assured the Canadian people that his government would make no external commitments – above all, no permanent external commitments – without the concurrence of the Canadian Parliament. But, on the evening of the 17th of August, the thought of Parliament apparently did not even cross his mind. He accepted Roosevelt's proposal at once, without asking for time to consult his own colleagues and to inform the British government; and Roosevelt drafted a statement which was immediately given to the press. The Canada–

United States Permanent Joint Board on Defence was set up very quickly and its members held their first meeting on the 26th of August. Eight months later, in April 1941, this close Canadian-American co-operation, which had begun in the planning of continental defence, was extended by the Hyde Park Declaration to cover the production of war materials.

In the meantime, the Battle of Britain had been won, and Hitler had dropped his plans for an invasion across the Channel. Neither side was now in a position to end the war by a knock-out blow. The Germans began the 'Blitz' over England; the British retaliated with the night bombing of Germany. At the moment, the only possible way in which Britain could strike against Germany was by air; but Italy, which had entered the war on Germany's side in June 1940, was vulnerable in the Mediterranean and in the Middle East. The British successes in North Africa and the prolonged resistance of the Greeks finally compelled Hitler to come to the rescue of his feeble and hard-pressed ally. The German offensives in Libya, Yugoslavia, and Greece were quick and dramatic successes; but the chief direction of Hitler's strategy in 1941 was not southeast, but east; and in June he launched the gigantic and terrible enterprise of the invasion of Russia. The whole character of the war was changing; it changed even more radically in December 1941, when the Japanese attacked Pearl Harbor and brought the United States into the conflict. The war had ceased to be a war between the British Commonwealth and Germany; it had become a world war in which every important power on earth was now engaged.

CHAPTER TWELVE

The Return to Colonial Status

ONCE THE WAR became a world war, the partnership of the United States and the United Kingdom was the dominant political fact in the western world; and the centre of this partnership was the close personal relationship between Churchill and Roosevelt. Together they ran the war for the combined forces of the British Empire and Commonwealth and the United States. The declaration of the United Nations, published on the 1st of January, 1942, gave precedence to the United States, Great Britain, Soviet Russia, and – at Roosevelt's insistence – China. Roosevelt and Churchill were ready to recognize the equality of the four great powers in the conduct of the world war as a whole; but they refused to share their exclusive control of the American, British, and Commonwealth war effort. In theory, the Americans were, and continued to be, intensely suspicious of 'British imperialism'; but, in practice, they found it extremely convenient to have Churchill speak for the whole Empire, in which Canada was, in American eyes, simply a North American colony. The Combined Chiefs of Staff Committees, which were set up in December 1941, when Roosevelt and Churchill met in Washington, were composed exclusively of British and American officials. Canada, it was explained, could not be given membership in these bodies for, if she were admitted, the other Commonwealth countries would have to be admitted also, and this would be administratively impossible. For the most part, Canada sought in vain for a place in the Anglo-American supreme directorate; the only combined boards to which she gained admittance were politically unimportant.

It was, in fact, only through the Commonwealth relationship that Canada could have participated effectively in the conduct of the war. The obvious precedent for Commonwealth co-operation in wartime was the Imperial War Cabinet of 1917-18; but the institution which Borden had sought, and Lloyd George and Milner created, during the First World War was not to be re-established during the Second. Neither Churchill nor King wanted it. Churchill, intent upon a virtual personal monopoly in his own government, was even less willing to share his authority with Dominion prime ministers; and King's morbid and unreasoning suspicion of 'imperial centralization', as well as his ingrained preference for domestic Canadian politics, made it easier for Churchill to get his way, despite the protests of Australia and New Zealand. The four Dominions, Churchill argued, would never be able to agree upon a single representative of their joint interests; and representatives from all four governments would make a far too large and unwieldy war cabinet. Churchill had little interest in, and not much regard for, the modern Commonwealth; his romantic attachment was reserved for the old Empire. In his mind, the Dominions were convenient sources of men and materials, and useful as a collective makeweight against the preponderating power of the United States. But the cause they served, he never doubted for a minute, was the cause of Britain's greatness. They were to do as they were told, and to be used with little compunction for their sensibilities.

Canada had become an autonomous Dominion during the First World War; she reverted to the position of a dependent colony during the Second. The few occasions on which she seemed to acquire a more dignified status were nothing more than the semblance of reality. There were allied conferences at Quebec City in 1943 and 1944. King was physically present at both meetings and talked with British and American leaders; but he had no part whatever in the vital discussions of the principals, Churchill and Roosevelt, and their staffs. To one onlooker, he was like 'a man who has lent his house for a party'; and he himself admitted that his role at the Quebec Citadel was very much like that of the general manager of the

Château Frontenac Hotel. But he was not seriously disappointed or disconcerted. The mere appearance of conferring with the great satisfied him; the Canadian electorate, he believed, would be convinced of his importance in the counsels of the grand alliance. The conference, he decided, would be 'a pretty good answer' to the Tory insinuations that Canada's leaders were Churchill and the President.

The fact that Canada had no share in the general direction of the war did not mean that she lacked all control over the disposition of her armed forces. King at times exerted considerable influence, particularly on the employment of the Canadian Army; and his interventions were invariably for political, not military, reasons. He was quite content to have the Canadian troops remain indefinitely in England. He feared the casualties of combat, for heavy casualties might revive the dreaded demand for conscription; and, though he believed firmly that Canadian forces ought to aid in the defence of Britain, he was equally convinced that they must not be used to protect and perpetuate 'British imperial interests' in the Middle East and Far East. He opposed the dispatch of Canadian troops to Egypt and Libya in 1940-1 and to India, Burma, and Singapore in the expected Pacific campaign of 1945. The Defence Ministers, Ralston, Power, and Macdonald, came increasingly to believe that at least some Canadian divisions should have battle experience. But General McNaughton, who had built up the Canadian Army on the expectation of leading it as a united whole in the final invasion of north-western Europe, was opposed to the division of his forces; and the controversy over this issue lasted down until nearly the end of the war.

To a considerable extent, the Canadian people identified the national war effort with the Army; but the other services played a much larger part in the Second World War than they had in the First. About 250,000 men and women served in the Royal Canadian Air Force, and about another 100,000 in the Royal Canadian Navy. The navy was essentially a small-ship fleet – destroyers, corvettes, frigates, and minesweepers – which did heavy convoy duty in the North Atlantic and took part in the landings at Dieppe, Sicily, Italy, and Normandy. The largest enterprise undertaken by the air force was the British Commonwealth Air Training Plan, in which about 100,000 of its personnel were involved. The R.C.A.F. also guarded the Pacific and Atlantic coasts of Canada, and contributed forty-eight squadrons to the great armadas of the allied bomber command. In addition, a very large number of Canadians served in the Royal Air Force, which, indeed, was the original intent of the plan; and Power's programme of 'Canadianization' – the attempt to transfer Canadian aircrew to Canadian national squadrons – encountered many difficulties including the resistance of the Canadian aircrew themselves. About 10,000 Canadians, members of either the R.A.F. or the R.C.A.F., lost their lives in night bombing over Germany.

The largest number of Canadian service men and women – approximately 730, 000 – served in the army. The first Canadian action was in the defence of Hong Kong, a defence undertaken in December 1941, despite Churchill's previous opinion that the place should not be reinforced. Two Canadian battalions, which had not had time to complete their advanced training or to accustom themselves to local conditions, were overwhelmed in the irresistible Japanese advance. The frontal attack on Dieppe on the 19th of August, 1942, in which the Second Canadian Division played by far the largest part, was a much more tragic failure than Hong Kong had been; 907 Canadians of all ranks were killed or died of wounds. This second disaster was followed by nearly a year of inaction for the Canadian force in Britain. It had now become a small army of two corps and five divisions, two of them armoured, and two independent armoured brigades. The demand that it should get into the fight had grown steadily in the meantime; and the Canadian government prevailed upon Churchill to include the First Canadian division in the assault on Sicily in July 1943. Four months later, under still more persistent pressure from Ralston and Lieutenant-General Kenneth Stuart, the Chief of the General Staff, a Canadian corps headquarters was set up in Italy and the Fifth Canadian Armoured Division was dispatched to join it. General McNaughton, who had opposed this more serious division of the army, found himself gravely at odds with his home government; and at the same time his fitness to lead the Canadians in the field was questioned by the British military authorities; he retired and was succeeded by Lieutenant-General H. D. G. Crerar. The Third Canadian Division took part in the invasion of Normandy on the 6th of June, 1944, and during July it was joined by the Second Canadian Infantry Division and the Fourth Armoured Division. These formed the main body of the Second Canadian Corps, under General G. G. Simonds, and, later in the summer, of the First Canadian Army, commanded by General H. D. G. Crerar. During the autumn and winter, the First Canadian Army was partly composed of British, Polish, and other Allied formations; but in the spring of 1945 these forces were replaced by the troops of the First Canadian Corps, which arrived from Italy. Thereafter, the reunited Canadians fought together as a Canadian army until the end of the long campaign in north-western Europe.

≫ II ≪

WHEN THE WAR opened in 1939, the Canadian economy had by no means crawled clear of the deep pit of the depression. The great expansion of the 1920s, which had left Canada with excessive capacity in several major industries, had induced a mood of caution; and investment in new construction, apart from housing, was slow to get under way. There was no quick revival for the staple industries and trades. Wheat, plagued by drought and crop failures, as well as by continuing low prices, was still in a very depressed state on the eve of the war. Exports of wood pulp and newsprint gradually climbed closer to their pre-depression volume, but prices and total values still lagged behind. Mineral exports made the best showing of all during the 1930s; but this was largely because of the rising demand, at steady prices, for Canadian nickel, and the assured and highly lucrative market for gold in the United States. As a whole, recovery was slow; and in 1937-8, when it was still far from complete, it was halted by a new recession. The Gross National Product, at market prices, was lower in 1939 than it had been in 1929.

The Second World War was destined to change all this; but it did not do so immediately. Canada had herself done very little to provide her armed services with modern equipment; and very few orders had come from Britain, since the United Kingdom treated the Dominion as a very marginal source of supply. Thus, when the crisis came in the summer of 1940, the Canadian armament industry expanded widely and at great speed from a very restricted base; and within a few months Canadian war production achieved a range and variety that it had never had before. Canadian manufacturing had, of course, developed enormously during the First World War; but its scope had been comparatively narrow, and it had concentrated heavily on the production of shells. The First World War was fought at the very beginning of the age of the internal combustion engine. The Second World War was armoured, mechanized, and motorized as the First had never been; and Canada, with subsidiaries of some of the leading American motor car companies, was well prepared to produce the new transport equipment. Canadian factories also turned out large quantities of small arms and guns, fighting ships and cargo vessels, training planes, bomber and fighter planes; but undoubtedly the nation's greatest contribution to the mechanized allied armies lay in the wide and varied category of mechanical transport and armoured vehicles – tanks, armoured cars, trucks, and carriers of all kinds. The production of passenger cars was totally suspended for two years, and virtually for four; and during the war close to a million motor vehicles were produced.

During the first eight months of the war, while the Canadian government held to its belief in a limited war effort, it had haggled tenaciously over every military item in the budget; but, with the collapse of France, and the British withdrawal from Europe, these inhibitions abruptly vanished. The cost of the war reached towering heights at an incredible speed. Canadian Mutual Aid, on a scale relatively higher than that of the American Lend-Lease, was extended to Britain, other Commonwealth countries, and to China and the Soviet Union. In 1939, defence had cost Canada $125.7 million; by 1943, total expenditures for defence and Mutual Aid reached $4,241.6 million; and the federal budget as a whole was nearly eight times as great as it had been in 1939. Revenue was needed, on a vaster scale than ever before; and the Canadian people, now in the full flush of wartime fervour and prosperity, was a not unwilling source. Direct taxation, including personal and corporation income tax, estate duties, and excess profits taxes, was sharply increased. In 1939, these sources had yielded only $134.4 million; in 1944 their proceeds amounted to $1,336.3, or slightly less than ten times as much. At the same time, the Canadian government was borrowing heavily, and as much as possible from individual Canadians in order to divert their purchasing power from consumers' goods; and the national direct debt, which more than quadrupled in six years, rose from $3,961.5 million in 1939 to $17,892.6 million in 1945.

The war restored the federal government to the paramountcy it had gradually lost after 1919, and had ever since failed to regain. The only permanent addition to the federal legislative powers was the amendment of 1940 which added unemployment insurance, subsection 2A, to section 91 of the British North America Act. This change was made possible by the agreement of Quebec, which was finally granted after Godbout's victory over Duplessis. The transference of unemployment insurance to the federal government had been recommended by the Rowell-Sirois Commission; but this was only one item in a vast comprehensive scheme of constitutional reform, which, it was now realized sadly, was very unlikely to be carried out. A Dominion-provincial conference, called apprehensively by the federal government early in January 1940 to discuss the commission's report, ended, after only two days' debate, in total disagreement. Hepburn of Ontario angrily denounced the report as a 'blueprint for the destruction of Confederation'; and, although the familiar support of Duplessis was lacking, both Aberhart of Alberta and Pattullo of British Columbia joined Hepburn in his rejection of the Rowell-Sirois recommendations. The constitution of Canada was not to be formally and permanently amended for the benefit of the postwar world; but the precedents of the First World War left no doubt of the federal paramountcy in wartime. In his budget speech in April 1940, Ilsley, the Minister of Finance, presented his financial proposals to the provinces; they were to surrender personal income and corporation taxes for a year beyond the duration of the war, and in return they would either receive the amount of revenue they had actually collected from these sources in the previous fiscal year or they would be paid the net cost of the service of their debt, plus a special subsidy for fiscal need. All the provinces signed the tax suspension agreements. A virtual monopoly of fiscal power fell into the hands of the federal government; and for the next five years it exercised a far more vigorous and effective control over the Canadian economy than it had ever succeeded in doing in the First World War. The chief of its many agencies was the Wartime Prices and Trade Board, which, in October 1941, imposed a general price ceiling on all goods, wages, and services. Rationing for sugar, tea, coffee, meat, spirits, and gasoline came into effect only later.

As the Canadian war effort grew greater, the association of the Canadian and American economies became closer. The trade agreement of 1938, a tripartite affair which involved Canada, Great Britain, and the United States, had continued a tendency already evident in the Canada-U.S. Treaty of 1935, and in the revised agreement with the United Kingdom in 1937. As in these two previous deals, Canada agreed to reduce its duties on a number of items below the treaty or intermediate rate, as well as to accept lower preferences in Great Britain, in return for a reduced tariff on agricultural produce, cattle, and lumber in the United States. This increasingly close relationship was still further strengthened by the Hyde Park Declaration of April 1941, which King regarded as the economic counterpart of the Ogdensburg Agreement. The aim of the declaration was to cut down the heavy drain on Canadian reserves of gold and U.S. dollars by encouraging greater American purchases in Canada; each country was to provide the other with the defence articles it could produce best, and all American equipment purchased by Canada, but destined for the United Kingdom, was to be charged to Lend-Lease. The results of these arrangements could be seen in the comparative figures of trade with the United Kingdom and the United States. Imports from Great Britain rose very little, if at all, from their low prewar level; imports from the United States nearly tripled in value from 1939 to 1945. In 1944, exports to the United Kingdom had risen to approximately four times their value in 1939; but, in sharp contrast to the trading patterns of the First World War, exports to the United States rivalled, and for the last four years of the war exceeded, these high totals to Britain. By 1945 the American share of the non-resident investment in Canada had risen to 70 per cent and the British had declined to 25 per cent.

→»» III «←

KING'S VICTORY in the election of April 1940 was so overwhelming that for the next eighteen months opposition to his rule was dismally ineffective. Even the crisis of the spring and summer of 1940 did not seriously disturb the prevailing political calm. It was the vast expansion of the war in 1941 – Hitler's invasion of Russia, and the Japanese attack on Pearl Harbor – which began a new and more agitated period in Canadian politics. The war had now become a world war, in which the fate of all mankind was involved. Victory would require a vastly greater effort to achieve; but victory might also open up a new and far better era in human history. Out of these changed circumstances, two political issues – the issue of conscription, which had lain dormant since the beginning of the war, and the issue of the welfare state, which had been virtually forgotten ever since Bennett's defeat in 1935 – emerged from the oblivion in which they were buried to deepen the interest and quicken the pace of Canadian politics. Conscription and the welfare state not only inspired attacks on King's government from both right and left; they also revealed deep divisions in the Liberal Party itself.

The first challenge to the government came, somewhat surprisingly, from the Conservative side. Since its defeat in the general election of 1940, the party had seemed broken and cowed by its misfortunes. Robert J. Manion, Bennett's amiable but singularly luckless successor, retired soon after his electoral failure; and R. B. Hanson, elected by caucus as temporary leader in the House of Commons, was far from a conspicuous success. In November 1941, the executive of the Dominion Conservative Association, nearly two hundred strong, met in Ottawa, ostensibly to plan for a new national convention. The meeting reached the unexpected conclusion that a national convention was unnecessary, and it invited Arthur Meighen to resume his old post as leader of the party. Meighen declined; and then, under the pressure of what he was led to believe was a unanimous invitation, reluctantly accepted. This was a mistake; and the platform on which he stood in the by-election in York South, in the northern suburbs of Toronto, early in 1942, was even more unwise. Its sole important plank was conscription and union government; and these were premature proposals. The war had become a world war only two months ago; public opinion had barely begun to harden in favour of compulsory military service; and already Mackenzie King had moved astutely to guard his government against the impending change of view. On the 22nd of January, 1942, at the opening of Parliament, the Speech from the Throne announced that a plebiscite would be held to determine whether the Canadian people wished to release the government from its pledge not to introduce compulsion for overseas service. This announcement took the force out of Meighen's denunciation of government policy. He found the weapons he had chosen singularly ineffective; and it was difficult to protect himself from the steady socialist fire of J. W. Noseworthy, the C.C.F. candidate, his only opponent. Meighen was not illiberal; but, as an outspoken and effective critic of the welfare state, he was inevitably the mortal enemy of the C.C.F. In a campaign of extreme virulence and mendacity, in which the federal Liberals came surreptitiously to the aid of the C.C.F., Meighen was attacked as the implacable foe of labour and the reactionary champion of unregulated and predatory capitalism. He was decisively beaten in a constituency which had returned Conservative members for decades.

Meighen's humiliating defeat by Noseworthy was a sign both of a growing popular support for the C.C.F. and of a growing general interest in programmes of social welfare. The Second World War was not characterized by the powerful but very vague idealism that had dominated the First. The hopes and expectations of Canadians in 1942 were not nearly so lofty as those of their fathers and mothers had been a quarter-century before. What the new generation had in mind was a much more definite and practical plan of reform. They wanted the state to increase welfare services, provide reasonable security, and stop the onset of a postwar depression; and they believed that the relative success of the wartime controls was proving that a regulated economy would work. The growth and spread of these wartime opinions helped, not only to improve the fortunes of the C.C.F., but also to inspire a revival and reorganization of the Conservative Party. Meighen, though without a seat in the Commons, continued to lead the party; but defeat had not induced him to change his views in the slightest; and the direction of party policy, which he shared with Hanson, the House leader, was divided and weak. The deepening dissatisfaction with this state of affairs prompted a group of reforming Conservative 'laymen', not members of Parliament, to meet at Port Hope in September 1942 to discuss the party's programme for the future. The 'Port Hopefuls' drew up a statement of aims and beliefs which included such novel items as a liberal code for labour, a long-range, low-cost housing plan, and an elaborate social security programme. Meighen was not impressed by the public welfare proposals; but he had come to believe that the rural electorate alone would save Canada from the menace of the C.C.F. and that the Conservative Party should have a new leader who could appeal to the farming population. His choice fell on John Bracken, a dry, humourless, but efficient administrator, who had proved at least that he could survive for twenty years as Progressive premier of Manitoba, and thus appeared to answer Meighen's requirements. At the last moment Bracken agreed to contest the leadership provided the party changed its name to Progressive Conservative, and modelled its platform on the Port Hope report. He was elected leader on the second ballot at the national convention in Winnipeg in December 1942.

The C.C.F., however, not the Conservative Party, was to be the principal beneficiary of the social changes and socialist hopes of wartime. Up to then the C.C.F. had won urban middle-class and rural support, but it had never captured labour; and the full employment of the war years had now made organized labour an extremely important and desirable political asset. Between 1939 and 1945 trade union membership increased from 359,000 to 711,100, almost exactly doubling its numbers. The lion's share of this huge increase went to a newly created trade union congress, the Canadian Congress of Labour, which had been formed in 1940, when the Canadian unions that were affiliated with the C.I.O. in the United States united with the All-Canadian Congress of Labour. In 1943, the C.C.L. convention passed a resolution endorsing the C.C.F. as 'the political arm of labour in Canada', and urging its member unions to affiliate with the new party. The C.C.F. had never done well in Ontario, a highly industrialized province; but now, under a new provincial leader, E. B. Jolliffe, its fortunes began to pick up. The greatest source of its rapidly growing membership was organized labour; and by the summer of 1943 forty union locals had affiliated with the C.C.F.

The first real test of the rejuvenated party's strength came in the Ontario provincial election of the 4th of August, 1943. The Liberals, with a new leader, H. C. Nixon, the second since Hepburn's retirement in the previous autumn, were divided and demoralized. The real contest was between the Conservatives, under George Drew, who had been provincial leader since 1938, and the C.C.F., led by Edward Jolliffe. The results were startling and portentous for the future. The Liberals, who had held sixty-three seats at the dissolution, were reduced to fifteen. The Conservatives won in thirty-eight constituencies, a gain of fifteen. The C.C.F., which had no members at all in the House at the dissolution, elected thirty-four of its candidates and just failed to elect two more. The political future in

Ontario looked highly discouraging for the Liberals; but, in a mysteriously ambiguous fashion, it seemed to offer almost equal good fortune to the Conservatives and the C.C.F.

·≫ IV ≪·

THE DEMAND for conscription and the growing interest in organized social welfare were the two new forces with which King had to contend. He succeeded in accommodating himself fairly easily to the idea of the welfare state; but the issue of conscription for overseas service nearly broke his government in pieces. The result of the plebiscite, held on the 27th of April, 1942, was a 64-per-cent to 36-per-cent affirmative vote in the nation as a whole, a 72-per-cent to 28-per-cent negative vote in Quebec, and an 80-per-cent to 20-per-cent affirmative vote in the other eight provinces. What was to be done on the basis of results so conclusive and yet so contradictory? One French-Canadian minister, Cardin, wanted no action at all. Ralston and Macdonald interpreted the plebiscite as a mandate for conscription, to be introduced at once, or as soon as the voluntary system had been proved a failure. King agreed to amend the National Resources Mobilization Act by repealing the pledge against conscription. He was prepared to extend compulsory service to the entire Western Hemisphere, but no further at that moment. And he insisted that parliamentary approval must be obtained before conscripts could be sent to Europe. The prolonged dispute between the determined Ralston and the unyielding King continued until, in July 1942, Ralston at last resigned. He was persuaded to remain in office, but King kept his letter of resignation.

The second, and infinitely more serious, crisis over conscription came over two years later, in the autumn of 1944. It was precipitated by the heavy infantry casualties in the campaign in north-west Europe, and the desperate need of reinforcements for the Canadian Army. On the 18th of October, Ralston returned from a personal inspection of the Canadian forces in Italy, Belgium, and the Netherlands. Urgently, he insisted to

Mackenzie King and the cabinet that 16,000 men conscripted under the National Resources Mobilization Act (the N.R.M.A. men, as they were called, or, more contemptuously, the 'zombies') should be dispatched overseas at once to reinforce the depleted Canadian divisions. King was determined to resist this desperate measure at what he mistakenly believed was the eleventh hour of the European conflict. At repeated and interminable meetings of the War Committee and the cabinet, he rehearsed, at enormous length, all conceivable arguments against Ralston's proposal. Without informing his colleagues, he even telegraphed privately to Churchill, hoping that Churchill would confirm his own assumption that the war would soon be over and that Canadian reinforcements were unnecessary. The reply that came from Downing Street was diplomatically cautious and therefore politically useless. King was profoundly depressed; and then, in his extremity, he thought of McNaughton. He had been seeing something of the General recently; he had even come to the conclusion that McNaughton would be a fine appointment as the first Canadian Governor General. Now he realized that he could make other and better uses of the General's services. McNaughton had always believed firmly in the principle of voluntary recruitment. As Minister of Defence, McNaughton would make a final and no doubt successful effort to avoid conscription for service in Europe.

On the 31st of October and the 1st of November, King saw McNaughton and obtained his consent. On the evening of the 1st, before his mesmerized cabinet colleagues, he recalled Ralston's two-year-old letter of resignation, dismissed him, and announced McNaughton's appointment as his successor. For three desperate weeks, the new Minister of Defence struggled vainly to persuade a sufficient number of N.R.M.A. conscripts to volunteer for general service. Then, on the 22nd of November, the headquarters staff announced that the aim could not be achieved. King affected to believe that this admission of failure was virtually a mutinous military defiance that threatened the constitutional relations between the army and civil government. This melodramatic fiction could be used to persuade others and to justify himself. But in reality he needed no convincing. For the past fortnight his cabinet had been on the verge of dissolution. He realized that conscription for overseas service must be accepted if his government were to survive. On the 23rd of November, an order in council authorizing the dispatch of 16,000 N.R.M.A. conscripts to Europe was tabled in Parliament. Power resigned, but Louis St. Laurent and the other Quebec ministers stood firm; and Ralston supported the new policy. And although thirty-four French-Canadian members voted against King, he won the vote of confidence by a vote of 143 to 70.

King had successfully overcome the greatest peril of his entire political career. In comparison, the second wartime threat to his government, the rising demand for social welfare, was easy to guard against. Nearly a quarter of a century earlier King had been elected to the leadership of the Liberal Party on a platform of industrial reform and social welfare; but, though he had held office for seventeen of those twenty-five years, he had done extremely little to carry out his promises. Now, when the competition from both socialists and socially conscious Conservatives was at last becoming serious, he began a definite and conscious attempt to turn the Liberal Party leftward towards social reform. In January 1943, the Speech from the Throne forecast 'a charter of social security for the whole of Canada'; and the four by-elections which the Liberals lost in the following summer convinced the government that it must quickly provide definite evidence of its determination to make good these paper prophecies. A labour relations code in wartime industry was adopted. The wage stabilization order was amended to permit a cost-of-living bonus. A floor for farm prices was announced. In an important national broadcast early in December, Mackenzie King proclaimed that 'the idea of a national minimum for the whole people' was the guiding principle of the Liberal programme of social security. In January 1944, the cabinet decided in favour of family allowances, though King cheerfully recognized that they would cost half of a prewar budget; and in the following summer the Department of National Health and Welfare was established and the Family Allowances Bill became law.

These sagacious manoeuvres put the other two parties at an obvious disadvantage. The new Progressive Conservative Party had been organized in the hope of gaining the agrarian west and of displacing the Liberal Party as the alternative to socialism in central Canada. It failed to accomplish either. Bracken, who made no attempt to win a seat in the Commons, did not bring with him any western Progressive or Liberal followers; and the Conservatives had nothing to show in competition with King's welfare measures. Apart from Dr. Herbert Bruce, they did not oppose family allowances; but they somehow managed to leave the unfortunate impression that they were comparatively lukewarm about social security. This failure to contend with the reviving popularity of the Liberals in industrial Canada was bad enough; but perhaps even more serious was the complete collapse of Bracken's hopes of winning the agrarian west. The Saskatchewan provincial election of June 1944 was a triumph for the C.C.F. In a province which was fondly supposed to be a part of Bracken's western empire, the C.C.F. won in forty-seven out of fifty-five constituencies, and the Conservatives did not capture a single seat. It is true that a Conservative candidate defeated General McNaughton in the Grey North federal by-election; but here it was the conscription issue, an issue of declining, not increasing, political importance, that won the victory.

In the meantime, the slow decline of the C.C.F. had also set in. It had reached the summit of its popularity in the summer and autumn of 1943; and its electoral triumph in Saskatchewan nine months later was a western *tour de force* which, by that time, could not have been duplicated anywhere in the urban and industrial east. The party's affiliation with the trade unions, backed openly by the Canadian Congress of Labour, had not strengthened it nearly as much as it had been expected to do. Approximately a hundred union locals, with a membership of between 40,000 and 50,000, became affiliated with the C.C.F.; but the affiliation was formal and tenuous and did not give the party either substantial funds or many active workers. This lack of money and supporters weakened the C.C.F.'s defences at the very moment when it was exposed to a financially strong propaganda campaign which sought to prove that socialism meant dictatorship, regimentation, and confiscation.

King's luck held. He had won the election of 1940 before the real war had begun. He won the election of 1945 after the war in Europe had ended. The issues of war, including conscription, were gradually fading – though they had not faded completely – from people's minds; the issues of peace and postwar reconstruction were slowly gaining their interest. King's campaign was centred on the future. He promised full employment and social security. 'Vote Liberal and Keep Building a New Social Order in Canada' was his slogan. He managed in this way to escape the fate which overtook Winston Churchill less than a month later in England; but his victory nevertheless was a narrow one. With only 40.9 per cent of the popular vote, the Liberals gained 125 seats in a House of 245; and once again it was Quebec, where 53 Liberal candidates were returned, which saved the day for the party. French Canada could not easily forgive King for enforcing conscription in the autumn of 1944; but French Canada also found it harder to forget that, while he had resisted compulsory service until almost the end of the war, his opponents, the Conservatives, had been advocating it from nearly the beginning.

->>> V <<<-

THE NATURE of the postwar international organization and of Canada's place in it had become fairly clear long before hostilities ended. The four great powers – the United States, the United Kingdom, Soviet Russia, and, again at Roosevelt's insistence, China – had controlled and directed the strategy and diplomacy of the war. They had also made it quite plain, from the beginning, that they intended to play an equally predominant part in both the planning and the running of the postwar international organization. To Lord Halifax, the British Ambassador to the United States, who spoke in Toronto in January 1944, it seemed obvious that Great Britain, apart from the

Commonwealth, could not claim equal partnership with the other three 'Titans'. He pleaded for 'closer unity of thought and action' in Commonwealth defence, foreign policy, and economic affairs. 'Not Great Britain only,' he declared, 'but the British Commonwealth and Empire must be the fourth power in that group upon which, under Providence, the peace of the world will henceforth depend.' This piece of political realism, with its truly prophetic forecast of the postwar world, was too much for the Canadians. It sinned against the naïve, idealistic assumption, most earnestly voiced by the C.C.F., that the future world order would be based, not on power politics, but on the peaceful co-operation of all nations, great and small. Even more seriously, it offended the Liberal nationalist dogma, systematically inculcated by King, and now an article of religious faith in the Department of External Affairs, that Commonwealth co-operation meant 'imperial centralization'. King was 'dumbfounded' by the Halifax speech; but he remained resolute. An old, wearied, but indomitable Canadian St. George, he buckled on his armour once again for a final encounter with the hideous imperialist dragon. A unified Commonwealth policy, he told Parliament a week later, 'runs counter to the establishment of effective world security'. He looked forward to collaboration in the interests of peace with all friendly nations, great and small, and outside, as well as inside, the British Commonwealth.

More than a year later, when the United Nations, great and small, met at San Francisco to establish their new international organization, its main lines had already been settled by the great powers, in a way that effectively ensured their continued predominance. The Big Five – now including France as a prospective member – were to have permanent seats in the Security Council of eleven; and, on almost all substantive matters, the concurrence of all five permanent members was to be necessary. Canada was already committed in principle to the idea of a new world organization. Its proposed membership realized Mackenzie King's old ideas of universality, and, above all, it included the United States. Even its name had been Americanized! Canada was even ready to accept the pre-eminence of the great powers as necessary and expedient since, as King observed, 'power and responsibility should coincide'. But the Canadian government disliked the arbitrary authority of the veto, and strongly objected to the evident assumption that, apart from the Big Five, all members of the United Nations should be relegated to a common level of inferiority. 'Secondary powers with world-wide interests', such as Canada, the Canadian government believed, should have a preference over smaller and weaker states in elections to the non-permanent seats in the Security Council; and some limitation ought to be placed upon the Security Council's authority to require secondary powers, not among its members, to supply armed forces, possibly against their wish, in support of its enforcement policies. This last Canadian amendment particularly interested Mackenzie King. His concern was a characteristic expression of his instinctive desire to protect Canada against the automatic commitments imposed by a centralized power.

The Canadian delegation did not play a very active, distinguished, or influential part at San Francisco. Mackenzie King, a tepid internationalist at best, was afflicted with a terrible cold, preoccupied with the composition of his V-E Day radio broadcast to the Canadian people, and increasingly worried about the general election campaign. St. Laurent, the other senior Canadian minister at the conference, was much more enthusiastic about the new organization than his chief; but, as a novice in international gatherings, he remained cautious and reserved. Neither of them could possibly have competed with H. V. Evatt, the Australian Minister for External Affairs, as the champion of the middle powers; and King, who might have felt obliged to try, had the good sense not to. After a stay of barely three weeks, they both departed for Canada and the general election; and the Canadian permanent officials, members of the Department of External Affairs, were left behind to give what aid they could in the only partly successful struggle for the interests of the middle powers. All efforts to limit the range of the veto failed. In elections to the non-permanent seats in the Security Council, due regard was to be paid to the capacity of the candidates to carry out the duties of the position; but, on the other hand, consideration was also to be given to 'equitable geographical distribution'. It was only in their efforts to limit the authority of the Security Council to command the use of their armed forces that the middle powers won any substantial success; and here their victory was a hollow one, for the attempt to create an international police force under the United Nations turned out to be a total failure.

The United Nations Charter had not yet been signed, when the Cold War began. The wartime alliance of the three great powers, Britain, the United States, and Soviet Russia, was succeeded by the peacetime confrontation of the two superpowers, Soviet Russia and the United States. Great Britain, exhausted by her efforts during the war, was increasingly incapable of exerting her old influence in world affairs; and the United States, which only a decade earlier had been intent upon strengthening her legal isolation from foreign quarrels, now moved forward to assume the aggressive leadership of the entire West European–American world. At first, the two superpowers sought, chiefly by diplomatic pressure and partisan intrigue, to extend their political influence and improve their strategic positions, in central and eastern Europe, at each other's expense; but rapidly, after 1946, the conflict spread along a far wider front, and was fought with more varied and much heavier weapons. In March 1947, the American President, Harry S. Truman, in a statement appropriately christened the 'Truman Doctrine', presumed to divide the entire population of the world into two completely different and fundamentally antagonistic societies, governed by two utterly irreconcilable philosophies of life. The Marshall Plan offered American aid in postwar rehabilitation to all European countries without distinction; but to the Soviet Union, which interpreted the new scheme in the light of the Truman Doctrine, Marshall Plan aid looked suspiciously like an attempt to use American economic power to extend American influence into eastern Europe; and, in the end, all the states under Russian influence declined the American offer.

By the end of the year, a line had been drawn through central Europe, with Czechoslovakia to the east, dividing the economic clients of the United States from the economic satellites of the Soviet Union. And, by February 1948, with the Communist *coup d'état* in Czechoslovakia, the economic division of Europe had become a political division as well.

Canada responded to these events in a characteristic western fashion, but much more cautiously and deliberately than the United States. As a first step towards his own retirement, Mackenzie King transferred the portfolio of External Affairs to St. Laurent in the autumn of 1946; but, although St. Laurent was much more inclined to an active foreign policy than King had been, his first moves were comparatively restrained. The discovery of a fairly extensive Soviet spy ring in Canada during the autumn and winter of 1945-6 was a shock to many Canadians; the subsequent investigation was conducted in an efficient, if arbitrary, fashion, but it was not followed by a popular Communist witch hunt. In February 1947, just a month before President Truman propounded his uncompromising new doctrine, the renewal of the Canadian-American Permanent Joint Board on Defence was announced; and this was undoubtedly the result of clamorous American demands for improved protection in the north against a Soviet invasion of the Arctic. The announcement of the renewal of the Permanent Joint Board was accepted favourably enough in Canada; but a month later the enunciation of the Truman Doctrine was greeted with a good deal of criticism; and, in the following summer, when the government introduced the Visiting Forces (U.S.A.) Bill, giving the American military authorities power over their personnel in Canada, it suddenly found itself assailed by indignant complaints that it had failed to protect Canadian independence against the pressure of American military imperialism. Actually the Visiting Forces Act of 1947 gave the Americans less power than they had been given by order in council during the war; and the new activities of the Permanent Joint Board were carried on on a greatly reduced scale, and with much more care for Canadian sovereignty than before.

The mood of the Canadian government changed considerably in the next six months. From the first, Canada had objected to the obstructive monopoly power which the veto gave the permanent members of the Security Council; and the first two frustrating years in the history of the United Nations had more than proved the justice of these objections. In his opening speech at the United Nations Assembly in September 1947, St. Laurent warned that the world would not indefinitely tolerate a Security Council which was 'frozen in futility and divided by dissension'; and he predicted that 'democratic and peace-loving states' might have to unite in a new association for greater security. It was the Communist *coup d'état* in February 1948 that forced the western countries into positive action. Early in March, on the day after Jan Masaryk's death, Prime Minister Attlee telegraphed to Ottawa proposing a united front by the democratic nations against renewed aggression and suggesting that British, American, and Canadian representatives should meet to plan an Atlantic regional organization. Mackenzie King had looked with great apprehension on some of the policies of his new Minister of External Affairs; but even he was reluctantly converted to St. Laurent's belief that a positive and affirmative answer must be sent to Attlee's proposal. In April, a month later, in an important general review of Canadian policy in the House of Commons, St. Laurent announced his support for a 'western union' of free states for greater collective security.

→≫ VI ≪←

DURING THE WAR, the federal government had exercised a national command far more complete and successful than it had ever possessed before. It had fought the war, controlled and regulated the Canadian economy, and greatly enlarged the scope of Canadian social services. The proposals of the Royal Commission on Dominion-Provincial Relations had not taken, and probably never would take, formal shape in substantial amendments to the British North America Act; but the federal control of fiscal policy, which was one of the commission's principal recommendations, had been completely realized, for all practical purposes, during the war. The federal government was very reluctant to surrender this wartime paramountcy. In the general election, it had promised to prevent a postwar recession and to create a new social order in Canada. Federal leadership, it was assumed at Ottawa, was just as desirable for peace as for war. But federal leadership would have to be accepted all over again, for the tax rental agreements would terminate one year after the end of the war.

This was the main inspiration of the plan which the federal government presented to the Dominion-Provincial Conference in August 1945. It proposed that the provinces surrender succession duties, as well as personal and corporation income tax (succession duties had not been included in the wartime tax agreements); and in return they would receive unconditional subsidies, which would vary with the Gross National Product, but would in no case fall below a guaranteed minimum of twelve dollars *per capita*, census of 1941. In addition, the federal government would bear an increased share of the burden of old-age pensions, provide extended coverage for unemployment insurance and assistance, and accept 60 per cent of the cost of a provincially operated health insurance scheme. Finally, in order to gain national control of public investment, the federal government offered financial assistance in the planning and timing of provincial public works. In this way, it hoped to be able to offset any serious decline in private investment and employment.

This elaborate and comprehensive plan was doomed to failure. Unlike the Dominion, which had flourished and prospered during the war, the provinces had endured five years of subordination, neglect, and frustration. They were full of pent-up grievances, resentments, and demands; and, in George Drew of Ontario and Maurice Duplessis of Quebec, they had two leaders determined to resist the continuation of federal direction and control. Drew's stunning electoral victory in Ontario, only two months before, had given him renewed confidence; and Duplessis, who had beaten Godbout in the Quebec provincial election of August 1944, knew very well that in Quebec, in the summer of 1945, an anti-federal stand was assured of popularity. Drew's opening speech was a complete rejection of the federal government's proposals. Duplessis, who followed Drew, claimed that Hitler was the first centralizer, and that centralization always led to Naziism. The wrangling continued for three days, and on the fourth the conference was adjourned. It met again in April 1946. The federal government increased its minimum *per capita* grant to fifteen dollars and offered other financial inducements. It was all in vain. The national health scheme and the plan for co-ordinated, countercyclical public investment were given up. In the following year, the Dominion negotiated much less ambitious tax rental agreements with seven of the nine provinces.

The great federal peacetime programme of 1945 was designed in large measure to maintain full employment and prevent a postwar recession. Events proved that for this purpose it was not needed; the expected and dreaded postwar slump never came. Unemployment rose slightly in 1945, and more sharply in 1946, from its low point in 1944; but, by 1948, the number of persons out of work and seeking jobs had sunk again nearly to the lowest levels of the war. The postwar boom had begun. Prices and wages were rising rapidly; in the three years from 1945 to 1948, the Gross National Product increased by over 25 per cent. On the surface, everything looked extremely prosperous; but beneath the still continuing favourable balance of trade a crisis in international exchange was rapidly developing. A very large part of postwar Canadian trade to Great Britain, Europe, and China was financed by credits of nearly $600 million, authorized by the Exports Credit Insurance Act, and by the $1.25 billion loan to the United Kingdom. The wartime practice of bulk buying by contract was continued by Great Britain in its purchases of Canadian foodstuffs after the war; and often, particularly in the case of the notorious Anglo-Canadian Wheat Agreement of 1946, the supplies were provided at well below market prices. The needs of the British and European borrowers were so voracious that the credits were used up much faster than had been expected; and the recovery of European and British industry was so slow that a large return flow of exports to Canada did not materialize. In these circumstances, Canada satisfied its demands chiefly in the United

States; imports from the Republic, at steeply rising prices, increased by over 60 per cent in the first two postwar years; and in 1947 the unfavourable balance of trade, on American account, was $918,082 million. Exports to Europe were financed on credit; imports from the United States had to be paid for in cash. The result was a rapid drain of American dollars and gold which reached critical proportions in the autumn of 1947; and in November the new Finance Minister, Douglas Abbott, announced a credit of $300 million from the Export-Import Bank and a long list of restrictions cutting down imports from the United States. The reserves of gold and American dollars began to increase almost at once and by the summer of 1948 had reached comfortable proportions.

In the meantime, Mackenzie King's long reign was drawing to its final close. In August 1948, Louis St. Laurent was elected leader of the Liberal Party on the first ballot, and in October George Drew gained the leadership of the Progressive Conservative Party with equal ease. On the 15th of November King finally resigned. He had claimed to be a Canadian nationalist; in reality, he was, from the beginning, a North American continentalist. He had systematically undermined Canada's connections with Britain; and, instead of strengthening her national self-sufficiency, he had simply replaced the broken imperial ties with infinitely stronger continental bonds, which had effectively shackled Canada to the United States. He fondly believed that he deserved Gladstone's reputation as a statesman who had based his political career on moral and religious principles. In fact, he was destined, fairly quickly, to acquire an unedifying reputation as one of the shrewdest, hardest, and most ruthless political operators in the entire history of the British Commonwealth.

CHAPTER THIRTEEN

The Rule of the Professionals

S T. LAURENT'S attainment of the prime-ministership
seemed to imply a definite change in the nation's programme, both domestic and external. Mackenzie King's
nationalist policies had, to the last, remained negative and
defensive in character. St. Laurent was more interested in the
outside world than King had ever been and much more inclined
towards definite decisions and positive action. Canada had
emerged from the Second World War a more powerful nation,
in every material sense of the word, than she had entered it;
and, on the surface at least, there was every reason to expect a
vigorous postwar assertion of new-found national strength. How
would it express itself and with what success? Canadians continued to be divided and uncertain about their goals and the
proper means of attaining them; and world circumstances were
by no means entirely favourable for a young nation trying to
realize its full potential as an independent and influential
'middle power'. The Second World War had, for a time at
least, exhausted the great nineteenth-century European powers,
and apparently opened the way for the advance of a new country
like Canada. But Great Britain had also been prostrated by the
war, and her decline and the imminent dissolution of her
empire still further weakened Canada's oldest alliance and left
her vulnerable to the preponderating power of the United
States. The entire western world was now dominated by the
United States, which had just set out on a great ideological
crusade for the 'containment' of international Communism.
Every nation west of the spiritual divide in central Europe was

expected to offer itself, an eager and submissive volunteer, in the fight for freedom under American leadership; and Canada, the Republic's nearest neighbour and closest relative, must obviously be the first to stand up and be counted.

Canada's acceptance of membership in the North Atlantic Treaty Organization was a striking illustration of the impact of American military leadership on Canadian policies. The treaty, which was approved by the Canadian Parliament late in March 1949, united Canada, the United States, the Brussels powers, and a third, rather ill-assorted group of nations – Portugal, Denmark, Norway, Iceland, and Italy – in a common defensive alliance. An armed attack against any member of the organization was to be regarded as an attack upon them all; and, in case of its occurrence, each signatory promised to assist 'by taking forthwith, individually and in concert with other parties, such action as it deems necessary, including the use of armed force'. It was a far larger commitment for the defence of Europe than Canada would have dreamed of accepting before 1939; and, if the United States had not joined the organization on the same terms as the other members, it was a bigger undertaking than she would have accepted in 1949. Canada's old and distinctive connections with Great Britain and Europe were no longer strong enough to induce her to commit herself to a possible European war without the support of the United States; and the very fact that she had engaged a part of her armed forces in Europe made her still more dependent upon American military assistance in North America. In NATO, the pressure of the American super-power would be distributed among a dozen different nations; but in North America it would be concentrated on Canada with all the force of a tragically unequal dual alliance.

The first and most immediate confrontation of the two power blocs had occurred in Europe, and Canada had taken her place in it. The Cold War came later to Asia; but its intrusion was made easy by the political turmoil and conflict which had continued for so long in the Far East. In continental Asia, the long, confused Chinese civil war was ending in the triumph of the Communists over the Nationalist government of Chiang

Kai-shek. In South-east Asia, the South Pacific, and the Indian Ocean, the vast and painful process of decolonization was already well on the way towards completion. The eastern empires which the great European powers – France, Britain, and the Netherlands – had established during the seventeenth and eighteenth centuries were yielding to the pressure of local nationalist forces. France and the Netherlands sought to delay or resist the movements for independence, and to make terms for the transfer of sovereignty. Great Britain, for whom colonial devolution was an old and familiar story, determined to hasten rather than delay the process in her own eastern Empire; and India, Pakistan, Ceylon, and Burma quickly became independent, with complete freedom to decide their own political future. Unlike the French and Dutch colonies and protectorates, which hoped to sever their old connection with their mother countries, three of the British successor states, India, Pakistan, and Ceylon, wished to retain it, though India was equally determined to become a republic.

If the Commonwealth were to survive, it could do so only as the result of a fundamental change in its character. Where before it had been dominated by the white-settlement Dominions – Canada, Australia, New Zealand, and South Africa – it must now become multi-racial in interests and leadership. Its imposing prewar military power was gone for ever; but, in compensation, the changes in its own nature might enable it in future to wield a new moral authority in world politics. These possibilities impressed both St. Laurent and L. B. Pearson, the new Secretary of State for External Affairs, who had left the civil service for a political career in the autumn of 1948. They welcomed the new Commonwealth with far more friendly interest than Mackenzie King had ever shown in the old. They saw it as a bridge between east and west, a link between different races and religions, a store of political experience in the difficult business of democratic nation-building from which the eastern successor states might draw inspiration and guidance, and, finally, as a source of assistance, technical knowledge, equipment, and capital, which they could use to develop and diversify their national economies.

Both St. Laurent and Pearson believed in making whatever adjustments were necessary to permit India to remain in the Commonwealth on her own terms. It was St. Laurent who suggested the amendment to the Royal Style and Titles which distinguished between the Crown as Head of the Commonwealth and the Crown as the chosen sovereign of its individual member states. This change in phraseology enabled India to combine republicanism at home with continuing membership in the Commonwealth; and it was clear, from the beginning, that she was likely to exert a potent influence on its counsels. The Indian leader, Pandit Jawaharlal Nehru, who visited Ottawa in the autumn of 1949 and much impressed St. Laurent, was obviously certain to play a prominent and influential part in Asian and world affairs. In January 1950 – a sign of the new importance of the eastern successor states – the foreign ministers of the Commonwealth met at Colombo, the capital of Ceylon; and there Nehru presented a positive programme designed to promote growth and preserve peace in South-east Asia. He pleaded for large-scale economic and technical assistance for the newly independent nations of the Far East; he also urged that the members of the Commonwealth recognize Communist China on the usual non-committal diplomatic terms as a member of the comity of nations. The result of Nehru's first proposal was the Colombo Plan for Co-operative Economic Development in South and South-east Asia. The response to his second urgent plea seemed equally favourable.

The Commonwealth foreign ministers inherited their views on the conduct of international affairs from Great Britain. To them diplomatic recognition meant neither approval nor disapproval of the Communist régime; it meant nothing more than acceptance of the undoubted fact that the Communist régime was the effective government of China. Failure or refusal to recognize would thus imply a positive and hostile attitude; it would, Nehru argued eloquently, have the unfortunate effect of separating the new China from its democratic Asian neighbours, including India, and driving it into a close defensive alliance with Soviet Russia. He hoped to use the Commonwealth as a shield against the intrusion of the Cold War into

Asia, and for a while it looked as if he had succeeded. In December 1949 and January 1950, Great Britain and the principal Asian states in the Commonwealth, India, Pakistan, and Ceylon, as well as a number of European nations, including the northern monarchies, Denmark, Norway, and Sweden, all recognized Communist China. Pearson came home from the Colombo Conference prepared to recommend that Canada should follow their example.

Yet in the end she did not. For in the next few months a remarkable change in attitude took place. The rapidly increasing Canadian reluctance was partly the result of the fact that British recognition had been followed, not by amicable communications between the United Kingdom and China, but by arguments over Taiwan, the island to which Chiang Kai-shek had retreated, and over the continued Nationalist occupation of the Chinese seat on the Security Council of the United Nations. These circumstances certainly might have given Canada pause; but they were not the real reason for her failure to recognize the People's Republic of China. The real reason was the rapid growth of a neurotic and implacable opposition to recognition in the United States. In the first confrontation between the Commonwealth and the West European–American power bloc, Canada had deserted the Commonwealth and followed the United States. She had implicitly accepted the American doctrine of diplomatic recognition and the American moral rejection of Communist government.

⇢⟫ II ⟪⇠

IN THE MEANTIME, on the 27th of June, 1949, Louis St. Laurent and George Drew had had their first encounter at the polls. Both were distinguished, even handsome men. Drew's great height, his large frame, well-shaped features, and flashing smile gave him an impressive presence. St. Laurent's personality was much less flamboyant; but his fine profile and restrained, courtly manner invested him with a simple, patrician dignity. Drew fought the campaign with all his enormous energy, aggressive self-confidence, and indiscriminate invective. He was charming, dashing, and indefatigable. At times, St. Laurent's style was much more reserved and formal; and yet, on other occasions, he became more direct and familiar in his approach. His set speeches sometimes sounded like a company chairman's opening remarks to the shareholders at the annual meeting, or like an old-fashioned pedagogue's instruction to a class of rather backward children. But, in the casual encounters and impromptu utterances of the campaign, he managed to convey an impression, partly paternal and partly avuncular, of a wise, kindly, and utterly trustworthy old gentleman. To many he was 'Uncle Louis' or 'the papa of us all'. Against this reassuring popular image, Drew fought courageously, but in vain. The Liberal total of 190 seats in the twenty-first Parliament of Canada was greater than any party had ever yet won in any Canadian general election. Drew had done much worse than the unimpressive Bracken and only a little better than the unlucky Manion. There would be only 41 Conservatives in the new House of Commons, and only 13 followers of the C.C.F. The C.C.F. could now almost be dismissed as the party whose great future had become its distinguished past.

In domestic affairs, the most important national achievement of the first years of St. Laurent's prime-ministership was the entry of Newfoundland into Confederation. Ever since the Quebec Conference of 1864, Canadians had believed and expected that ultimately Newfoundland would join the union; and to Newfoundlanders the postwar years brought, for the first time in more than a decade, a real opportunity to reconsider their own political future. During the depression, the oldest Dominion had become bankrupt; responsible government was supended; and since 1934 the island had been administered by a Commission of Government appointed by the United Kingdom. The Second World War had restored Newfoundland's old importance as a strategic outpost; and heavy American and Canadian military expenditures helped to bring back its solvency. Newfoundland had now earned the right to determine its own destiny. In the autumn of 1946, a popularly elected convention had met at St. John's to consider the various constitutional courses which now lay open; and in the following summer a delegation of Newfoundlanders arrived in Ottawa to discuss union with Canada. The island delegates were properly discreet and cautious in their approach, for they were well aware that considerable opposition to Confederation existed in Newfoundland. Equally wary and calculating, but for far less legitimate reasons, was the team of ministers and civil servants, led by St. Laurent, which represented Canada in the negotiations. The cost of bringing federal and provincial services in Newfoundland to something like the national level would be extremely large. Would the nation be willing to pay the price? Would the truculent Premier Duplessis oppose the admission of a province which would enter with large territories in Labrador, territories awarded to it by the Judicial Committee of the Privy Council against the rival claims of Quebec? St. Laurent shared the common French-Canadian prejudice against this decision; and at one point he actually studied a proposal to drop union and instead to purchase Labrador for Canada, thereby creating a capital fund for Newfoundland and mollifying the injured feelings of Quebec at one and the same time.

Canada was ready to drop the original design of Confederation in order to purchase its peace with Quebec. But fortunately Newfoundland was not willing to sell its birthright to Canada. It declined to consider the outrageous Canadian proposal. The negotiations for union were resumed; and, by the autumn of 1947, the terms had been settled. Newfoundland, including Labrador, could enter Confederation, with six senators, seven members in the House of Commons, and generous subsidy provisions. It was now up to the people of Newfoundland to make a choice among the three possible courses that lay open to them: a continuation of the existing Commission of Government, responsible government as it had existed in 1933, and union with Canada. The first referendum, held in June 1948, eliminated Commission government, but placed the other two choices in a near tie, with responsible government on the old model slightly leading. The second referendum, which took place a month later, gave Confederation with Canada a small majority. This 'near run thing' left Mackenzie King doubtful;

but a decision had been made, and, at the end of March 1949, Newfoundland became Canada's tenth province.

The complete realization of Canada's original territorial aims was not the only nationalist advance of the early postwar years. For a long time, independent sovereignty had been a more important goal than geographical expansion; and, to St. Laurent and Mackenzie King, constitutional maturity was conceived almost solely as change in Canada's relations with the United Kingdom. They both wanted a Canadian Governor General, a distinctive Canadian flag, and a separate Canadian citizenship; and the last two of these items appeared openly in the postwar programme which King had presented as early as the first sessions of the twentieth Parliament. The Canadian Citizenship Act of 1946 distinguished for the first time between Canadian citizenship and the common national status which Canadians shared with all the other citizens of the Commonwealth as subjects of the Crown. The Act defined Canadian citizenship; it also declared that a Canadian citizen was a British subject; and, in thus preserving the old dual allegiance, it managed to combine innovation and continuity.

A similar attempt at a compromise on the dangerous question of a distinctive Canadian flag, launched as early as the autumn of 1945, broke down completely. English-speaking M.P.s insisted that the Union Jack must form an essential part of the new flag, and French-speaking M.P.s demanded its total elimination. A parliamentary committee, appointed to consider the problem, adopted a compromise design which reduced the size of the Union Jack, changed the colour of the background from red to white, and substituted a gold maple leaf for the shield in the fly. At this point, a group of French-Canadian members, headed by Jean Lesage, uncompromisingly warned the Prime Minister that they would vote against the new design, even if it meant bringing down the government. Mackenzie King did not hesitate for more than a moment. He yielded to the private threats of a small French-Canadian pressure group and disavowed the majority recommendation of an official parliamentary committee. The committee's report was presented; but the government made no move to implement it. The shaky

Liberal majority in the twentieth Parliament was the reason for this inaction; but St. Laurent's great victory in the 1949 election completely invalidated this excuse. Yet, oddly enough, the new Prime Minister let this important item in the nationalist programme lie unnoticed where his predecessor had dropped it.

When the tokens of nationality were conspicuous and emotionally evocative, the government had declined to take a firm stand. But the vocabulary of sovereign status was less noticeable and inflammatory than its public symbols; and, in the change of national nomenclature, King and St. Laurent showed a determined, but surreptitious, and even secretive, persistence. Ever since Confederation, 'Dominion of Canada' had been used, officially as well as unofficially, as the nation's title. It had been well-known and well-loved by generations of Canadians; but now, as a result of the postwar revolution in the constitution of the Commonwealth, the word 'Dominion', in the eyes of doctrinaire Liberal nationalists, had sunk into unfashionable disrepute. No statute or order in council authorizing a change of title was ever passed; and no frank statement of government policy in the matter was ever issued. Quietly, unostentatiously, the word 'Dominion' was simply dropped, at every opportunity, from public documents; and the 'Dominion of Canada' became 'Canada' or 'the Government of Canada'.

The effort to nationalize the emblems of state had had mixed and by no means impressive results. The attempt to complete the nation's legal sovereignty was equally a very qualified and partial success. In the autumn of 1949, acts were passed abolishing appeals to the Judicial Committee of the Privy Council and empowering Parliament to amend the constitution in the purely federal field of jurisdiction. The federal field of jurisdiction was, of course, only one of several categories of legislative power; and, by a constitutional convention which was now well established, the concurrence of the provinces would be required before any general amending formula, covering all sections of the British North America Act, could be adopted. In January 1950, when a Federal-Provincial Conference met, it quickly became clear that agreement about amendment was highly unlikely. Duplessis of Quebec declared that the constitution was sacrosanct and could not be altered. Douglas of Saskatchewan insisted that the constitution was archaic and must be changed. In the end, the committee of Attorneys General did little more than complete and refine the division of the clauses of the British North America Act into six different categories, a task which had been begun by a similar committee fourteen years before.

In the spring of 1949, another and a very different national enterprise had been begun. Vincent Massey, former High Commissioner to the United Kingdom, was appointed chairman of a Royal Commission on National Development in the Arts, Letters, and Sciences. The commissioners were asked to make a survey of the institutions which helped to 'express national feeling, promote common understanding, and add to the variety and richness of Canadian life'. Their report, an imaginative and daring document, published two years later, examined such federal institutions and agencies as the Canadian Broadcasting Corporation, the National Film Board, the National Museum, the Parliamentary Library, and the Public Archives; it also analysed, sympathetically and at length, the position and problems of the scholar and scientist, the writer and artist, in Canada. The Commission's recommendations were many and varied; but the grant of federal aid to Canadian universities and the creation of a Canada Council for the encouragement of the arts, letters, humanities, and social sciences were the two most striking and ambitious proposals. The Massey Commission was the crowning achievement of Vincent Massey's long career as a public servant; and early in 1952 he became the first native-born Governor General of Canada.

→》 III 《←

THE CANADIAN nationalist programme was well under way when the outbreak of the Korean War abruptly called into question, for all but the super-powers themselves, the validity of the whole conception of national independence and self-determination.

Since the announcement of the Truman Doctrine in 1947, the United States had been committed to a Manichaean belief in the existence of two irreconcilable ideologies and ways of life, one liberal, democratic, and absolutely good, and the other totalitarian, Communistic, and totally evil. Logically this fundamental division of humanity must be world-wide; but so far only Europe and North America had obeyed the brutal compulsions of the conflict and separated into two hostile, armed camps. The Cold War had not yet spread to Asia, and the United States had not intervened directly in the Chinese civil war; but in 1949, when the war ended in the triumph of the Communists and the creation of the Chinese People's Republic, the American sense of mortification, injury, and loss became intolerable. China was America's political foster child, its favourite protégé, its potential ally; and China's rejection of the good American way of life in preference for Communism was almost as if a prize pupil or an angelic choir boy had suddenly and unaccountably taken to a career of crime. The Chinese revolution could not be a 'good' revolution, as the American Revolution had been, of course. It was inconceivable that it could be the genuine wish of the Chinese people; it must be the evil fruit of a conspiracy, engineered by Communist spies and agents and undoubtedly inspired from Moscow. Communism was a world-wide conspiracy; it was the enemy that worked from within as well as from without. It was present in the United States; it even existed, as Senator Joseph McCarthy charged in his sweeping attacks on the loyalty of the Truman administration, in the American government itself. An hysterical fear and hatred of Communism mounted in the United States.

On the 25th of June, fighting broke out along the 38th parallel, which was the boundary dividing the People's Republic of Korea, dominated by Soviet Russia, from the Republic of Korea, dominated equally by the United States. On the same day, in response to an American request, and on the basis of most inadequate information, the Security Council of the United Nations met and adopted a resolution condemning the attack on the Republic of Korea, demanding the withdrawal of the North Korean forces to the 38th parallel, and calling on all members of the United Nations to render every assistance in the execution of this resolution. The Truman administration quickly decided that, so far as the United States was concerned, 'assistance' meant armed assistance. The United States was determined to intervene unilaterally and at once; and the respectable cover of a United Nations resolution would be useful, but not essential. On the 27th of June, at midday, President Truman announced that he had ordered American naval and air units to give support to the South Korean forces, and that the Seventh Fleet had been commanded to insulate Taiwan from the Communist-controlled mainland of China. It was only after these orders had been made public that the Security Council met, and, on a motion of the United States, recommended that the United Nations give 'such assistance to the Republic of Korea as may be necessary to repel the armed attack and restore peace and security in the area'. This resolution passed with the bare minimum of seven votes. The representative of Soviet Russia was absent; Yugoslavia voted no; India and Egypt abstained (India later concurred).

Canada had been a member of the United Nations Temporary Commission created in 1947 to supervise the establishment of an independent and united Korea; but she had withdrawn when it had been decided to hold elections in the southern division of the country alone. At that time the Canadian government had dissociated itself from what had obviously become a struggle between the United States and the Soviet Union for power and influence in Korea; but this position had subsequently been compromised when Canada recognized the southern republic as an independent state. In June 1950, when the crisis broke, she risked her integrity much more seriously; her efforts to separate the achievement of peace in Korea from the now world-wide American crusade against Communism proved weak and ineffectual. The United Nations could not itself take action in Korea; its international police force, to which all member nations were supposed to contribute according to article 43 of the Charter, had never materialized. If there was to be quick intervention in Korea, it could be undertaken only by the United States; and, as the American authorities made quite plain from the beginning, it would be carried out solely on their terms. In the morning hours of the 27th of June, Pearson tried to persuade the Truman administration to delay its announcement of armed aid to South Korea until intervention had been authorized by the Security Council. He argued also that the invasion of South Korea should be publicly regarded as a single and local attack, and not as a manifestation of world-wide Communist aggression. This early Canadian essay at 'quiet diplomacy' at Washington failed as such efforts were to fail so often in the future. The United States decided unilaterally to take armed action in Korea; and, by announcing this decision at the same time as the publication of its policy for Taiwan, the Truman administration acknowledged that these were two closely related parts of a single great operation.

If St. Laurent and Pearson felt troubled and uncertain about this highly equivocal enterprise and its dubious beneficiary, Syngman Rhee, the President of the Republic of Korea, they did not trouble the Canadian Parliament and people with their doubts. Three Canadian destroyers and a unit of the Royal Canadian Air Force were promptly dispatched to the scene of action; and, before the war was over, Canada had contributed a brigade to the ground forces under the U.S.-U.N. command. Pearson admitted that the United States had first offered aid to Korea on its own authority; but he argued blandly that the American action was 'in accordance with the spirit and letter of the Charter of the United Nations'. He even attempted the difficult feat of justifying the American insulation of Taiwan and, at the same time, dissociating Canada from any part in it. When the U.S.-U.N. forces crossed the 38th parallel and thus committed exactly the crime of which North Korea had originally been judged guilty, he apparently assumed that the fight was nearly over and elections could soon be held in a united Korea. When MacArthur's forces swept up to the borders of Manchuria, and China angrily reacted in much the same way as the United States would have reacted if a Communist-dominated United Nations had invaded north-western Mexico in an attempt to extend the rule of a 'people's republic' at

Mexico City, Pearson seemed to regard the Chinese intervention as an act of unjustified aggression. By the middle of November, he had so far imbibed the crusading American spirit that he was prepared to accept, with apparent equanimity, a vast extension of the war into a full-scale conflict between the United States and the United Nations on the one hand and China on the other. It was not until President Truman suggested to a group of American journalists that the United States might have to use the atom bomb to win the war that this complacency was seriously disturbed; and even then it was Prime Minister Attlee who flew to Washington and first protested against any unilateral American decision to use the bomb.

From then on, Canadian, British, and Indian policies drew closer together; and Canada tried, though not consistently, to limit the war and bring it to an end as quickly as possible. Pearson was made a member of the original cease-fire committee, appointed in December 1950; but, in February 1951, Canada voted in favour of the resolution, sponsored by the United States, naming China an aggressor, a resolution that logically implied a war with the Chinese People's Republic. In reality the United Nations was unwilling to incur this gigantic risk; and, in April, that incorrigible expansionist, General MacArthur, the United Nations commander, was dismissed by President Truman. The cease-fire negotiations, which finally began in July, were interminably prolonged by the dispute over the repatriation of prisoners; and there were times, particularly after Eisenhower succeeded Truman as President in 1953, when American exasperation and impatience at this delay brought a general war as close as it had been in the autumn of 1950. By this time, Canadian leaders were speaking a language very different from that in which they had indulged three years before; St. Laurent and Pearson stressed the war's limited objective, denied all intention of unifying Korea by force, and, in private, tried to temper American indignation.

-≫≫ IV ≪≪-

THE POST-WAR recession, which everybody had been expecting and dreading, finally arrived in 1948 on the heels of the exchange crisis. Unemployment increased during 1949 and kept increasing until June of the following year. For the three years 1948-50, the total annual value of exports scarcely varied, despite a growing rise in prices. Yet the effects of the slump were not too serious or prolonged, and by the middle of 1950 it had run its course. At that point, strong expansionary forces recovered their control of the economy; and for the next seven years, broken only by another slight recession in 1953-4, the nation experienced a period of sustained economic growth. Employment reached the highest level in Canada's history. National income continued its steady rise. All divisions in the private sector of the economy participated, though unequally, in the general development; and, between 1950 and 1957, the annual expenditure of all Canadian governments – federal, provincial, and municipal – more than doubled. It was as satisfactory an upswing as any that had gone before; and yet it differed profoundly from all the booms that had preceded it. It expressed in economic terms – terms as significant as the language of politics – the rapidly changing nature of the new Canada and its place in the world.

To a very large extent, the explanation of the upswing lay in the postwar discovery of new and important natural resources, and the rapid development of the resource industries, old and new. In 1947 came the first oil strike in the Edmonton region of Alberta and the opening up of the immense iron-ore deposits on the Quebec-Labrador boundary. In the next ten years production of iron rose from less than 2 million to more than 21 million tons; the output of crude petroleum mounted from 8 million to more than 181 million barrels; and the volume of natural gas increased from 52 to 220 billion cubic feet. These were the most spectacular developments of the period; but the growth of the older resource industries, some of them also encouraged by important new discoveries, and all stimulated by rising prices, was almost equally impressive. The value of exports of non-ferrous metals, rising to $982 million in 1957, had tripled in a decade; and yet the pulp-and-paper industry, though its growth was less spectacular, still kept its leading position in Canada's external trade. On the whole, most of the significant economic developments of the postwar period simply confirmed and emphasized Canada's traditional role as an exploiter of her own natural resources and a producer of raw and partly processed materials for more populous and industrialized nations.

The second important factor in the upward surge of the early 1950s was the Korean War. In 1949, federal government expenditure on defence had totalled $387.2 million. The first year of the Korean War saw this amount doubled; and by 1952 it had reached a total of nearly $2 billion. The newly established Department of Defence Production, over which the energetic and ruthless C. D. Howe presided, stimulated the revival and expansion of the aircraft and electronics industries and brought shipbuilding back to something like its level of importance during the Second World War. Considerable quantities of this wartime production were supplied to the United States and Canada's other NATO allies; but manufacturing in general, though it expanded more rapidly than the economy as a whole, never recovered the prominent place in Canada's external trade that it had acquired during the Second World War and held for a few years after its conclusion. By 1950 Japan and the countries of Western Europe had completed the absorbing task of reconstruction and had regained their former competitive efficiency and vigour as industrial and trading nations. Exports of manufactured goods had made up nearly 55 per cent of total Canadian commodity exports at the end of the Second World War; but, in the fiercer rivalry of postwar international trade, the proportion dropped to 40 per cent and 35 per cent. Once again, the domestic market had become the only great market of Canadian secondary industry – the market in which it disposed of over 90 per cent of its production. Canada, in fact, had reverted to the state of industrial immaturity out of which she had first emerged during the First World War, nearly half a century earlier. This relative decline in the sale of Canadian manufactures abroad and the accompanying enormous increase in the export of raw staple products and industrial materials were the twin expressions of Canada's return to a condition of economic colonialism.

In the economic as in the political world, Canada had gained autonomy in one empire only to become the colony of another. Her dependence upon American markets and American capital steadily increased. From 1948 to 1958, the nation's export trade to all countries had advanced in a satisfactory but very uneven fashion; her stake in the commerce of North America had grown by leaps and bounds. Exports to the United Kingdom had increased in value by only 7 per cent, exports to all countries by less than 60 per cent, and exports to the United States by over 90 per cent. The share of the United States in Canada's external trade had by 1958 reached formidable proportions; 60 per cent of Canadian exports were sold to the American Republic, and over 70 per cent of imports were bought from it. As in the past, the large deficit in the balance of payments with the United States was met to some extent by a surplus in the account with the United Kingdom; but a considerable and increasingly unfavourable balance remained and, as the decade of the 1950s went on, this was settled by larger and larger imports of American capital.

This huge investment of American funds was the final and conclusive sign of Canada's increasing subordination in a North American empire, organized, developed, and financed on a continental scale by the United States. In 1945 foreigners had invested $7.1 billion in Canada; by 1957, this total had grown to $17.5 billion. In 1945, Americans had contributed 70 per cent of the whole; by 1957 their share had grown to 76 per cent. A considerable part of this vast commitment had, of course, gone into such 'portfolio' investments as bonds, debentures, and minority holdings of equities listed on the stock exchanges; but, at the same time, a second substantial portion, which during the 1950s increased to over 50 per cent of the whole, was put into 'direct' investment, investment in which American ownership was so concentrated as to constitute American control. In the textile and iron and steel industries, the American interest had always been relatively small; it rivalled or slightly exceeded the Canadian interest in the pulp-and-paper and agricultural machinery industries; but in the manufacture of rubber, and automobiles and parts it was completely dominant. In 1948, Americans had owned 35 per cent and controlled 39 per cent of the total capital in Canadian manufacturing; by 1957, ownership had increased to 39 per cent and control to 43 per cent of the whole. The steady advance of the American stake in Canadian manufacturing was one of the conspicuous features of the period; but it was not the only, nor the most striking, evidence of the progressive penetration of the Canadian economy by American capital. American money continued to pour into the smelting and refining of Canadian base metals, and from the first it acquired a dominating influence in the new resource industries of petroleum and natural gas. In 1957, Americans owned 57 per cent and controlled 70 per cent of the Canadian petroleum and natural gas industries.

Canada had always welcomed the influx of foreign capital on terms more liberal than those offered by any other industrialized nation in the world. Canadians assumed that American capital had enabled them to develop their resources and expand their industries more quickly than they could have done with their own means. They were equally convinced that American scientific knowledge, technological expertise, and managerial skill had helped to lift Canadian industrial productivity to a high level otherwise impossible of attainment. The Liberal government watched the massive postwar accumulation of American capital in Canada apparently without a tremor of apprehension; and C. D. Howe, who was himself an American import and who had held all the vital cabinet posts in industrial development, personified the whole dynamic process. The Canadian economy had become a branch-plant economy. Canada was developing a branch-plant government and a branch-plant state of mind. Canadians had learnt to identify postwar prosperity with American capital, just as they had been taught to identify the defence of liberty and democracy with American foreign policy. They looked to New York and Chicago for industrial direction just as they looked to Washington for diplomatic leadership. The great American multi-national corporation had never yet come under critical scrutiny in Canada. Canadians had scarcely begun to suspect that massive American investment might be impeding the growth of a native Canadian capital market, lowering the quality of Canadian industrial management and entrepreneurship, reducing the time and money spent in Canada on scientific and technological research, deepening the traditional national tendency towards timidity and conservatism in business, and transferring the power – and finally the capacity – to make important decisions out of the hands of Canadians and into those of foreigners.

⊰⊱ V ⊰⊱

IN 1953, DWIGHT D. EISENHOWER became President of the United States and the Soviet Union exploded its first hydrogen bomb. The western world was brought to the frightening realization that the American Republic no longer possessed a monopoly of these terrible engines of mass destruction and that a major war would threaten the annihilation of the entire human race. The peoples of all nations were shocked and horrified by the thought of this awful possibility; but even the prospect of total human obliteration seemed to have little effect on the aggressive foreign policy of the new American President and his Secretary of State, John Foster Dulles. In January 1954, Dulles announced that the United States would defy 'the conspiracy against freedom' with 'massive retaliation', inflicted whenever and wherever the American government chose. For the next twelve months, he continued to exhibit his daring virtuosity at 'brinkmanship' at the edge of every diplomatic cliff in Europe or Asia. He attempted, with the threat of an 'agonizing reappraisal' of American foreign policy, to compel France to join the European defence community. He proposed military intervention by Britain and the United States in support of French power in Indo-China; sponsored the formation of the South-East Asia Treaty Organization, despite the reluctance of Britain and the opposition of several Asian states whose 'freedom' the organization was supposedly designed to protect; and negotiated a mutual defence treaty with Chiang Kai-shek's Nationalist Chinese government, a treaty which quickly provoked hostilities about Taiwan and threatened a general war between China and the United States.

Canada had accepted American leadership in the West European–American defence system; but she watched Dulles's intensification of the Cold War with a good deal less of the crusading ardour that she had shown during the first months of the 'collective resistance to aggression' in Korea. The sorry enterprise of the Korean War, in which Canada had suffered 1,557 casualties, had finally come to the futile conclusion of a complete stalemate. By the middle of 1954, it was perfectly apparent that a unified, independent, and democratic Korea was impossible of achievement, and that the two republics into which the Korean peninsula was divided would continue on their separate ways exactly as they had done before the war began. It was highly unlikely, in existing international circumstances, that the Security Council of the United Nations would ever again attempt to 'restore international peace and security' by force; and Canada, freed from the obligations of collective security, was in no hurry to become involved in even more obvious American exercises in the Cold War. The Canadian government remained quite detached from the South-East Asia Treaty Organization. Pearson repeatedly insisted that Canada was not bound by the American commitment to Taiwan, although he did agree, instinctively adopting the conceptions and phraseology of the Cold War, that positions of strategic importance in the struggle against world Communism should not be lightly abandoned. At first he was equally firm in his assertions that Canada was not concerned in the problem of Indo-China, since it had never been submitted to the United Nations; but when an invitation came to work out the cease-fire agreement which had just been negotiated by the Geneva Conference, the Canadian government somewhat reluctantly accepted; and Canada, along with India and Poland, joined the three-nation Supervisory Commission appointed to watch over the settlement in Vietnam, Laos, and Cambodia.

)ieppe, August 1942

*'uebec Conference, 1943: Eden, King, Roosevelt, Princess Alice, Cadogan,
racken, Churchill*
. . [Mackenzie King] admitted that his role at the Quebec Citadel was very much
ke that of the general manager of the Château Frontenac Hotel."

Louis St. Laurent
". . . he managed to convey an impression, partly paternal and partly avuncular, of a wise, kindly, and utterly trustworthy old gentleman."

C. D. Howe
". . . [he] had never known what it was to be in opposition and did not intend to find out."

ohn Diefenbaker
". . . the inspiring vision of the prophet, the burning sincerity of an evangelist,
nd the annihilating attack of a prosecuting counsel determined on the conviction
f a monstrous criminal."

*James E. Coyne: at the University of
Manitoba, 1961*
"Academic economists, the reverend episcopate of Canadian laissez-faire capitalism, denounced Coyne as a contumacious
heretic, and demanded that he be unfrocked and deprived of all his priestly
functions."

L. B. Pearson cuts his centennial year birthday cake aided by J. W. Pickersgill (left) and Mrs. Pearson (right)
"Their feelings found outlets in a large number of 'centennial projects'."

The United States had disliked and resisted the Geneva settlement and some Canadians feared that Canada courted American disapproval if she accepted the appointment to the Supervisory Commission. The Canadian government was even more acutely aware of the fact that it risked the sovereign displeasure of the United States if it made any move to recognize the Peking government or to support its inclusion in the United Nations. To the American people, 'Red' China, as it was invariably called, was the central enormity and abomination of Asia, the mere thought of which, even after seven years, was still insupportable; and President Eisenhower, reiterating his unalterable opposition to China's admission to the United Nations, claimed that he had the support of 95 per cent of his fellow citizens. To Canada, recognition was simply a practical diplomatic necessity and not a good-conduct prize awarded for adherence to the American way of life. In North America, these were dangerous thoughts which the Canadian government intimated only very discreetly. The nearest any Canadian politician came to a frank avowal was when Prime Minister St. Laurent, at the end of the Asian stage of his world tour in 1954, declared candidly at Seoul that 'some day we will have to be realistic and admit that the government of China is the government of the people'. For the next week, he was kept busy explaining away his sensible but 'unfortunate' remark to the Canadian Parliament and press.

The influence of American example was potent in Asia; the power of American authority was dominant in North America. At times and in ways which the American government thought desirable or expedient, the whole continent was, in fact, being organized on an integrated continental scale. Co-operative undertakings for continental defence, which were an essential part of American grand strategy in the Cold War, were carried forward with the utmost promptitude and vigour; but joint commercial enterprises, such as the St. Lawrence Seaway, which for decades had been a favourite project of Canadian economic planning, were repeatedly postponed to suit American convenience. The Canadian commitment to NATO in Europe drastically weakened Canada's powers of self-protection; and at the frenzied height of the Dulles crusade against Communism, the American demand for the improved defence of the far north became imperative and irresistible. A radar screen, the Pine Tree Line, had already been built across the continent through the northern United States and southern Canada; and, in 1954, the two countries decided to construct two further, more northerly screens, one of which, the so-called Distant Early Warning Line (or DEW Line), was to be installed and manned by the United States. This revelation of Canada's military weakness and compromised sovereignty apparently did not disturb the complacency of the Canadian government; but it mortified and angered many Canadians. And their sense of national self-reliance and self-sufficiency suffered another serious injury when, at the eleventh hour, and on the ungenerous terms of its own choosing, the United States decided to participate in the St. Lawrence scheme, and the hope of an all-Canadian Seaway was gone for ever.

->» VI «-

IN AUGUST 1953, St. Laurent won his second general election. He had made no promises; he simply stood, with comfortable self-satisfaction, upon his government's record. His campaign was relaxed and casual. The electorate was apathetic, or away on summer holidays, and only 67 per cent of the voters went to the polls. Everybody apparently assumed that the results would contain no surprises; and they did not. The Conservatives increased their strength in the House of Commons to 51 seats; but many of these gains had already been won in the by-elections of the previous two years. Both the Co-operative Commonwealth Federation and the Social Credit Party had slightly improved their positions; but the opposition as a whole, even in the unlikely event of its uniting in a vote of want of confidence, could muster only 95 votes. St. Laurent had a following of 170 members and a majority of 75.

For the next two years, the St. Laurent government relapsed into a state of complacent inactivity very reminiscent of that in which Mackenzie King had rested so comfortably from 1926 to 1929. The St. Lawrence Seaway, begun at long last in the autumn of 1954, was the only great new undertaking of the period; but the division of its construction and ownership between Canada and the United States reduced its significance as a national Canadian achievement. Unemployment, the most politically dangerous symptom of the post-Korean War recession, increased sharply in 1954 and early 1955; but the government proposed no special measures for its alleviation, and the project of the South Saskatchewan Dam had been indefinitely postponed. Still older Liberal policies, the unfinished business of the great nationalist campaign of 1945-9, had, it seemed, been even more completely forgotten. The Canada Council, recommended by the Massey Commission in 1951 as a means of giving national support to the arts, letters, humanities, and social sciences, had not yet been established. A new federal-provincial tax-sharing agreement, which gave the provinces a rebate on federal taxes amounting to 10 per cent on personal incomes, 9 per cent on corporation incomes, and 50 per cent on succession duties, was adopted in 1956; but, after the abortive effort of 1950, the government had dropped the search for a method of amending the Canadian constitution, and had not resumed it since. Nobody apparently dreamed of removing the flag from the deep cupboard in which it had been hidden.

For a time it seemed as if the government might continue indefinitely, and with complete impunity, on its unhurried, self-assured, and authoritative way. In both provincial and federal politics, there appeared to be almost no signs of serious opposition to its rule. The majority of the provinces were now governed by parties professedly hostile to the Liberals; but the running feud with Ottawa, which had been such a popular feature of provincial politics during the 1930s, was now kept up by Quebec virtually alone. At Ottawa itself, resistance to the Liberal dynasty seemed even feebler. George Drew was ill during 1954; and his inability to put the government on the defensive in a single major issue, as well as his relative failure in two general elections, brought about the inevitable demands for his resignation. The opposition was divided and discouraged. And then, during the session of 1955, it was suddenly given a real chance. The act creating the Ministry of Defence Production provided for its termination in 1956; but now, though the Korean armistice was nearly two years old and almost all the Canadian soldiers had returned to Canada, St. Laurent proposed that the Ministry be continued, as an ordinary department of government, but with all its original wartime emergency powers. The Conservatives, leaping upon this bill as a blatant example of the government's authoritarian instincts and arbitrary conduct, found, to their pleased astonishment, that they had press and public opinion on their side. In the end, St. Laurent yielded to the determined opposition filibuster; and, in C. D. Howe's absence, he accepted Drew's suggestion of a definite terminal date for the emergency powers.

Howe was furious; but he soon recovered all his old enthusiasm in a new peacetime project as vast and spectacular as any he had ever tackled during two wars. On the 1st of September 1955, he and St. Laurent reached an agreement with representatives of Ontario, Alberta, and a new commercial company, Trans-Canada Pipe Lines, for the transmission of natural gas from the Alberta fields to the markets of eastern Canada.

CHAPTER FOURTEEN

Point of No Return

IN HIS TRIUMPHANT statement of September 1955, announcing the pipeline agreement, St. Laurent declared that the new project ranked in importance with that first great transcontinental Canadian enterprise, the Canadian Pacific Railway. There were, in fact, several disquieting ways in which the pipeline undertaking resembled Sir Hugh Allan's fated first attempt to build the railway to the Pacific; and the most obvious of these was the heavy dependence of both upon American entrepreneurs and American capital. Though Trans-Canada Pipe Lines had been formed, under federal government pressure, by the union of two companies, one substantially Canadian-owned and the other an American subsidiary, the controlling interest in the joint organization lay securely in the hands of American capitalists. The company which was to supply most of the natural gas was also American-controlled; and, while one of the markets which Trans-Canada Pipe Lines hoped to exploit lay in the urban centres of Ontario and Quebec, the other was located south of the boundary in the state of Minnesota. The preliminary requirements for such a vast and varied enterprise were many. Authority for this or that phase of its operations had to be obtained from the governments of Alberta, Canada, and the United States. Contracts had to be negotiated with the construction companies which would build the pipeline, the oil companies which would supply the gas, and the Canadian and American customers who would use it. In the eyes of Canadian financial houses, these complicated, interrelated necessities lent a dangerous air of uncertainty to the whole vast scheme; and, when Trans-Canada Pipe Lines proposed a large bond issue to cover the major part of the cost of construction, they declined to underwrite it.

At this point, the officials of Trans-Canada Pipe Lines appealed to the government of Canada; they asked it to guarantee the interest on a first mortgage bond issue of $275 million. A question of first-class national interest was raised by this request; why should the Canadian government be called upon to give the financial assistance necessary to start a commercial company which was continental rather than Canadian in character, which was controlled by American capitalists, and sought markets in the United States as well as in Canada? The Canadian Parliament, press, and people became quickly and passionately involved in the controversy over this issue; but the first important result of Trans-Canada's request was a division of opinion within the Liberal government itself. Howe, Minister of Trade and Commerce and Defence Production, was enthusiastically in favour of assistance to the company; Walter Harris, the Minister of Finance, was doubtful and critical of it. St. Laurent tried in vain to mediate between these two formidable colleagues; and the first attempt to arrange an agreement between the government and the company broke down completely.

Howe was disappointed but indomitable. The Trans-Canada project appealed irresistibly to every significant element in his character and personality. He liked vast undertakings; he enjoyed quick decisions and strenuous action; he was prepared to take large risks. The close integration of Canada into a North American economy dominated by the United States was, to a very large extent, a development of the two decades in which he had watched over Canada's economic progress; and Canada's new continental orientation was in effect a gigantic amplification of his own continental outlook. Orthodox financial considerations and simple nationalist fears were powerless to restrain his impetuous enthusiasm for a project which promised to be the supreme achievement of his career. He produced plan after plan to save the pipeline; and, finally, in August 1955, a new proposal gained St. Laurent's consent. The governments of Canada and Ontario would themselves construct the costly division of the line through northern Ontario at their own expense, and later, when the financial success of the enterprise was assured, they would sell it to Trans-Canada Pipe Lines.

This was the scheme which Howe first submitted to Parliament in March 1956; but, before the debate was resumed in May, its terms had been significantly and questionably altered. In the United States, the Federal Power Commission, pressed by other competing suppliers of energy, had not yet approved the import of Canadian natural gas into the Republic; and, in these still uncertain circumstances, Trans-Canada Pipe Lines had not been able to obtain the funds necessary for the construction of its own division of the line in western Canada. This probably meant no more than a delay of a few months or at the most a year; but to Howe, who was by now completely obsessed by his project, all delay had become insupportable. He was determined that the enterprise should begin during the summer of 1956; and, with a fervid energy which was strange in him, he persuaded his colleagues to advance Trans-Canada up to 90 per cent of the cost of the western section of the pipeline as far east as Winnipeg. He also succeeded in convincing the reluctant cabinet that the 5th of June must be the deadline for the passage of the revised measure, and that, if necessary, closure would be used to push it through the House of Commons in time.

Howe submitted the new proposal to the House on the afternoon of the 8th of May. The government's rigid timetable allowed less than a month for parliamentary approval. The Progressive Conservatives and the C.C.F. members, united in opposition and confident of widespread popular support, began at once to prolong the debate and resist the passage of the bill by every conceivable parliamentary device. But Howe was equally determined to push the scheme through by whatever arbitrary methods were required. On six of the seven clauses proposed by the government at the resolution stage, the entire discussion consisted of 207 words uttered by Howe himself! Closure, a Conservative invention piously denounced by the

Liberals as politically immoral, had to be employed; and its use on four separate occasions enlarged the scope and meaning of the pipeline debate by another huge dimension. The popular opposition to the alienation of Canadian industry and natural resources was now strengthened by resentment at the offences of Liberal rule and concern for the integrity of the Canadian Parliament. Two decades in office had apparently bred in the Liberal government a complacent belief in its own wisdom, a contemptuous disregard of criticism, and a truculent impatience at all delay. To a rapidly increasing number of Canadians, Liberal rule had become autocratic rule, and the rude and presumptuous Howe was its personification. The Progressive Conservative and C.C.F. members realized that they were fighting for a cause which was both constitutionally dignified and politically popular; and the knowledge strengthened their determination and their pertinacity. The debate continued for long, acrimonious days and nights of procedural wrangles, questions of privilege, and appeals of the Speaker's rulings, all enlivened by the furious exchange of insinuations, charges, insults, recriminations, and abuse. In the end, early in the morning of the 6th of June, the Pipeline Bill passed, only a few hours after the deadline set by the government. It was a sorry victory. The pipeline debate had discredited Howe, tarnished the prestige of the Prime Minister, humiliated the Speaker, exhausted and demoralized the Commons, and stained the dignity and repute of Parliament.

⇥⟫ II ⟪⇤

THE PIPELINE DEBATE and the Suez crisis were the obverse and reverse sides of the same medal. The Liberal government's sponsorship of the pipeline project was an unmistakable sign of Canada's close identification with a continental North American economy, dominated by the United States. The Suez crisis was an equally plain revelation of the disintegration of the postwar Commonwealth and the submission of its members, including Canada, to American leadership in world politics.

Traditionally the Middle East was a British and French sphere of influence; but, since the beginning of the Eisenhower administration, the United States had interfered more actively in the politics of the region, with distinctly unsettling effects. The High Dam at Aswan on the Nile River was the darling nationalist project of Gamal Abdel Nasser, the new dictator of Egypt. The United States had offered financial aid for the construction of the dam; and then Dulles, annoyed by Nasser's ostentatiously 'neutralist' attitude and his increasing contacts with Communist countries, abruptly withdrew the offer. One week later, on the 26th of July, 1956, Nasser defiantly announced that the Suez Canal, the one great foreign asset in Egypt, had been nationalized. The canal was an international waterway operated by the Suez Maritime Company under a ninety-nine-year lease, which in 1956 still had twelve years to run. It was territorially a part of Egypt and subject to Egyptian sovereignty; but its independence as an international waterway, open to the ships of all nations in war as well as in peace, had originally been guaranteed by the Convention of 1888, and subsequently confirmed, when Great Britain abandoned its Egyptian base, by the Anglo-Egyptian Treaty of 1954. Disraeli's purchase of the Khedive Ismail's shares in 1875 had given Great Britain a 44-per-cent interest in the Suez Maritime Company; and the free passage of the canal was of enormous importance to British commerce. To the government of the United Kingdom and particularly its new Prime Minister, Sir Anthony Eden, who was completely obsessed with the seizure, Nasser was a cheating, thieving fascist dictator who exercised a dangerously disturbing influence in the politics of the Middle East. The barefaced theft of the canal, the British government concluded, must be resisted and, if necessary, by force.

The attitude of the United States was, of course, very different. The Republic had gained its exclusive property rights in the Panama Canal by pressure politics which contrasted very unfavourably with the ordinary commercial methods by which Britain had acquired her interest in the Suez Canal. But while the United States government had for generations regarded American diplomatic imperialism in South and Central America as an eminently respectable activity, it looked with grave disapproval on the old-fashioned 'European' type of imperialism which Britain had exercised in the Middle East. Dulles's suspicion of Nasser's 'neutralist' behaviour was balanced by his instinctive sympathy with Egypt's long 'subjection' to British colonial rule. The United States had not the slightest intention of surrendering her territorial sovereignty in the Panama Canal zone; but it was owing in considerable measure to American pressure that Britain had withdrawn her troops from Egypt in 1954. The abandonment of the Egyptian military base meant that Britain had no means on the spot to resist Nasser's seizure. She hoped, with the aid of a large number of maritime nations, including the United States, to establish a permanent international control of the canal. But, apart from force, what sanctions could be employed to compel Nasser to accept such an arrangement? Dulles, though he denounced the seizure of the canal and agreed to join a common front of protest, was from the first opposed to the use of force.

Like Mackenzie King, who had prevented the use of Canadian troops in North Africa during the Second World War, St. Laurent shared this characteristically American suspicion of 'British imperial interests' in the Middle East; and nothing could irritate his prickly French-Canadian susceptibilities faster than the operations of British diplomacy. He was annoyed at Eden's calm assumption that Canada would share Britain's indignation at Nasser's act; and the Canadian government would go no further than to give its detached approval to the plans for the establishment of an international administration for the canal. As might have been expected, Nasser unaccommodatingly rejected the first proposal for such an international body, and was certain to reject the second, in the sure knowledge that the United States would not intervene to enforce it. What was to be done? Like Dulles, St. Laurent and Pearson were totally opposed to the use of force against Egypt. They may have hoped, like Dulles, that the affair could be spun out, through one abortive solution after another, until Britain and France grew weary and gave up their claims. The furthest Pearson would go was to suggest that France and Britain might be invited to bring the question before the Security Council; but this move was certain to be blocked by the United States. Dulles objected that the United Nations must not be converted into a mere agency for the enforcement of British policy in the Middle East, though it was true, of course, that six years earlier the United Nations had played the part of an agency in carrying out American policy in Korea.

Britain and France had had enough of procrastination and frustration. They determined to act. They brought the issue of the canal before the Security Council; but, in the meantime, while they practised open but vain diplomacy at New York, they were making an elaborate and secret arrangement with Ben-Gurion of Israel. Israel was to attack Egypt; Great Britain and France would then intervene, and, on the pretext of protecting the free navigation of the canal, order the withdrawal of the Egyptian and Israeli forces and themselves occupy Port Said and Suez. This, of course, was a plot, a plot which bore a noticeable resemblance to another highly successful conspiracy, in which, two years earlier, the United States had assisted Honduras and Nicaragua in the planning and equipping of a military invasion of Guatemala and the overthrow of its reformist Arbenz government. Some of the Arbenz reforms had affected the interests of that powerful American capitalist organization, the United Fruit Company; and, in the view of the Eisenhower administration, this was sufficient proof that Arbenz had become the tool of international Communism. A calculated act of aggression in support of the United Fruit Company was regarded, in the United States, as a necessary part of the great crusade for liberty and democracy; but, oddly enough, this ideological imperative could not justify Anglo-French action in Egypt in defence of their treaty rights in the Suez Canal. In Ottawa, these fine distinctions seemed unquestionable. So far as the Canadian government was concerned, the invasion of Guatemala might have occurred on the moon, instead of in the Americas. But when St. Laurent heard that Britain and France were moving planes and ships to Egypt, the news threw him into a violent access of righteous indignation. His draft reply to Eden's message announcing the Anglo-French *démarche* was softened at the instance of the English-speaking moderates in the cabinet; but it plainly declared that Canada would not endorse the British military adventure in Egypt. British and American policy had openly diverged, and Canada had taken its stand with the United States and against the United Kingdom.

At New York, in a special session of the General Assembly, Pearson proposed and carried a plan for the formation of a United Nations force to impose a cease-fire in Egypt. At first Eden hoped that British and French troops would be accepted as part of this police force, but this face-saving plan was summarily rejected by the United States. Urged on by the French, Eden pressed forward with the Anglo-French expedition, but by this time its failure had become inevitable. The threats of Soviet Russia, the implacable hostility of the United States, and, finally, the imminent collapse of the pound sterling, compelled the British Prime Minister to accept the cease-fire unconditionally. In the Canadian House of Commons St. Laurent angrily exulted in the humiliation of those he called 'the supermen of Europe' and in the end of the era in which they had governed 'the whole world'. In reality, as he ought to have known very well, there were no 'supermen' in Europe; the real supermen were the leaders of the Soviet Union and the United States. They had imposed their joint solution on 'the whole world'; and the Commonwealth – with Australia and New Zealand supporting and Canada and India opposing Britain – had been seriously divided.

⇥⟫ III ⟪⇤

THE PIPELINE DEBATE was the last, as well as the greatest, parliamentary battle that George Drew ever fought. Ill and exhausted, he retired from the leadership of the Progressive Conservative Party in September 1956; and, in December, a convention met to elect a new leader, the fifth in only eighteen years. Of the three candidates for the office, Donald M. Fleming, E. Davie Fulton, and John G. Diefenbaker, Diefenbaker seemed from the first the probable winner; but he was, in many ways, an unusual Conservative, and a still more unlikely Conservative leader. Boyhood on a prairie farm, undergraduate life at the University of Saskatchewan, and legal practice in western villages and small towns had made him a westerner such as no previous Conservative leader, not even Bracken, had ever been. In his early, unsuccessful ventures into federal and provincial politics, he showed a strong interest in popular causes; and when he finally won a seat in the Commons in the election of 1940, he stood out from the first as an earnest and determined champion of civil liberties and welfare services. Politics was the monopolizing interest of his life; but his ascent up the ladder of the party hierarchy was slow. He tried for the leadership in 1942 and again in 1948, and was twice beaten, though in 1948 he ran in second place. The party's Old Guard managed to hold him back until Drew's retirement; but after that he rapidly gained influential and active supporters. At the national convention in December 1956, he won easily on the first ballot.

At sixty-one, Diefenbaker was older than any of his predecessors had been at the time of their election to the leadership. More than once during his long career of defeats, rebuffs, and frustrations, he had almost decided to give up politics completely. But there was one immense gain among the losses of this prolonged and discouraging delay. Diefenbaker's real aim was not the leadership of the Progressive Conservative Party, but the prime-ministership of Canada. If he had won in 1942 or 1948, he would probably have worn himself out, and strained the loyalty of the party, in fruitless years of opposition, just as Bracken and Drew had done. But in 1956 he faced a prospect, not of lengthy and exhausting struggle, but of quick and easy success. The pipeline debate and the Suez crisis had undeniably injured the prestige of the Liberal government; and the curious fact was that the Liberal government seemed absolutely oblivious to the damage it had sustained. Well into the fourth year of the twenty-second Parliament, it had singularly little to offer a nation of restive, critical, and angry voters. The Canada Council, with an endowment of $100 million, was at last established; but the Saskatchewan Dam had been postponed once more, and there was apparently no money for advances to farmers against their unsold grain. A long line of annual surpluses was not followed by a burst of pre-election generosity. Walter Harris's last budget cut taxes by only $50 million, added only a dollar to the family allowances and six dollars to the old-age pension – increases which did no more than cover the rise in the cost of living since 1949.

The Liberals entered the election campaign of 1957 in a mood of complacent optimism. Not unnaturally, St. Laurent assumed that he was fighting the Conservative Party, an old, familiar, and not very formidable enemy; but in fact, his antagonist was not a political party at all, but a man, John George Diefenbaker; and Diefenbaker was a novel and extraordinary phenomenon – a positive prodigy – in Canadian politics. In some mysterious but compelling fashion which was peculiarly his own, he seemed to combine the inspiring vision of the prophet, the burning sincerity of an evangelist, and the annihilating attack of a prosecuting counsel determined on the conviction of a monstrous criminal. His eloquence was somewhat old-fashioned in a florid, fervent, nineteenth-century manner. His long, involved sentences, with their frequent interjections and parenthetical remarks, were often confused and ungrammatical. His rhetorical devices – his gestures, the lifted and lowered tones of his voice, the changing pace of his delivery – were all very obvious. Yet, increasingly, as the campaign went on, he succeeded in capturing his audiences. He had a gift for devastating phrases and verbal burlesque. He impressed people with his absolute sincerity and invincible determination. He excited them with his vague, splendid visions of the future.

St. Laurent had not the remotest idea of how to cope with this fabulous personage. The best he could do was to appear in his accustomed role, with the familiar make-up and the well-known lines of 1949 and 1953. This reassuring portrait of a benevolent elder statesman talking over public affairs in a friendly and informal fashion, like a wise father discussing the problems of home-management and child-rearing with a group of interested parents, had apparently pleased everybody before; but now, strangely enough, it seemed to be losing its appeal. St. Laurent's meetings were thinly attended and marred by unfortunate incidents. Several of his cabinet ministers discovered, to their great surprise and discomfiture, that they were in trouble in their constituencies. The confident estimates of Liberal strength in the twenty-third Parliament were revised slightly downward; but nobody dreamed for a moment that the St. Laurent government might be defeated.

The result, for everybody, was an immense surprise; for the Liberals, it was a crushing blow. With a larger percentage of the popular vote than their adversaries had gained, and with 105 members in the new House as opposed to 112 Progressive Conservatives, their defeat was far from a rout. But these things scarcely mattered. In the minds of the Liberals, the government of Canada had become synonymous – or, more accurately, identical – with Liberal government; and the staggering fact that the Canadian electorate had shown a preference, even if only a small preference, for the opponents of the Liberals meant not only the rejection of a political party, but virtually an anarchistic repudiation of all Canadian government! The white, stricken countenance which St. Laurent presented to the television cameras in the Château Frontenac Hotel on the evening of the 10th of June was a strained mask of incredulity and consternation. He quickly placed the resignation of his government in the hands of the Governor General, and, less than three months later, retired from the leadership of the Liberal Party. A number of his cabinet colleagues abandoned public life even more abruptly. If God was going to alter the accepted rules of Canadian politics to such an outrageous extent that the Conservatives might actually win, then Liberal ministers were simply not going to play such a discreditable game any longer! Led by C. D. Howe, who had never known what it was to be in opposition and did not intend to find out, eight former Liberal cabinet ministers left politics for private professional practice or highly lucrative jobs in industry and finance.

More than six months later, in January 1958, when the Liberals met in convention to elect a new leader, Pearson was clearly the favourite. Paul Martin, his only important rival, had won his seat in the Commons in 1935, thirteen years before Pearson; but, for most of those years, Pearson, as a senior officer in the Department of External Affairs, had been making policy, rather than merely implementing it; and, for the next nine years, he had been St. Laurent's closest associate in the cabinet. His stature had been notably increased by his diplomacy during the Suez crisis, and his reputation as a world statesman had apparently been confirmed by the award of the Nobel Peace Prize. He won the Liberal leadership easily enough; but, four days later, when he got up to move a want-of-confidence amendment to a supply motion, he made a particularly sorry parliamentary beginning. Urged on by Pickersgill, who could never quite accustom himself to the astonishing fact that the Liberals were not still in office, he moved that the Conservatives should resign forthwith, without the trouble and expense of an election. Diefenbaker covered this fatuous amendment with cartloads of ridicule. By the end of the month he had decided on an immediate dissolution and a new general election. This time his all-embracing vision of Canada's future had been localized and focused. He saw a new Canada – a Canada of the North! With this as its principal slogan, the Progressive Conservative Party won 208 seats and a majority of 151 over all parties in the House of Commons. It was the greatest electoral victory in the history of the Canadian Parliament.

⇥⇥ IV ⇤⇤

THE 1950S WERE DRAWING to a close. It had been a wonderful ten years for Canada in ways that were gratifyingly familiar. Once again, as in the days of the Laurier boom, the mood of exuberant national confidence had its strong roots in the incontestible material facts of economic expansion, increasing prosperity, and rapidly growing numbers. The census of 1961 recorded a total population of 18,238,247. There were 4,228,818 more people in Canada in 1961 than there had been in 1951, an increase of 30 per cent, made up of a substantial net migration and a much larger natural increase. The birth rate, which had sunk as low as 20.1 in the last years of the depression, rose suddenly to 27.2 in 1946 and remained at 27 or 28 during the next fourteen years. Only 22,722 immigrants had arrived in Canada in 1945; 1957 brought 282,164, which was a larger number than had come in any year since 1913, forty-four years earlier. The huge total immigration of the 1950s was offset by the large emigration, chiefly of native Canadians, who departed, as in the past, mainly to the United States; but, even so, there was a net gain of over a million people.

The four million new Canadians were distributed in a very unequal fashion across the ten provinces that now made up the nation. As usual, the two central provinces, Ontario and Quebec, gained the great majority, over 2,800,000, of the new citizens; Ontario's share was 35 per cent of the whole, a percentage five points higher than Quebec's. In comparison with these huge totals, the advances in the middle west and the Atlantic provinces were extremely modest. Not one of the Atlantic provinces grew by more than 100,000 people, though both Newfoundland and Nova Scotia came very close to it. Saskatchewan, which had lost population during the two previous decades, also made a gain of nearly 100,000; and Manitoba, whose growth in the same twenty years had been very slow, managed to add nearly 150,000 to its numbers. The only region which exceeded the central provinces in its rate of increase was the far west – Alberta and British Columbia. Alberta, with nearly 400,000 new citizens, and British Columbia with more than 450,000, had each grown by approximately 40 per cent. The new west, the west of oil, natural gas, newsprint, and base metals, whose metropolitan centres were Calgary, Edmonton, and Vancouver, now represented the new orientation and the chief drive of the Canadian economy. The first west, the west of wheatlands and grain growers, had ceased to be the common interest and joint enterprise of Canadians.

The arrival of approximately 1,500,000 immigrants notably increased the rich variety of Canada's tessellated social pavement. The new Canadians, who came from the Netherlands, Italy, Czechoslovakia, Yugoslavia, and Hungary, as well as from

England and Scotland, differed markedly from their forerunners, the European peasants or Canadian and American farmers, who had settled in Canada during the first decade of the century. Not infrequently, the newcomers of the 1950s were middle-class city-dwellers, trained in various crafts or educated for the professions. In 1911, Europeans of ethnic origin other than British or French had formed about 13 per cent of the population; in 1961, half a century later, but chiefly as a result of the immigration of the previous fifteen years, the proportion had almost doubled to a little less than 26 per cent. It was true that nearly half of this third ethnic division of Canadian society had abandoned their native languages, mainly for English, and, to a very small extent, for French; but this wholesale adoption of the master language of North America did not imply that the new Canadians had lost their cultural identity or cohesion. With better-educated leaders, who quickly came to occupy positions of prominence and influence in Canadian life, without ever losing their contacts with their own people, the third great ethnic division of Canadian society became more conscious of itself and more determined and articulate in its own defence.

This vast human influx from Western Europe had had its disturbing effects upon the position of the two founding ethnic groups in Canada, British and French; but, on the surface at least, it looked as if the British had yielded most. In 1961, Canadians of French descent amounted to 30.37 per cent of the total population, a loss of less than one point from their percentage in 1871; but the British, who in 1871 had held pride of place with 60 per cent of the new nation's human resources, had now declined to 43.84 per cent. The relative reduction of the strength of British stocks was a characteristic feature of the new Canada; but its importance was greatly modified by the steady advance of the English language, at the expense of French as well as of the other European languages. Nearly 2,250,000 'New Canadians' now spoke English as their mother tongue; over 400,000 Canadians of French origin had also abandoned French for English. In Quebec itself, the retention of French as a mother tongue had been scarcely weakened at all; but, in other provinces and particularly in Ontario and the west, the shift to the dominant language of North America was steadily increasing. It was a progressive assimilation, constantly growing with each succeeding generation.

For all Canadians, whether of British, French, or other West European origins, the city had become the centre of economic and social life. The urge towards urban living had lost much of its force during the 1930s, when the farm at least saved its dependants from the hunger and destitution that overtook the unemployed city worker. The drift to the cities was not resumed during the 1940s, for the war and the first postwar years, with their voracious markets and high prices for Canadian agricultural products, made commercial farming a highly rewarding occupation. These conditions preserved the importance of the rural community in Canadian life down to the middle of the century; but after that the farm began to lose its manpower and change its character. In 1951, the rural population of Canada amounted to 38.4 per cent of the whole; ten years later it had declined to 29 per cent. Farms were larger in size and smaller in number, more mechanized, with more paid labour; and the change which had overtaken the ancient business of agriculture was only one manifestation of the technological revolution that was shifting Canadians from primary manual labour to other categories of gainful occupation. The large division of the Canadian labour force which made a living by hard manual tasks dropped from 39 per cent of the total in 1911 to 21 per cent in 1955. Those engaged in the more skilled jobs in secondary industry had increased slightly to about a third of the gainfully employed. The third and highest level of economic activity – the professional, managerial, and clerical occupations – included, in 1955, about 46 per cent of the total working population.

For a whole decade, Canadians, like other Europeans and American peoples, had been repeatedly informed, by politicians and other interested parties, that they were living in an age of affluence, and 'had never had it so good'. Many of them were living at least with more ease, in greater comfort, and with the help of more mechanical equipment than they had ever done before. Oil- and gas-fired furnaces had to a large extent ended the dirt and labour of heating with coal and wood. Electric refrigerators, stoves, and washing and drying equipment had mitigated the ancient drudgery of the kitchen. There were 4,104,400 passenger automobiles registered in Canada in 1960, more than twice as many as there had been ten years earlier; and although the Canadian Broadcasting Corporation had barely begun television broadcasting in the autumn of 1952, some 2,600,000 receiving sets had been sold by the beginning of 1957. Evidences of prosperity were everywhere; but the 'national minimum for the whole people', which Mackenzie King had promised during the Second World War, was still appallingly low. Despite fairly full employment and continuing inflation, 25 per cent of all Canadian families could be classified as 'low-income families' in 1961.

These gross inequalities were not peculiar to Canada. The affluent upper reaches of Canadian society, as well as its drab subsistence level and its deep pockets of misery, differed only relatively from those in the United States. In fact, the most significant development of the Canadian community after the Second World War was, paradoxically, the steady approximation of its activities, interests, and values to those of the Republic. Ten years ago, at the beginning of the decade, the Massey Commission had solemnly warned the Canadian people of the strength of 'the forces of geography' and the dangers of cultural continentalism. By the end of the 1950s, the Canada Council was giving support to Canadian ballet, theatre, and opera, as well as encouragement to the Canadian artist, musician, writer, and scholar. But the real danger to the Canadian identity lay in the enormous pressure of the American mass media – radio, television, motion pictures, and periodicals – which were busily turning the nation into a cultural colony of the United States in the same way as it was already becoming a branch-plant economy and a military satellite.

Only the state could challenge this apparently irresistible continentalism; but, in a free-enterprise country such as Canada, the state's accepted functions and its financial resources were limited; and, equally important, it was inhibited by the known inclination of large numbers of Canadians for American commercial entertainment. The Board of Broadcast Governors, established in 1958 to control all Canadian broadcasting, ruled that 'Canadian content' in radio and television must at least reach a modest 55 per cent, with 40 per cent in 'prime time'; but the Canadian Broadcasting Corporation, in its struggle to concentrate on Canadian themes and promote Canadian talent, was hampered by its own financial weakness, by the growth of a competing commercial television system, and by the voracious Canadian appetite for American programmes. The recommendations of the Royal Commission on Publications, which was set up in 1960 to study 'measures which could contribute to the further development of a Canadian identity through a genuinely Canadian periodical press', were never implemented. And Canadian sport, especially Canada's own game, hockey, had been largely integrated into a continental sports entertainment industry which was controlled in the United States.

⟫ V ⟪

DIEFENBAKER had promised many things; many other things were vaguely expected of him; but his main purposes were four in number. The north, he declared, was Canada's last great untouched inheritance; and, under his administration, the north would repeat the success which the west had brought Canada half a century before. The federal government's authoritarian disregard of Parliament and its centralization of power at Ottawa were evils which he would stop. He would attempt to halt the transfer of Canadian industry and natural resources into the control of American capital; and he would restore Canada's traditional close relations with the Commonwealth and put an end to its subservient acceptance of American foreign policy. He had awakened great expectations, expectations probably too great for any government to realize, and certainly greater than his Progressive Conservative government could make good in a single Parliament.

John Diefenbaker had sought power with admirable courage and persistence; but his political genius lay in its achievement, not in its exercise. He could inspire a popular crusade or animate an impetuous attack; but, even with the largest parliamentary majority in Canadian history, he could not plan and carry through a general, integrated programme of reform. Davie Fulton, Alvin Hamilton, and George Hees were as devoted and able public servants as any in Canadian history; but they remained gifted individuals, rather than members of a well-organized team. Diefenbaker dominated but could not direct his cabinet; the talents which had shone so brightly in election campaigning and parliamentary debate flickered uncertainly in the Privy Council Chamber and the Prime Minister's Office. The government lacked positive leadership in the service of a definite plan; it also found, at least at first, great difficulty in establishing a congenial and beneficial relationship with the civil service. The senior civil servants, whose character had been subtly changed by long years of close co-operation with Liberal ministers in the formation of government policy, were only too apt to regard those curious interlopers, the Conservative ministers, with doubt and apprehension. The Conservative ministers, who could not help but feel intruders in an unsympathetic if not alien city, looked on the civil servants with some suspicion.

These were not the only weaknesses and deficiencies. A central misfortune of the Conservative Party of the 1950s lay in the fact that it lacked a comprehensive and coherent body of doctrine. Diefenbaker's populism, like Bennett's Christian socialism, was firmly rooted in the traditional Conservative use of the powers of a centralized federation for national purposes, economic or social. Diefenbaker's resentment of American control and leadership, his instinctive urge towards a renewal of the old Anglo-Canadian alliance, were also natural modern developments of the historic Conservative policies. But there were other elements in modern Conservative thought, derived from nineteenth-century liberalism and fortified by dogmas currently fashionable in the United States, which weakened the influence of the main tradition. Diefenbaker's support of provincial rights conflicted with the party's basic belief in centralization. His humanitarian radicalism was confronted by the fiscal orthodoxy of some of his cabinet ministers. The urge to escape from American domination in foreign affairs was held back by an uncritical acceptance of the validity of the Cold War and the justice of the American claim to leadership of the 'Free World' in the struggle against Communism.

At home, there were inhibitions that weakened the force of Diefenbaker's drive; abroad there were obstacles that were almost certain to prevent the realization of his hopes. The decline and fall of the British Empire-Commonwealth and the growth of a continentally organized North America were twin processes which had been going on now for over four decades and which successive Liberal governments in Canada had actively encouraged and assisted. To arrest these powerful tendencies at this late stage would require the invention of novel and daring policies designed to defend Canadian integrity and independence against continentalism. Even more important and difficult, it would require the recreation of something which had virtually ceased to exist, the British Commonwealth. The Suez crisis had disrupted the old organization and ended its influence as a cohesive force in international affairs; and the expulsion of South Africa in 1961 continued the process of disintegration. On his own sincerely held principles, Diefenbaker could have done nothing else but join the Asian and African leaders in their condemnation of South Africa's racial policies; but the exclusion of the Union was one more sign of the Commonwealth's vanishing solidarity. Never again would Britain see in it a possible source for the reinforcement of her own declining strength. She would renew her 'special political relationship' with the United States, which Churchill had first forged during the Second World War. She would seek her economic future in Europe. The Anglo-Canadian alliance had gone; and Canada no longer regarded the Commonwealth very seriously as a medium for the promotion of her interests abroad.

Only a few weeks after he had taken office, Diefenbaker was made painfully aware of the compelling force of these historical tendencies. A plan for Canadian-American co-operation in air defence, the North American Air Defence Agreement (NORAD), which had first been discussed over a year earlier, was virtually ready for formal acceptance by both countries, just before the general election of 1957. This arrangement was, of course, the logical outcome of the Ogdensburg Agreement and the co-operative radar screens established in the 1950s, and agreed perfectly with the continental bias of Liberal defence policy. Pearson, it was true, attempted to evade responsibility by insisting that the St. Laurent government had reached no final decision before the election; but the available evidence implied that a definite commitment had been made; and, whatever he may have thought about the advisability of the agreement, Diefenbaker evidently assumed that the negotiations had gone too far to be reversed. The pact, which was presented to Parliament in the spring of 1958, provided for a joint air defence system, with an American commander-in-chief, and a Canadian second in command, both of whom were to be responsible to their respective chiefs of staff and hence ultimately to the civilian control of ministers. It was apparently assumed that both governments would agree about the gravity of any particular crisis and would alert all divisions of the defence system at the same time.

Diefenbaker had found it hard to escape from the powerful tentacles of continentalism. He soon discovered that it was equally difficult to strengthen the slack ties of the Commonwealth. Early in July 1957, on his return from his first Commonwealth Conference, he announced that his government planned to divert 15 per cent of Canada's imports from the United States to the United Kingdom. This announcement, which, in reality, was a declaration of hopeful intent rather than a statement of settled policy, was couched in imprudently precise terms, and had apparently been made in ignorance, or disregard, of two important and relevant circumstances. The first of these was the restrictions imposed by the General Agreement on Tariffs and Trade, to which both Canada and the United Kingdom were parties; and the second was the growing British interest in the newly formed European Common Market. GATT prevented the introduction of any additional preferences for British goods such as those granted by the Ottawa Agreements of 1932. There were other possible ways of increasing the British market in Canada, although the Canadian government did not specifically suggest any; but the most obvious way was to set up a free-trade area between the two countries; and this was what the British proposed, first privately in discussions with Canadian ministers and then publicly through Peter Thorneycroft, the British Chancellor of the Exchequer, at a press conference. When Thorneycroft made this off-hand announcement, he was perfectly well aware of the fact that the Canadian government disliked the free-trade plan and could not possibly accept it. Britain may have considered Diefenbaker's 15 per cent proposal an unwelcome intrusion at a time when her best markets seemed increasingly to lie in Europe and when she wished to keep her hands completely free for negotiations with the Common Market countries. Apparently the best way to get rid of Canada and its inconvenient suggestions was to call its bluff publicly.

Diefenbaker's overture had failed. The new Conservative régime had not brought any improvement in Anglo-Canadian relations; on the contrary, it had seen Canada's more complete identification in a continental defence system dominated by the United States. Some of the dangerous implications of this unequal partnership gradually became evident in 1959 after Fidel Castro's revolutionary movement had triumphed in Cuba. Castro's agrarian reforms, which affected American properties on the island, soon aroused the hostility of the United States; and American punitive measures drove Castro into closer relations with Soviet Russia. In American eyes, Cuba was simply a more dangerous Guatemala, to be dealt with by the same methods; and, in April 1961, six months after an American embargo of trade with the island had been proclaimed, the Central Intelligence Agency of the United States sponsored and directed an open invasion of Cuba, on the approved Guatemalan model, an invasion which, this time, was a complete and humiliating failure. The Canadian government continued to prohibit the export of strategic materials to Cuba and took steps to prevent the transshipment through Canada of American goods prohibited by the American embargo; but it declined to join the United States in its virtually complete suspension of trade with Cuba. Official Canadian comment on the invasion was muted; but among Canadian citizens there was widespread disquiet at the apparent American assumption of a right to confront and challenge the growth of socialism or Communism anywhere in the Americas.

➤➤ VI ◄◄

IN ANY ORDINARY circumstances, Diefenbaker's apocalyptic vision of Canada's future would have been hard to realize and his passionate crusade for social justice and human rights would probably have produced no more than modest human results. In the depressed state of affairs that followed his accession to power, the difficulties in the way of manifest success increased, and the gap between promise and performance widened accordingly. The drive which had sustained the Canadian economy, with only few and brief intervals, ever since the beginning of the Second World War, began at last to falter. The whole period 1957-61 was one of slow and interrupted growth; 1958 and 1961 were years of positive recession. Unemployment rose to levels higher than those of any period since the beginning of the Second World War. The gratifying annual rise in the value of exports flattened out; and the unfavourable balance of trade, which had begun to increase sharply in 1956, maintained unprecedented and alarming heights until 1960 brought some improvement.

In such conditions, what might have been a spectacular advance turned out to be a not unsuccessful holding operation. As a result of the 'roads to resources' programme, carried out in conjunction with the provinces, over 4,000 miles of new roads were laid down in the Canadian northland. The bulk sales to Russia and China, which cleared up most of the huge carry-over of Canadian wheat, were the gifts of good fortune rather than the gains of government initiative; but the reforming statutes for Canadian agriculture, sponsored by Alvin Hamilton, were the results of careful and imaginative planning. Very large sums of money were put into the development of natural resources, and the promotion and rationalization of primary industries. The cost of welfare and social security also mounted rapidly, partly through the increase of unemployment assistance and relief projects, and largely through a major expansion of the national health services. Many of these developmental and welfare policies were carried out jointly by the federal and provincial governments on a shared-cost basis; the provinces all gained from an increase in their rebate of the income tax, and the Atlantic provinces were awarded a special supplement to their equalization grants.

At the same time, the costs of administration mounted steeply. Financial rivalries threatened the amicable federal-provincial relations which Diefenbaker had hoped to establish. As 1962, the terminal date of the five-year tax rental agreements, approached, federal and provincial governments began to quarrel seriously over the division of tax revenues. In February 1961, after two inconclusive fiscal conferences, Diefenbaker proposed, as the two major changes in the existing financial arrangements, a new formula for the calculation of the equalization payments and an increase to 20 per cent over a five-year period of the provincial rebate of the income tax. This settlement, which disappointed and angered more provinces than it pleased, was finally imposed by Ottawa; but, if the federal government could act independently in fiscal matters, it needed the consent of the provinces for constitutional change. And Diefenbaker could not expect provincial acquiescence even in his most cherished piece of legislation, the Bill of Rights. He did not seek, and probably could not have obtained, provincial agreement to its entrenchment as an amendment to the British North America Act. It remained simply a statute of the Parliament of Canada whose safeguards applied only to matters within federal legislative authority.

The years 1960-1 had witnessed a remarkable resurgence of provincial opposition to federal policies. And the gravity of this widespread discontent was ominously deepened by a series of rapid changes which in less than a year took place in the province of Quebec. Maurice Duplessis died in September 1959, and his death ended the reactionary, repressive, and corrupt régime which Union Nationale had come to mean. Paul Sauvé, Duplessis's successor as premier, might have led his party back to the old reform programme which Duplessis himself and Paul Gouin had drawn up a quarter-century earlier; but Sauvé died suddenly in January 1960, and Union Nationale lost its best leader and the federal Conservatives their last real hope in Quebec. In the provincial general election of June 1960, the Liberals, led by Jean Lesage, won a narrow victory over Union Nationale. Their success may have surprised them, but they knew exactly what they wanted to do with political power. At the fiscal conference in July, which he attended only a few weeks after he had gained office, Lesage made large demands and assertions and talked spaciously about Quebec's provincial sovereignty. It was his urgent request that prompted the federal government to resume the long-abandoned search for a method of amending the British North America Act which could be carried out and completed in Canada. But Lesage was less interested in constitutional methodology than he was in the acquisition of power and revenue. He intended to use the government of Quebec – the Quebec 'state' – as the positive and virtually exclusive political agency for the defence of French-Canadian rights and the promotion of French-Canadian interests. His programme carried with it an undefined but real menace to Confederation. His provincial separatism conflicted directly with the pan-Canadianism of that 'unhyphenated Canadian', John Diefenbaker.

In the summer of 1961, when these outward attacks were already threatening the Progressive Conservative government, its inward contradictions and weaknesses were glaringly made public in a humiliating controversy with James Coyne, the Governor of the Bank of Canada. Coyne had been pursuing a tight monetary policy at the very time when Donald Fleming, the Minister of Finance, with his large expenditures and budget deficits, was relying on expansionary methods to sustain the flagging economy. During the past eighteen months, while Coyne had been making his views known in a series of outspoken public addresses, the contradiction between Canadian fiscal and monetary policy had become increasingly obvious;

but this was not the only issue which separated the Governor from the Conservative government and from orthodox economic and financial opinion in Canada. Coyne was a strong economic nationalist who for months had been telling Canadians that they were losing control of their own industries and natural resources as a result of the import of American capital, and that they must learn to 'live within their own means' if they wished to maintain their own national identity and their power of self-determination.

This heroic proposal might have helped to give Canada that freedom from American domination which Diefenbaker had declared he desired; but it would have run counter to his hope for the rapid expansion of the welfare of the common man; and it would have conflicted even more seriously, but for very different reasons, with the orthodox beliefs of the economic and financial establishment of Canada. Canadian financiers and manufacturers, who instinctively assumed that anyone objecting to the import of American capital must be insane, attacked Coyne's 'dangerous' ideas and privately hoped for his dismissal. Academic economists, the reverend episcopate of Canadian laissez-faire capitalism, denounced Coyne as a contumacious heretic, and demanded that he be unfrocked and deprived of all his priestly functions. In the end, the government demanded Coyne's resignation; and, when he refused to submit it, introduced a bill in the House of Commons declaring his office vacant. The Senate, which was dominated by Liberals, rejected the bill and vindicated the Governor's conduct. Immediately after their vote was taken, Coyne resigned.

It had been a particularly inglorious and depressing episode. The muddle of the government's economic policy and the ineptitude of its methods had been equally exposed. And the revelation had come at a peculiarly unfortunate time. The twenty-fourth Parliament of Canada was well into its fourth year, and newspapers were already talking about a new general election.

CHAPTER FIFTEEN

Obscure Destiny

B Y THE BEGINNING of 1962, two of the strongest forces in Canadian politics, one peculiar to Canada and one common to the whole of North America, had turned against Diefenbaker. He had totally alienated the business community, and he was steadily losing the capricious support of French Canada. In 1958, both Quebec and industrial and financial Canada had jumped on the Progressive Conservative bandwaggon chiefly because Diefenbaker looked like a certain winner; but, four years later, in the light of his obviously declining prestige, there was no longer any need for these two powerful interests to hedge their bets. Quebec, now in the full career of its reforming and nationalist programme, was fundamentally opposed to Diefenbaker's pan-Canadianism; and Diefenbaker's fiscal and monetary bungles, his populist inclinations, his unconcealed preference for small businessmen, villagers, and countryfolk, exasperated and disgusted Toronto and Montreal. Diefenbaker might win without Quebec – he had done so in 1958; but the disaffection of the two great metropolitan centres of eastern Canada was a serious loss. Toronto and Montreal meant more than the banks, the industrial corporations, the trust companies, the investment houses, and their long coiling train of brokers, salesmen, and advertisers. Toronto and Montreal represented the whole of modern urban life, with its good schools, reputable universities, national newspapers and periodicals, radio and television centres. Toronto and Montreal stood for millions of prosperous and sophisticated city-dwellers and townsfolk, who now formed the bulk of Canada's population and who monopolized the mass media of the mid twentieth century and used them to promote their own increasingly continentalist interests and values.

How far could Pearson, the new Liberal leader, capture the support of the two dominant forces which Diefenbaker was almost certain to lose? The recovery of Quebec, which for most of the past sixty years had been a Liberal stronghold, seemed probable; but, until Pearson and the federal Liberals had come to terms with the current revolution in French Canada, it was by no means certain. The return of high finance and industry to their historic and rewarding position in the Liberal forces seemed much more likely. Their allegiance, which went back to the first decade of the century, had been broken reluctantly, for prudential considerations only, in 1958; and the business community, completely disillusioned with Diefenbaker, was anxious to renew it. Outwardly, at least, the new Liberal leader looked as if he might be the man destined to bring about the happy reconciliation of Canadian capital and Canadian government. For one thing – and this, in itself, was almost a sufficient recommendation – Pearson was so utterly unlike Diefenbaker. To the horrified gaze of financiers and manufacturers, Diefenbaker had appeared as some frightful combination of prophet, religious fanatic, and prosecuting counsel; but Pearson, with his slight lisp, his pleasant, slightly deprecating manner, and the mild idiosyncrasy of his bow tie, seemed the picture of commonplace but reassuring normality. His favourite indoor relaxation was watching western dramas and football and hockey games on television, and his devotion to these popular products of the American sports and entertainment industry was one significant indication of his bland acceptance of the orthodox assumptions on which North American life was built. His long experience in 'quiet diplomacy' had comfortably adjusted him to the postwar world of super-power politics. He was, in fact, a characteristic example of the new Canadian political style – a joint creation of Liberal politicians and Liberal civil servants – which had reduced Canadian government to a cautious, prosaic routine. He was not in the least likely to dream vain dreams and see grandiose visions about Canada. He would not indulge in pretentious notions about Canadian sovereignty or nostalgic longings for the old Britannic connection. The invasion of American capital and the authority of American leadership in international affairs would seem just as natural and beneficial to him as they had to King, St. Laurent, and Howe.

The support of the dominant urban classes was certain to go to Pearson; but they did not constitute the whole of the Canadian people; and, in the general election of June 1962, he showed a singular ineptitude in trying to win over the remainder. His opponent, the Prime Minister, had chosen to campaign on the record of his government as a promise of still more wonderful things to come; and this strategy left the Conservative leader wide open to ridicule and insult. Urban newspapers heaped abuse upon Diefenbaker's childish self-esteem, his blatant demagoguery, and his fumbling indecision. His five years in power were pictured as an uninterrupted chronicle of bungling, mismanagement, and disaster. Pearson and his followers presented themselves as the trained team that would bring this incompetence to an end. The Conservatives were made to appear as rank amateurs, the Liberals as gifted and experienced professionals. This campaign, which implied that the art of government was a branch of technology understood only by sophisticated professional technocrats, was a considerable success in cities and large towns; but the rest of the country remained unimpressed. Of the fifty-eight constituencies in Toronto, Montreal, Vancouver, Winnipeg, and Ottawa, the Conservatives gained only nine. Yet their percentage of the popular vote was a shade better than that of the Liberals and they won 116 seats to the Liberals 100.

These, for both parties, were disappointingly indecisive results; and their ambiguity was increased by the performance of two new parties, the New Democratic Party and the Créditistes, the French-Canadian branch of the Social Credit movement. The New Democratic Party was a recreation of the old Cooperative Commonwealth Federation, with a discreetly modern name and programme designed to attract a wider support from trade unionists and reforming Liberals. Led by T. C. Douglas, the former premier of Saskatchewan, the N.D.P. trailed dismally in its first general election, winning no more than nineteen seats; and the only real surprise of the contest was the success of Réal Caouette and his Quebec Créditistes, who, with their twenty-six seats, would hold the balance of power in the twenty-fifth Parliament. Quebec, though disillusioned with the Conservatives, was not yet prepared to trust the Liberals. Its preference for its own eccentric brand of Social Credit revealed a stubborn disbelief in all national parties.

-≫ II 〔〔-

THE PRIME MINISTER was shaken, but not altered. The weaknesses in his leadership persisted, the divisions among his cabinet ministers grew more serious; and at the same time the gravity and danger of Canada's external circumstances steadily increased. The immediate financial problem – the decline of the Canadian dollar and the drain of Canada's reserves of gold and American funds – a problem intensified by the ambiguous results of the election, was solved with comparative ease. The Canadian dollar was pegged at 92.5 cents American; and, with tariff surcharges on a variety of imports, and a line of credit from the International Monetary Fund and other sources, the nation emerged from its exchange difficulties fairly quickly. The uncertain balance of payments was one significant index of Canada's subordinate and insecure position in a continental economy; but there were other political and military signs of her dependence which cut deeper into the national assumption of autonomy and self-determination, and could provoke far more violent public controversy. Diefenbaker had tried in the past, with little persistence or consistency and without much success, to safeguard Canada's independence; and now the forces upon which he could count in his defence against the United States were growing steadily feebler. Canadian capitalism, with its now unalterable American orientation, was against him. He had failed to restore the solidarity of the Commonwealth; and the collapse of the old Anglo-Canadian alliance was now manifest in Britain's application for membership in the European

Economic Community. Finally, his appeasement of the provinces – a tacit repudiation of the historic Conservative policy of national centralization – had not materially modified the growing provincial assertiveness. Quebec threatened trouble; British Columbia had already created it. And British Columbia's resistance to federal policies in the Columbia River Treaty with the United States showed clearly how provincial obstruction could weaken the federal government's power to protect the national interest in the face of American demands.

The Columbia River, which has its origin in Canada and flows into the Pacific Ocean through the United States, is the fourth largest river in North America and a vast potential source of electric power. The dilemma which confronted Canada in its negotiations with the United States for the development of the river's energy was the customary painful Canadian choice between a national and a continental plan. At first, the Canadian government, doubtless inspired by General A. G. L. McNaughton, the veteran chairman of the Canadian section of the International Joint Commission, proposed to act independently and construct all the dams and installations that Canada required on the Canadian side of the line. The Boundary Waters Treaty of 1909 gave Canada the right to proceed alone; but her attempt to do so met the joint resistance of the governments of British Columbia and the United States. The United States was certain to demand heavy compensation for the diversion of the Kootenay River into the Columbia, an essential part of the Canadian national plan; and Premier W. A. C. Bennett of British Columbia, the province which would have to build and operate the dams and market the power, argued that the development of the Canadian Columbia alone would be too difficult and expensive.

In the end, the Canadian government gave way; and the Columbia River Treaty, signed as early as January 1961, provided for a co-operative Canadian-American undertaking, with a series of dams on both sides of the boundary, and a share for Canada in the power generated in the United States. Continentalism had won its first, but not its last, victory on the Columbia River. Out of the bitter experience of the past, the Canadian governments had for many years prohibited the long-term sale of electric power in the United States; but Bennett hoped to finance the development of the Peace River with the proceeds of the sale of Columbia River power, and the west-coast cities of the United States were eager to purchase it. The Diefenbaker cabinet began to give uncertain indications that it was prepared to abandon a principle that Canada had long considered vital to the national interest. It looked as if the continental power grid, like the continental development project, was likely to triumph.

This was not all. The Canadian government was acutely conscious of pressure from British Columbia; it was even more painfully conscious of the prospective withdrawal of the United Kingdom. In July 1961, Britain had announced that it intended to seek admission to the European Common Market; and, at that point, the vague apprehensions which the Canadian ministers had felt ever since the breakdown of the Anglo-Canadian trade talks in the autumn of 1957 quickly became positive fears. Britain's entry into this European protectionist bloc would almost certainly mean the end of Canada's surviving preferences in the British market; but, for Diefenbaker and some of his ministers, the political implications of Britain's new departure may have been just as disquieting as its probable economic consequences. Diefenbaker had regarded the Commonwealth relationship in the old Canadian way, as one of the best available correctives for the dangerous imbalance of power on the North American continent. But, for nearly fifteen years, the cohesion of the postwar Commonwealth had been steadily weakening; and now Britain's shift to Europe seemed like a public declaration that, in the judgment of her government, the old association had ceased to have any validity or importance.

It was a disturbing revelation, all the more disturbing because Britain's European policy was vigorously endorsed by the United States; and Canada faced a solid Anglo-American front with the support of only the old Australasian Dominions and the new African states. In September 1961, when the Commonwealth Economic Consultative Council met at Accra, Ghana, George Hees and Donald Fleming openly attacked the British request for admission to the E.E.C.; and, a year later, at the

Commonwealth Prime Ministers' Conference in London, Diefenbaker repeated the same criticisms, in somewhat more measured tones. Although the proposed terms of the British entry
largely justified his complaints, and although they were echoed
by almost all the delegations at the conference, Diefenbaker
quickly became the chief butt of the British government's angry
resentment. Without the slightest scruple, British ministers betrayed the secrets of the conference to their own newspaper cor-
respondents and deliberately organized a vindictive campaign
against Canada in the British press.

The abuse of Diefenbaker in London was one aspect of his
vulnerable isolation; another, still more significant, was his
growing unpopularity and disparagement in Washington. Almost from the beginning, the Prime Minister's relations with
the new President of the United States, John F. Kennedy, had
been unpleasant; but it was the build-up of American nuclear
missile strength and the American confrontation with the Soviet
Union over Cuba which brought about the open and acute
divergence of the two governments. Diefenbaker accepted the
ideology of the Cold War and even the American assumption of
the leadership of the 'Free World', but with important qualifications, the roots of which were deep in the Canadian past. He
resented the American claim to a special and exclusive protec-
torate over the affairs of the Americas; and, in common with
many Canadians, he disliked the fanatical excesses of the American antipathy to Communism, and disapproved of the extreme
methods – commercial embargo and military intervention – by
which the United States had tried to bully Cuba into conformity
with the American way of life.

Further American pressure on Fidel Castro's government was
highly unlikely to win Diefenbaker's support. Unfortunately,
by this time, Cuba had become a fixed obsession of the American government; and, in October 1962, the establishment of
Soviet missile bases on the island gave Kennedy the opportunity
of retrieving his previous failures by a bold stroke which would
at once compel the withdrawal of Russia and the submission of
Castro. On the 22nd of October, without waiting for the action
of the United Nations and with only an hour and a half advance

notice to the Canadian government, the President unilaterally announced a naval blockade of Cuba – a blockade which he described by the healing, medical term 'quarantine', but which was, in fact, an act of war. Clearly the American government and people expected an instant, automatic, and loyal Canadian response. It did not come. The Canadian divisions of NORAD were not placed in an advanced state of alert; and, in the Commons, Diefenbaker suggested an impartial inquiry into the state of affairs in Cuba, thereby impiously questioning the dogma that the voice of the President of the United States, speaking *ex cathedra*, was the voice of God, revealing God's perfect truth.

Canada had stood almost alone in its obstinate reluctance to support the American stand in the Cuban crisis; but, in the eyes of the Kennedy administration, this was not the only, nor perhaps the most important, sign of Canada's insubordinate deviation from American policy in the Cold War. A 'missile gap' of massive proportions already existed, in favour of the United States; but the American government was anxious that Canada, its partner in NATO and NORAD, should play its dutiful minor part in the vast American system of thermonuclear defence and counterattack. There was never any thought of Canada's acquiring possession and control of its own nuclear weapons; the question was rather whether she would accept nuclear ammunition, on the basis of American ownership and management, for her NATO forces in Europe and her anti-bomber defences in North America. Already Bomarc-B missiles, originally intended to be capped with nuclear warheads, had been established by the Americans at two bases in Canada, and Starfighter planes, equipped to carry small nuclear bombs, had been ordered for the Royal Canadian Air Force in Europe. But the essential technical agreement with the United States, which would alone permit the Canadian use of this nuclear equipment, had not yet been made; and, in the meantime, while the Conservative government showed reluctance, and then unwillingness, to complete its own defence programme, the whole nation became involved in an earnest debate over the wisdom and morality of Canadian participation in nuclear warfare. A substantial number of responsible and important groups and organizations, including the Liberal Party and the New Democratic Party, were largely or wholly in favour of nuclear disarmament. The government by now had effectively taken the same stand; but the government, like the nation, was not all of one mind. Ever since the relative failure of the general election of 1962, a group within the cabinet had questioned the continuance of Diefenbaker's leadership; and a division of opinion over nuclear policy now deepened the significance of this clash of personalities. Douglas Harkness, the Minister of Defence, believed that Canada should complete its defence programme by the acquisition of nuclear arms. Howard Green, the Secretary for External Affairs, was a devoted believer in nuclear disarmament.

Upon this divided people and its divided government, the full weight of American reprimand and injunction now fell with shattering force; the Kennedy administration regarded Canada with a cold fury of impatience. If the Canadians could not make up their minds on this vital subject, they must be taught to do so! On the 3rd of January, General Lauris Norstad, the American officer who had just resigned his post as commander-in-chief of the NATO forces in Europe, arrived in Ottawa and frankly informed Canadian newspapermen that, if Canada did not equip her Starfighter squadrons with nuclear ammunition, she would not be fulfilling her NATO commitments. Nine days later, on the 12th of January, Pearson announced, to the surprise and discomfiture of some of his followers, that he had changed his mind and now supported nuclear arms. This abrupt reversal of Liberal policy ensured that the nuclear question would become the main, and probably the decisive, issue when Parliament met on the 21st of January. Diefenbaker's long speech on the 25th of January was confused, and, to some extent, contradictory and misleading; but his appeal to the need for delay and reconsideration as a necessary prelude to any final commitment in such a momentous question was basically an effective defence of his policy. This evidence of Canada's obstinate determination to decide its own course in the NATO and NORAD alliances was too much for the American Department of State. On the 30th of January, without troubling to convey its criticisms through the normal diplomatic channels, it published a press release which coldly corrected some of the statements in Diefenbaker's speech and flatly contradicted others. This intervention in the public affairs of a friendly nation, this deliberate attempt to put foreign pressure on the political decisions of the Canadian people, was the savage blow which brought about the break-up of the Conservative government. On the 3rd of February, Harkness resigned. On the 5th, the three opposition parties combined to defeat the government on a want-of-confidence amendment.

In the election campaign that followed, the Liberals concentrated their ridicule on the broad target of the Prime Minister's procrastination and irresolution. 'The first sixty days of a new Liberal administration,' they promised, 'will be sixty days of decision.' And at first their easy victory seemed guaranteed by the support of virtually all the opinion-making forces of a united North America. In Canada, almost the whole of the newspaper press, the entire business community, the urban executive and professional classes, the army, and the civil service were opposed to Diefenbaker; and in the United States, President John F. Kennedy, keeping up the good work which his general and his State Department had begun, gave an unofficial presidential blessing to the external activities of his chief election expert, who secretly came up to Canada to aid the Liberals in their campaign. In the face of the combined resources of the North American established order, Diefenbaker seemed a negligible figure. Hees and Sévigny had followed Harkness in resigning; Fulton and Fleming declined to run for re-election. Yet Diefenbaker's weakness and isolation seemed to re-inspire him with the audacious ingenuity he had shown in the 1957 and 1958 campaigns. In the general election of the 8th of April, 1963, he won a surprising 95 seats; and Pearson, with a following of 129 Liberals, was seven votes short of a majority over all parties in the new Parliament.

⟫ III ⟪

THE NEW Prime Minister's electoral overtures to French Canada – his promise of a Canadian flag and his offer of a royal commission on bilingualism and biculturalism – had gained him twelve additional seats in Quebec, but had apparently not done very much to appease that province's political discontent. The so-called 'quiet revolution', now nearly at the close of its third year, rushed impetuously forward on the riptide of success. The 'quiet revolutionaries' themselves and their English-Canadian sympathizers liked to assume that their movement was a totally new phenomenon in Quebec politics; but, in reality, it differed from its predecessors only where its scope and intensity had been increased by the special circumstances of the past quarter-century. The 'quiet revolution' was, in fact, the tumultuous outbreak of economic grievances and social discontents which for twenty-five years had been held in check by the petrified incubus of Union Nationale. The deaths of Duplessis and Sauvé and the disintegration of their party had suddenly liberated the long-pent-up energies of mid-twentieth-century Quebec.

Since the Second World War, the influence of industrialization upon the province of Quebec had been steadily increasing. It had weakened the rural and clerical interests and values which had so long dominated the life of the province; and it had lowered the protective barriers which for generations had kept it in relative isolation from the rest of Canada. By the beginning of the 1960s, the 'French fact' in Canada, both within Quebec and beyond its borders, had greatly altered. In one important sense, it had greatly gained; but, in other equally significant ways, it had lost and was steadily losing. For a very long period the French language had gradually been extending its sway over the province of Quebec itself; English Canadians, once numerous in the Eastern Townships, had gradually retreated to the cities; and, by the middle of the twentieth century, nearly 75 per cent of the declining English-speaking minority in the province lived in Montreal. In the eyes of French-Canadian leaders, this expansion of French power in

the ancient kingdom of their race was an encouraging and fortifying circumstance; but their confidence was seriously qualified by two other disturbing facts. Outside Quebec, except for
a north-western extension into Ontario and a north-eastern
extension into New Brunswick, the progressive assimilation of
the French-speaking communities into English Canada had
driven the French language into a steep decline. Inside Quebec,
the triumph of French had remained largely a triumph of
language, and the growing preponderance of the French-speaking majority had not enabled it to wrest control of the new
industrial machine from the dwindling English-speaking minority. On the contrary, the dominance of the English in the
financial and managerial levels of provincial society had actually
increased.

In 1960, for the first time in literally a generation, a new
group of French-Canadian leaders had an opportunity of grappling with the problems posed by French Canada's new position
in an industrialized nation. There were two fields, one provincial and one federal, in which much would have to be done
for the modernization of the French-Canadian community and
the protection and promotion of its interests; but Quebec
itself, where the French-speaking majority held unquestioned
control, was obviously the place to begin. Quebec, in many
ways, was a singularly backward province, with laws, institutions, and customs, long unquestioned and unaltered, which
were extremely ill-adapted to modern industrial life. For the
first few years of the new Liberal administration, the Premier,
Jean Lesage, and his two principal associates, René Lévesque
and Paul Gérin-Lajoie, busied themselves with necessary provincial reforms. For the first time in Quebec's history since
Confederation, the state began to play a major energizing part
in the whole economic, social, and cultural life of the province.
Free compulsory education was provided for all up to the age
of fifteen; the antiquated labour laws were reformed. Finally,
after a new election had, in 1962, confirmed and strengthened
Lesage's hold on power, the Quebec hydro-electric companies –
the long execrated English 'trusts' – were nationalized and
incorporated in a provincially owned Quebec Hydro.

These were radical changes; but they did not satisfy the revolutionary spirit that now animated Quebec. The removal of the old repressive restrictions, the realization of the freer, fuller, richer life that the rest of industrial North America enjoyed, was a central aim of the movement; but equally important was the insistent demand that these achievements should be the work of French Canadians, done in their own ways and on their own terms. Along with a joyous sense of release at the absence of restraint and the end of deprivation, there went a new pride and confidence in the fact of being French. From the first, the reforming urge and the national spirit went hand in hand, and strengthened each other. But, in existing circumstances, there was no single political entity in which they could fully express themselves. In Canada, sovereignty was divided between the federal and the provincial governments; and this fact had, and always had had, important implications for French Canadians. In the nation as a whole, where they were a minority, their political influence was limited; and in the province of Quebec, where they were the majority, their constitutional jurisdiction was limited. The growth of the nationalist movement would have to take place within the Canadian federal system and the limits of the British North America Act. The realization of these constitutional impediments quickly aroused an angry sense of frustration in the French-Canadian nationalists. Their nationalism, acutely irritated by the obstacles imposed by the existing all-Canadian nationality, became the dominant theme of their protest movements. Its chief aim was the drastic reform of the Canadian federal system.

Obviously there were two principal ways in which Canadian federalism could be altered in the interest of French-Canadian nationalism. On the one hand, Canada could be officially declared a bilingual and bicultural country and the position of the French language improved throughout the nation as a whole; or, on the other, Quebec, as the particular homeland of the French-Canadian people, could be accepted as a province different from all the others, and granted a special detached position in Canadian Confederation. There were, of course, ambitious French Canadians who hoped to obtain both objects; but there was a basic logical contradiction between a bilingual but united Canada and a virtually independent Quebec; and, if only one nationalist goal were attainable, there was little doubt which was easier of achievement. To make Canada a constitutionally bilingual state would be hard enough; to make it a country in which French Canadians could speak their own language and feel at home everywhere was quite impossible. In continental Canada, there could never be more than a limited and partial satisfaction for French-Canadian nationalism; but surely its complete, or nearly complete, fulfilment was possible in an autonomous Quebec, increasingly detached from the rest of Canada? A minority in Canada as a whole, French Canadians constituted over 80 per cent of the population of Quebec; they securely dominated the provincial legislature; and, if the jurisdiction of the province could be extended to cover nearly the whole range of the life of its inhabitants, then the purposes of French-Canadian nationalism could be substantially accomplished. From the beginning, there were various political groups – Le Rassemblement pour L'Indépendance Nationale (R.I.N.) was an early example–which proposed to push this aim to its logical conclusion in complete separation from Canada. Lesage and his lieutenants did not go this far; but, egged on by Daniel Johnson, the new leader of Union Nationale, who was now vigorously competing for nationalist support, they began to threaten that, if Canadian Confederation were not drastically changed so as to satisfy French Canada's needs and aspirations, Quebec would secede from the union.

The threat of separation drew its force from two basic assumptions about the nature of Canadian federalism. It was assumed, in the first place, that ethnic and cultural values ought to be considered basic in Canadian Confederation, and that the most important fact about Canada was its cultural duality. It was taken for granted, in the second place, that the inadequate recognition and application of these principles in the existing Canadian constitution was the main, or even the sole, reason for the inferior part which French Canadians were obliged to play in national life. The first sweeping proposition

332 ->>> CANADA'S FIRST CENTURY

relegated all other Canadian interests – political stability, economic growth, national independence – to an inferior level of importance. The second assertion disregarded or dismissed all other explanations of the position in which French Canada now found itself. To a very large extent, the liberation of French Canadians had always lain in their own hands; and the crumbling walls of the medieval fortress in which they had lived submissively for so long had been maintained and repaired by their own church, their schools, their narrow professional education, their unenterprising capitalists, and their venal and obscurantist politicians. All these relevant considerations were brushed contemptuously aside. The nationalists insisted that the English-Canadian majority and the centralist constitution it had imposed were the sufficient causes of their misfortunes; and by an aggressive campaign of propaganda, in which every form of persuasion, shock, and menace was employed, they succeeded in convincing a surprisingly large number of English Canadians that the plight of French Canada was a crime of which they were guilty.

What followed was a vociferous and incessant discussion of the nature of Canadian Confederation and the justice and wisdom of the Canadian constitution. The strident uproar was popularly called a 'dialogue' – a conversation, that is, between English and French Canada; but, in fact, the last thing it resembled was a genuine debate. The acceptance of the French-Canadian nationalist case by an influential English-Canadian minority and its dissemination by most of the country's opinion-making mass media effectively prevented it from ever becoming a dialogue. It remained a monologue, shrill, continuous, confident, aggressive, and self-righteous. Criticisms and counter-arguments were given no space, no time, and no attention; protests were lost in the vast hubbub of complacent approval. If, despite everything, a few critics did succeed in exposing the historical myths and factual distortions on which the 'dialogue' relied, they were promptly rebuked as narrow-minded bigots or denounced as disloyal Canadians. If they imprudently ventured to treat the whole subject in a bantering, satirical vain, their guilt was judged even more severely. Such conduct was regarded as the near-equivalent of sacrilege or blasphemy!

By the time the Liberals gained power at Ottawa in the spring of 1963, the validity of the French-Canadian grievances, the need for reparation by English Canada, and the deficiencies of the Canadian constitution had become the nation's three most popular dogmas. They dangerously undermined Canada's cohesive strength at the very moment when its continued existence as an independent nation was threatened by the pressure of external forces.

»»» IV «««

THE 'OLD FIRM' – that easy, long-established combination of politicians and bureaucrats, the unique creation of the Liberal Party – was back once again at the old stand. The Prime Minister himself, Pickersgill, Sharp, Drury, and Lamontagne contributed the acquired expertise of the civil service. Martin, Chevrier, and Winters represented the seasoned experience of professional politics. It was, apparently, a happy, harmonious company; and its only incongruous member, who stood out all the more conspicuously as the solitary exception to the prevailing uniformity, was the new Minister of Finance, Walter L. Gordon. Gordon, who had entered Parliament as late as 1962, was a relatively new member of the Liberal team; but it was his beliefs, even more than his inexperience and unprofessional insouciance, that marked him out from his highly conventional colleagues. He was a convinced economic nationalist, in a group which, for either political or economic reasons, was firmly committed to North American continentalism.

Gordon, however, was not permitted to interfere in diplomacy; Pearson, the veteran professional, kept that department to himself. His visit to London in the first days of May 1963 was little more than a social duty call; but the meeting with President Kennedy, at the presidential house at Hyannis Port a week later, was full of meaning. The talks took place in the easy, cosy atmosphere of an opulent North American home; and Pearson's encyclopaedic knowledge of American baseball statistics quickly established him as a very solid North American citizen. 'He'll do!' Kennedy remarked approvingly, and Pearson proceeded to 'do' all the vital things for which the American government had been waiting so impatiently and so long. All hesitations and reservations about Canada's participation in nuclear warfare were swept aside with friendly dispatch; the Bomarcs were to be capped with nuclear warheads and the Starfighters armed with nuclear bombs. The communiqué which was issued after the meeting talked spaciously about the need of continental security, the joint use of strategic natural resources in continental defence, and the 'co-operative development' of the Columbia River.

A month later, on the 13th of June – the fifty-third of the 'sixty days of decision' – Gordon presented a budget which, in its decisive nationalist emphasis, contrasted very oddly with the Prime Minister's sweeping continentalism. The budget was vulnerable in several important ways; for one thing, Gordon had employed three outside economists in its preparation and had failed to take the advice of his experienced officials on the administrative problems presented by some of his proposals. But, without any doubt, the most controversial features of this first Liberal financial programme were the very positive recommendations for reversing the steady American acquisition of the control of Canadian industry. Gordon proposed a takeover tax of 30 per cent on the sales of shares in Canadian companies to non-resident individuals or corporations; he also varied the withholding tax on dividends paid to non-residents in accordance with the extent of the Canadian share in the ownership of each particular company. These measures created consternation in Toronto and Montreal. Led by Eric Kierans, the president of the Montreal Stock Exchange, the entire Canadian business community denounced Gordon's proposals in tones of mingled scorn and outrage. The takeover tax was abandoned; the withholding taxes on non-resident dividends were modified. Gordon had apparently been cured of his fit of nationalist madness; and the business community, breathing a sigh of relief, assumed that American investment would continue as bountifully as before. But the free flow of American capital into

Canada depended not only on the willingness of Americans to buy and lend, and the eagerness of Canadians to sell and borrow. It was also contingent upon the fiscal and monetary policies of the American government. The Kennedy administration, worried by the increasing deficit in the American balance of payments, decided to impose an 'interest equalization' tax, which would make it more expensive for Americans to invest in Canada and more expensive for Canadians to borrow in New York. Stocks, which had declined on the Canadian exchanges at the news of Gordon's takeover tax, plunged swiftly downward on the announcement of Kennedy's 'interest equalization' duty. Alarmed Canadian officials, hurrying to Washington, obtained a partial and discretionary exemption for Canada from the new rules. The nation retained its subordinate and privileged position in the continental economy, but on terms which limited its own monetary freedom and increased its dependence on American policy.

Gordon's spirited defence of Canadian economic independence was an aberration from traditional Liberal policy which was hurriedly given up in alarm when the dreadful consequences of restraints on American investment were revealed. For the next few years, the Pearson government dropped external affairs and gave its almost undivided attention to the alarming division within the country. For over sixty years, Quebec had been the main source of Liberal power and the chief beneficiary of Liberal largesse; and now the angry turmoil in French Canada and Lesage's grandiose conception of the status and responsibilities of his province made Quebec the main focus of Liberal interest once again. Ontario, in an intermittent and indistinct fashion, came just within Pearson's range of vision; but for him the rest of the nation could hardly be said to exist at all. Beyond the eastern boundary of Quebec and the western boundary of Ontario, Canada simply fell away, like the world in an early medieval map, into vacant outer space; and if, beyond this point, land was suspected to exist, it was believed to be inhabited by half-fabulous monsters, vaguely known as Westerners or Maritimers. These creatures were dismissed as irrelevant and unimportant. The whole effort of the

Pearson government was concentrated on Quebec. For Quebec it made plans, reversed plans, dropped plans, and invented new plans. For Quebec it stumbled from one crisis to another in a frantic search for appeasement.

The appointment of the Royal Commission on Bilingualism and Biculturalism, the first step in the government's programme, was an implicit recognition of the claim that federal action was necessary to make Canada a more truly bilingual and bicultural nation. The composition of the commission was based, with mathematical exactitude, upon the absolute equality of the cultures of the two 'founding races'. Davidson Dunton, the president of Carleton University, and André Laurendeau, the editor of Le Devoir, were joint chairmen; in addition, there were three other English Canadians, three more French Canadians, and two 'New Canadians', one of whom spoke English and the other French. The four French-Canadian members of the commission were able, even distinguished people. The four English-Canadian commissioners, one of whom was a former federal civil servant and another a resident of Quebec known for his sympathetic attitude to the 'quiet revolution', formed, as a group, an obviously partial and inadequate representation of the values and interests of English Canada. By its terms of reference, as well as by its composition and its very title, the commission assumed the validity and supreme importance of the 'equal partnership' of the two cultures. The commissioners were likely to have little interest in, and less respect for, the conception of Canadian nationality on which Confederation had originally been based and with which it had continued for over ninety years.

The 'Bi-and-Bi Commission' was the first pledge of the Pearson government's commitment to the ideal of a bilingual, bicultural, but united Canada. The 'distinctive' Canadian flag was offered as a guarantee that the 'new Canada' had already begun its existence. The Prime Minister's original proposal – a design of three red maple leaves on a white ground with a broad blue bar at either end – was pertinaciously debated until an exhausted House of Commons set up a fifteen-man committee to study the question in the hope of reaching general agreement. Late in the autumn of 1964 the majority of the committee reported in favour of a design of a single red maple leaf, on a white ground, with a red bar at either side. The new flag, with its deliberate rejection of Canada's history and its British and French legacies, bore a disturbingly close resemblance to the flag of a new 'instant' African nation, a nation without a past, and with a highly uncertain future. The exclusive reliance on the maple leaf, an heraldic symbol appropriate only to a national or provincial shield or escutcheon, revealed the committee's, and the government's, poverty of invention, and their total failure to provide effective substitutes for the historical traditions they had summarily dismissed. The simple arrangement of red and white was, as two members of the Group of Seven vainly tried to point out, a vapid and monotonous colour combination. Yet, after further futile weeks of debate, Parliament finally adopted the single maple leaf flag; and on the 15th of February, 1965, a grey, cold, cheerless winter day, it was raised for the first time on Parliament Hill.

The new flag, like the Royal Commission on Bilingualism and Biculturalism, was born of the belief that the aims and aspirations of French Canada could be satisfied within an altered but still united nation. In fact, the great majority of the Quebec nationalists had fixed their hopes, not on a reformed Canada, but on a separate or virtually independent Quebec. In their eyes, the prospect of a truly bilingual and bicultural country was too remote and unlikely to merit serious consideration; it was completely immaterial what flag was chosen to represent a federation whose central government deserved no more loyalty than that accorded to a tax-collecting agency. What they wanted from English-Canadians was not co-operation in the creation of a new bicultural Canada but money for the building of a new autonomous Quebec; and the Lesage government, with its ambitious and extremely expensive programme for the extension of government controls and services over the entire range of provincial life, was the vital embodiment of this dominant purpose. Lesage intended to preserve and increase the provincial sphere of jurisdiction, to expel the federal government from the fields in which it had tried to promote national development and maintain national standards of welfare, and finally – and perhaps most important of all – to appropriate all the funds which the federal government would have expended on these projects in Quebec, and thus to augment Quebec's provincial revenues, extend its services, and increase its prestige.

In 1964-5, two new measures – the Canada Pension Plan and a federal-provincial fiscal arrangement based on the 'opting-out' principle in joint or shared-cost programmes – revealed the impressive success of Lesage's campaign. By the 'opting-out' formula a province could assume full financial responsibility for a continuing joint federal-provincial scheme and at the same time receive the equivalent of the previous federal contribution to its cost, either through an increased share in direct taxes or in other ways. Federal initiative in the planning of these co-operative programmes had sometimes annoyed the provinces, for it could derange their own priorities and saddle them with unwanted burdens; but Quebec was the only province which opposed the system on principle. It proceeded to withdraw, taking its tax equivalent with it, from most of the continuing shared-cost programmes already in existence.

It had made good its claim to financial exclusiveness; but its success did not end there. A constitutional amendment of 1951 had made the provinces paramount in pension legislation; and Lesage used this legislative superiority to force the rest of Canada into a reluctant acquiescence in still another of Quebec's demands. The announcement of the federal government's proposed extension of the national welfare system, the Canada Pension Plan, provoked an immediate declaration that Quebec must have a pension plan of its own. The federal scheme, conceived on pay-as-you-go lines, with relatively small contributions from employees and employers, failed completely to satisfy Lesage or his new Minister of Revenue, Eric Kierans. They wanted larger contributions, which could be funded and which, under provincial administration, would provide capital for an ambitious expansion of public ownership – the means by which French Canadians could gain control of provincial industry. Obviously the two schemes would have to be integrated in order to ensure national coverage and 'portability'. In the end, it was the provincial rather than the federal scheme that triumphed.

Quebec had succeeded in imposing its will on Canada in an important issue of public policy; but the power which it was now exercising with such confident determination could be used for negative as well as positive purposes. Quebec could gain its own ends; it could also prevent Canada as a whole from getting its way. This veto was employed to block the realization of a long-held Canadian aim – the provision of a method by which the amendment of the Canadian constitution could be completed in Canada – just at the moment when its final achievement seemed inevitable. The pursuit of this crowning power of national sovereignty, interrupted after the constitutional conference of 1950, was resumed by the Diefenbaker government, under Davie Fulton's leadership; and, by the end of 1961, a series of federal-provincial conferences had produced a comprehensive amending formula. A different procedure was devised for each of the five categories into which the clauses of the British North America Act were divided; and, in order to modify the admitted rigidity of a part of the plan, it was provided that Parliament, under certain restrictions, could delegate legislative power to the provincial legislatures, and the provincial legislatures delegate power to Parliament.

In 1964, the Pearson government, with Guy Favreau as Minister of Justice, took up the still incomplete project; a series of meetings in early October made the last changes in what was beginning to be called the 'Fulton-Favreau formula'; and on the 14th of October it was unanimously accepted at a conference of prime ministers and premiers. Parliament approved the new formula; so did nine of the ten provincial legislatures. But Quebec, surprisingly, declined to concur. Lesage had declared himself satisfied; but Lesage soon discovered that his rival, Daniel Johnson, the leader of Union Nationale, could outbid him in nationalist demands. The new amending formula, Johnson insisted, might safeguard Quebec's existing powers, but would effectively prevent the acquisition of those important additional powers which, in his view, were essential to the completion of full provincial sovereignty. Lesage, having tried for a while to defend his position, was gradually forced into a retreat. The Quebec legislature was not invited to approve the formula; and once again the thirty-year-old effort to make the Canadian constitution 'truly and wholly' Canadian had come to a dead stop.

->>> V <<<-

THE EFFORT to satisfy the aims and aspirations of French Canada had not brought national concord. The extent of the nationalist demands had shocked, alarmed, and angered many English Canadians; many French Canadians felt frustrated and exasperated by the slow progress of their separatist movement. A strange new spirit, curiously compounded of discontent, discouragement, impatience, and intransigence, began to pervade the country. It was not that there were any serious signs of an interruption or a decline in the nation's growth and prosperity. The pace of economic activity was swift in both 1965 and most of 1966; and in 1966 the population reached the satisfying round figure of twenty million. The origins of the Canadian malaise lay, not in any decrease in its material success or physical well-being, but in a profound loss of conviction in Canada's future as a nation. A despairing uncertainty about the prospect of English-French relations, disillusionment in both Canadian political parties and even in Canadian political institutions, disappointment at the role to which Canada had been reduced in world politics, and doubt of its ability to survive as an independent nation on the North American continent – all combined to create a complex, contradictory, and deeply pessimistic mood.

In Quebec, the separatist movement grew more outspoken in its rejection of Canada and its federal institutions, and more defiant in its use of extra-legal methods. Empty streets, drawn blinds, and little groups of people with their backs turned greeted Queen Elizabeth when she came to celebrate the centenary of the Charlottetown and Quebec conferences in the autumn of 1964. The establishment of a new body, the Estates General of the French Canadian Nation, plainly implied that the existing parliamentary system could no longer be accepted as satisfactory and that the representatives of the people must meet in convention to draft a new constitution. Two terrorist organizations – Front de Libération Québécoise (FLQ) and Armée pour la Libération de Québec (ALQ) – openly advocated and practised the politics of force. Armouries were robbed of guns and ammunition, bombs exploded, gangs of separatists and hooligans battled with the police. It was all a little frightening, even in Quebec; and Lesage, having called up the nationalist wind, felt uneasily obliged to moderate the separatist whirlwind. Daniel Johnson, the leader of Union Nationale, was rapidly proving himself to be more skilful in his manipulation of the nationalist issue; and also, by steady emphasis on the cost and the anticlerical implications of Lesage's educational reforms, he was recapturing many of his party's old conservative supporters. In June 1966, Union Nationale won an unexpected victory over the Liberals in the provincial general election.

At Ottawa, the Liberals were almost as harassed and insecure as they were at Quebec. The Pearson régime had begun its existence with an embarrassing sequence of ineptitudes and blunders; it continued its unhappy career with a particularly unsavoury series of scandals. To the Canadian people, the Pearson cabinet presented the appearance of a highly respectable, if somewhat undistinguished, group of experienced professional administrators; but the Pearson cabinet was the creation of the victorious Liberal Party, and the Liberal Party was, and had been for generations, dependent upon Quebec. In Quebec, political corruption had become a recognized part of the provincial way of life; and the scandals of 1964-5 differed from their predecessors only in so far as they reflected the changes which industrialization and urbanization had brought to the province. Since the end of the Second World War, the roots of the Liberal Party organization had worked their way through Quebec's organized political corruption and deep into Montreal's organized crime.

The Prime Minister, four French-Canadian cabinet ministers,

and a group of senior civil servants – executive assistants, special assistants, and parliamentary secretaries – were directly or indirectly involved in the scandals of 1964-5. Sometimes, with a return to the more simple, old-fashioned practices of the past, the culprits did nothing more than sell their political influence for bribes or purchase furniture on compromisingly easy terms from dubious companies. Often they acted in response to the pressure or the influence of the criminal underworld; and two departments in particular – the Department of Justice and the Department of Citizenship and Immigration – seemed only too ready to do substantial favours for highly suspect characters. One notorious gangster escaped the country on inadequate bail; another's deportation order was mysteriously delayed; still another, who ought to have been promptly deported, almost acquired status as a landed immigrant. These discreditable episodes were bad enough; but they were dwarfed in comparison by the huge disgrace of the Rivard affair. Lucien Rivard, a ringleader in the North American criminal narcotics trade, had been arrested in Montreal on information from Washington, and the American authorities had applied for his extradition to the United States. With arrogant assurance, the agents of the Mafia-controlled drug trade then attempted to arrange bail for Rivard, who would, of course, take advantage of his freedom to flee the country. Incredibly enough, they found sympathetic accomplices in Ottawa. A small group of civil servants in the Departments of Justice and Citizenship and Immigration, as well as the Prime Minister's parliamentary secretary, were implicated in this conspiracy to defeat the ends of justice. The long, insinuating tentacles of the Mafia had reached right into the office of the Prime Minister of Canada.

The increasing violence and moral degradation of Canadian politics were not the only guilty burdens which weighed down the spirits of Canadians as they approached the centenary of Confederation. The debasement of Canadian domestic affairs was fully matched by the humiliating futility of Canada's position in world politics. For fifteen years the Canadian government had gone on apparently accepting the simple ideology of the Cold War, the myth of the international Communist conspiracy, and the American claim to leadership, in 'the struggle for democracy and freedom'. In 1962-3, when Diefenbaker attempted to break through the walls of Canada's mental prison, these ideological assumptions had already grown very suspect; and, by the middle of the 1960s, their invalidity had become notorious, even to a large minority of American citizens. During 1965, the United States revealed herself once again as the opponent of nationalism and reform and the defendant of imperialism and reaction. Without the authority of the United Nations and even without consultation with the Organization of American States, American forces were dispatched to put down a revolt in the Dominican Republic, which thus became the third victim of the American determination to suppress socialism or Communism in the western hemisphere. In Viet Nam, the United States had by this time completely replaced France as the conservative buttress against the postwar nationalist movement in the former Indo-China. The old European colonialism – for generations the favourite object of American democratic disapproval – had now been totally supplanted by the new American military imperialism. In February 1965, when the United States began the systematic bombing of selected targets in North Viet Nam, the dimensions of the struggle were enormously enlarged.

As the bombing continued, with only one short interruption, Canadian concern over the implications of this barbarous conflict mounted rapidly. In volume and fervour, the outcry against the war in Viet Nam soon equalled, and then exceeded, the earlier protest over the use of nuclear weapons. Canada was the immediate neighbour of the United States, its ally in NATO and NORAD, and its most readily available external source of explosives and chemicals for the American armed forces. Canadians could not help feeling involved in the tragedy in Viet Nam; but the Canadian government lacked the power to stop the carnage, and equally lacked the conviction and courage to appeal to others for its cessation. The International Control Commission, of which Canada, along with Poland and India, was a member, was immobilized in futility; and when, in April 1965, the Prime Minister for once broke through the cautious restraints of his government's policy and openly advocated 'a suspension of air strikes against North Viet Nam', he was quickly made aware of the sovereign displeasure of the American President, Lyndon Johnson. Once again, Canadians learnt that what the United States expected from its North American ally was not advice, or even tentative suggestions, but silent and instant obedience.

⇢≫ VI ≪⇠

THE MOOD in which Canadians reached and passed the mid-point of the 1960s was troubled, disillusioned, and baffled. The general election of the 8th of November, 1965 – the third general election in fewer than four years – brought out once more the deep discouragement, the chronic division and uncertainty which had seemingly paralysed the national will. The Pearson minority government, hounded by Diefenbaker's debating skill and never sure of its survival in the Commons, was eager to end this agonizing parliamentary stalemate; and at last, after two uneasy years in power, the prospects of a real electoral victory seemed to brighten. In the winter of 1965 the quarrel in the Conservative Party over Diefenbaker's leadership grew more acute; and, in September, Pierre Elliott Trudeau, Jean Marchand, and Gérard Pelletier, three prominent left-wing French Canadians, who had become convinced that the federal pendulum had swung too far towards a separatist Quebec, went over to the Liberal Party. Pearson assumed that the replacement of the corrupt Quebec Old Guard by three promising new leaders would restore his party's respectability and increase its strength. He took it for granted that the dispute over Diefenbaker's leadership had demoralized the Conservative Party and scattered its support. His campaign was based on an appeal for stable government; but, once again, the solid majority that would ensure stable government was denied him. The Liberals, their share of the popular vote slightly pared, won only two additional seats in the House of Commons. The Conservatives gained exactly the same number. For the third time in a row, the nation had suspended judgment. The divisions which separated urban from rural Canada, which isolated the west and the Atlantic region from the central provinces, had become more glaringly conspicuous than ever.

The Liberals had been reprimanded, if not censured; the Conservatives had been tolerated but not approved. The results of the election were a plain admonition to both parties to reform their morals, if not to change their policies. Neither party paid much attention to the warning; and 1966, with the Spencer scandal and the Gerda Munsinger affair, was almost as discreditable a year as 1964-5 had been. The questionable case of George Victor Spencer, a Vancouver postal clerk who had been dismissed without a proper trial on a charge of selling information to Soviet agents, prompted the Conservative Party to demand a judicial investigation; and the Liberal Minister of Justice, Lucien Cardin, infuriated by this renewed Conservative attempt to blacken his department's administrative record, retaliated by charging that former Conservative ministers, in their relations with Gerda Munsinger, a German woman suspected of Communist affiliations, had endangered Canadian security regulations. The Munsinger affair bespattered both parties with mud. The Prime Minister's abrupt consent to a judicial inquiry in the Spencer case nearly led to Cardin's resignation and threatened a serious division in the cabinet; the Liberals, in their turn, were beginning to feel that they might do better with a new and younger leader. Among the Conservatives, the dissatisfaction with Diefenbaker increased; in November 1966, Dalton Camp, the national president of the Conservative Association, finally won executive approval for the holding of a national leadership convention.

Meanwhile, as the centenary of Confederation drew closer, the Pearson government continued on its uncertain and embarrassed way. It offered federal assistance in the establishment of a provincially administered medical insurance scheme (Medicare); and it began the integration of the Canadian armed forces. Every other important aspect of Canadian defence or foreign policy remained unchanged. NORAD, now ten years old, and NATO, nearly twenty, were apparently regarded as untouchable. American influence frustrated Paul Martin's attempts to seat continental China in the General Assembly or the Security Council of the United Nations; and his bland, platitudinous circumlocutions about the war in Viet Nam had remained unaffected by the growing intensity of Canadian criticism. The government resisted the demand of the First National City Bank of New York, on behalf of its subsidiary, the Mercantile Bank of Canada, for exemption from the provisions limiting the non-Canadian interest in any Canadian chartered bank; but otherwise its efforts to combat the American takeover of Canadian industry were purely exploratory and tentative. The unrepentant Walter Gordon, who had not been retained in the cabinet after the election of 1965, set out his views in a new publication, *A Choice for Canada: Independence or Colonial Status*. He totally failed to win over his fellow Liberals at the party policy convention in the autumn of 1966; the prairie delegates, in particular, vigorously asserted the need of the west for American capital in the development of its resources and American markets for the sale of its oil and natural gas. Three months later, when he rejoined the cabinet as Minister without Portfolio, he was ostensibly conceded no more than the supervision of a special task force appointed to investigate the impact of American capital on Canadian independence. The most important new factor in Canadian-American trade relations – the automotive agreement of 1965 – was, in effect, a move away from the direction which Gordon wished Canada to travel. Under certain stringent conditions, designed to safeguard the continuance of the Canadian motor industry, the automotive agreement established free trade in cars and parts between the two countries, and thus gave Canada a special privileged position in a continental industry.

Quebec remained the first priority of the Pearson government, which continued, as in the past, to give its best efforts to the satisfaction of French Canada. From the outset it was clear that the French-Canadian triumvirate, Trudeau, Marchand, and Pelletier, was likely to have a profound influence on this endeavour. The new ministers set their faces against further concessions towards a separatist Quebec; they believed instead in a bicultural, bilingual, but united Canada. For over two years, the Pearson government had concentrated almost exclusively on the first of these two possible ways of satisfying French-Canadian nationalist aims; but now, abandoning this alternative, it fixed its hopes upon a united Canada acceptable to both languages and cultures. A detailed programme to this end would have to wait until the Royal Commission on Bilingualism and Biculturalism presented its report; but, in the meantime, Pearson committed himself to the ominous principle of bilingualism in the civil service, and promised a bill of rights in which languages would be given special guarantees.

The elevation of bilingualism to the status of a condition of employment and promotion in the public service was certain to put the small number of truly bilingual persons, most of them French Canadians, in a highly preferred position, and to penalize a large number of able English Canadians and 'New Canadians' anxious to serve their country, who had never had any reason to learn French and might find some difficulty in doing so. Without doubt, this serious departure from the merit system would foment grievances and resentments among government employees, and weaken the morale and damage the efficiency of the public service. The attempt to carry out the promise of legal protection for the French language was also sure to provoke criticism and disaffection. In the Atlantic provinces, apart from New Brunswick, such guarantees would have little meaning; they would be equally irrelevant in Ontario, except along the Ottawa River and in the north-west. But proximity had made Maritimers and Ontarians aware of French Canada and its distinctive culture; and they had learnt to accept the concessions which successive federal and provincial governments had granted the French-speaking minority in the hope of keeping its vote. Thus the Atlantic provinces and Ontario had to some extent been prepared for the new federal programme of legal protection and administrative preferment for the French language; but the west had not. From the western border of Ontario to the Pacific, the decline of French and the increase of English continued in steady progression. Almost from the beginning, the west had been unilingual. It had successfully defeated the early attempts of the federal government, in the Manitoba Act and the North-West Territories Act, to entrench confessional schools and the French language in the western provincial constitutions; and it was half a century now since it had freed itself from the last of these legal fetters. The west had rejected bilingualism and biculturalism once; it was not likely to submit to them a second time.

There were clear indications of the federal government's positive plans for a bilingual, bicultural, but united Canada. Its negative anti-separatist policies became even more explicit in the autumn of 1966, when a series of federal-provincial conferences took up the contentious fiscal problem once again. A strict adherence to the existing division of legislative power and a corresponding acceptance of separate financial responsibility was the severely clean-cut proposal of the federal government. Ottawa would continue to sponsor shared-cost programmes in the economic field, for there its powers and duties were basic; but in the social services, where jurisdiction rested primarily with the provinces, it would retire from co-operative plans, leaving all the provinces in the same position as Quebec, with Quebec's rate of tax abatement. Johnson was indignant both because Quebec would get no more revenue and because the other provinces would get exactly as much; but this angry dissatisfaction was shared, for one reason or another, by all of the provincial governments. Federal hints of approaching constitutional changes were now followed by even more pointed provincial suggestions. Early in 1967, Prime Minister Robarts of Ontario, who had revived the old Toronto-Quebec axis of the days of Hepburn and Duplessis, announced that his province would call a conference on 'The Confederation of Tomorrow'.

Before that great day arrived, the Confederation of yesterday reached the end of its hundred years. Celebrations, from which the province of Quebec and the vast majority of its citizens stood ostentatiously aloof, were held, in one way or another, all over the rest of the country. If English Canadians could not look forward to the future with confidence, they could at least look back to the past with pride. Their feelings found outlets in a large number of 'centennial projects' – provincial, municipal, and personal; but, apart from the centennial train, which travelled through the entire country, there was no national embodiment of the record of the past and no national expression of the elation which a century of struggle and achievement had inspired. The only splendid public enterprise of 1967 was the Montreal World's Fair, 'Expo 67: Man and His World', the huge cost of which, supposedly divided among the city of Montreal, the province of Quebec, and the federal government, was ultimately discharged by the federal government alone. Expo 67 was an enormous success and drew large crowds of people; but, like every world's fair, where a particular city throws its gates open to the people of all nations, Expo 67 was a municipal and international, but not a national, event. Apart from the fact that it showed the world what Canadians could do at the end of their nation's first century, the fair had no connection with the centenary and deliberately excluded all reference to it. English Canadians may have imagined that Expo 67 was a memorial to Confederation; French Canadians saw it as a demonstration of the prowess of French Canada and as a tribute to the glory of Montreal.

Epilogue: Ottawa, 1967

THE CENTENNIAL celebrations had not centred on Ottawa; but Ottawa was perhaps the most impressive creation of Canada's first hundred years. The little town of 1867, cowering like an overgrown lumber camp at the edge of the pine forest, had become a large city of close to 500,000 people. The three stone buildings on Parliament Hill which an impressed George Brown had declared in 1864 were 'five hundred years in advance of the time' had, in fact, ceased to accommodate all the operations of the federal government within the first two decades of its history. For many years, new buildings were added slowly, one by one, and at long intervals; but the coming of the welfare and interventionist state, whose permanency was clinched by the Second World War, vastly enlarged the sphere of government; and, from then on, building construction hardly ever ceased its struggle to keep up with the insatiable demands of constantly increasing masses of civil servants for office space and houses. The original Victorian small town – its shabby shops and houses and its few opulent residences incongruously interspersed with imposing public buildings and huge office blocks – was now surrounded, on three sides, by a new and populous city, which stretched out along scenic drives and highways lined with plazas, shopping centres, and motels, through miles of neat new streets, bright new houses, and towering new apartments. On its fourth side, across the Ottawa River in Quebec, was the town of Hull, the neglected and slatternly survivor of the old lumbering days, a town still dominated and disfigured by the pulp-and-paper industry, which had gradually become a dormitory suburb for many French-Canadian civil servants and was now included in the area over which the National Capital Commission exercised its sway.

The passage of time had added a new justification to the choice of Ottawa as the capital. The city had, in several important ways, become a microcosm of the nation as a whole, a typical illustration of a number of its current problems. The spread of suburban Ottawa into adjacent municipalities brought out, once again, the inadequacy of the existing divisions of local government; and, in Ottawa's case, the need for the reorganization of the metropolitan area – a need which it shared with many other cities – was complicated by the growing demands of its distinct ethnic and cultural communities. Ottawa was about one-fifth and Hull over four-fifths French-speaking; and, in a decade when bilingualism and biculturalism had suddenly become potent concepts, the presence of such large numbers of both the 'founding races' in the capital area took on a fresh significance. Some Canadians came to believe that Ottawa, precisely because it was the capital city, should recognize and express, in a more formal fashion, the nation's cultural duality. This proposal, like other recommendations of those who took a national approach to the French-Canadian issue, encountered formidable obstacles. Unlike Washington and Canberra, the Ottawa capital area had not been made a separate district under federal control. The provinces of Ontario and Quebec, the municipalities on both sides of the Ottawa River, as well as the government of Canada, would necessarily all be involved in any political reorganization of the Ottawa region.

In 1867, it would have seemed highly unlikely – and even incredible – that either metropolitanism or bilingualism could ever come to be regarded as a serious problem in Ottawa. The men of 1867 had other things on their minds. The capital they had chosen was surrounded by forest, and the forest symbolized the vast, ungainly, and intractable presence of northern North America. To the north and west of the river lay the enormous expanse of rock and water, forest and plain, which made up the half-continent that the Dominion of Canada had inherited and hoped to occupy as its own. To the south stood the Parliament which must try to bring this new nation into effective being. In 1867, the contradiction of man and nature had been Canada's basic issue, and generations had passed before it began to seem possible that politics might in the end triumph over geography. In 1967, the vanquished forest seemed to have retreated before the steady advance of suburban Ottawa; and it was perhaps only on dark winter nights that the fierce breath from the north suddenly reminded parliamentarians of the harsh difficulties and dangers of Canada's half-continent and of the prolonged and exacting labour that had gone into its subjugation. In 1967, they could comfort themselves with the reflection that the long struggle was finally over and that Parliament had won.

But had it? In 1967, the nation's good southern lands had been occupied and its buried northern riches discovered and exploited. Within the limits of a precarious system of international trade and exchange, and with all the uncertainties of a continuing world inflation, Canada was an extremely prosperous country; and Canadians enjoyed a material standard of living which was as high, or nearly as high, as that of any other people on earth. These were very substantial achievements; but in themselves they did not by any means fulfil the aims of the Fathers of Confederation. The purposes of the Fathers were political and social as well as economic. Their primary object had been the establishment of a separate British-American nation and an independent northern economy based on a transcontinental east-west axis. From the first they had been acutely aware of the fact that the preponderating power of the United States and its instinct for continental domination represented the greatest danger to their main ambition; and they had realized equally clearly that the political connection with Great Britain gave them an ally whose support could alone redress the ominous imbalance of power on the North American continent.

For half a century, Britain provided markets, capital, immigrants, and diplomatic protection. For half a century, Canadians held to the belief that membership in the British Empire, which had ensured their own survival as a nation, would in the end enable them to play an influential part in world affairs. This first phase of the national existence lasted down until the First World War; but thereafter its essential elements began to decay or were deliberately impaired. The main direction of Canadian economic activity shifted from east to south. The American market became increasingly important in Canadian trade and American capital increasingly dominant in Canadian development. Along with this gradual dwindling of the old economic ties with the United Kingdom there went a corresponding decline in the historic Anglo-Canadian alliance and the virtual dissolution of the British Commonwealth. Mackenzie King, the archetypal Canadian continentalist, broke up the Britannic union without even attempting to devise policies for a separate and independent Canada. Since 1940, Canada has stood alone, its independence exposed to the penetrative power of American economic and military imperialism, its identity subjected to the continual hammering of American mass media.

It was at this crucial point, when the pressures of continentalism were growing steadily greater, that the first serious rejection of the settlement of Confederation created a dangerous fissure in Canadian national unity. French Canada, alarmed by the impact of industrial North America upon its distinctive culture, demanded drastic changes which would ensure its survival; and these claims started a revolutionary change in the way in which Canadians regarded their federal system. Confederation had been a political union of several provinces, not a cultural compact between two ethnic communities, English and French. But now many Canadians were brought to believe that the fundamental and essential feature of Canada was its cultural duality and that the proper official recognition of this postulate in the Canadian federal system was the first priority of the national interest. The grant of a separate and virtually independent status to Quebec or the slow promotion of cultural dualism throughout united Canada – the two methods by which this aim might conceivably be realized – were both certain to create divisions among Canadian governments and strain and tension among the Canadian people. The first hasty and ill-conceived attempts to gain these objectives had, in fact, begun a period of dissension, acrimony, and violence which threatened at times to end in the dissolution of the union. The damage which these experiments had already done to the fabric of the nation did not intimidate the separatists or the cultural dualists. They pressed their case relentlessly. And finally, in 1967, the Canadian people learnt that their rulers had committed them to the dangerous and monopolizing task of the wholesale revision of the Canadian constitution.

Not one of the provincial and federal rulers pointed out – perhaps none realized – that the settlement of Confederation had been adopted, after a long period of dissension exactly similar to that of the 1960s, as the only compromise that was likely to endure. And in 1967 no one could claim the existence of any general agreement on the nature and extent of the proposed revision. Some provincial premiers wanted no changes at all in the existing system; others never got beyond a vague, complacent assumption that perhaps some changes were necessary; and, apart from a few fatuous generalizations, the only positive proposals came from the federal government and the province of Quebec. The federal government, too intimidated to raise the vital issue of the redivision of legislative powers and too cowed to urge the need of wider federal jurisdiction, busied itself mainly with individual and group rights, language guarantees, and changes in the composition and functions of the Senate – 'Senate reform' being one of the stalest and most fraudulent of all exercises in Canadian politics. The province of Quebec, for whom the government of Canada was nothing more than a convenient and tractable source of revenue, concentrated exclusively on ways of magnifying its own importance as a separate nation state. The fact was that the body of political theory and social and moral philosophy which was common to the whole of British North America in 1867 had by this time completely broken down; and its final disintegration was the long-delayed but inevitable deferred payment of the price of Canada's rapid development. The settlement and exploitation of northern North America had been a continental, not a national, achievement. The long association of Canadians with the government and people of the United States, their dependence upon American capital, their reliance upon American initiative and technology, their gradual acceptance of American standards and values, had given the Republic a huge equity in the Canadian nation and a potent influence on the Canadian national character. Continentalism had divorced Canadians from their history, crippled their creative capacity, and left them without the power to fashion a new future for themselves. Even the will to defend their independence and protect their national identity had been weakened; they seemed scarcely to be aware of the danger in which they stood. The problem of a separatist Quebec had come to obsess and monopolize the minds of both English Canadians and French Canadians. It had distracted them from other and more vital national tasks. It had blinded them to the peril that threatened their existence as a separate nation in North America.

In 1867, Canada's position in the Western Hemisphere had been unique; alone of all the nations of the continents of North and South America, she had retained her connection with her Mother Country. Her original endowment had been British, but she had modified it to suit her North American needs, and, in the process, had made it Canadian. The settlement at Confederation had thus been a characteristically native product – an expression of both the political inheritance and the political experience of Canadians. From Great Britain, they had acquired constitutional monarchy and representative institutions; they had gained responsible government and colonial autonomy through their own political development in the century from the British conquest to Confederation. Their new federal system was a distinctively Canadian creation, shaped by their own history, designed for their own purposes, and consciously independent of foreign models. They believed that they had avoided what they took to be the fatal weaknesses of American federalism; and they were convinced that constitutional monarchy, on the British model, would long outlast the republican régimes which in the mid nineteenth century seemed likely to founder in both Europe and North America.

They put their trust, not in written constitutions or bills of rights, but in the long-established conventions of parliamentary government and the common law. And they had preferred the public order and private restraint of the Canadian community to what they believed was the anarchy and licence of the neighbouring republic.

By 1967, these institutions were already on the defensive, and these convictions and assumptions were losing their vital force. Their decay, in fact, had gone so far that Canadians were almost incapable of realizing that their great nineteenth-century creations had been lost or destroyed and that they had literally nothing of their own to replace what had irrevocably vanished. They had permitted their government to turn its back on their past and to repudiate their history; and in the bankruptcy of their own national philosophy, they turned instinctively to the nearest available creditor, the United States. The distinctive features of Canadian federalism, already eroded by legal decisions and provincial exactions, were attacked for their failure to conform to 'classical' – that is, American – federal principles. The critics of the monarchy, parliamentary institutions, and the common law simply took over their proposed improvements from the checks and balances of American congressional government and the principles of the American Bill of Rights. Imitation and plagiarism had become deep-seated Canadian instincts; economic and political dependence had grown into a settled way of life. It was only through a great collective effort, in which both English Canadians and French Canadians fully participated, that the nation could have escaped from its mental vassalage and recovered its independent powers of creation and self-determination. But the new dominance of ethnic values in Canadian domestic politics and the resulting outbreak of cultural conflict had destroyed national unity at the moment when it was desperately needed. The review of the Canadian constitution, begun in confusion and irresolution, with conflicting purposes and no common goal in sight, was likely to end in futility; and the failure of this unavailing effort was certain to bring continentalism one long stage further towards its final triumph.

Index

Index